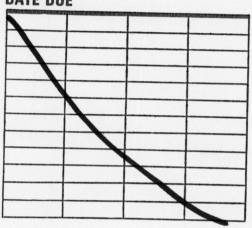

WORLD POLITICS

WORLD POLITICS
SECOND EDITION

*THE WRITINGS OF THEORISTS AND
PRACTITIONERS, CLASSICAL AND MODERN*

EDITED BY **AREND LIJPHART**
UNIVERSITY OF LEIDEN

ALLYN AND BACON, INC. BOSTON

Library of Congress Catalog Card No.: 70–139293
Printed in the United States of America.

To Antony Sune

The Teaching of International Relations in the

CONTENTS

Part IV. The Search for Order and Peace

PREFACE TO THE
SECOND EDITION

The analysis of international relations requires close attention both to the elements of change and to the elements of continuity. The second edition of this book is designed with this twofold requirement in mind. While retaining the principles and aims of the first edition, it has been revised in order to keep the readings up-to-date and relevant for world politics in the 1970s, and to strengthen the coverage of the basic concepts and theories that have proved useful guides to understanding in the past and that have maintained their utility and relevance for contemporary world politics. The principal revisions are the following:

1. The element of classical theory has been strengthened considerably. In addition to the theorists already represented in the first edition, the second edition includes analyses by Erasmus, Rousseau (excerpts from *The State of War*), Hamilton, Bentham, John Stuart Mill, and Engels.

2. The second edition includes two new stimulating discussions by contemporary theorists: Inis Claude's comparison of preventive diplomacy with collective security and Herman Kahn's examination of the nature of nuclear war.

3. The views of a number of important political practitioners are also presented in the new edition: Napoleon, Richard Nixon, Mao Tse-tung, and Lin Piao.

4. An entirely new concluding chapter on the future of international politics was added. It contains famous predictions made in the past as well as an outstanding analysis of future trends and developments by Karl Deutsch.

Finally, several relatively minor revisions were made such as the updating of some of the selections where necessary (including the replacement of some selections by later writings by the same authors), slight organizational adjustments, and the improvement of some of the translations.

A.L.

PREFACE TO THE
FIRST EDITION

This book of readings is designed specifically for use in the introductory course in International Relations as a companion volume to the textbook. It presents provocative and authoritative materials on the basic concepts and persistent issues of world politics. Among the authors are the classical political theorists— Plato, Thucydides, Machiavelli, Dante, Bodin, Grotius, Hobbes, Hume, Rousseau, Kant, Von Clausewitz, and De Tocqueville; the acknowledged leaders among contemporary theorists—political scientists Deutsch, Haas, Hoffmann, Kaplan, Mitrany, Thompson, and Wright; theologian Niebuhr; historian Langer; geographer Jones; psychiatrist Frank; and political practitioners who can speak authoritatively on world affairs, from Theodore Roosevelt and Woodrow Wilson to Kennedy, De Gaulle, Hallstein, U Thant, and Khrushchev.

The readings are supplementary in nature, and do not attempt to substitute for the International Relations text or the tasks of the instructor. The introductory sections in each of the chapters are deliberately kept very brief; they are introductory only, rather than full expositions or outlines of the topic under consideration or interpretations and summaries of the readings which follow.

Any book of readings on world politics can only include an infinitesimal portion of the vast and ever-growing literature in the field; the selection of specific readings was, therefore, no simple task. In compiling this reader, I was guided by several criteria, not all of which were easily reconcilable. The most important criterion was over-all quality of analysis and exposition. The selections had to treat the fundamental concepts and issues in an intellectually challenging and stimulating fashion. Furthermore, I thought it desirable to present the authors' ideas in their entirety rather than in truncated form. This goal conflicted with the aims of comprehensiveness and balance of topics, viewpoints, and approaches, and with the practical necessity of keeping the length of this volume within reasonable bounds. The inevitable result was a compromise. Wherever possible, entire articles, speeches, or chapters from books are reprinted. And when any pieces had to be abridged, the excerpts represent consecutive material as much as possible.

I acknowledge with gratitude the helpful comments and suggestions I have received from my colleagues Professors Saul N. Silverman and M. George Zaninovich. And my wife deserves special thanks, in particular for her help with translations.

A.L.

WORLD POLITICS

part I
THE STUDY OF INTERNATIONAL RELATIONS

1

INTERNATIONAL RELATIONS
AS AN ACADEMIC DISCIPLINE

What is the academic discipline variously labeled "International Relations," "International Politics," "International Studies," "Foreign Affairs," "World Affairs," or "World Politics"? What are its distinguishing characteristics? What is its scope? Is it truly an academic discipline? These and other fundamental questions are discussed in the first selection by Morton A. Kaplan of the University of Chicago. Kaplan is the author of *System and Process in International Politics* and many other books and articles.

In the second selection, which is an excerpt from a longer article, William T. R. Fox and Annette Baker Fox analyze the teaching of International Relations at both the undergraduate and graduate level in

American colleges and universities. William T. R. Fox is Professor of International Relations at Columbia University. Annette Baker Fox is a member of the Department of Political Science at Hunter College. She is the author of *The Power of Small States* and other scholarly publications.

1. *IS INTERNATIONAL RELATIONS A DISCIPLINE?* * /
MORTON A. KAPLAN

Is international relations a distinctive discipline—different from sociology, for instance, in the same way in which sociology is distinctive from political science or economics? Can it be studied independently, or must it be studied as a sub-discipline of some other discipline such as political science? Is the subject matter of international relations susceptible to disciplinary study in some coherent fashion or is it a mere grab bag from which we pick and choose according to momentary interests and to which we can apply no coherent theory, sets of generalizations, or standardized methods?

That we are asked to discuss the topic "Is International Relations a Discipline?" is indicative of a state of unease in the profession. One would find it difficult to imagine similar questions asked of economics, sociology, or political science in general. The practitioners in these fields assume that they practice a discipline and turn their attention immediately to the important substantive and methodological questions raised by their subject matter. They may be concerned with the proper methods of conducting research but not with their title to conduct research. The difficulties that cause students of international relations to raise such a fundamental question must be sought, I believe, in the nature of the subject matter and the history of the discipline.

Before raising the problem in a more general way, I should like briefly and in an over-simplified fashion to mention one aspect of

* Morton A. Kaplan, "Is International Relations a Discipline?" *The Journal of Politics*, Vol. 23, No. 3 (August 1961), pp. 462–76. Reprinted by permission.

the history of international relations studies that is perhaps in part responsible for this state of affairs. When political science separated itself from historical or legal studies, it turned to factual studies of existing political institutions. Then it began to raise questions about comparative institutional differences and to study the inter-relationships between different kinds and levels of political organizations. When interdisciplinary political scientists came on the scene, they were able to apply their theories and insights to an established body of factual data and an established body of theory. Although in their time, they were controversial, they enriched both our factual knowledge and our theoretical understanding. They permitted us to develop broader and more complex theories and to investigate new and interesting factual problems. The relationships between politics and boundary conditions, for example, political personality, elite structures, and voting behavior, could be explored systematically and scientifically for the first time. But however revolutionary these inter-disciplinary methods appeared at the time, they were related to the traditional problems of political science. They were concerned ultimately with institutional and organizational regularities of a political nature even where these problems were raised and studied in novel ways. And findings based on these new methods have been absorbed so successfully by the discipline that they are now even regarded by some as "old hat."

International relations broke away from its historical base at the time when interdisciplinary research in political science first began to develop. It inherited the new approach without having a traditional body of theory or factual data to apply it to (aside perhaps from some earlier and rather vague generalities about the "balance of power"). It could not use interdisciplinary data and theories to enrich and deepen our knowledge of international politics because that was still largely an unexplored subject. In addition, international relations broke loose as an independent discipline during a period in the 1920's when idealism was high and the urge to solve practical problems great. As a consequence, there were sometimes fantastic schemes for world government. The object was to produce international peace rather than disciplinary knowledge. Some scholars did recognize the need for theory and data if such objectives were to be achieved; although this led to an occasional monumental work, such as Quincy Wright's *The Study of War*, the international system as a complex social and political system still remained largely unexplored. This is not to deny that very useful knowledge was sometimes attained. Staley's *War and the Private Investor* added to our knowledge of imperialism and Lasswell's *World Politics and Personal Insecurity* was a major contribution to our knowledge of the psychodynamics of aggressive international behavior. There were of course other important pieces of research that could have been named in place of these examples. But, at least in my opinion, all these works, however valuable they may have been individually, did not add up to a discipline of international relations because there was no common disciplinary core to be enriched as there had been in the companion subject matter of political science.

In short, international relations, although a subject matter, had not become a discipline. Now, although this distinction is perhaps elementary, it might be useful to say a few words about it. Different abstract phases of the same concrete subject matter can be studied by different disciplines. For instance, the economic institutions of society can be studied by the economist, sociologist, psychologist, political scientist, and so forth. The economist studies the flow of resources and the allocative mechanisms; the psychologist may study the effects of different economic systems on personality; the sociologist may study the interrelationships of the economic sub-system with other sub-systems of the society; the political scientist may study the relationships between political and economic organization or the political aspects of economic organization. But only the study by the economist concerns economics.

A discipline implies a set of skills and techniques; a body of theory and of propositions; and a subject matter. This assertion is perhaps necessarily a bit vague and subject to judgmental discriminations, for the astrophysicist, the biophysicist, and the microphysicist share some skills and techniques, some matters of theory and of propositional import, and the common subject matter of physics only at an appropriate level of generalization. This vagueness at the boundary, however, need not distress us, for when we turn to international relations, as the subject matter involving transactions across national boundaries, it is immediately evident that these transactions come within the purview of many different recognized disciplines. For example, international trade comes within the purview of economics; international religious movements and cultural diffusion patterns may be studied by the sociologist; international tensions may come within the province of the psychologist; and wars, international political movements, and patterns of alliance fall within the realm of political science.

The Problem of a Discipline of International Relations

The preceding discussion, discursive as it may have been, raises at least two general questions worth some discussion and exploration. Are any international transactions properly to be studied by a discipline that is specifically international or do we merely apply an already existing discipline to some aspects of international transactions? If there is any such discipline, then it deserves to become the focus of international relations research. If there is no such discipline, then there is no discipline of international relations although there may be disciplines of political science, economics, sociology, and so forth, that can be applied to the study of international relations. In this case, as political scientists, we would expect the student of political science to be concerned primarily with political aspects of international relations. And although as modern political scientists we would also expect him to have some knowledge of economics, sociology, and psychology, we would expect him to use this knowledge in structuring primarily political research problems. We might, however, recognize international politics as a sub-discipline of political science in the same sense in which astrophysics is a sub-discipline of physics.

I know of no convincing discussion that a specifically international relations discipline exists. But, before we can therefore assume that international politics can be studied as a sub-discipline of political science, we must ask whether the conditions appropriate for the existence of such a sub-discipline exist. There are at least three sets of circumstances which would suffice to contra-indicate this. If international events were epiphenomena of national events, that is, mere consequences of national events not requiring for their understanding study of the international matrix, we would deny the validity of a sub-discipline. If international events were to be studied primarily by non-political techniques, we would deny the existence of such a sub-discipline. And, if the subject matter of international politics were recalcitrant to systematic political exploration, we might be led to deny the feasibility of a sub-discipline of international politics. In this latter case, we might have to restrict ourselves to historical investigations.

I am under no illusions concerning my ability to settle defini-
tively the question raised above, particularly within the limitations
of the present paper. None the less some partial answers may be
attempted. There is no doubt that some wars were caused in some
important sense by intra-national considerations, by the need for
markets, because of internal political crises, or even perhaps by the
influence of a king's mistress. The last illustration is not intended in
any sense as humorous, for in those cases where such an influence
operated, the failure to take it into account would impoverish our
understanding of the actual event. If and to the extent to which
some intra-national factor played a systematic role in international
events, the study of international relations would have to rely upon
the discipline or body of factual information that elucidated this
matter and, if possible, would have to incorporate such findings into
its own analysis. But it is difficult to believe that the differences
between the Italian city state system, the national state politics of
nineteenth century Europe, and the present bipolar system can be
accounted for in all important senses without an analysis of the
number of participating actors, their relationship to non-members
of the system and to their environment, their capabilities and
geographic relations, and their modes of political intercourse. And,
to the extent that this is true, non-political or non-international
analyses, although perhaps important and even essential supplements
to the analysis of international political events, are not substitutes
for such analysis.

Nor, do I think, can international relations be reduced to a
discipline other than political science. Even if Lenin's theory of
imperialism were correct—and the evidence is conclusively against
it—the fact that the declining rate of profit inspired the drive for
colonies and trade wars would only serve to provide a motivating
factor for international politics and would no more eliminate the
need for studying the specifically international political factors than
would any of the intra-national factors mentioned in the paragraph
above. Lenin's was perhaps the most sophisticated attempt that has
been made to reduce international relations to a discipline other than
politics, in this case economics. Other attempts have been made in
the case of psychological factors. Harold Lasswell pioneered in
showing the relationship between personality and behavior within
institutional settings. With particular reference to our subject, he
explored the shadowland area in which personality has its effects
upon aggressive and warlike behavior. Unfortunately, in the hands

of psychologists and sociologists who lacked Lasswell's political knowledge and sophistication, Lasswell's theories were misused and attempts were made to reduce wars and arms races to personality maladjustments, as if rational or non-psychological factors never could account for such behavior. Such attempts suffered from grave theoretical and factual faults. No account of international events which leaves out the political can provide satisfactory systematic knowledge.

There is finally a third possibility, namely that the subject matter of international politics, although important, is recalcitrant to the kinds of studies that would have to be made if systematic knowledge were to become available. It might be argued that there is only one international system (except perhaps in time) and that therefore comparative analysis could not be used. The changes that occur through time may occur in so many aspects of the action pattern that ascription of the change in international politics to a particular factor may not be capable of even imprecise empirical confirmation. These factors may include weapons technology, transportation and communication improvements, changes in national economic strength, changes in the number of significant nations, changes in the form of international organization and formal governmental organization, and changes in national values and belief patterns, and so forth. In addition, in the international system, there are a smaller number of events than within the domestic arena; we cannot gamble on the general run, but usually must bank our fate on particular decisions. Thus one cannot necessarily expect the kind of generalized system of roles and role expectations one finds within national systems. This means more unpredictability for individual decisions and less in common between successive decisions. The "deviant" decision is less likely to wash out in the general average and a "deviant" actor has a greater potential for revolutionizing the system than within national systems.

One could multiply the reasons just given. They explain the preference of some for historical investigation or case study. But such investigation or studies are not and cannot be substitutes for political analysis of a systematic nature. A historical study represents an attempt to account for a particular historical sequence of events. In making his study, the historian may employ knowledge from economics, politics, psychology, sociology, technology, and so forth, in evaluating his data. The problem of how he engineers his data when considering the combined effects of events analyzed from the standpoint of many different disciplines is still largely unexplored in the methodological literature and is an art. This means the historian's results are limited by his intuitive ability and judgment in handling combinations of factors. To the extent that factors other than the international political influence the historic sequence of events, the historian is not embarrassed by the absence of a discipline of international politics. To the extent that events are influenced by international political factors—and in the discussion of the first two objections an attempt was made to show briefly that they will be in most important cases—he cannot make his generalizations without employing the same methods which a discipline of international politics would employ. And if such a discipline is not possible, the generalization of the historian is not possible either.

Although this is obvious theoretically, it is not obvious practically for reasons that are easy to understand. The historian or the case study analyst, because he analyzes a concrete sequence of events and tries to take into account all factors influencing that event rather than the class of factors influencing the type of event as in scientific disciplinary studies, engages in a pseudo-recreation of the event and, if he is able, employs the skill of a novelist to create an atmosphere of reality that is psychologically compelling. The nature of his generalizations is hidden by his inexplicit and unsystematic—at least from the standpoint of a generalized science—mode of analysis; and indeed his style of story telling is not conducive to making such analysis explicit or systematic. As a consequence he is usually unaware that his generalization does not follow from the concrete story but can only follow from an abstract argument which, if it is consistent, will be isomorphic with the model that a political scientist would employ.

There can be no quarrel with good historical studies. They do a job that has to be done and for which no other discipline is a substitute. If the historian is not always as sophisticated as he should be with respect to the ways in which he uses scientific theories, the social scientist is often neglectful of the complexity of historical life. And if the historian often fails to provide the social scientist with the data he requires, this is sometimes at least the fault of the social scientist for failing to state his theories in ways that encourage and facilitate related historical investigation. But, when all this is said, the historical investigation is not a substitute for the job a discipline of international politics would be required to perform.

Of course the fact that no substitute exists and that the task such a discipline would perform is quite important does not imply that such a discipline is possible. But the arguments against it are by no means definitive. Nor is it really clear that we are really so much worse off than the other social science disciplines that an effort in this direction would not be worthwhile.

The Requirements of a Discipline of International Politics

It seems to me that regardless of how advanced some of us may consider the techniques we employ, the primary focus of a discipline of international politics must be related to the traditional focus of political science in general. If we cannot escape the methodological advances that have been made in the last thirty years—and there is no reason why we should want to—it may still be important for us to direct these methods and techniques to the study of traditional political problems, at least as they are relevant to international politics. These core problems, so to speak, involve the institutional means by which political problems are solved and political values distributed within the international system.

We are interested in patterns of actions, not with particular cases. Just as we might be interested in a particular cabinet dispute for the light it sheds on the means by which cabinet disputes might be settled in Great Britain or on the range of solution formulas and the constraining factors that predispose toward a particular type of solution, so a study of international conflict or problem settlement would be concerned primarily not with elucidating the particular case but with elucidating the general mode of settlement or the range of settlement and the relevant constraining factors. Even though these institutional patterns may be informal rather than formal, we are concerned with human behavior as it manifests itself in institutions with respect to political matters. That these problems look somewhat different substantively from the problems we are normally used to in political science stems from the fact that the institutional setting of international politics is somewhat different from that of national politics. And, to the extent that this is the case, the sub-discipline of international politics may differ from that of political science in general as much as that of astrophysics differs from microphysics.

The differences between international politics and national politics are fairly obvious. They can be exaggerated and many of these differences may fail to apply to unstable national systems. But the statement of the major differences still should help to clarify the situation. The state as we know it is in some sense the ultimate seat of political authority within which political decisions are made and political values allocated. It attempts to maintain its jurisdiction at the expense of any external or putatively superior authority. The quest for control of the state gives rise to the traditional problems of the form of government, the authority and scope of jurisdiction of officials, the rights of citizens, problems of responsibility and accountability, and so forth. International politics, on the other hand, is the arena in which these ultimately authoritative states, almost like Leibnizian monads, have to come into contact with each other and settle their conflicts without the supravention of any external political authority or master monad. Standardized rules of behavior, if they develop at all, must occur as a consequence of coordination rather than of imposition.

Within national political systems, political organization is formal and durable. Its maintenance does not require explanation although its working processes require study. The organizational forms of international politics, at least those of central importance, like the alliance or bloc, are more often than not of an informal nature, if not with respect to their own organization then at least with respect to relations among them. The memberships of such alignments may be shifting and, although alliances may be a recurrent feature of a particular kind of international system, particular alliances may come into and pass out of existence with relative rapidity. The maintenance of a particular kind of alliance system through changes in actual alliances may indeed require explanation and hence different techniques of investigation from those applied to formal governmental organizations operating within nation states.

Within most national systems, decisions normally are made by voting, whether for candidates for office or on legislative matters. The character of the voting may depend on the kind of electoral or on legislative system; surely votes in the American Congress, the British House of Commons, and the Supreme Soviet are of a different order. But, even where decisions do not occur as a consequence of voting, there are formally determined methods for making the decisions. And in all cases political scientists have developed techniques for studying these processes. In international politics, decisions are made as a consequence of formal or informal bargaining, inexplicit coordination of policy, or the application of force. Techniques for studying these procedures have not been well developed in political science, although the economist has paid considerable attention to bargaining problems that may be considered similar.

Political scientists have paid careful attention to the pressure group in their study of decision processes in national politics. Certainly the pressure group has played an important role in the making of international decisions. The Southern cotton lobby played a role in the revocation of the Aswan Dam offer by John Foster Dulles, the oil lobby plays a role in the current coddling of the Arab states, and the sugar lobby influences American relations with Cuba and the Philippines. Yet, when this is admitted, it remains true that foreign policy is oriented more toward problems produced by the international environment than toward demands of self-interested domestic pressure groups. This is not to say that foreign policy is not responsive to domestic pressures. Unfortunately the ill-advised interwar neutrality legislation was in large part a response to such pressures. But these pressures were based more upon a conception of what American interests were than upon a consideration of what a particular group gained from the legislation. Although their differences are not absolute, it is possible that at least somewhat different methods may be required in investigating the two fields of legislation.

Within the nation state there are millions of voters and still additional millions of citizens. There are parties, labor unions, industrial organizations, religious groups, and so on. They participate in a web of social relations by means of cross-cutting social roles. In the international system, the primary actor is the nation state. In the nineteenth century the number of the most important actors could have been counted on the fingers of one's hands. In the present bipolar system, the United States and the Soviet Union are the most important actors, there is a small number in the second rank, and a total of over one hundred nations. With such small numbers, the statistical averaging out that can occur in domestic social and political processes is not to be expected. This point, however, was made earlier, and need not be expanded here.

Although perhaps overemphasized in earlier writings, nations are characterized by a certain amount of consensus and many of the cross-cutting social roles within them are solidary, that is, based on diffuse affective support or loyalty, rather than of an instrumental character. The relations of individuals and groups toward the nation are themselves solidary; loyal support is expected and those from whom it is expected themselves expect to give it. In general the relations of nations toward each other or toward the international system tend to be instrumental, that is, to be based on considerations of immediate advantage rather than of loyalty, duty, and so forth.

In domestic politics, strategic analysis is not central to investigation. Although the techniques for pushing bills through the legislature may involve a number of strategic elements, the character of the political system is not at stake and the general content of most domestic legislation is oriented toward the broad middle spectrum of opinion in democratic countries or toward the objectives of a dominant party or dictatorship. Ultimate strategic considerations govern domestic politics primarily in transitional periods, for example, the Chinese Civil War, and the periods in Soviet party politics after the deaths of Lenin and Stalin. In the first case, the form of the governmental system was at stake; in the latter, the specification of the winning dictator. It is normally the case in international politics that the major decisions involve the existence of the parties to the decision and the nature of the international political system. And for this reason the decisions are of a highly strategic character. In a general sense the participants in the international political process are engaged in a game or struggle involving honor, fortune, and life. The fact that there are only a small number of them and hence that the system is subsystem dominant, that is, that the patterns of behavior are not parametric givens for the actors but may be influenced by the actions of the actors, reinforces the strategic nature of the decision process, and requires a strategic focus to the analysis of these matters.

If the preceding factors are taken not as absolutes but merely as indications of important differences between national and international politics, they may help to indicate some respects in which the problems of international politics may differ from those of national politics—even though in both cases, we are concerned with institutional patterns of political behavior—and the ways in which somewhat different techniques of analysis profitably may be employed. In general in the international system the most important organizational forms and patterns are the informal rather than the formal. As far as governmental features of the international system are concerned, formally organized systems like the League of Nations and the United Nations, at least so far as past history is concerned, have been peripheral rather than central. The absence of a formal political system in the international arena does not imply the absence of the political management of problems. This political management, with its informal organizational forms, should be regarded as the central focus of the discipline of international politics.

The primary techniques of international government are bargaining and conflict. Bargaining may involve not merely the withholding of the item offered in exchange but the implicit or explicit threat of the use of force. An important instrument in the imposition of goals and goal patterns is the coalition, alignment, bloc, or concert. These are the means by which particular objectives are attained or which may be used to maintain norms of conduct. The criteria for admission to membership, the duration of membership, the types of goals pursued by given kinds of organized international groupings, the limits placed upon these goals, and the factors that constrain all the preceding subjects are among the most important items of the subject matter of the discipline of international politics.

But it is not enough merely to name these features; they must be studied as part of a coherent system of international political relations. The political scientist studying the American legislative system can understand it only as part of a presidential system of government and a federal system of political relationships, for these other aspects of the American political system constrain and qualify the legislative system. In the same way alliance patterns, with respect to durability of specific memberships and goal patterning, depend upon the kinds of national actors who participate, the number of national actors in the entire international system, their relative capabilities, the state of military technology and economic growth, scales of capabilities, the existence or non-existence of supranational types of political organization, and the political organization and goal systems of the participating national actors. The shifting membership and limited goal pattern of most eighteenth and nineteenth century international politics and the rigid membership patterns and relatively unlimited objectives of late nineteenth and early twentieth century international politics must have some relationship to specifiable differences in the international system if there is to be a discipline of international politics. This holds also for present-day bipolar developments.

The study of the discipline of international politics probably will make use of many of the same kinds of institutional analysis as does the discipline of political science in general. But the strategic nature of the activity in the international system indicates that considerable insights may possibly be gained from strategic theory. The absence of durable formal organization, the small number of important or essential actors, and the strategic character of decision making indicate that normative models may be useful to explore the subject matter. The fact that the international system is subsystem dominant and the consequent influence of the decisions of the particular actor upon the state of equilibrium of the system—a situation quite different from that of national politics—tend to reinforce this conclusion. A normative model employs motivational assumptions (in this sense there is a similarity to economic theory) and permits us to study abstractly the relations between a few selected variables of the system. This may be an aid to analysis for, although a change in formal organizational patternings requires explanation in the study of national political systems, it is the maintenance of the informal organizational patterns of international politics that requires explanation. The coordination of independent nation states on particular patterns of alignment and on certain kinds of goal limitations for reasonably long periods of time is not at all easy to understand. A normative model possibly may help to explain how independently chosen strategies converge toward a particular equilibrium—an equilibrium with respect to types of alignment patterns, types and limits of goal objectives, and norms and normative patterns.

There is an important difference, however, between the situation facing the economist and that encountered by the student of international politics. Most economic analysis deals with systems in which irrational behavior by an entrepreneur has the effect only of driving him out of business. If the market is perfect—in our terms, system dominant—this affects only the individual entrepreneur and not the nature of the market. If the market is oligopolistic—subsystem dominant—then individual irrationality may drive the economic system toward a more monopolistic situation. But the irrational entrepreneur does not weaken the position of any of his competitors by collapsing unless his collapse, for specific reasons, favors a particular one of his competitors. Moreover, the economist tends not to analyze these situations because he is more interested in types of markets than in changes from one form of market to another; and present day economies provide him with an abundance of types.

In the international arena, there is only one market, so to speak, rather than many markets co-existing within an economic system. That market is the market of nation states. A change in the configuration of the market is usually a change once and for all. And therefore dynamic aspects of the international system are of the greatest importance. In addition, an irrational strategy in a situation like that of international politics may have a direct effect on the viability of the other actors. Although cartels are known in economics, they do not play the same vital role as alliances, for instance, in the "balance of power" system. Irrationality here of one nation may make ineffective the protective devices normally employed by other nations to maintain the system.

For these reasons the student of international politics cannot assume parametric or environmental conditions in the same way that the economist assumes, for instance, economic rationality. He must be cognizant of all the boundary factors that may produce a dynamic change in the nature of the international system. Although his discipline focuses on the inter-relationships of nations, he does not deify the nation and recognizes that under the skin of the nation, individuals, groups, elites, various kinds of processes, factors, and so forth, may produce novel kinds of international behavior that have the profoundest effect upon the pattern of international politics. And although the discipline of international politics generally assumes the primacy of international factors in its analysis, it is necessary to recognize that occasionally other factors may play a dominant role. The nationalism and anti-Westernism of many of the new nations presents a case in point.

As a consequence the student of international politics will be sensitive to related disciplines that enable him to understand these boundary conditions. Such collateral disciplines include, among others, military science, comparative politics, administrative science and organization theory, economics and studies of economic capabilities, geography, decision-making theory and strategic theory, sociology and related cultural science, and law. No attempt will be made here to specify the role they play in enriching the discipline of international politics other than to assert that they do have a role to play.

I realize that I have merely indicated what the subject matter and methods of the discipline of international politics might look like. I have not established that research in this area can be as successful as in political science generally. But although our methods may have to differ from general political science, we will probably have to turn toward our own version of the traditional problems of politics if we are to succeed in strengthening the discipline. It is not necessary to argue over how fast we should proceed theoretically or formally. Some of the reasons advanced earlier with respect to the need for normative models would seem to indicate at least some effort in a theoretical and at least semi-formal direction. But different political scientists may bring different insights and skills into play in conducting their research. Some research problems may seem to demand more or less theory. And it would seem more fruitful to see what speed turns out best for particular kinds of tasks by applying our insights to these problems than to engage in a methodological debate, which in practice may produce only verbal acrobatics. The discipline should have enough "give" to accommodate different insights, methods, theories, and skills. We have too often seen rejected methods gain new vigor at a new stage of development of a discipline. None of us has achieved such success with his methods that he should be prepared to read others out of court.

2. THE TEACHING OF INTERNATIONAL RELATIONS IN THE UNITED STATES* / WILLIAM T. R. FOX AND ANNETTE BAKER FOX

. . . Of the 750 or more accredited American universities and colleges, about 300 have separate departments of political science or of international relations. Only these institutions are likely to offer international relations courses. John Gange estimates that nearly all the significant international relations research comes from forty or fifty of them.[48] This is only a little larger than the number offering the Ph.D. degree in either political science or international relations. For most of the rest, the scope of the international relations courses is largely dictated by the content of the available general textbooks.

* William T. R. Fox and Annette Baker Fox, "The Teaching of International Relations in the United States," *World Politics*, Vol. 13, No. 3 (April 1961), pp. 348–55. Reprinted by permission.

[48] John Gange, *University Research on International Affairs*, Washington, D.C., American Council on Education, 1958, p. 12.

The content of the subject, especially in undergraduate courses, is sharply affected by the goals of the teacher. Although training for citizenship is probably as much of a goal in undergraduate international relations teaching as in the teaching of American government, few professors today see their function as the preaching of salvation via the adoption of some particular grand design for world organization or for American foreign policy. Converting the unwashed isolationist masses to the secular religion of internationalism is not the dominant teaching goal of the international relations scholar. His public service motivation and his voluntaristic predispositions do, however, affect his selection of topics for teaching and research.

Whether because the subject is new or because the world is changing so rapidly, there are few acknowledged classics which every serious American student of international relations will be expected to have read; there are as yet no Paretos or Durkheims, no Marshalls or Keyneses, no Bagehots or Diceys. With no core of acknowledged classics and no system of central examinations, each teacher is free to choose his own approach to a general course in international relations. The large number of introductory textbooks is perhaps one indication of the dissatisfaction which most of their writers have felt with the books written prior to their own. Even the size of the American market cannot by itself account for the continuing production of such books and of collections of annotated readings to supplement or to substitute for them.

Several attempts have been made to classify approaches to international relations teaching and research. In Vernon Van Dyke's 1956 summer seminar on the teaching of international politics, four approaches to the study were identified: the institutional, the historical, the philosophical, and the behavioral.[49] It is noteworthy that the social scientists cited to illustrate these four approaches were as often outside the field of international relations as inside. Heterogeneity of approach is apparently characteristic not just of international relations but of the whole of American social science.

Arnold Wolfers has distinguished the "states as actors," "minds of men," and "corporate actors" approaches.[50] The first takes the nation-states as given and concentrates on the multiple-sovereignty

[49] Vernon Van Dyke, ed., *Some Approaches and Concepts Used in the Teaching of International Politics*, Iowa City, State University of Iowa, 1957.
[50] Arnold Wolfers, "The Actors in International Politics," in William T. R. Fox, ed., *Theoretical Aspects of International Relations*, Notre Dame, Ind., University of Notre Dame Press, 1959, pp. 83–106.

system as an interaction system;[51] it finds the richest materials for study in diplomatic history. The second stresses the unity of intranational and world politics, and makes more use of sociology and social psychology.[52] The third puts "government" rather than "politics" at the center of the study and gives more emphasis to international organization.[53] There are no pure examples of any one of these three approaches at the general textbook level, but the books do differ significantly in their relative emphases.

Still another way of characterizing approaches to the study of international relations is to distinguish the "principles," the "country-by-country," and the "transformations" approaches. Most of the general textbooks exemplify the "principles" approach, although those with a strong historical or geographical emphasis[54] illustrate the second. The experiment at San Francisco State College has emphasized the third, as does the recent text by A. F. K. Organski.[55] These three approaches are complementary rather than incompatible, but the study of such "transformations" as are being wrought by bipolarity, atomic age technology, and the rise of the Afro-Asian nations will receive increasing attention.[56]

Practical limits in approach are set by the gaps in the students'

[51] E.g., Morgenthau, *Politics Among Nations.*

[52] E.g., Harold D. Laswell, *World Politics and Personal Insecurity,* New York, McGraw-Hill, 1935; and Frederick S. Dunn, *War and the Minds of Men,* New York, Council on Foreign Relations, 1951.

[53] E.g., Clyde Eagleton, *International Government,* 3rd ed., New York, Ronald Press, 1957.

[54] A recent example is Lennox A. Mills and Charles H. N. McLaughlin, *World Politics in Transition* (New York, Henry Holt, 1956), in which about half the text is devoted to the foreign policies of particular states; an influential earlier work is Harold and Margaret Sprout, eds., *Foundations of National Power* (2nd ed., New York, Van Nostrand, 1951).

[55] See "San Francisco International Studies Project" and "International Studies," San Francisco State College, 1959 and 1960 (mimeographed); and A. F. K. Organski, *World Politics,* New York, Alfred A. Knopf, 1958.

[56] Among the major transformations, that brought about by scientific and technological change has perhaps been least systematically analyzed. The short-run impact on military policy and strategic theory has been widely discussed, but non-military and long-run aspects have been generally neglected in both teaching and research. A few exceptions are John Herz, *International Politics in the Atomic Age,* New York, Columbia University Press, 1959; Philip C. Jessup and Howard Taubenfeld, *Controls for Outer Space and the Antarctic Analogy,* New York, Columbia University Press, 1959; "Science and World Politics" (a symposium), *Journal of International Affairs,* xiii, No. 1 (1959); and John G. Stoessinger, "Atoms for Peace: The International Atomic Energy Agency," in Commission to Study the Organization of Peace, *Organizing Peace in the Nuclear Age,* New York University Press, 1959, pp. 117–233.

previous historical or social science training.[57] Sometimes this leads the teacher to "do-it-yourself" efforts to be his own historian,[58] his own student of comparative politics, his own sociologist,[59] his own geographer,[60] his own demographer,[61] his own political philosopher,[62] etc. Extensive digressions to make up for the students' presumed deficiencies make it difficult in many cases to discover the integrating approach and sometimes create doubt that the unexplicated approach is even implicit.[63] Texts with a sustained point of view and closely reasoned argument are likely to be addressed to and most suitable for students who begin their study of international relations at a more advanced stage in their educational careers and who have the factual and intellectual resources to evaluate the argument.

There are many subjects which appear in almost all the treatises and course syllabi we have examined, whatever the basic approach of the particular scholar. Grayson Kirk in 1947 identified "five ingredients" which appeared in almost all the treatises and syllabi: (1) the nature and operation of the state system; (2) basic power factors; (3) the special position and policies of the first-ranking powers; (4) the history of international relations since World War I; and (5) the building of a better world order.[64] Richard N. Swift has summarized the changes since 1947 in the following terms: "Courses today stress power and the complexity of world affairs rather than the state system: they probe deeper into the elements of national power, and in so doing take account of the theoretical and

[57] Cf. Grayson Kirk, *The Study of International Relations in American Colleges and Universities*, New York, Council on Foreign Relations, 1947, p. 34: "All social studies are so interrelated that each can best be studied if the beginning student has already studied all the others."

[58] Frederick L. Schuman, *International Politics* (New York, McGraw-Hill, 1st ed., 1933; 6th ed., 1960), is distinctive for its long historical introduction.

[59] Ernst B. Haas and Allen S. Whiting, *Dynamics of International Relations* (New York, McGraw-Hill, 1956), draws on both comparative politics and sociology.

[60] H. and M. Sprout, eds., *op. cit.*

[61] Robert Strausz-Hupé and Stefan T. Possony, *International Relations*, 2nd ed., New York, McGraw-Hill, 1954; and Organski, *World Politics, op.cit.*

[62] Hans J. Morgenthau, *Politics Among Nations*, 3rd ed., New York, Alfred A. Knopf, 1960.

[63] Fred A. Sondermann, in "The Study of International Relations: 1956 Version" (*World Politics*, x, No. 1, October 1957, pp. 102–11), distinguishes the texts with a unified conceptual framework from those "strung together . . . in a more or less random fashion." The latter group often contains more factual data than the former.

[64] Kirk, *op. cit.*, pp. 27–29.

practical results of research in economics, psychology, and sociology. In debating the position of the realists and idealists and
presenting the cold war, instructors now pay more attention to
theoretical presuppositions; and in presenting accurately the picture
of world politics today, they have had to give a larger place than
ever before to Africa and Asia."[65] Evidently, fashions in teaching
have followed the fashions in research . . . , but usually only after
an interval.

In a student's field of undergraduate concentration, courses in
international politics, law, and organization are commonly offered.
In the more advanced work in the major, students may pursue a
variety of courses in non-domestic aspects of economics, law,
geography, and possibly other social sciences, and study European
and American diplomatic history.

Beyond that, the student often takes special courses in the
problems of non-European areas. So little even yet, however, is
taught about the non-European world that it is difficult to fill the
gaps in knowledge of the history, culture, economy, and politics of
various parts of Asia and Africa to the point at which serious
analysis becomes possible.[66] Acquiring expertness in any one area is
so great a task that it is ususual for a student to be required to do
special work in more than one of the areas of non-European culture.

A variety of teaching devices are used to bind together and
apply some of the kinds of knowledge that the student has acquired
from these varying combinations of courses in international relations, cognate subjects, and area studies. In one sense the course in
American foreign policy, which ordinarily deals both with the
conduct of American foreign relations and with the analysis of
alternative American foreign policies, represents an effort to apply
the knowledge previously acquired in courses presented from a
"world" point of view. The student looks at the world as seen from
Washington, at the situation in which the makers of American
foreign policy find themselves, and at the choices which they have
to make. Other teaching techniques also have this objective. For

[65] Richard N. Swift, *World Affairs and the College Curriculum*, Washington, D.C., American Council on Education, 1959, pp. 118-19.

[66] Enthusiasm for area studies sometimes goes so far that the task of filling
in the gaps of knowledge about unfamiliar parts of the world may be mistaken for the whole study of international relations. This results from a genuine confusion between "foreign" and "international." If "international" were
synonymous with "everything foreign," then one would only have to add up
his knowledge of individual areas and call the sum total "international relations."

example, there are the recent experiments with political gaming as a teaching device in which the students play roles as representatives of various countries negotiating with each other under specified circumstances and do the research to enable them to play these roles.[67]

Another and more widely used method to promote a vicarious sense of participation is the staging of mock political meetings of various kinds. For example, a mock United Nations General Assembly or a mock disarmament commission or a mock Congressional committee hearing is held in which each student or group of students purports to represent a different country or a different point of view.

Only a relatively small proportion of American students are able to travel abroad and, of these, few in any way that is very helpful to their academic study of international relations. Only a small proportion have the opportunity even to visit Washington. Five institutions, with a grant from the Carnegie Corporation— Colgate, Columbia, Princeton, Rutgers, and Swarthmore—have developed a program to send undergraduate honors students to Europe for independent summer research. The results will be carefully watched for the light they throw on a difficult teaching problem.[68]

At the postgraduate level there are two kinds of programs of study in international relations.[69] One is the program which leads toward the Ph.D. degree and university teaching and research. The other is a quasi-professional program which leads toward a master's degree and employment in government or such private fields of

[67] See Lincoln P. Bloomfield and Norman J. Padelford, "Three Experiments in Political Gaming," *American Political Science Review*, LIII, No. 4 (December 1959), pp. 1105-15; and Herbert Goldhamer and Hans Speier, "Some Observations on Political Gaming," *World Politics*, XII, No. 1 (October 1959), pp. 71-83.

[68] The difficulty of teaching undergraduate students with no foreign travel experience, no direct observation of politics in the national capital, and no simulated international relations experiences in mock meetings and political gaming may be lessened by the rise in standards of television news reporting on world affairs. Documentary presentations on such topics as "The Population Explosion" or "The Munich Crisis" and the showing in full of Nikita Khrushchev's two-hour press conference on the occasion of the abortive summit conference of May 1960 are examples. Harlan Cleveland, "The Real International World and the Academic Lag," in Roy A. Price, ed., *New Viewpoints in the Social Sciences* (28th Yearbook, Washington, D.C., National Council for the Social Studies, 1958, pp. 172-88), emphasizes the importance of immersion in some foreign culture as a "necessary modern supplement" to the education of every American, not just the student with a specialized concern in the field of international relations.

[69] Cf. C. Dale Fuller, *Training of Specialists in International Relations*, Washington, D. C., American Council on Education, 1957.

international affairs as journalism, finance, or trade. The former program culminates in the writing of a dissertation to test the student's independent research abilities. The latter is likely to have a curriculum which is interdisciplinary and largely prescribed and calls for no comparable experience in independent research.[70]

The two types of postgraduate training are not so separate that there are no "cross-over" points. A substantial fraction of the terminal master's degree candidates develop a deeper scholarly interest and become candidates for the Ph.D. degree. On the other hand, many of the Ph.D.'s find careers in government; this appears to be especially true of those with scarce skills in foreign area studies and those with intensive training in economic aspects of international relations.

The traditional three-year period for earning the Ph.D. degree has not ordinarily proved long enough. For the international relations student, all kinds of social science disciplines seem to have tantalizing relevance. More often than not, at least a fourth post-graduate year is required. For the student who is simultaneously pursuing a second program of specialized studies in the problems of some Asian or African or Russian area, it seems to be physically impossible to prepare for the general subjects examinations and to complete a dissertation within the allotted three-year period.

There is no apparent correlation between the organization of international studies within a given university and the availability of courses in special aspects of international relations. Probably, the independent department of international relations or the interdepartmental supervising committee offering a Ph.D. in international relations requires fewer supporting graduate courses in comparative government and political theory and more supporting graduate courses in diplomatic history and the other social sciences. In either case, the choice of options in specialized sub-fields is wide. Each of the leading graduate schools is accordingly turning out men and women of widely varying interests.

[70] It is possible to earn a Ph.D. specializing in international relations and an M.A. as a way-station on the road to the Ph.D. in most of the leading universities, whether in political science or under a separately organized international relations program. The University of Chicago and Yale University were among the first to develop a separately organized Ph.D. program in international relations. The quasi-professional terminal master's degree is offered in a smaller number of institutions. There are separately organized programs for training specialists, for example, at American University, Columbia University, Johns Hopkins University, Princeton University, and Tufts University (Fletcher School of Law and Diplomacy).

One practical consideration may have tended to keep the graduate student in international relations anchored in an established department—usually political science. That consideration is the practical necessity of being employable as an instructor in a department of political science. With the American pattern of requiring the beginning instructor to teach some sections of the introductory course and with that course normally "American Government" if his is a political science department, the prudent graduate student has often combined his international relations studies with enough other political science to compete with political scientists for the available academic vacancies. If there is an increase in the number of independent departments of international relations, prudence may not operate in exactly the same way. . . .

2
REALISM AND IDEALISM

Should statesmen be "idealists" or "realists"? Should students of International Relations be "idealistic" or "realistic" in their analysis of world affairs? Are the two approaches mutually exclusive? Or can one achieve a judicious combination of the two and be a "realist" and an "idealist" at the same time? The selections in this chapter deal with this fundamental and persistent controversy.

Niccolo Machiavelli (1469–1527) gained the reputation of being the realist *par excellence* mainly as a result of his most famous work, *The Prince*. The first selection juxtaposes two chapters breathing vastly different spirits from this one book.

The second selection is a speech by Dean Acheson, a leading critic of the alleged idealism of United States foreign policy, delivered at Amherst College on December 9, 1964. Acheson was Secretary of State from 1949 to 1953, and is the author of *A Citizen Looks at Congress and Power and Diplomacy*.

In the third selection, Stanley H. Hoffmann subjects the realist theory of International Relations, particularly as expounded by Professor Hans J. Morgenthau, to a searching analysis. The selection is an excerpt from his article in *World Politics*. Hoffmann is Professor of Government at Harvard University. He has also written *Contemporary Theory in International Relations* and other works.

3. *THE PRINCE** / *NICCOLO MACHIAVELLI*

Whether Princes Ought to Be Faithful to Their Engagements

It is unquestionably very praiseworthy in princes to be faithful to their engagements; but among those of the present day that have been distinguished for great exploits, few indeed have been remarkable for this virtue, or have scrupled to deceive others who may have relied on their good faith.

It should, therefore, be known that there are two ways of deciding any contest: the one by laws, the other by force. The first is peculiar to men, the second to beasts; but when laws are not sufficiently powerful, it is necessary to recur to force. A prince ought, therefore, to understand how to use both these means. This doctrine is admirably illustrated to us by the ancient poets in the allegorical history of the education of Achilles and many other princes of antiquity by the centaur Chiron, who, under the double form of man and beast, taught those that were destined to govern, that it was their duty to use by turns the arms adapted to both these natures, seeing that one without the other cannot be of any durable advantage. As a prince must learn how to act the part of a beast sometimes, he should make the fox and the lion his patterns. The first can but feebly defend himself against the wolf, and the latter readily falls into such snares as are laid for him. From the fox, therefore, a prince will learn dexterity in avoiding snares; and from

* Niccolo Machiavelli, *The Prince* (New York: The National Alumni, 1907), Chap.'s 18 and 26, slightly revised by the editor.

the lion, how to employ his strength to keep the wolves in awe. But they that entirely rely upon the lion's strength, will not always meet with success: in other words, a prudent prince cannot and ought not to keep his word, except when he can do it without injury to himself, or when the circumstances under which he contracted the engagement still exist.

I should be cautious in inculcating such a precept if all men were good; but as the generality of mankind are wicked, and ever ready to break their word, a prince should not keep his more scrupulously, especially as it is always easy to justify a breach of faith on his part. I could give numerous proofs of this, and show numberless engagements and treaties that have been violated by the treachery of princes, and that those who enacted the part of the fox have always succeeded best in their affairs. But it is necessary to disguise the appearance of craft, and thoroughly to understand the art of feigning and dissembling; for men generally are so simple and so weak that he who wishes to deceive easily finds dupes.

One example, taken from the history of our own times, will be sufficient. Pope Alexander VI played during his whole life a game of deception; and though his faithless conduct was extremely well known, his artifices always proved successful. Oaths and protestations cost him nothing; never did a prince so often break his word or pay less regard to his engagements. This was because he so well understood this chapter in the art of government.

It is not necessary, however, for a prince to possess all the good qualities I have enumerated, but it is indispensable that he should appear to have them. I will even venture to affirm, that it is sometimes dangerous to use them, though it is always useful to appear to possess them. A prince should earnestly endeavor to gain the reputation of kindness, clemency, piety, justice, and fidelity to his engagements. He should possess all these good qualities, but still retain such power over himself as to display their opposites whenever it may be expedient. I maintain that a prince, and especially a new prince, cannot with impunity exercise all the virtues, because his own self-preservation will often compel him to violate the laws of charity, religion and humanity. He should habituate himself to bend easily to the various circumstances that may from time to time surround him. In a word, it will be as useful to him to persevere in the path of rectitude, while he feels no inconvenience in doing so, as to know how to deviate from it when circumstances dictate such a course. He should make it a rule, above all things, never to utter anything that does not breathe of kindness, justice, good faith and piety. This last quality it is most important for him to appear to possess, as men in general judge more from appearances than from reality. All men have eyes, but few have the gift of penetration. Everyone sees your exterior, but few can discern what you have in your heart; and those few dare not oppose the voice of the multitude, who have the majesty of their prince on their side. In the actions of men, and especially of princes, from which there is no appeal, the end justifies the means. Let it then be the prince's chief care to maintain his authority; the means he employs, be they what they may, will, for this purpose, always appear honorable and meet applause; for the vulgar are ever caught by appearances, and judge only by the event. And as the world is chiefly composed of such as are called the vulgar, the voice of the few is seldom if ever heard or regarded.

There is a prince now living (whose name it may not be proper to mention) who ever preaches the doctrines of peace and good faith; but if he had observed either the one or the other, he would long ago have lost both his reputation and his dominions.*

Exhortation to Deliver Italy from Foreign Powers

When I take a review of the subject-matter treated of in this book, and examine whether the circumstances in which we are now placed would be favorable to the establishment of a new government, alike honorable to its founder and advantageous to Italy, it appears to me that there never was, nor ever will be, a period more appropriate for the execution of so glorious an undertaking.

If it was necessary that the people of Israel should be slaves to Egypt, in order to elicit the rare talents of Moses; that the Persians should groan under the oppression of the Medes, in order to prove the courage and magnanimity of Cyrus; and that the Athenians should be scattered and dispersed, in order to make manifest the rare virtues of Theseus, it will be likewise necessary, for the glory of some Italian hero, that his country should be reduced to its present miserable condition, that the Italians should be greater slaves than the Israelites, more oppressed than the Persians, and still more

* Ferdinand V, King of Aragon and Castile, who thus acquired the kingdoms of Naples and Navarre.

dispersed than the Athenians; in a word, that they should be without laws and without chiefs, pillaged, torn to pieces, and enslaved by foreign powers.

And though it has sometimes unquestionably happened that men have arisen who appeared to be sent by Heaven to achieve our deliverance; yet jealous fortune has ever abandoned them in the midst of their career; so that our unfortunate country still groans and pines away in the expectation of a deliverer that may put an end to the devastations in Lombardy, Tuscany, and the kingdom of Naples. She supplicates Heaven to raise up a prince that may free her from the odious and humiliating yoke of foreigners, may close the numberless wounds with which she has been so long afflicted, and under whose standard she may march against her cruel oppressors.

But on whom can Italy cast her eyes except upon your illustrious house, which, visibly favored by Heaven and the Church, the government of which is confided to its care, possesses also the wisdom and the power necessary to undertake so glorious an enterprise? And I cannot think that the execution of this project will seem difficult if you reflect on the actions and conduct of the heroes whose examples I have adduced. Though their exploits were indeed wonderful, they were still but men; and although their merit raised them above the others, yet none of them certainly were placed in a situation so favorable as that in which you now stand. You have justice on your side; their cause was not more lawful than yours, and the blessing of God will attend you no less than them. Every war that is necessary is just; and it is humanity to take up arms for the defense of a people to whom no other resource is left.

All circumstances concur to facilitate the execution of so noble a project, for the accomplishment of which it will be necessary only to tread in the steps of those great men whom I have mentioned in the course of this work. For though some of them, it is true, were conducted by the hand of God in a wonderful manner—though the sea divided to let them pass, a cloud directed their course, a rock streamed with water to assuage their thirst, and manna fell from heaven to appease their hunger—yet there is no occasion for such miracles at present, as you possess in yourself sufficient power to execute a plan you ought by no means to neglect. God will not do everything for us; much is left to ourselves, and the free exercise of will, that so our own actions may not be wholly destitute of merit.

If none of our princes have hitherto been able to effect what is now expected from your illustrious house, and if Italy has continually been unfortunate in her wars, the evil has arisen from the defects in military discipline, which no person has been able to reform.

Nothing reflects so much honor on a new prince as the new laws and institutions established under his direction, especially when they are good and bear the character of grandeur. It must be acknowledged that Italy soon accommodates herself to new forms. Her inhabitants are by no means deficient in courage, but they are destitute of proper chiefs; the proof of this is in the duels and other individual combats in which the Italians have always evinced consummate ability, while their valor in battle has appeared wellnigh extinguished. This can be attributed only to the weakness of the officers, who are unable to ensure obedience from those who know, or think they know, the art of war. Thus we have seen the greatest generals of the present day whose orders never were executed with exactness and celerity. These are the reasons why, in the wars in which we have been engaged for the last twenty years, the armies raised in Italy have been almost always defeated. Witness Tarus, Alexandria, Capua, Genoa, Vaila, Bologna, and Mestri.

If, therefore, your illustrious house is willing to follow the example of our ancestors, who have delivered their country from the rule of foreigners, it is necessary, above all things, as the only true foundation of every enterprise, to raise a national army. You cannot have better or more faithful soldiers, and though every one of them may be a good man, yet they will become still better when they are all united, and see themselves rewarded by a prince of their own.

It is therefore absolutely necessary to have troops raised in our own country, if we wish to protect it from the invasion of foreign powers. The Swiss as well as the Spanish infantry are highly esteemed, but both have defects that may be avoided in the formation of our troops, which would render them superior to both of those powers. The Spaniards cannot withstand the shock of cavalry, and the Swiss cannot maintain their ground against infantry that is equally resolute.

Experience has fully shown that the Spanish battalions cannot resist the French cavalry, and that the Swiss have been defeated by the infantry of Spain. And though there has not been any thorough trial with regard to the Swiss on this point, yet there was a sort of specimen at the battle of Ravenna, where the Spanish infantry came in contact with the German troops, who fought in the same order as the Swiss. Upon that occasion, the Spanish having, with their accustomed impetuosity, and under the protection of their bucklers, thrown themselves across the pikes of the Germans, the latter were obliged to give way, and would have been decisively defeated, but for their cavalry.

It is necessary, therefore, to institute a military force possessing the defects of neither the Swiss nor the Spanish infantry, and that may be able to maintain its ground against the French cavalry, and this is to be effected, not by changing their arms, but by altering their discipline. Nothing is more likely to make a new prince esteemed and to render his reign illustrious.

Such an opportunity should be embraced eagerly that Italy, after her long sufferings, may at least behold her deliverer appear. With what demonstrations of joy and gratitude, with what affection, with what impatience for revenge, would he not be received by those unfortunate provinces that have so long groaned under such odious oppression? What city would shut her gates against him, and what people would be so blind as to refuse him obedience? What rivals would he have to dread? Is there one Italian that would not hasten to pay him homage? All are weary of the tyranny of these barbarians. May your illustrious house, strong in all the hopes that justice gives our cause, deign to undertake this noble enterprise, that so, under your banners, our nation may resume its ancient splendor, and behold the prophecy of Petrarch at last fulfilled.

> When virtue takes the field,
>   Short will the conflict be,
> Barbarian rage shall yield
>   The palm to Italy:
> For patriot blood still warms Italian veins;
> Though low the fire, a spark at least remains.

4. *ETHICS IN INTERNATIONAL RELATIONS TODAY: OUR STANDARD OF CONDUCT* / DEAN ACHESON

The discussion of ethics or morality in our relations with other states is a prolific cause of confusion. The righteous who seek to deduce foreign policy from ethical or moral principles are as

* Dean Acheson, "Ethics in International Relations Today: Our Standard of Conduct," *Vital Speeches of the Day*, Vol. 31, No. 8 (February 1, 1965), pp. 226–28. Reprinted by permission.

misleading and misled as the modern Machiavellis who would conduct our foreign relations without regard to them.

Most of what we, and a good part of the noncommunist world, regard as ethical principles relates to conduct, the behavior of individuals toward one another. There is pretty general agreement that it is better to act straightforwardly, candidly, honorably, and courageously than duplicitously, conspiratorially, or treacherously. This is true of conduct toward friends and toward those who are ill-disposed to us. It is well that our government should give to foreigners as well as to our own people as clear an idea as possible of its intentions. To do so should inspire confidence and increase stability. One need not counsel perfection—for instance, to tell the whole truth; but it ought not to be too much to advise telling nothing but the truth—advise which might usefully have been given to President Eisenhower before he began issuing statements about the U-2 aircraft shot down some years ago over the Soviet Union.

The French school of diplomacy, founded by Cardinal Richelieu, the dominant school for nearly three centuries, and probably still the best ever devised, was based, as François de Callières stated, upon the principle that "open dealing is the basis of confidence" (a very different idea from President Wilson's ill-considered maxim, "open covenants openly arrived at"). He adds, "The negotiator therefore must be a man of probity and one who loves truth; otherwise he will fail to inspire confidence." And again, "Deceit is the measure of the smallness of mind of him who uses it . . . a lie always leaves behind it a drop of poison. . . . Menaces always do harm to negotiation. . . ."

It does not detract from the purity of his morals that he supports them with worldly wisdom:

> The diplomatist must be . . . a good listener, courteous, and agreeable. He should not seek to gain a reputation as a wit, nor should he be so disputatious as to divulge secret information in order to clinch an argument. Above all the good negotiator must possess enough self control to resist the longing to speak before he has thought out what he wants to say. . . . He should pay attention to women but never lose his heart . . . , possess the patience of a watch-maker . . . should not be given to drink . . . and be able to tell where, in any foreign country, the real sovereignty lies. . . . Finally . . . a good cook is often an excellent conciliator.

For any of you who are contemplating a career in the Foreign Service, François de Callières is as sound an adviser today as he was in 1716.

Without laboring the point further, I take it as clear that, where an important purpose of diplomacy is to further enduring good relations between states, the methods—the modes of conduct—by which relations between states are carried on must be designed to inspire trust and confidence. To achieve this result the conduct of diplomacy should conform to the same moral and ethical principles which inspire trust and confidence when followed by and between individuals.

The purpose of our own diplomacy, as of the French school, requires the inspiring of trust and confidence, for our governmental goal for many years has been to preserve and foster an environment in which free societies may exist and flourish. When we have said this, we had better stop and think before concluding that the policies which will advance us toward this goal can usefully be discussed or evaluated in terms of moral or ethical principles.

In the first place, a little reflection will convince us that the same conduct is not moral under all circumstances. Its moral propriety seems to depend, certainly in many cases, upon the relationship of those concerned with the conduct. For instance, parents have the moral right, indeed duty, to instill moral and religious ideas in their children and correct moral error. Ministers, priests, rabbis, and mullahs have much the same duties to their flocks, including that of correcting heresy, when they can make up their minds what it is.

But these same acts on the part of public officials—certainly in the United States—would be both wrong and a denial of the fundamental rights of the citizen. Indeed, even prayer prescribed and led by teachers in our public schools is condemned by our courts with the approval of some of our churches. The attempt of both governmental and religious bodies to censor literature, painting, sculpture, the theater, and the movies, under the aegis of those alliterative adjectives, lewd and lascivious, seems to me intolerable. Parents, if they are any good, can shield their children from whatever they choose. The rest of us had better take our chances with mortal sin, rather than to have policemen, trained to handle traffic and arrest criminals, become judges of what art we may see or read. And it is just as bad when the local watch and ward society or church body tries to do the same thing.

So, acts, moral in one human relationship, may become quite the reverse in another. Generally speaking, morality often imposes upon those who exercise the powers of government standards of conduct quite different from what might seem right to them as private citizens. For instance, the moral, and indeed the legal, duty of a judge in bringing to bear upon a party before him the coercive power of the state is not to do "what he thinks is right," or by his decision to mould the kind of society which seems to him to accord with divine will or high human aspiration. He has not been given this great power so that he might administer personal justice, even though his conscience be as clear as that of Harun al-Rashid or Henry the Second when they decided disputes by virtuous inspiration. Our courts are supposed to be courts of law; and whatever justice may be (I know of no satisfactory definition of it), it is to be achieved, as the phrase goes, "under law." It is our hope that the consciences of our judges will be guided, not by what they think is right, but what they believe the law requires them to decide, whether they like it or not.

So, too, what may be quite proper and moral for a private citizen—for instance, the pursuit of personal advantage, or the advantage of a group—often, and rightly, is condemned if done when he assumes legislative or executive office. This distinction is not always perceived and has gotten many people into trouble. Even a candidate for office cannot expect the same latitude given private individuals in exposing his ignorance and stupidity. November 3rd last [1964] made that rather clear.

Moreover, the vocabulary of morals and ethics is inadequate to discuss or test foreign policies of states. We are told that what is ethical is characterized by what is excellent in conduct and that excellence may be judged by what is right and proper, as against what is wrong, by existing standards. But when we look for standards we find that none exist. What passes for ethical standards for governmental policies in foreign affairs is a collection of moralisms, maxims, and slogans, which neither help nor guide, but only confuse, decision on such complicated matters as the multilateral nuclear force, a common grain price in Europe, policy in Southeast Asia, or exceptions and disparities under the Kennedy Round of tariff negotiations.

One of the most often invoked and delusive of these maxims is the so-called principle of self-determination. In the continuing dispute over Cyprus it has been invoked by nearly all parties to the struggle to support whatever they were temporarily seeking to achieve—by all Cypriots to justify revolt against British rule, by Archbishop Makarios to support an independent government for the whole island, by Greek Cypriots as foundation for enosis (union) with Greece, and by Turkish Cypriots for partition of the island and double enosis, union of one part with Greece and the other with Turkey.

Despite its approval by Woodrow Wilson, this maxim has a doubtful moral history. He used it against our enemies in the First World War to dismember the Austro-Hungarian and Ottoman Empires with results which hardly inspire enthusiasm today. After the Second World War the doctrine was invoked against our friends in the dissolution of their colonial connections. In all probability these connections would inevitably have been dissolved. But the results were immeasurably improved when considerations other than moralistic maxims were brought to bear on the process.

On the one occasion when the right of self-determination— then called secession—was invoked against our own government by the Confederate States of America, it was rejected with a good deal of bloodshed and moral fervor. Probably you agree that it was rightly rejected. You would doubtless also agree that the dialogue now in progress between the British and French speaking sections of Canada upon the problems of a common national life together would not be helped by conducting it in terms of the principle of self-determination.

Furthermore, this moralistic doctrine is not merely no help to wise policy decisions, it can be a positive menace to them. "Hitler's appeal to national self-determination in the Sudeten crisis in 1938," writes Henry Kissinger, "was an invocation of 'justice,' and thereby contributed to the indecisiveness of the resistance; it induced the Western powers to attempt to construct a 'truly' legitimate order by satisfying Germany's 'just' claims. Only after Hitler annexed Bohemia and Moravia was it clear that he was aiming for dominion, not legitimacy; only then did the contest become one of pure power."

Another set of moralisms and maxims crops up to bedevil discussion and decisions about what is broadly called "foreign aid." A good deal of trouble comes from the anthropomorphic urge to regard nations as individuals and apply to our own national conduct vague maxims for individual conduct—for instance, the Golden Rule—even though in practice individuals rarely adopt it. The fact is that nations are not individuals; the cause and effect of their actions are wholly different; and what a government can and should do with the resources which it takes from its citizens must be governed by wholly different considerations from those which properly determine an individual's use of his own.

This does not mean that considerations of compassion have no place in governmental decisions. It does mean that the criteria are generally quite different and far more complicated. Some of these criteria will determine what funds can be made available; others will determine their allocation among uses always exceeding amounts available.

The overriding guide must be achievement of a major goal of policy—in this case, creating an environment in which free societies may flourish and undeveloped nations who want to work on their own development may find the means to do so. This is an exceedingly difficult matter for both aiding and aided governments. The criteria should be hard-headed in the extreme. Decisions are not helped by considering them in terms of sharing, brotherly love, the Golden Rule, or inducting our citizens into the Kingdom of Heaven.

But, you will say to me, at least one moral standard of right and wrong has been pretty well agreed to be applicable to foreign policy. Surely, the opinion of the world has condemned the use and threat of force by one state against another, as the United Nations Charter bears witness. Does this not give us firm ground on which to stand? Well, does it? Ever since the Charter was signed, those whose interests are opposed to ours have used force, or the threat of it, whenever it seemed to them advisable and safe—in Greece, Czechoslovakia, Palestine, Berlin, Korea, Indochina, and Hungary. Each side used it in regard to Suez.

Is it moral to deny ourselves the use of force in all circumstances, when our adversaries employ it, under handy excuses, whenever it seems useful to tip the scales of power against every value we think of as moral and as making life worth living? It seems to me not only a bad bargain, but a stupid one. I would almost say an immoral one. For the very conception of morality seems to me to involve a duty to preserve values outside the contour of our own skins, and at the expense of foregoing much that is desired and pleasant, including—it may be—our own fortunes and lives.

But, however that may be, those involved in the Cuban crisis of October, 1962, will remember the irrelevance of the supposed moral considerations brought out in the discussions. Judgment centered about the appraisal of dangers and risks, the weighing of the need for decisive and effective action against considerations of prudence; the need to do enough, against the consequences of doing too much. Moral talk did not bear on the problem. Nor did it bear upon the decision of those called upon to advise the President in 1949 whether and with what degree of urgency to press the attempt to produce a thermonuclear weapon. A respected colleague advised me that it would be better that our whole nation and people should perish rather than be party to a course so evil as producing that weapon. I told him that on the Day of Judgment his view might be confirmed and that he was free to go forth and preach the necessity for salvation. It was not, however, a view which I could entertain as a public servant.

What, then, is the sound approach to questions of foreign policy? I suggest that it is what we might call the strategic approach—to consider various courses of action from the point of view of their bearing upon major objectives. On August 22, 1862, President Lincoln wrote to Horace Greeley in response to the latter's question as to how the President viewed the question of slavery in relation to the war then in progress, "my paramount object in this struggle is to save the Union, and is not either to save or destroy slavery. If I could save the Union without freeing any slave, I would do it; and if I could save it by freeing all the slaves, I would do it; and if I could do it by freeing some and leaving others alone, I would also do that. What I do about slavery and the colored race, I do because I believe it helps to save this Union; and what I forbear, I forbear because I do not believe it would help to save the Union. I shall do less whenever I shall believe what I am doing hurts the cause, and I shall do more whenever I shall believe doing more will help the cause."

This is what I mean by the strategic approach. If you object that is no different from saying that the end justifies the means, I must answer that in foreign affairs only the end can justify the means; that this is not to say that the end justifies any means, or that some ends can justify anything. The shifting "combinazioni," sought by the weak Italian city states of the Renaissance to plunder one another, not only failed to justify the means they used, but gave their diplomacy and its expounder, Niccolo Machiavelli, the bad name they have today.

The end sought by our foreign policy, the purpose for which we carry on relations with foreign states, is, as I have said, to preserve and foster an environment in which free societies may exist and flourish. Our policies and actions must be tested by whether they contribute to or detract from achievement of this end. They need no other justification or moral or ethical embellishment. To oppose powerful and brutal states which threaten the independence of others is not less admirable because it helps secure our own as well; nor is it less good to help others improve their lot because it is necessary to keep the free world free and to strengthen it.

In conducting our foreign affairs we can use any amount of intelligence, perseverance, nerve, and luck. But if we have an excess of moral or ethical enthusiasm or idealism, let us not try to find an outlet for it in the formulation of foreign policies. Rather in how we carry them out. In this country we have an unfortunate tendency to do fine and noble things in a thoroughly churlish way. Let us remember that often what we do may be less important than how we do it. "What one lives for may be uncertain," writes Lord Robert Cecil; "How one lives is not." We can be faulted far less in what we do, than in how we do it.

5. *INTERNATIONAL RELATIONS: THE LONG ROAD TO THEORY* / STANLEY H. HOFFMANN*

. . . The theory which has occupied the center of the scene in this country during the last ten years is Professor Morgenthau's "realist" theory of power politics. It tries to give us a reliable map of the landscape of world affairs,[9] to catch the essence of world politics. The master key is the concept of interest defined in terms of power. The theory succeeds in focusing attention on the principal actors in world affairs: the states, and on the factors that account for the autonomy of international relations: the differences between domestic and world politics which thwart the operation in the latter of ideas and institutions that flourish in the former, the drastic imperatives of survival, self-preservation, and self-help which are both the causes and the products of such differences.

However, as a general theory, the realist analysis fails because it

---

* Stanley H. Hoffmann, "International Relations: The Long Road to Theory," *World Politics,* Vol. 11, No. 3 (April 1959), pp. 349–54. Reprinted by permission.
[9] Hans J. Morgenthau, "Reflections on the State of Political Science," *Review of Politics,* XVII, No. 4 (October 1955), pp. 455ff.

sees the world as a static field in which power relations reproduce themselves in timeless monotony. The map is inadequate for two main reasons. First, the realist analysis of power is a very debatable one. The decision to equate politics and the effects of man's "lust for power," and the tendency to equate power and evil or violence, mutilate reality.[10] A "power monism" does not account for all politics, when power is so somberly defined. Furthermore, the extent to which power as a carrier of evil and violence expresses a basic human instinct is questionable, for much of the international (or domestic) evil of power is rooted not in the sinfulness of man but in a context, a constellation, a situation, in which even good men are forced to act selfishly or immorally. The discrimination between the inherent or instinctive aspects of the "power drive," and the situational or accidental ones, is an important task, neglected by the theory.

Also, it is dangerous to put in a key position a concept which is merely instrumental. Power is a means toward any of a large number of ends (including power itself): the quality and quantity of power used by men are determined by men's purposes. Now, the realist theory neglects all the factors that influence or define purposes. Why statesmen choose at times to act in a certain way rather than in another is not made clear. The domestic considerations that define national power are either left out or brushed aside. So is the role of internationally shared values and purposes. We get a somewhat mechanistic view of international affairs in which the statesmen's role consists of adjusting national power to an almost immutable set of external "givens." The realist world is a frozen universe of separate essences.[11]

Even if the role of power were as determining as the theory postulates, the question arises whether any scheme can put so much methodological weight upon one concept, even a crucial one; for it seems to me that the concept of power collapses under the burden. Power is a most complex product of other variables which should be allowed to see the light of the theory instead of remaining hidden in

[10] Hans J. Morgenthau, *Scientific Man versus Power Politics*, Chicago, 1946, pp. 50–51 and 188–202.

[11] On these points, see John H. Herz, *Political Realism and Political Idealism*, Chicago, 1951, pp. 3–15 and 63ff.; Robert W. Tucker, "Professor Morgenthau's Theory of Political 'Realism,'" *American Political Science Review*, XLVI, No. 1 (March 1952), pp. 214–24; Herbert Butterfield, "The Scientific versus the Moralistic Approach," *International Affairs*, XXVII, No. 4 (October 1951), pp. 411–22; Harold Sprout, "In Defense of Diplomacy," *World Politics*, I, No. 3, (April 1949), pp. 404–13.

the shadow of power.[12] Otherwise, the theory is bound either to mean different things at different steps of the analysis (or when dealing with different periods), or to end by selecting for emphasis only one aspect of power: either military force or economic strength.[13] Thus, instead of a map which simplifies the landscape so that we can understand it, we are left with a distortion.

There is a second reason for the inadequacy of the map. The clumsiness that comes from the timeless concept of power is compounded by the confusing use of other concepts that are dated in more ways than one, and which the theory applies to situations in which they do not fit. The model of the realists is a highly embellished ideal-type of eighteenth- and nineteenth-century international relations. This vision of the golden age is taken as a norm, both for empirical analysis, and for evaluation. A number of oddities of the theory are explained thereby. First, the lack of an adequate discussion of ends. For when all the actors have almost the same credo, it becomes easy to forget the effects of the common credo on the actors' behavior, and to omit from among the main variables of the theory a factor whose role seems constant.[14] It is nevertheless an optical illusion to mistake a particular pattern for the norm of a scientific system. Secondly, the conception of an objective and easily recognizable national interest is one which makes sense only in a stable period in which the participants play for limited ends, with limited means, and without domestic kibitzers to disrupt the players' moves. In such a period, the survival of the main players is rarely at stake in the game, and a hierarchy can rather easily be established among the other and far less vital interests that are at stake. Today, survival is almost always in question, and the most divergent courses of action can be recommended as choices for survival.[15] An attempt at using the theory as a key to the under-

[12] It is impossible to subsume under one word variables as different as power as a condition of policy and power as a criterion of policy; power as a sum of resources and power as a set of processes; power as a potential and power in use.

[13] On this last point, see, e.g., A. F. K. Organski's "economic power monism" in his *World Politics*, New York, 1958.

[14] Morgenthau's views on the role of motives and of ideological preferences are to be found in *Politics Among Nations*, New York, 1955, pp. 6–7 and 8off. Similar views are expressed by Kenneth W. Thompson in Roy Macridis, ed., *Foreign Policy in World Politics*, New York, 1958, pp. 351–55.

[15] See Thomas I. Cook and Malcolm Moos, "Foreign Policy: The Realism of Idealism," *American Political Science Review*, XLVI, No. 2 (June 1952), pp. 342–56; Raymond Aron, "En quête d'une philosophie de la politique étrangère," *Revue Française de Science Politique*, III, No. 1 (January–March 1953), pp. 69–91.

standing of contemporary realities puts one in the position of a Tiresias who recognizes interests which the parties refuse to see, who diagnoses permanence where the parties find confusing change, and whose ex post facto omniscience is both irritating and irrelevant.

Thirdly, the idea that the national interest carries its own morality is also one which makes sense only in a stable period (although it is strangely phrased). For it is in such a period that an international consensus assures at least the possibility of accommodation of national objectives: the conflicts of interests which are involved are not struggles between competing international moralities. The philosophical pluralism implicit in the realist theory (which purports to be both normative and empirical) is hardly tolerable in periods of "nationalistic universalism," and it is unnecessary in periods of stability and moderation, which bloom only because of a basic agreement on values. Fourth, the emphasis on the rationality of foreign policy and the desire to brush aside the irrational elements as intrusions or pathological deviations are understandable only in terms of cabinet diplomacy, where such deviations appear (especially with the benefit of hindsight) to have been rare. There, rationality seemed like the simple adjustment of means to stable and generally recognized ends. These concepts are far less applicable to a period in which the political struggles involve primarily the determination of ends.[16] Thus, behind the claim to realism, we find a reactionary utopia.

The consequence of this inadequacy of the map is that the theory's usefulness as a general theory for the discipline is limited. In the first place, from the point of view of systematic empirical analysis, the theory stresses the autonomy of international relations to the point of leaving beyond its pale the forces which work for change and which, cutting across the states, affect the states' behavior.[17] We are presented both with a single key to the closed room of politics among nations, and with a warning that the room is in a house whose key we cannot have, or whose opening must be

[16] These arguments are developed by Henry A. Kissinger in *A World Restored,* Boston, 1957. The application of a rationality of means to the selection of ends is, it seems to me, one of the fallacies that mar the argument for limited nuclear war.

[17] See Hans J. Morgenthau, "Another 'Great Debate': The National Interest of the United States," *American Political Science Review,* XLVI, No. 4 (December 1952), pp. 973–76; and a critique of this attitude in Reinhold Niebuhr, *The Children of Light and the Children of Darkness,* New York, 1944, pp. 173ff.

left to the "workman-like manipulation of perennial forces."[18] We are not told what they are, or how they operate. We reach at this point one of the most fundamental ambiguities of the theory. The postulate of the permanence of power politics among nations as the core of international relations tends to become a goal. The static qualities of the theory lead to confusion between the phenomenon of power conflicts and the transitory forms and institutions in which such conflicts have been taking place in recent centuries. Why should the sound reminder that power is here to stay mean that the present system of nation-states will continue, or change only through forces that are of no concern to us? Such an attitude is a double evasion: from the empirical duty of accounting for change, and from the normative task of assessing whether the present system should indeed continue. One cannot help but feel that, in spite of Mr. Morgenthau's qualifying statements, there is behind his theory the old position that whatever has been, must continue.

This brings us to a second limitation, which concerns the usefulness of the scheme as a normative theory. It is something of a success philosophy. The criterion of a good foreign policy is its rationality, but the touchstone of rationality is success. Unfortunately the standards of success and failure are not made clear. First, how will we distinguish between the follies of straight utopianism and the fallacies of wrong realism—realism that did not work?[19] Secondly, from what viewpoint shall we decide whether a statesman has succeeded or failed? Shall we turn to history alone? But at what stage? Metternich had succeeded by 1825, failed by 1848, and writers disagree as to whether he had succeeded or failed by 1914.[20] If we set our standards outside and above history, we must avoid trying to prove that history will inevitably recompense policies that meet our standards. Otherwise, we become salesmen for a philosophical stand who travel the roads of history in search of a clientele of confirmations, rather than scholars testing a hypothesis or philosophers interested in an ideal which history cannot promise to bless at all times.

The former position we wish to avoid. It is particularly uncomfortable when one's basic postulate about human nature is such that history cannot be anything but a tale full of sound and fury,

[18] Morgenthau, *Politics Among Nations*, p. 9.
[19] Aron, *op. cit.*; David Thomson in *Contemporary Political Science*, Paris, UNESCO, 1950, pp. 588–89.
[20] See E. H. Carr, *The Twenty Years' Crisis*, London, 1951, pp. 89–91.

signifying nothing.[21] This view makes it impossible to understand how there could be a rational theory of rational human behavior. This is not the last contradiction: the realist theory combines a Hobbesian image of naked power politics with an attempt to show that states are nevertheless not condemned to a life that is "nasty, brutish, and short." Realism thus puts its faith in voluntary restraints, moderation, and the underlying assumption of possible harmony among national interests—points scarcely admitted by the original postulate. Finally, there is a sharp contrast between this postulate, whose logic is a permanent clash of forces of evil, and the norm of eighteenth- and nineteenth-century international relations— the period in which the world's state of nature was most Lockian, and Morgenthau's view of human nature most unjustified.

With such flaws and contradictions, the policy guidance which the realist theory is able to afford is limited. Realism allows us to eliminate those policies that would foolishly forget the prerequisite of power; but it does not go much further. Too many factors are left out for realist advice to avoid the dilemma of homilies and admonishments, or suggestions inappropriate for revolutionary periods.[22] The light that illuminated the landscape in the quiet obscurity of nineteenth-century politics is blown out by today's tempest. . . .

[21] Reason, "far from following its own inherent impulses, is driven toward its goal by the irrational forces the ends of which it serves" (Morgenthau, *Scientific Man versus Power Politics*, p. 154). See Alfred Grosser, "L'étude des relations internationales, spécialité américaine?" *Revue Française de Science Politique*, vi, No. 3 (July–September 1956), pp. 634–51.

[22] This is frequently the case with George Kennan. See William G. Carleton, "Braintrusters of American Foreign Policy," *World Politics*, vii, No. 4 (July 1955), pp. 627–39. On the possibility of justifying in realist terms a policy that can also be advocated on utopian grounds, see Warner R. Schilling, "The Clarification of Ends, or, Which Interest Is the National?" *ibid.*, viii, No. 4 (July 1956), pp. 566–78.

part **II**
THE MODERN
STATE SYSTEM

3
SOVEREIGNTY

The prime characteristic of the modern state system is sovereignty. Jean Bodin (1530–96) thoroughly defined and analyzed this concept in his *Six Books of the Commonwealth*, first published in 1576. He wrote this work at a time of political disorders in France, which explains his horror of anarchy and his concern for the establishment of strong governmental authority. The excerpts included in this chapter show, however, that he did not think of sovereignty as completely unlimited power.

Bodin's principal concern was sovereignty within the state. What effect does the existence of many states, each sovereign and under no higher authority, have on the international system? Thomas Hobbes (1588–1679) in his famous work *Leviathan*, from which the second selection is drawn, compared international relations with those of individuals in a "state of nature," which he described as a situation of perpetual conflict. Jean Jacques Rousseau (1712–78) sharply disagreed with Hobbes' concept of the state of nature as applied to individuals. But, following a different line of argument, he arrives at a very similar conclusion regarding the state of nature among states in the international system. Rousseau expounded these ideas in *The State of War*. Although this essay is only a relatively brief fragment of an unfinished work, it is one of the most significant classical writings in the field of international relations.

Clement Attlee, British Prime Minister from 1945 to 1951 and Labor Party leader until 1955, also equated sovereignty with international anarchy, and therefore regarded it as the root of the world's troubles. The final selection in this chapter is the Annual Memorial Lecture of the David Davies Memorial Institute of International Studies delivered by Lord Attlee in the House of Commons in 1958.

6. ON SOVEREIGNTY* / JEAN BODIN

Sovereignty is the absolute and perpetual power of a state which in Latin is termed *maiestas* . . . It is perpetual because one may give absolute power to one or more persons for a certain length of time, but once that time has expired they become merely subjects again themselves; even while they are in power, they cannot call themselves sovereign rulers, but only the agents of that power until it pleases the people or the prince to revoke it. The true sovereign always retains his power. Just as he who lends his goods to another remains the lord and owner of them, so he who grants to others the power and authority to judge and command either for a limited time or for as long as it pleases him, actually retains the power and the jurisdiction merely borrowed by those exercising it. That is why the law stipulates that local governors or the prince's lieutenants, as agents of the prince's power, surrender their authority at the end of their terms of office. And in this respect there is no difference between the highest and the lowest officials. For if it were otherwise, and the absolute power granted by a prince to his

---

* Jean Bodin, *Les Six Livres de la République* (Paris, 1583), Chap. 8. Translated by Eva Tamm Lijphart and Arend Lijphart.

lieutenant should be called sovereignty, he could use it against his prince who would then be a prince in name only: the subject would command his lord and the servant his master. Nothing could be more absurd, because the person of the sovereign is always excepted, as a matter of right, in all grants of power and authority to others. However much he gives, he always keeps more himself. He is never deprived of his power to command or intervene in all matters delegated to his magistrates or officers by way of prevention, confirmation, evocation, or any other way it pleases him. He may also revoke any delegated power or allow it to be exercised only as long as he thinks fit. . . .

Let us now consider the other part of our definition and explain what is meant by the term "absolute power." The people or the lords of a state may simply give to someone the sovereign and perpetual power to dispose of their goods and persons and of the whole state at his pleasure and then leave it to a successor of his choice, in the same way that a property owner may generously make a pure and unconditional gift of his goods to someone. Such a gift is the only true gift—unconditional, unqualified, and irrevocable. Other gifts, burdened by obligations and conditions, are not true gifts. Similarly, sovereignty given to a prince with obligations and conditions attached is neither true sovereignty nor absolute power, unless the conditions of his appointment are only those of the laws of God and of nature . . . If we state that he who has absolute power is not subject to any laws, there is no sovereign prince at all in the world because all the princes of the earth are subject to the laws of God and of nature and to certain human laws common to all nations. . . .

The sovereign cannot in any way be subject to the commands of others, for it is he who makes law for his subjects, abrogates laws that are no longer needed, and replaces them with new laws. No one who is subject to the law or under some other person's authority can do this. That is why according to law the prince is exempt from all laws. The word "law" in Latin also implies the command of the holder of sovereignty. Furthermore, we find in all decrees and statutes the following clause: "Notwithstanding all decrees and statutes from which we have derogated or do hereby derogate." This clause was always added to the ancient laws whether the former law had been promulgated by the prince himself or by his predecessors. For it is quite certain that all laws, ordinances, letters patent, privileges, and grants issued by the prince are in force only during his lifetime, unless they are expressly or at least tacitly confirmed by his successors . . .

If, therefore, the sovereign prince is exempt from the laws of his predecessors, still less can he be bound by his own laws and ordinances. One may impose a law on someone else, but it is impossible to impose a law on oneself or to bind oneself in any matter which depends on one's own free will. As the law states, *Nulla obligatio consistere potest, quae a voluntate promittentis statum capit.* It follows, therefore, that the king cannot be subject to his own laws. Just as, according to the canonists, the Pope can never tie his own hands, the sovereign prince cannot tie his own hands even if he should want to do so. Therefore, we find the following phrase at the end of decrees and statutes: "For such is our good pleasure," indicating that the laws of a sovereign prince, even though founded on good reasons, depend solely on his own free will.

The divine and natural laws present a different case. All princes of the earth are subject to them, and cannot infringe them without being guilty of treason and war against God, under whose majesty all monarchs of the earth must be subjugated and must bow their heads in fear and reverence. Hence the absolute power of princes and sovereign lords does not extend to the laws of God and of nature. He who best understood the meaning of absolute power and made kings and emperors submit to his power [Innocent IV], defined it as being above the ordinary law, but not above the divine and natural laws.

But is not the prince subject to the laws of his country if he has sworn to uphold them? Here we have to distinguish. If the prince swears to himself that he will uphold the law, he is not bound by his oath any more than by a promise to himself. Even subjects are not bound in any way by private oaths to keep agreements. The law permits a breach of such agreements even though they may be fair and reasonable. However, if one sovereign prince promises another prince, whether under oath or not, to uphold the laws which he or his predecessors have made, he is bound to do so if the other prince's interests are involved. If they are not involved, neither the promise nor the oath can bind him.

The same rule applies to promises made by the sovereign prince to his subjects, even if they were made before his election, for this makes no difference. It is not that the prince is bound by his own laws or those of his predecessors. But he is bound by the just covenants and promises he has made, whether under oath or not, just as a private person is bound in such a case. For the same reasons that a private person can be released from a promise which was unjust, unreasonable, or too burdensome, or which was extracted by fraud, error, or force, a sovereign prince can act to reverse any encroachments on his sovereign rights. Hence our maxim stands, that the prince is neither subject to his own laws nor to those of his predecessors, but is bound by the just and reasonable covenants which affect the interests of all or some of his subjects. . . .

We must not confuse laws with covenants. Laws proceed from the sovereign who can bind the subject but cannot bind himself. Covenants are mutually and reciprocally binding on both the prince and his subjects, and cannot be contravened by either party to the prejudice of the other without his consent. In this case, the prince has no more rights than his subjects. . . .

The constitutional laws and the laws concerning the King's estate are, like the salic laws, annexed and united to the Crown, and cannot be infringed by the prince. If he should do so, his successor can always nullify any act prejudicial to the constitutional laws and those of the royal estate on which his sovereign majesty is based. . . .

Is the prince bound to uphold the law of nations? . . . The prince is not bound by the law of nations to a greater extent than by his own laws. If the law of nations is iniquitous, the prince can disregard it when making laws for his own kingdom and can forbid his subjects to observe it, even when it is truly common to all peoples, as was done in this kingdom [France] with regard to slavery. He can also disregard any similar provisions of the law of nations, provided that he does nothing against the law of God. For if justice is the end of the law, the law the work of the prince, and the prince the image of God, the law of the prince should be patterned after the law of God.

7. *THE STATE OF NATURE** / *THOMAS HOBBES*

. . . in the nature of man we find three principal causes of quarrel. First, competition; secondly, diffidence; thirdly, glory.

* Thomas Hobbes, *Leviathan* (London: Andrew Crooke, 1651), Part I, Chap. 13. (Spelling and punctuation modernized.)

The first maketh man invade for gain; the second, for safety; and the third, for reputation. The first use violence, to make themselves masters of other men's persons, wives, children, and cattle; the second, to defend them; the third, for trifles, as a word, a smile, a different opinion, and any other sign of undervalue, either direct in their persons, or by reflection in their kindred, their friends, their nation, their profession, or their name.

Hereby it is manifest that, during the time men live without a common power to keep them all in awe, they are in that condition which is called war, and such a war as is of every man against every man. For "war" consisteth not in battle only or the act of fighting, but in a tract of time wherein the will to contend by battle is sufficiently known, and therefore the notion of "time" is to be considered in the nature of war, as it is in the nature of weather. For as the nature of foul weather lieth not in a shower or two of rain, but in an inclination thereto of many days together, so the nature of war consisteth not in actual fighting, but in the known disposition thereto during all the time there is no assurance to the contrary. All other time is "peace."

Whatsoever therefore is consequent to a time of war, where every man is enemy to every man, the same is consequent to the time wherein men live without other security than what their own strength and their own invention shall furnish them withal. In such condition there is no place for industry, because the fruit thereof is uncertain, and consequently no culture of the earth, no navigation nor use of the commodities that may be imported by sea, no commodious building, no instruments of moving and removing such things as require much force, no knowledge of the face of the earth; no account of time, no arts, no letters, no society, and, which is worst of all, continual fear and danger of violent death, and the life of man solitary, poor, nasty, brutish, and short.

It may seem strange to some man that has not well weighed these things, that Nature should thus dissociate and render men apt to invade and destroy one another; and he may therefore, not trusting to this inference made from the passions, desire perhaps to have the same confirmed by experience. Let him therefore consider with himself, when taking a journey, he arms himself and seeks to go well accompanied; when going to sleep, he locks his doors; when even in his house, he locks his chests; and this when he knows there be laws and public officers armed to revenge all injuries shall be done him; what opinion he has of his fellow-subjects, when he rides armed; of his fellow-citizens, when he locks his doors; and of his children and servants, when he locks his chests. Does he not there as much accuse mankind by his actions as I do by my words? But neither of us accuse man's nature in it. The desires and other passions of man are in themselves no sin. No more are the actions that proceed from those passions, till they know a law that forbids them; which, till laws be made, they cannot know, nor can any law be made till they have agreed upon the person that shall make it.

It may peradventure be thought there was never such a time nor condition of war as this; and I believe it was never generally so over all the world, but there are many places where they live so now. For the savage people in many places of America, except the government of small families the concord whereof dependeth on natural lust, have no government at all, and live at this day in that brutish manner as I said before. Howsoever, it may be perceived what manner of life there would be where there were no common power to fear, by the manner of life which men that have formerly lived under a peaceful government, use to degenerate into in a civil war.

But, though there had never been any time wherein particular men were in a condition of war one against another, yet in all times kings and persons of sovereign authority, because of their independence, are in continual jealousies and in the state and posture of gladiators, having their weapons pointing, and their eyes fixed on one another, that is, their forts, garrisons, and guns, upon the frontiers of their kingdoms, and continual spies upon their neighbours; which is a posture of war. But because they uphold thereby the industry of their subjects, there does not follow from it that misery which accompanies the liberty of particular men. . . .

8. *THE STATE OF WAR** / *JEAN JACQUES ROUSSEAU*

Even if Hobbes' assumption that an unlimited and indomitable greed has developed in all men were true, it would still not produce that universal war of every man against every man, of which he paints

* Jean Jacques Rousseau, *L'État de Guerre* (approx. 1755). Translated by Eva Tamm Lijphart and Arend Lijphart.

such an odious picture. This uncontrolled desire to take possession of everything is incompatible with the desire to destroy all one's fellow-men. Because the victor has killed everyone, he has the misfortune of living alone in the world, and cannot enjoy anything for the very reason that he owns everything. What is the use of wealth if there is nobody else who can know about it? What is the use of owning the whole universe, if the owner is its only inhabitant? Will his stomach devour all the products of the earth? And who will collect the products of all the different climates for him? Who will bear witness to his empire in the vast regions of the earth in which he will never live? What will he do with his treasures? Who will eat all his food? To which eyes will he show his power? Instead of massacring everyone, he will put everyone in chains in order to at least have slaves. That immediately changes the whole nature of the question; since there is no urge to destroy one's fellow-men, a state of war in this sense does not exist.

Man is by nature peaceful and timid; at the least sign of danger, his first instinct is to flee. He acquires boldness only by experience and habit. Honor, self-interest, prejudice, vengeance—all the passions which enable him to face death and peril—are feelings foreign to him in the state of nature. Only when he has established a social bond with another man, will he decide to attack someone else. And he only becomes a soldier after having been a citizen first. One cannot discern any strong natural disposition to make war on all one's fellow-men. But I have already spent too much time discussing a philosophy which is as revolting as it is absurd, and which has already been refuted a hundred times.

Therefore, there is no general war of every man against every man. And the human race was not created for the single purpose of destroying itself. . . .

Now we enter into a new order of things. We shall see men united by an artificial bond, but united to destroy each other; and all the horrors of war stem from men's efforts to prevent it. But it is important that we first get a clearer explanation of the essential nature of the body politic than has been given heretofore. The reader should remember that we are concerned less with particular historical facts than with right and justice in general, and that I want to examine the subject objectively and without prejudice.

The formation of the first society necessarily led to the formation of all the others. It was necessary to join it or to unite in order to resist it. It was necessary to imitate it or else be devoured by it.

Thus, the entire surface of the earth was changed: everywhere nature disappeared, and everywhere human art took its place; independence and natural freedom made way for laws and slavery. It is no longer possible to be free; the philosopher looking for the true man is unable to find him. But we are mistaken if we think that the state of nature has disappeared altogether; it reappears and shows itself where we least expect it. The independence which is taken away from men as individuals, takes refuge in their societies; and these great bodies, left to their own impulses, produce clashes that are all the more terrible because their weights exceed those of individual people.

But, it will be said, how is it possible that these bodies, which are equally solidly based, ever collide with each other? Should not their very constitution maintain them in a condition of perpetual peace? Are they obligated, like men, to seek more than they need? Don't they have within themselves all that they require for their preservation? Are competition and trade an inevitable source of discord? And haven't the inhabitants of all countries existed before the beginning of commerce—irrefutable proof that they can live without it?

These questions I could answer merely on the basis of facts, and I would not have to fear any rejoinder. But I have not forgotten that I argue here about the general nature of things—not about individual events, which may have a thousand special causes, unrelated to the common principle. Let us consider carefully the structure of political bodies; even though each one has sufficient means to preserve itself, we find that their mutual relations are not much closer than those of individuals. Basically, man does not need any contact with his fellow-men; he can enjoy a healthy and vigorous existence without their help; he does not need human care as much as he needs the products of the earth; and the earth produces more than enough to feed all its inhabitants. Moreover, man's size and the extent of his power are fixed by nature and cannot be exceeded. All his faculties are limited in every respect. His life is short, and his days are counted. His stomach does not expand in proportion to his wealth; his passions may grow, but his pleasures are not without measure; his heart is limited like the rest of him; his capacity for enjoyment is always the same. Although he may think of himself in grand terms, in reality he always remains small.

The state, on the contrary, is an artificial body, and consequently does not have any definite limits; the size that is appropriate to it, cannot be defined, and can always be increased. The state feels weak as long as there are others which are stronger. Its security and its preservation demand that it becomes more powerful than all its neighbors. It cannot maintain, increase, and exercise its power except at their expense; and if it does not need to seek its sustenance abroad, it must continuously try to gain new members to reinforce its might. For the inequality among men has limits imposed by the hands of nature, but the inequality of societies can continue to grow, until one absorbs all the others.

Thus, because the power of the body politic is purely relative, it is forced to compare itself in order to know itself; it depends on everything surrounding it, and must take an interest in all that happens there. Even if a state should aim merely at self-preservation within its own borders, without either gaining or losing anything, it still becomes small or large, weak or strong, according to whether its neighbor expands or contracts, is strengthened or weakened. . . .

The most remarkable aspect of the situation of mankind is a manifest contradiction in its constitution which makes it vacillate between two conditions. Among men, we live in the civil state and are subject to the laws; among peoples, each enjoys its natural freedom. This renders our situation fundamentally worse than if these distinctions were unknown. For, living at the same time in the social order and in the state of nature, we are subjected to the inconveniences of both without finding security in either. . . .

Let us take a moment to contrast these ideas with the horrible system of Hobbes; we find that, completely contrary to his absurd doctrine, the state of war is not at all natural to man. War stems from peace, or at least from the precautions which men have taken for the purpose of securing a lasting peace.

9. *THE PERILS OF ABSOLUTE SOVEREIGNTY* / CLEMENT ATTLEE*

The root of the trouble in today's world is that we believe in anarchy. We believe in the complete, or almost complete, right of

* Clement Attlee, "The Perils of Absolute Sovereignty," *The Saturday Review* (August 23, 1958), pp. 22–23. Reprinted by permission of the David Davies Memorial Institute of International Studies and *The Saturday Review*.

every nation to do what it chooses. One still has the feeling that anything like a surrender of sovereignty is contrary to our human nature. Although every day individuals surrender their sovereignty inside a country for the sake of a larger freedom, we still talk as if we were detached individuals when it comes to international affairs.

What is needed in the world today is the rule of enforceable law enforced. You will find some people who say that all this is high-flying idealistic nonsense. So long as human nature remains human nature this idea of world government will remain nothing but a comfortable dream. I wonder how many people have said that in their time with regard to every possible innovation. But you cannot afford to take that view today. Unless mankind meets the challenge of the present day it will not survive.

The United Nations doesn't yet fill the bill. The U.N. has not yet meant the surrender of sovereignty; it is not an authoritative force—it has no instrument. I am not denying that it is a very powerful forum of public opinion, nor am I denying that it does all kinds of good things, but it doesn't do the *essential* things. But there are some hopeful signs. Leaders in our own country and others no longer shrink from world government. It has been proclaimed by our Government that we must work towards world government—that is a great step forward from the old days when collective security was called midsummer madness. They also declare for absolute disarmament. Thirty or forty years ago anyone who preached that would have been answered, "Human nature never changes—people always fight." Today we have plans for disarmament.

But why do all these admirable plans break down? The late Arthur Henderson worked with great devotion between the wars on disarmament proposals. Other experts are working constantly. Yet why don't we get disarmament? I think the answer is that we always found that between the wars you cannot get disarmament without some security—it always broke down on that. How can you get security? You cannot get security internationally today. You may get a partial security in arrangements of one kind and another—such as NATO and SEATO. But I don't believe we will get real disarmament without an approach to an international force. I say it for this reason: at the present time we are held in uneasy equilibrium by the possession of two groups in the world of nuclear weapons. We hope this means that nuclear warfare will never come to the world. We hope that, but it may be that the mere fact that either side would hesitate to use these nuclear weapons may make them take a chance with what are called "conventional weapons." A good definition of an unconventional weapon was given by Sir Winston Churchill the other day: "Those the other side have got and you have not got." I don't much believe in this distinction. I don't believe that when you arm your forces with nuclear weapons you can then talk of them as conventional weapons. I think the distinction has to do with their mass destructiveness, as contrasted to comparatively light weapons for police purposes.

I think the time has come when, if we are realists, we should say that no major war would be won with nuclear weapons, and therefore if any minor trouble develops we don't want forces which would lead inevitably to the use of nuclear weapons. We want something much smaller and lighter—a form of armed police force. If we had that you could, I believe, have enough to stop incidents where there was danger developing, but we would also be saved all the immense business of these huge land armies that I believe will never fight at all.

How are you going to get such a force? People say that there is not today the necessary unity in the world; power politics are played all the way. I don't see any reason why, apart from power politics, some of these problems that oppress us in various parts of the world should not be settled peaceably, but there are people who have an interest in stirring it up.

Can we get away from this? Let's be realists. If it is really true that the Soviet Union is inspired by a complete desire to enslave the whole world, as a combination of the old-fashioned Russian imperialism and the new Communist ideological imperialism, then the outlook is pretty bad; but I always think we are rather inclined to overestimate the solidarity and strength of the people with whom we can necessarily have only a limited contact. Looking back at the war and reading the memoirs, it is most illuminating to see what they were thinking on the "other side." At the time we were all impressed by the fact of this great military force of Germany, absolutely on top, and yet you find that the inside was quite doubtful. And the idea of an absolutely strong, monolithic power in Russia may be wrong.

I believe that despite the possession of nuclear weapons, the dominating feeling in Russia today is fear. I believe the trouble in America is fear. If we could lift off that fear we might get much further. I don't believe that the holding of the satellite states is essentially due to an imperialist desire to spread Communism. I think it is a desire to have an expendable bursting layer between East and West. I don't think that any of us, any country, even in the most extremist circles in America, imagines that one could conquer Communism by an attack on Russia. I hope Russia also realizes that they will not conquer the world by force, because the forces will be too strong for them—the spiritual forces. They are already finding difficulties in the satellite countries. That is why, I think, that if you could lift off this fear of Russia today an approach might be made which would reconcile things. And even if the nuclear weapons are held by the two rival groups instead of by a world authority it might be possible that the Russians, like everybody else, do not want to have localized little wars because they may not remain localized.

One of our difficulties in all these matters is that it is not as if the world was a very peaceful place. There are an awful lot of sore places. Any suggestion you have to stabilize the world as it is would cause a great outcry from the people under a rule they don't like. Again I don't believe, with all our sympathy for the Hungarians, Poles, Rumanians, and the rest, that one would contemplate embarking on a nuclear war to rescue them, nor do I think they would contemplate it either, because after the rescue there might be very little left of the rescued or the rescuer.

We need to make a start on the idea of an international force. That force would not be European solely, or American or Australian, but should cover Africa and Asia as well. One of the dangers I see today in the world is that out-of-date ideas still hang on. There are still out-of-date ideas about the primacy of Europe. I don't think we have shown an awful lot of commonsense in nearly committing suicide in two world wars, so we might be a bit humble on that.

I think that a world force might make the best approach to world government. I know all the difficulties of world government. You can say, "Where are you going to draw the line between what nations can do and what they cannot do?" But our aim would be to begin with the minimum, just as we did in our own domestic affairs. Our early force was really just to keep law and order, the King's peace, the Police Force gradually coming about, and it has taken very many years before we met society's other needs.

I would like to continue on the widest possible scale the work that is being done to try and raise the standards in the undeveloped countries of the world. I am all for that, but I think one cannot continue without any surrender of sovereignty. Surrender of sovereignty is what you want if you look only at this one aspect of war and peace. Could we make a start on that? I would like to see it pressed further, rather more vigorously than at present. So many of the smaller issues are pressed, but the big major one is not. I don't want it to be done by acrimonious disputes in the U.N.—there are far too many acrimonious debates. I would like it seriously discussed everywhere what the reality is—the reality that faces us, simply, is our civilization going to continue? This question was always at the back of my mind when I was in office. There was always this looming danger. Yet nationalism persists. I refer to the hope that nations may grow upon the question of sovereignty. Sixty years ago, who would have thought of the surrender of sovereignty in the British Commonwealth? Now today in India, Pakistan, Ceylon, Ghana, Malaya and elsewhere we have seen a surrender of sovereignty.

But to whom should sovereignty be surrendered? I believe we must have a wide authority and that that wide authority must cease to be based just on power. All the arguments (we had them all at San Francisco) as to why the power must be placed in the hands of a few big states—are true only if we are going to depend on action of individual states to support the law. If you get away from that there is no reason why we need have this predominance of the bigger states. The interests of the smaller ones are just as great as our own. I am not going to argue on the subject of world government in its detail. I have never felt that technical details were so important. If people want to get these things, they will. I would like a movement in this country and every country in favor of world government, not on the grounds of commonsense. It is commonsense that we who live in a city like London should have all kinds of things controlled—motorists must not pass a red light; drains must be looked after and all that. It is time we realized that the world is also a close-locked community today. We just cannot afford to have the exercise of individual sovereignty.

To whom are you going to hand it over? I am democratic; I am prepared to submit to the will of a properly constituted body representing the world. I am not prepared to submit to a kind of junta of three or four of the strongest powers. I have been accustomed for many years to accept the will of the majority, and I am prepared to do it again. I would like Britain and America and Russia also to be prepared to do it, because I believe that unless we can get this we shall not get peace.

4
INTERNATIONAL ANARCHY AND WORLD-GOVERNMENT

The preceding chapter discussed the consequences of state sovereignty for international politics; this discussion is continued in the present chapter. If state sovereignty means anarchy and war, should one conclude that the solution lies in the creation of a single world-state under a single world-government?

The first two selections answer this question affirmatively. In his *De Monarchia* or *On World-Government*, Dante Alighieri (1265–1321) argues that world-government is indeed the only possible solution. It is interesting to note that he relies not only on deductive reasoning and on the authority of the Bible and Aristotle, but also on the empirical example of the Roman Empire as a "world-government." Alexander Hamilton (1757–1804) also argued that sovereign states necessarily come into conflict with

each other, and that the only way to avert this danger is their unification under a single government. He advocated this solution in
the sixth *Federalist Paper* specifically for the American states, but
his arguments are equally applicable to the world as a whole.

Reinhold Niebuhr arrives at the opposite conclusion in a well-
known article in *Foreign Affairs*. World-government, according to
him, is an illusion. Theologian Niebuhr, who has written extensively
on international politics, is Professor Emeritus at Union Theological
Seminary.

10. *ON WORLD-GOVERNMENT* * / *DANTE ALIGHIERI*

The proper function of the human race, taken as a whole, is to
exercise constantly the entire capacity of its intellectual potential,
primarily for speculation, and secondarily, as an extension of speculation, for action. And since whatever applies to the part also applies
to the whole, and since individual men grow perfect in knowledge
and wisdom when they can sit quietly, it is evident that the human
race also performs its tasks most freely and most easily in the calm
and tranquillity of peace. That man's work is almost divine is revealed in the words: "Thou hast made him a little lower than the
angels." It is clear, therefore, that universal peace is the best of all
things which are ordained for our happiness. That is why there
rang out to the shepherds from on high the message not of riches,
nor pleasures, nor honors, nor length of life, nor health, nor strength,
nor beauty, but the message of peace. For the heavenly host proclaimed: "Glory to God in the highest, and on earth peace to men
of good will." Hence, also, "Peace be with you" was the salutation
of the Saviour of men; it befitted the supreme Saviour to utter the
supreme salutation. His disciples took care to preserve this custom,
and so did Paul in his salutations, as must be evident to all.

It is clear, then, from these considerations what is the better
way, or rather the best way for the human race to do its work. And,
consequently, it is also clear that the nearest approach to the ultimate
goal of all our work is universal peace. Let this be the principle

* Dante Alighieri, *De Monarchia*, C. Witte, ed. (Vienna, Braumüller, 1874),
Book I, Chap. 4, 5, 10, 16. Translated by Eva Tamm Lijphart and Arend
Lijphart.

guiding our subsequent arguments and the standard which we need to test the truth of whatever we try to prove. . . .

The first question is whether a temporal world-government is necessary for the well-being of the world. There is no weight of argument or authority against its necessity, and there are very powerful and clear arguments for it. The first of these arguments is given by the Philosopher in his *Politics*. For there this venerable authority asserts that, whenever several things are ordained for a single purpose, one of them must regulate and rule, and the others must be regulated and ruled. This demands credence not only because of the glorious name of the author, but also because of inductive reasoning.

For, if we consider an individual man, we see that this applies to him: while all his faculties are directed toward happiness, he can only attain it when his intellectual faculty regulates and rules all the others. If we consider a household, whose aim is to prepare the members of the family to live rightly, there must be one who regulates and rules: the father of the family or someone who takes his place. The Philosopher states that "every household is ruled by the eldest." And it is his task, as Homer says, to govern and make laws for all others. Hence the proverbial curse: "May you have an equal in your house." If we consider a neighborhood, whose aim is to give mutual help with regard to persons and property, there must again be one who rules the others, either an outstanding person from among them who rules with their consent, or someone imposed on them by another. Otherwise the community will not only fail to provide mutual support, but may be completely destroyed if many members strive for pre-eminence. Again, if we consider a city, whose aim is to provide a good and sufficient life, there must be a single government, not only in well-governed cities but also in those that are badly ruled. Otherwise, civil life fails to reach its goal altogether, and the city itself ceases to be what it was. Finally, if we consider a kingdom, whose aim is the same as that of a city but also includes the maintenance of peace, there must be one king who rules and governs. Otherwise, not only the inhabitants of the kingdom fail to live well, but also the kingdom itself falls apart, in accordance with the infallible truth that "every kingdom divided against itself shall be laid waste." If, then, this is true of all cases in which there is a single aim, the proposition stated above must also be true.

Since the whole human race is ordained for one end, as we

showed above, there must be one ruling and governing power, which should be called monarch or emperor. And thus it is clear that for the well-being of the world there must be a world-government or empire. . . .

Wherever there can be strife, there must be judgment. Otherwise, imperfection would exist without its own means of correction, which is impossible because God and Nature possess all necessary means. It is evident that between any two governments that are completely independent of each other, conflicts may arise either through their own fault or that of their subjects. In such cases, there must be judgment. And because they are not subordinate to each other and cannot know each other's affairs (for among equals there is no authority), there must be a third government under whose wider jurisdiction the other two are ruled. And this third government is either the world-government or it is not. If it is, we have reached our conclusion. If it is not, it will again have its equal beyond the boundary of its jurisdiction, and again a higher government will be necessary—and so *ad infinitum*, which is impossible. Thus we arrive at a first and highest judge by whose judgment all conflicts are settled either directly or indirectly. And this will be the monarch or emperor of the world. Therefore, world-government is necessary for the world. The Philosopher saw this argument when he said: "Things do not want to be in disorder; because a multitude of governments is disorder, there must be one government." . . .

Memorable experience confirms the deductive arguments set forth above, namely, the condition of mankind which the Son of God either awaited or arranged himself according to his will, when he assumed human form for man's salvation. For if we survey all the conditions and times of men since the fall of our first parents, which was the beginning of all our errors, we shall find no true world-government and no complete peace in the world except under the divine Monarch Augustus. And that in his time mankind was blessed with the tranquillity of universal peace is affirmed by all historians, by all illustrious poets, as well as by the evangelist of the gentleness of Christ; and Paul called that most happy condition "the fullness of time." Truly the time and all temporal things were full, for all services toward our happiness were properly fulfilled. But what the state of the world has been since that day the seamless robe was rent by the nail of greed, we can all read and, unfortunately, behold ourselves. O human race, how many storms and shipwrecks must thou endure, so long as thou, like a beast of many heads, strivest after diverse ends! Thou art sick in intellect and likewise sick in affection: thou healest not the higher intellect by irrefutable arguments, nor the lower by the lessons of experience, nor even the affection by the sweetness of divine persuasion which sounds to thee from the trumpet of the Holy Spirit: "Behold, how good and how pleasant it is for brethren to dwell together in unity."

11. *CONCERNING DANGERS FROM WAR BETWEEN THE STATES* * / *ALEXANDER HAMILTON*

The three last numbers of this work have been dedicated to an enumeration of the dangers to which we shall be exposed, in a state of disunion, from the arms and arts of foreign nations. I shall now proceed to delineate dangers of a different, and perhaps, still more alarming kind; those which will in all probability flow from dissensions between the states themselves, and from domestic factions and convulsions. These have been already in some instances slightly anticipated; but they deserve a more particular and more full investigation.

If these states should either be wholly disunited, or only united in partial confederacies, a man must be far gone in Utopian speculations, who can seriously doubt that the subdivisions into which they might be thrown would have frequent and violent contests with each other. To presume a want of motives for such contests, as an argument against their existence, would be to forget that men are ambitious, vindictive and rapacious. To look for a continuation of harmony between a number of independent, unconnected sovereignties, situated in the same neighborhood, would be to disregard the uniform course of human events, and to set at defiance the accumulated experience of ages.

The causes of hostility among nations are innumerable. There are some which have a general and almost constant operation upon the collective bodies of society. Of this description are the love of power, or the desire of preëminence and dominion—the jealousy of

* Alexander Hamilton, James Madison, and John Jay, *The Federalist* (Hallowell: Masters, Smith & Co., 1857), No. 6.

power, or the desire of equality and safety. There are others which have a more circumscribed, though an equally operative influence within their spheres; such are the rivalships and competitions of commerce between commercial nations. And there are others, not less numerous than either of the former, which take their origin entirely in private passions; in the attachments, enmities, interests, hopes, and fears of leading individuals in the communities of which they are members. Men of this class, whether the favorites of a king or of a people, have in too many instances abused the confidence they possessed; and assuming the pretext of some public motive, have not scrupled to sacrifice the national tranquillity to personal advantage, or personal gratification.

The celebrated Pericles, in compliance with the resentment of a prostitute,[1] at the expense of much of the blood and treasure of his countrymen, attacked, vanquished, and destroyed the city of the *Samnians*. The same man, stimulated by private pique against the *Magarensians*, another nation of Greece, or to avoid a prosecution with which he was threatened as an accomplice in a supposed theft of the statuary *Phidias*, or to get rid of the accusations prepared to be brought against him for dissipating the funds of the state in the purchase of popularity, or from a combination of all these causes, was the primitive author of that famous and fatal war, distinguished in the Grecian annals by the name of the *Peloponnesian* war; which after various vicissitudes, intermissions and renewals, terminated in the ruin of the Athenian commonwealth.

The ambitious cardinal, who was prime minister to Henry VIIIth, permitting his vanity to aspire to the triple crown, entertained hopes of succeeding in the acquisition of that splendid prize by the influence of the emperor Charles Vth. To secure the favor and interest of this enterprising and powerful monarch, he precipitated England into a war with France, contrary to the plainest dictates of policy, and at the hazard of the safety and independence, as well of the kingdom over which he presided by his counsels, as of Europe in general. For if there ever was a sovereign who bid fair to realize the project of universal monarchy, it was the emperor Charles Vth, of whose intrigues Wolsey was at once the instrument and the dupe.

The influence which the bigotry of one female,[2] the petulance

---

[1] Aspasia, vide Plutarch's life of Pericles.
[2] Madame de Maintenon.

of another,[3] and the cabals of a third,[4] had in the contemporary policy, ferments and pacifications, of a considerable part of Europe, are topics that have been too often descanted upon not to be generally known.

To multiply examples of the agency of personal considerations in the production of great national events, either foreign or domestic, according to their direction, would be an unnecessary waste of time. Those who have but a superficial acquaintance with the sources from which they are to be drawn, will themselves recollect a variety of instances; and those who have a tolerable knowledge of human nature, will not stand in need of such lights, to form their opinion either of the reality or extent of that agency. Perhaps, however, a reference, tending to illustrate the general principle, may with propriety be made to a case which has lately happened among ourselves. If SHAYS had not been a *desperate debtor*, it is much to be doubted whether Massachusetts would have been plunged into a civil war.

But notwithstanding the concurring testimony of experience, in this particular, there are still to be found visionary or designing men, who stand ready to advocate the paradox of perpetual peace between the states, though dismembered and alienated from each other—the genius of republics, say they, is pacific; the spirit of commerce has a tendency to soften the manners of men, and to extinguish those inflammable humors which have so often kindled into wars. Commercial republics, like ours, will never be disposed to waste themselves in ruinous contentions with each other. They will be governed by mutual interest, and will cultivate a spirit of mutual amity and concord.

We may ask these projectors in politics, whether it is not the true interest of all nations to cultivate the same benevolent and philosophic spirit? If this be their true interest, have they in fact pursued it? Has it not, on the contrary, invariably been found that momentary passions, and immediate interests, have a more active and imperious control over human conduct than general or remote considerations of policy, utility or justice? Have republics in practice been less addicted to war than monarchies? Are not the former administered by men as well as the latter? Are there not aversions, predilections, rivalships and desires of unjust acquisition,

[3] Dutchess of Marlborough.
[4] Madame de Pompadoure.

that affect nations as well as kings? Are not popular assemblies frequently subject to the impulses of rage, resentment, jealousy, avarice, and of other irregular and violent propensities? Is it not well known, that their determinations are often governed by a few individuals in whom they place confidence, and that they are of course liable to be tinctured by the passions and views of those individuals? Has commerce hitherto done any thing more than changed the objects of war? Is not the love of wealth as domineering and enterprising a passion as that of power or glory? Have there not been as many wars founded upon commercial motives, since that has become the prevailing system of nations, as were before occasioned by the cupidity of territory or dominion? Has not the spirit of commerce, in many instances, administered new incentives to the appetite, both for the one and for the other? Let experience, the least fallible guide of human opinions, be appealed to for an answer to these inquiries.

Sparta, Athens, Rome and Carthage, were all republics; two of them, Athens and Carthage, of the commercial kind. Yet were they as often engaged in wars offensive and defensive, as the neighboring monarchies of the same times. Sparta was little better than a well regulated camp; and Rome was never sated of carnage and conquest.

Carthage, though a commercial republic, was the aggressor in the very war that ended in her destruction. Hannibal had carried her arms into the heart of Italy, and even to the gates of Rome, before Scipio, in turn, gave him an overthrow in the territories of Carthage, and made a conquest of the commonwealth.

Venice, in latter times, figured more than once in wars of ambition; till becoming an object of terror to the other Italian states, Pope Julius the second found means to accomplish that formidable league,[5] which gave a deadly blow to the power and pride of that haughty republic.

The provinces of Holland, till they were overwhelmed in debts and taxes, took a leading and conspicuous part in the wars of Europe. They had furious contests with England for the dominion of the sea; and were among the most persevering and most implacable of the opponents of Louis XIV.

In the government of Britain the representatives of the people compose one branch of the national legislature. Commerce has been

[5] The LEAGUE OF CAMBRAY, comprehending the emperor, the king of France, the king of Aragon, and most of the Italian princes and States.

for ages the predominant pursuit of that country. Yet few nations have been more frequently engaged in war; and the wars in which that kingdom has been engaged, have in numerous instances proceeded from the people. There have been, if I may so express it, almost as many popular as royal wars. The cries of the nation and the importunities of their representatives have, upon various occasions, dragged their monarchs into war, or continued them in it, contrary to their inclinations, and sometimes contrary to the real interests of the state. In that memorable struggle for superiority, between the rival houses of *Austria* and *Bourbon,* which so long kept Europe in a flame, it is well known that the antipathies of the English against the French, seconding the ambition, or rather the avarice of a favorite leader,[6] protracted the war beyond the limits marked out by sound policy, and for a considerable time in opposition to the views of the court.

The wars of these two last mentioned nations have in a great measure grown out of commercial considerations: the desire of supplanting, and the fear of being supplanted, either in particular branches of traffic, or in the general advantages of trade and navigation; and sometimes even the more culpable desire of sharing in the commerce of other nations, without their consent.

The last war but two between Britain and Spain, sprang from the attempts of the English merchants, to prosecute an illicit trade with the Spanish main. These unjustifiable practices, on their part, produced severities on the part of the Spaniards, towards the subjects of Great Britain, which were not more justifiable; because they exceeded the bounds of a just retaliation, and were chargeable with inhumanity and cruelty. Many of the English who were taken on the Spanish coasts, were sent to dig in the mines of Potosi; and by the usual progress of a spirit of resentment, the innocent were after a while confounded with the guilty in indiscriminate punishment. The complaints of the merchants kindled a violent flame throughout the nation, which soon after broke out in the house of commons, and was communicated from that body to the ministry. Letters of reprisal were granted and a war ensued, which, in its consequences, overthrew all the alliances that but twenty years before had been formed, with sanguine expectations of the most beneficial fruits.

From this summary of what has taken place in other countries,

---

[6] The Duke of Marlborough.

whose situations have borne the nearest resemblance to our own, what reason can we have to confide in those reveries, which would seduce us into the expectation of peace and cordiality between the members of the present confederacy, in a state of separation? Have we not already seen enough of the fallacy and extravagance of those idle theories which have amused us with promises of an exemption from the imperfections, the weaknesses, and the evils incident to society in every shape? Is it not time to awake from the deceitful dream of a golden age, and to adopt as a practical maxim for the direction of our political conduct, that we, as well as the other inhabitants of the globe, are yet remote from the happy empire of perfect wisdom and perfect virtue?

Let the point of extreme depression to which our national dignity and credit have sunk; let the inconveniences felt everywhere from a lax and ill-administration of government; let the revolt of a part of the state of North Carolina; the late menacing disturbances in Pennsylvania, and the actual insurrections and rebellions in Massachusetts, declare!

So far is the general sense of mankind from corresponding with the tenets of those, who endeavor to lull asleep our apprehensions of discord and hostility between the states, in the event of disunion, that it has from long observation of the progress of society become a sort of axiom in politics, that vicinity or nearness of situation, constitutes nations natural enemies. An intelligent writer expresses himself on this subject to this effect: "NEIGHBORING "NATIONS (says he) are naturally ENEMIES of each other, unless "their common weakness forces them to league in a CONFEDERATIVE "REPUBLIC, and their constitution prevents the differences that "neighborhood occasions, extinguishing that secret jealousy, which "disposes all states to aggrandize themselves at the expense of their "neighbors."[7] This passage, at the same time, points out the EVIL, and suggests the REMEDY.

[7] Vide Principles des Negotiations par l'Abbe de Mably.

12. *THE ILLUSION OF WORLD-GOVERNMENT** / *REINHOLD NIEBUHR*

The trustful acceptance of false solutions for our perplexing problems adds a touch of pathos to the tragedy of our age.

The tragic character of our age is revealed in the world-wide insecurity which is the fate of modern man. Technical achievements, which a previous generation had believed capable of solving every ill to which the human flesh is heir, have created, or at least accentuated, our insecurity. For the growth of technics has given the perennial problems of our common life a more complex form and a scope that has grown to be worldwide.

Our problem is that technics have established a rudimentary world community but have not integrated it organically, morally or politically. They have created a community of mutual dependence, but not one of mutual trust and respect. Without this higher integration, advancing technics tend to sharpen economic rivalries within a general framework of economic interdependence; they change the ocean barriers of yesterday into the battlegrounds of today; and they increase the deadly efficacy of the instruments of war so that vicious circles of mutual fear may end in atomic conflicts and mutual destruction. To these perplexities an ideological conflict has been added, which divides the world into hostile camps.

It is both necessary and laudable that men of good will should, in this situation, seek to strengthen every moral and political force which might give a rudimentary world community a higher degree of integration. It was probably inevitable that the desperate plight of our age should persuade some well meaning men that the gap between a technically integrated and politically divided community could be closed by the simple expedient of establishing a world government through the fiat of the human will and creating world community by the fiat of world government. It is this hope which adds a touch of pathos to already tragic experiences. The hope not only beguiles some men from urgent moral and political responsi-

* "The Illusion of World Government" (Copyright 1949 Reinhold Niebuhr) is reprinted with the permission of Charles Scribner's Sons and of Faber & Faber Ltd. from *Christian Realism and Political Problems* by Reinhold Niebuhr.

bilities. It tempts others into irresponsible criticisms of the necessarily minimal constitutional structure which we have embodied in the United Nations and which is as bad as its critics aver only if a better one is within the realm of possibilities.

Virtually all arguments for world government rest upon the simple presupposition that the desirability of world order proves the attainability of world government. Our precarious situation is unfortunately no proof, either of the moral ability of mankind to create a world government by an act of the will, nor of the political ability of such a government to integrate a world community in advance of a more gradual growth of the "social tissue" which every community requires more than government.

Most advocates of world government also assume that nations need merely follow the alleged example of the individuals of another age who are supposed to have achieved community by codifying their agreements into law and by providing an agency of some kind for law enforcement. This assumption ignores the historic fact that the mutual respect for each other's rights in particular communities is older than any code of law; and that machinery for the enforcement of law can be efficacious only when a community as a whole obeys its laws implicitly, so that coercive enforcement may be limited to a recalcitrant minority.

The fallacy of world government can be stated in two simple propositions. The first is that governments are not created by fiat (though sometimes they can be imposed by tyranny). The second is that governments have only limited efficacy in integrating a community.

II

The advocates of world government talk of calling a world constitutional convention which would set up the machinery of a global constitutional order and would then call upon the nations to abrogate or abridge their sovereignty in order that this newly created universal sovereignty could have unchallenged sway. No such explicit abnegation has ever taken place in the history of the world. Explicit governmental authority has developed historically from the implicit authority of patriarchal or matriarchal tribal forms. Governments, so established, have extended their dominion over weaker neighbors. But the abridgment of sovereignty has always been indirect rather than direct; or it has been attained by the super-imposition of power.

The notion that world government is a fairly simple possibility is the final and most absurd form of the "social contract" conception of government which has confused modern political thought since Hobbes. It must certainly be obvious by this time that the conception of a state of nature in which all men were at war with all, and of a subsequent social contract through which men established a power over themselves to avoid mutual annihilation, is a pure fiction. A small human community is as primordial as the individual. No group of individuals has ever created either government or community out of whole cloth. One reason why the social contract conception of government has a particular plausibility with us is because the United States came closer to a birth by "contract" than any other nation. But the preamble of our constitution declares that its purpose is to establish a "more perfect union." That is a very telling phrase which presupposes a previous union. This previous union was in fact established on the battlefield in a common struggle against a common foe; it needed only to be made "more perfect." It may be observed in passing that, though the 13 colonies had never enjoyed sovereignty, they did not find it too easy to submit what had only been potential, and not actual, sovereignty to the authority of the federal union. We fought a civil war before it was proved that they had in fact done this without reservations.

When the question is raised whether the nations of the world would voluntarily first create, and then submit to, a super-national authority, the possible reluctance of nations, other than Russia, to take this step is fortunately or unfortunately obscured by the Russian intransigence. The Russians have declared again and again that they would leave the United Nations if the veto power were abolished. This means that Russia, as a prospective minority in a world community, is not ready to submit her fate to the will of a majority, even in such a loose organization as the United Nations. It is therefore obvious that she would be even more unwilling to submit her sovereignty to a more highly integrated constitutional order.

The proponents of world government have two answers to the problem posed by Russian intransigence. One is to assert that the Russians never have had the chance to accept or reject a genuinely constitutional world order; and that there are real possibilities of her acceptance of a constitution which is not weighted against her. This answer contains in a nutshell the rationalist illusion implicit in world government theories. It assumes that constitutions can insure the mutual trust upon which community rests. Actually, even the best constitution must, if it is democratic, set up some kind of majority rule. It is not workable if there is not enough common ground between majority and minority to assure that a majority will not take advantage of a minority, or that the minority will not suspect the majority of injustice, even though without cause. There are republics in South America with quite nice constitutions in which a defeated minority starts conspiracies against the government, usually through military channels, on the day after election.

The other answer to the problem of Russian intransigeance is a proposed creation of a "world" government without Russia. Thus in the name of "one world" the world would be divided in two. Proponents of world government are always ready with criticisms of the ambiguities in the Charter of the United Nations, without recognizing that those ambiguities correspond to the actual historical situation. The Security Council is, for instance, a bridge of a sort between the segments of a divided world. They would destroy that bridge for the sake of creating a more logical constitutional system. This done, they look forward to one of two possibilities.

One is that Russia, faced with a united opposition, and concluding that she would not have to sacrifice her Communist Government but only her ambition to spread Communism, would ultimately capitulate and join the world federation. This abstract approach to political problems is completely oblivious of the dynamism of Communism.

The other course chosen by some advocates of world government is to create such a government without Russia and to divide the world more consistently in the name of the principle of "one" world. If this should lead to a world conflict they believe that the agonies of war will be assuaged for us by our knowledge that we are at least fighting for a principle of ultimate validity.

There is, of course, a possibility that a closer political integration of the non-Communist nations may save the world from war by the creation of an adequate preponderance of power in the west. But such an objective is not to be reached by loftily disavowing "power politics" in favor of "law." The world federalists who accept the inevitability of war walk bravely up the hill of pure idealism and down again into the realm of pure power politics. In this journey they rid themselves of the logical and moral ambiguities of the much despised quasi-constitutional system of the United Nations. Their brethren who are in a less exalted frame of mind will continue to put up with the Charter for the sake of preserving a bridge, however slight, between Russia and the west, making the best arrangements they can to restrain Russia, while trying at the same time to strengthen the existing world security agencies.

The ambiguities in the Charter of the United Nations which so outrage the advocates of world government are in fact the consequence of seeking to guarantee two, rather than one, objectives. The one objective is to preserve the unity of one world, even though it be seriously divided, and to provide a meeting ground between east and west where some of the tensions and frictions may be resolved. The other is to preserve the integrity of our "way of life" against a tyrannical system which we abhor. The Russians, in so far as they are honest devotees of a Marxist dream of world order, are presumably in the same position. Each of us hopes ultimately to create a world order upon the basis of our conception of justice. Neither of us is ready, at the moment, to submit our fate to a world authority without reservation, so long as the possibility remains that such an authority could annul a system of law and justice to which we are deeply committed.

III

So far we have considered only the difficulties of creating a world government by constitutional fiat. But a much more serious defect in world government theories is to be found in their conception of the relation of government to community. Governments cannot create communities for the simple reason that the authority of government is not primarily the authority of law nor the authority of force, but the authority of the community itself. Laws are obeyed because the community accepts them as corresponding, on the whole, to its conception of justice. This is particularly true of democratically-organized communities. But it is well to observe that even in traditional, non-democratic communities of the past there was a discernible difference between tyranny and legitimate government. It consisted precisely in the fact that a legitimate government relied primarily upon the implicit consent of the community.

Even in a national constitutional system, such as our own, we have seen how limited is the power of law whenever a portion of the community adheres to moral standards which differ from those of the total community. We have had this experience both with the prohibition movement and with the question of civil rights for Negroes in southern states. And where is the police force, loyal to a world state, to come from? The police power of a government cannot be a pure political artifact. It is an arm of the community's body. If the body is in pieces, the arm cannot integrate it.

The priority of the community to its laws and its use of force does not mean that both law and force may not have limited efficacy in perfecting the organization and preserving the integrity of the community. Good constitutions provide for the rational arbitrament of many conflicting and competing forces which might otherwise tear the community apart. Preponderant force in one part of the community may also so shape the social forces of the total community that its use need not be perpetual. Thus the preponderant force of the northern states decided the issue whether our nation was a nation or merely a federation of states. But force is no longer necessary to guarantee the loyalty of the southern states to our union. The ancient empires of Egypt, Babylon and Persia were created through the preponderant force of a particular city-state; but they finally achieved a unity which did not require the constant application of force. It must be noted that this pattern of coalescence of communities gives us no analogy for the creation of a world community in democratic terms, that is, without the imposition of preponderant power. The best analogy for our present world situation is to be found in Greece rather than in Egypt or Babylon. The Greek city-states never achieved the imperial unity of the oriental empires. The threat of Persia did finally prompt the organization of the Delian League; but the rivalry of Sparta and Athens for the hegemony in the League resulted in its disintegration. The unity of Greece was finally achieved under Philip and Alexander of Macedon. But this imperial unity was also a tyrannical nemesis for Greek culture. The analogy in present global terms would be the final unification of the world through the preponderant power of either America or Russia, whichever proved herself victorious in a final global struggle. The analogy teaches us nothing about the possibilities of a constitutional world state. It may teach us that though the perils of international anarchy are very great, they may still be preferable to international tyranny.

The coalescence of communities from city-states to empires in the ancient world, and from feudal entities to nations in the modern period, was frequently accomplished only by the imposition of preponderant power. The fact is particularly significant, since all of these communities could rely upon all sorts of "organic" factors for their force of cohesion which the rudimentary world community lacks. By organic factors, I mean such forces as the power of ethnic kinship, the force of a common history—particularly the memory of joint struggles against a common foe—a common language, a common culture and a common religion. We do have examples of ethnically and religiously pluralistic nations and empires, but they possess a basic homegeneity of some kind, underlying the differences. In modern India, where religious differences are thoroughgoing and highly localized, it proved impossible to construct a constitutional system which could allay the mutual fears of Hindus and Moslems. The birth in blood of these two nations, once the unifying force of an imperial power was removed, ought to teach our world planners more about the limited efficacy of constitutions than they have evidently learned. There were certainly more common elements in the situation in India than the world community will possess for a long time to come. Despite these common elements, the unity of India proved to be unattainable.

Sometimes the world planners recognize the absence of organic forces of cohesion in the world community. Thus Erich Kahler[1] sees that a world constitution lacks the "substratum" of organic and historical forces, which characterize the constitutions of national governments. But he draws the conclusion that a world constitution "must create the substratum to which it is to be applied." The proposed method of creating the substratum, according to Mr. Kahler, is to use "regions" rather than "extant states" as electoral units in the world constitution, for "if we base the world government on the states, we will fail in the essential task of creating the substratum." The illusions of omnipotence which infect the thought of this kind of political idealism could not be more vividly portrayed. There is no explanation of how states, who have a sovereign voice, would be persuaded to grant this electoral power to "regions" which would have no such voice in a world constitutional convention. The idea probably is that there would be a nonrepresentative constitutional convention of "experts" and the hope is that sovereign states will meekly accept the dictum of the experts that regions

[1] Erich Kahler, "The Question of a 'Minimum Constitution.'" *Common Cause*, June 1948.

offer a better "substratum" for the world community than extant
states. Nor is any attempt made to deal with the difficulty that many
of the regions which would hopefully be created are so little
integrated that an electoral canvass would be completely meaningless in them.

The fact is that even the wisest statecraft cannot create social
tissue. It can cut, sew and redesign social fabric to a limited degree.
But the social fabric upon which it works must be "given."

IV

The international community is not totally lacking in social tissue;
but it is very scant, compared with that of particular states. Let us
briefly assess the various factors in it. Most important as a force of
social cohesion in the world community is the increasing economic
interdependence of peoples of the world. But it is important to
contrast this economic interdependence immediately with the wide
disparity in the economic strength of various nations. At the
climactic dinner of the World Republic convention, held in
Chicago in October 1948, Professor Urey, the atomic scientist,
expressed the conviction that the "inclusion of the illiterate, poverty-
stricken, overnumerous masses of the Far East" constituted the
major problem of the world state. He believed that the white race
would not tolerate being outvoted by Asiatics. He therefore proposed a system of weighted votes in favor of nations with high
literacy and abundance of raw materials and industrial production.
He felt certain that the more "enlightened" Orientals would not
object to this procedure. But an objection, from Thomas Tchou,
sitting two places to the left of Professor Urey, was immediately
forthcoming. Weighted representation, he declared, was immoral.[2]
Thus the real problems have an inconvenient habit of peeking
through, even at a dinner of a World Republic convention.

A second factor in the social tissue of the world community is
the fear of mutual annihilation, heightened in recent years by the
new dimension which atomic discoveries have given to mankind's
instruments of death. We must not underestimate this fear as a
social force, even as we must recognize that some culturally pluralistic communities of past history have achieved some cohesion
through the minimal conviction that order is to be preferred to

[2] *Common Cause*, December 1948, p. 199.

anarchy. But the fear of destruction in itself is less potent than the fear of specific peril from a particular foe. There is no record in history of peoples establishing a common community because they feared each other, though there are many instances when the fear of a common foe acted as the cement of cohesion.

The final and most important factor in the social tissue of the world community is a moral one. Enlightened men in all nations have some sense of obligation to their fellow-men, beyond the limits of their nation-state. There is at least an inchoate sense of obligation to the inchoate community of mankind. The desperate necessity for a more integrated world community has undoubtedly increased this sense of obligation, inculcated in the conscience of mankind since the rise of universal, rather than parochial, philosophies and religions. This common moral sense is of tremendous importance for the moral and religious life of mankind; but it does not have as much immediate political relevance as is sometimes supposed. Political cohesion requires common convictions on particular issues of justice; and these are lacking. If there is a "natural law" which is "self-evident" to all men, it certainly does not contain very much specific content beyond such minimal rules as the prohibition of murder and theft and such general principles of justice as the dictum that each man is to have his due. There is little agreement on the criteria by which the due of each man is to be measured.

There is a special irony in the fact that the primary differences in the conceptions of justice in the world do not, however, spring from religious and cultural differences between east and west. They can, therefore, not be resolved by elaborate efforts at cultural syncretism between east and west. The primary differences arise from a civil war in the heart of western civilization, in which a fanatical equalitarian creed has been pitted against a libertarian one. This civil war has become nationally localized. Russia has become the national center of the equalitarian creed, while America is the outstanding proponent of the libertarian one. The common use of the word "democracy," together with the contradictory interpretations of the meaning of that word, is the semantic symbol of the conflict. The idea that this conflict could be resolved by greater semantic accuracy is, however, one of the illusions of a too rationalistic culture which fails to understand the power of the social forces expressed in contradictory symbols.

In short, the forces which are operating to integrate the world community are limited. To call attention to this fact does not mean that all striving for a higher and wider integration of the world community is vain. That task must and will engage the conscience of mankind for ages to come. But the edifice of government which we build will be sound and useful if its height is proportionate to the strength of the materials from which it is constructed. The immediate political situation requires that we seek not only peace, but also the preservation of a civilization which we hold to be preferable to the universal tyranny with which Soviet aggression threatens us. Success in this double task is the goal; let us not be diverted from it by the pretense that there is a simple alternative.

We would, I think, have a better chance of success in our struggle against a fanatical foe if we were less sure of our purity and virtue. The pride and self-righteousness of powerful nations are a greater hazard to their success in statecraft than the machinations of their foes. If we could combine a greater degree of humility with our stubborn resolution, we might not only be more successful in holding the dyke against tyranny, but we might also gradually establish a genuine sense of community with our foe, however small. No matter how stubbornly we resist Russian pressure, we should still have a marginal sense of community with the Soviet Union, derived from our sense of being involved in a common fate of tragic proportions and from a recognition of a common guilt of mutual fear. If community in basic terms is established by various organic forces of history, it must finally be preserved by mutual forbearance and forgiveness.

There is obviously no political program which can offer us, in our situation, perfect security against either war or tyranny. Nevertheless we are not prisoners of historical destiny. We shall have constant opportunity to perfect instruments of peace and justice if we succeed in creating some communal foundation upon which constitutional structures can rest. We shall exploit our opportunities the more successfully, however, if we have knowledge of the limits of the will in creating government, and of the limits of government in creating community. We may have pity upon, but can have no sympathy with, those who flee to the illusory security of the impossible from the insecurities and ambiguities of the possible.

5
NATIONALISM

What is nationalism and what is its role in world affairs? The first selection presents Ernest Renan's classic definition of nationalism. Historian Renan (1823–92) delivered the lecture entitled "What Is a Nation?" at the Sorbonne on March 11, 1882.

The second selection is by the Italian nationalist Giuseppe Mazzini (1805–72). Mazzini is a typical spokesman of nineteenth-century liberal nationalism. It is particularly interesting to note that he regards nationalism not as a factor producing international tension and hostility, but rather as a prerequisite for the establishment of an international brotherhood of free nations. The essay "Duties Toward Your Country" appeared in *Pensiero ed Azione* in 1858.

The final selection in this chapter is taken from an article by Karl W. Deutsch. The excerpts presented here emphasize the aggressive and imperialistic tendencies of successful nationalism. The author, Professor of Government at Harvard University, is the outstanding contemporary theorist on the question of nationalism. Among his many books and articles are *Nationalism and Social Communication* and *The Nerves of Government*.

13. WHAT IS A NATION?* / ERNEST RENAN

I propose to ask you to join with me in analysing an idea which, though it appears simple, yet lends itself to the most dangerous misunderstandings. Human society assumes the most varied forms, great masses of human beings, such as we see in China, in Egypt and in the older Babylonia; the tribe as exemplified by the Hebrews and Arabs; the city, as in Athens and Sparta; the unions of various countries, as in the Achaemenian, Roman and Carlovingian empires; communities having no mother country but held together by the bond of religion, as the Israelites and the Parsees; nations such as France, England and most modern European autonomous States; confederations, as in Switzerland and America; relationships, such as those set up by race, or rather by language, between the different branches of Germans or Slavs: all these various groupings exist, or have existed, and to ignore the differences between them is to create a serious confusion. At the time of the French Revolution it was believed that the institutions of small independent towns, such as Sparta and Rome, could be applied to our great nations comprising thirty or forty million inhabitants. Nowadays, we observe a graver error. The terms "race" and "nation" are confused, and we see attributed to ethnographic, or rather linguistic, groups a sovereignty analogous to that of actually existing peoples. Let us try to arrive at some degree of exactness with regard to these difficult questions in which the least confusion at the outset of the argument as to the meaning of words may lead in the end to the most fatal errors. Our task is a delicate one; it amounts almost to vivisection; and we are going to treat the living as usually we treat the dead. We shall proceed coldly and with the most complete impartiality. . . .

We are told by certain political theorists that a nation is, above

* Alfred Zimmern, ed., *Modern Political Doctrines* (London: Oxford University Press, 1939), pp. 186, 192–96, 198–203. Reprinted by permission.

all, a dynasty representing a former conquest that has been at first accepted, and then forgotten, by the mass of the people. According to these politicians, the grouping of provinces effected by a dynasty, its wars, marriages and treaties, ends with the dynasty that has formed it. It is quite true that most modern nations have been made by a family of feudal origin, which has married into the country and provided some sort of centralizing nucleus. The boundaries of France in 1789 were in no way natural or necessary. The large area that the House of Capet had added to the narrow strip accorded by the Treaty of Verdun was indeed the personal acquisition of that family. At the time when the annexations were made no one thought about natural limits, the right of nations or the wishes of provinces. Similarly, the union of England, Ireland and Scotland was a dynastic performance. The only reason why Italy took so long to become a nation was that, until the present century, none of her numerous reigning families became a centre of union. It is an odd fact that she derives the royal[1] title from the obscure island of Sardinia, a land which is scarcely Italian. Holland, self-created by an act of heroic resolution, has none the less entered into a close bond of marriage with the House of Orange, and would run serious risks, should this union ever be endangered.

Is, however, such a law absolute? Doubtless, it is not. Switzerland and the United States which have been formed, like conglomerates, by successive additions, are based on no dynasty. I will not discuss the question in so far as it concerns France. One would have to be able to read the future in order to do so. Let us merely observe that this great French line of kings had become so thoroughly identified with the national life that, on the morrow of its downfall, the nation was able to subsist without it. Furthermore, the eighteenth century had entirely changed the situation. After centuries of humiliation, man had recovered his ancient spirit, his self-respect and the idea of his rights. The words "mother country" and "citizen" had regained their meaning. Thus it was possible to carry out the boldest operation ever performed in history—an operation that may be compared to what, in physiology, would be an attempt to bring back to its former life a body from which brain and heart had been removed.

It must, therefore, be admitted that a nation can exist without any dynastic principle, and even that nations formed by dynasties

[1] The House of Savoy owes its royal title solely to the possession of Sardinia (1720).

can be separated from them without thereby ceasing to exist. The old principle, which takes into account only the right of princes, can no longer be maintained: and, besides dynastic right, there exists also national right. On what criterion is this national right to be based? By what sign is it to be known? And from what tangible fact is it properly to be derived?

1. Many will boldly reply, from race. The artificial divisions, they say, the results of feudalism, royal marriages and diplomatic congresses, have broken down. Race is what remains stable and fixed; and this it is that constitutes a right and a lawful title. The Germanic race, for example, according to this theory, has the right to retake the scattered members of the Germanic family, even when these members do not ask for reunion. The right of the Germanic family over such-and-such a province is better than the right of its inhabitants over themselves. A sort of primordial right is thus created analogous to the divine right of kings; and the principle of ethnography is substituted for that of nations. This is a very grave error, and if it should prevail, it would spell the ruin of European civilization. The principle of the primordial right of race is as narrow and as fraught with danger for true progress as the principle of nations is just and legitimate.

We admit that, among the tribes and cities of the ancient world, the fact of race was of capital importance. The ancient tribe and city were but an extension of the family. In Sparta and Athens all citizens were related more or less closely to each other. It was the same among the Beni-Israel; and it is still so among the Arab tribes. But let us leave Athens, Sparta and the Jewish tribe and turn to the Roman Empire. Here we have quite a different state of affairs. This great agglomeration of completely diverse towns and provinces, formed in the first place by violence and then held together by common interests, cuts at the very root of the racial idea. Christianity, characteristically universal and absolute, works even more effectively in the same direction. It contracts a close alliance with the Roman Empire, and, under the influence of these two incomparable unifying agents, the ethnographic argument is for centuries dismissed from the government of human affairs.

In spite of appearances, the barbarian invasions were a step further on this road. The barbarian kingdoms which were then cut out have nothing ethnographic about them; they were decided by the forces or whims of the conquerors, who were completely indifferent with regard to the race of the peoples whom they subjugated. Charlemagne reconstructed in his own way what Rome had already built, viz., a single empire composed of the most diverse races. The authors of the Treaty of Verdun, calmly drawing their two long lines from north to south, did not pay the slightest attention to the race of the peoples to right or left of them. The frontier changes which took place in the later Middle Ages were also devoid of all ethnographic tendencies. Let it be granted that the consistent policy of the Capets managed more or less to gather together, under the name of France, the territories of ancient Gaul; yet this was by no means the consequence of any tendency on the part of their inhabitants to unite themselves with their kindred. Dauphiné, Bresse, Provence and Franche-Comté no longer remembered any common origin. The consciousness of Gallic race had been lost since the second century A.D., and it is only in modern times, and retrospectively, that the erudite have unearthed the peculiarities of the Gallic character.

Ethnographic considerations have, therefore, played no part in the formation of modern nations. France is Celtic, Iberic and Germanic. Germany is Germanic, Celtic and Slav. Italy is the country in which ethnography finds its greatest difficulties. Here Gauls, Etruscans, Pelasgians and Greeks are crossed in an unintelligible medley. The British Isles, taken as a whole, exhibit a mixture of Celtic and Germanic blood, the proportions of which are particularly difficult to define.

The truth is that no race is pure, and that to base politics on ethnographic analysis is tantamount to basing it on a chimera. The noblest countries, England, France and Italy, are those where breeds are most mixed. Is Germany an exception in this respect? Is she a purely Germanic country? What a delusion to suppose it! All the South was Gallic; and all the East, starting from the Elbe, is Slav.

2. What we have said about race, applies also to language. Language invites union, without, however, compelling it. The United States and England, as also Spanish America and Spain, speak the same language without forming a single nation. Switzerland, on the contrary, whose foundations are solid because they are based on the assent of the various parties, contains three of four languages. There exists in man a something which is above language: and that is his will. The will of Switzerland to be united, in spite of the variety of these forms of speech, is a much more important fact than a similarity of language, often attained by vexatious measures.

It is to the honour of France that she has never tried to attain unity of language by the use of coercion. Is it impossible to cherish the same feelings and thoughts and to love the same things in different languages? We were talking just now of the objections to making international politics dependent on ethnography. It would be no less objectionable to make them depend on comparative philology. Let us allow full liberty of discussion to these interesting branches of learning, and not mix them up with what would disturb their serenity. The political importance ascribed to languages comes from regarding them as tokens of race. Nothing could be more unsound. In Prussia, where nothing but German is now spoken, Russian was spoken a few centuries ago; in Wales, English is spoken; in Gaul and Spain, the original speech of Alba Longa; in Egypt, Arabic; and we could cite any number of other examples. Even in the beginning of things, similarity of language did not imply that of race. Take the proto-Aryan or proto-Semitic tribe. It contained slaves speaking the same language as their masters, whereas the slave very often differed from his master in race. We must repeat that these divisions into Indo-European, Semitic and other languages, which have been laid down by comparative philologists with such admirable acumen, do not coincide with those laid down by anthropology. Languages are historical formations which afford little clue to the descent of those who speak them and which, in any case, cannot be permitted to fetter human liberty, when it is a question of deciding with what family one is to be linked for life and death.

This exclusive importance attributed to language has, like the exaggerated attention paid to race, its dangers and its objections. If you overdo it, you shut yourself up within a prescribed culture which you regard as the national culture. You are confined and immured, having left the open air of the great world outside to shut yourself up in a conventicle together with your compatriots. Nothing could be worse for the mind; and nothing could be more untoward for civilization. Let us not lose sight of this fundamental principle that man, apart from being penned up within the bounds of one language or another, apart from being a member of one race or another, or the follower of one culture or another, is above all a reasonable moral being. Above French, German or Italian culture, there stands human culture. Consider the great men of the Renaissance. They were neither French, nor Italian, nor German. By their intercourse with the ancient world, they had rediscovered the secret of the true education of the human mind, and to that they devoted themselves body and soul. How well they did!

3. Nor can religion provide a satisfactory basis for a modern nationality. In its origin, religion was connected with the very existence of the social group, which itself was an extension of the family. The rites of religion were family rites. The religion of Athens was the cult of Athens itself, of its mythical founders, its laws and customs. This religion, which did not involve any dogmatic theology, was, in the full sense of the words, a state religion. Those who refused to practice it were not Athenians. At bottom it was the cult of the personified Acropolis; and to swear on the altar of Aglauros[1] amounted to an oath to die for one's country. This religion was the equivalent of our drawing lots for military service or of our cult of the national flag. To refuse to participate in such cult would have been tantamount to a refusal nowadays to serve in the army, and to a declaration that one was not an Athenian. On the other hand, it is clear that such a cult as this meant nothing for those who were not Athenians; so there was no proselytising to compel foreigners to accept it, and the slaves of Athens did not practice it. The same was the case in certain small republics of the Middle Ages. No man was a good Venetian if he did not swear by St. Mark; nor a good citizen of Amalfi if he did not set St. Andrew above all the other saints in Paradise. In these small societies, acts, which in later times became the grounds for persecution and tyranny, were justifiable and were as trivial as it is with us to wish the father of the family many happy returns of his birthday or a happy new year.

What was true of Sparta and Athens was no longer so in the kingdoms that emerged from the conquests of Alexander, and still less so in the Roman Empire. The persecutions carried out by Antiochus Epiphanes to induce the Eastern world to worship the Olympian Jove, like those of the Roman Empire to maintain the farce of a state religion, were mistaken, criminal and really absurd. Nowadays the situation is perfectly clear, since the masses no longer have any uniform belief. Every one believes and practices religion in his own way according to his capacities and wishes. State religion has ceased to exist; and a man can be a Frenchman, an Englishman or a German, and at the same time a Catholic, a Protestant or a Jew, or practice no form of worship at all. Religion has become a matter to be decided by the individual according to his conscience, and

[1] Aglauros, who gave her life to save her country, represents the Acropolis itself.

nations are no longer divided into Catholic and Protestant. Religion which, fifty-two years ago, was so important a factor in the formation of Belgium, is still equally so in the heart of every man; but it is now barely to be reckoned among the reasons that determine national frontiers.

4. Community of interest is certainly a powerful bond between men. But do interests suffice to make a nation? I do not believe it. Community of interest brings about commercial treaties. Nationality, which is body and soul both together, has its sentimental side: and a Customs Union is not a country.

5. Geography, and what we call natural frontiers, certainly plays a considerable part in the division of nations. Geography is one of the essential factors of history. Rivers have guided races: mountains have impeded them. The former have favoured, while the latter have restricted, historic movements. But can one say, as some people believe, that a nation's boundaries are to be found written on the map, and that it has the right to award itself as much as is necessary to round off certain outlines, or to reach such-and-such a mountain or river, which are regarded as in some way dispensing the frontier *à priori?* I know no doctrine more arbitrary or fatal than this, which can be used to justify all kinds of violence. In the first place, is it the mountains, or is it the rivers that constitute these alleged natural frontiers? It is indisputable that mountains separate; but rivers tend rather to bring together. Then again all mountains cannot divide states. Which are those that separate and those that do not? From Biarritz to Tornea there is not one estuary which is more like a boundary than another. If History had so decreed, then the Loire, the Seine, the Meuse, the Elbe and the Oder would have, as much as the Rhine has, this character of national frontier, which has been the cause of so many infringements of that fundamental right, which is the will of men. People talk of strategic grounds. Nothing is absolute; and it is evident that much must be conceded to necessity. But these concessions must not go too far. Otherwise, every one will demand what suits him from a military point of view and we shall have endless warfare. No; it is not the soil any more than the race which makes a nation. The soil provides the substratum, the field for struggle and labour: man provides the soul. Man is everything in the formation of this sacred thing that we call a people. Nothing that is material suffices here. A nation is a spiritual principle, the result of the intricate workings of

history; a spiritual family and not a group determined by the configuration of the earth.

We have now seen those things which do not suffice to create such a spiritual principle. They are race, language, interests, religious affinity, geography and military necessity. What more then is required? In view of what I have already said, I shall not have to detain you very much longer.

III

A nation is a soul, a spiritual principle. Two things, which are really only one, go to make up this soul or spiritual principle. One of these things lies in the past, the other in the present. The one is the possession in common of a rich heritage of memories; and the other is actual agreement, the desire to live together, and the will to continue to make the most of the joint inheritance. Man, gentlemen, cannot be improvised. The nation, like the individual, is the fruit of a long past spent in toil, sacrifice and devotion. Ancestor-worship is of all forms the most justifiable, since our ancestors have made us what we are. A heroic past, great men and glory—I mean real glory—these should be the capital of our company when we come to found a national idea. To share the glories of the past, and a common will in the present; to have done great deeds together, and to desire to do more—these are the essential conditions of a people's being. Love is in proportion to the sacrifices one has made and the evils one has borne. We love the house that we have built and that we hand down to our successors. The Spartan song "We are what ye were, and we shall be what ye are," is, in its simplicity, the abridged version of every national anthem.

In the past, a heritage of glory and of grief to be shared; in the future, one common plan to be realized; to have suffered, rejoiced and hoped together; these are things of greater value than identity of custom-houses and frontiers in accordance with strategic notions. These are things which are understood, in spite of differences in race and language. I said just now "to have suffered together," for indeed common suffering unites more strongly than common rejoicing. Among national memories, sorrows have greater value than victories; for they impose duties and demand common effort.

Thus we see that a nation is a great solid unit, formed by the realization of sacrifices in the past, as well as of those one is prepared to make in the future. A nation implies a past; while, as regards the present, it is all contained in one tangible fact, viz., the agreement and clearly expressed desire to continue a life in common. The existence of a nation is (if you will forgive me the metaphor) a daily plebiscite, just as that of the individual is a continual affirmation of life. . . .

14. *DUTIES TOWARD YOUR COUNTRY* /
GIUSEPPE MAZZINI

Your first duties—first as regards importance—are . . . towards Humanity. You are *men* before you are either citizens or fathers. If you do not embrace the whole human family in your affection, if you do not bear witness to your belief in the Unity of that family—consequent upon the Unity of God;—and in that fraternity among the peoples which is destined to reduce that Unity to action; if, wheresoever a fellow-creature suffers, or the dignity of human nature is violated by falsehood or tyranny—you are not ready, if able, to aid the unhappy, and do not feel called upon to combat, if able, for the redemption of the betrayed or oppressed—you violate your Law of life, you comprehend not that Religion which will be the guide and blessing of the future.

But what can each of you, singly, *do* for the moral improvement and progress of Humanity? You can from time to time give sterile utterance to your belief; you may, on some rare occasions, perform some act of *charity* towards a brother man not belonging to your own land;—no more. But charity is not the watchword of the Faith of the future. The watchword of the Faith of the future is *association* and fraternal co-operation of all towards a common aim, and this is as far superior to all charity, as the edifice which all of you should unite to raise would be superior to the humble hut each one of you might build alone or with the mere assistance of lending and borrowing stone, mortar, and tools.

But, you tell me, you cannot attempt united action, distinct and

* Giuseppe Mazzini, "Duties Toward Your Country," in *Introduction to Contemporary Civilization in the West*, 3rd ed. (New York: Columbia University Press, 1961), Vol. II, pp. 540–43. Reprinted by permission.

divided as you are in language, customs, tendencies, and capacity. The individual is too insignificant, and Humanity too vast. The mariner of Brittany prays to God as he puts to sea: *Help me, my God! my boat is so small and Thy ocean so wide!* And this prayer is the true expression of the condition of each one of you, until you find the means of infinitely multiplying your forces and powers of action.

This means was provided for you by God when he gave you a country; when, even as a wise overseer of labour distributes the various branches of employment according to the different capacities of the workmen, he divided Humanity into distinct groups or nuclei upon the face of the earth, thus creating the germ of Nationalities. Evil governments have disfigured the Divine design. Nevertheless you may still trace it, distinctly marked out—at least as far as Europe is concerned—by the course of the great rivers, the direction of the higher mountains, and other geographical conditions. They have disfigured it by their conquests, their greed, and their jealousy even of the righteous power of others; disfigured it so far that, if we except England and France—there is not perhaps a single country whose present boundaries correspond to that Design.

These governments did not, and do not, recognise any country save their own families or dynasty, the egotism of caste. But the Divine design will infallibly be realised. Natural divisions, and the spontaneous innate tendencies of the peoples, will take the place of the arbitrary divisions sanctioned by evil governments. The map of Europe will be re-drawn. The countries of the Peoples, defined by the vote of free men, will arise upon the ruins of the countries of kings and privileged castes, and between these countries harmony and fraternity will exist. And the common work of Humanity, of great amelioration, and the gradual discovery and application of its law of life, being distributed according to local and general capacities, will be wrought out in peaceful and progressive development and advance.

Then may each one of you, fortified by the power and the affection of many millions, all speaking the same language, gifted with the same tendencies, and educated by the same historical tradition, hope even by your own single effort to be able to benefit all Humanity.

O my brothers, love your Country! Our country is our Home, the House that God has given us, placing therein a numerous family that loves us, and whom we love; a family with whom we sympathize more readily, and whom we understand more quickly, than we do others; and which, from its being centred round a given spot, and from the homogeneous nature of its elements, is adapted to a special branch of activity.

Our Country is our common workshop, whence the products of our activity are sent forth for the benefit of the whole world; wherein the tools and implements of labour we can most usefully employ are gathered together; nor may we reject them without disobeying the play of the Almighty, and diminishing our own strength.

In labouring for our own country on the right principle, we labour for Humanity. Our country is the fulcrum of the lever we have to wield for the common good. In abandoning that fulcrum, we run the risk of rendering ourselves useless not only to humanity but to our country itself.

Before men can *associate* with the nations of which humanity is composed, they must have a National existence. There is no true association except among equals. It is only through our country that we can have a recognizeed *collective* existence.

Humanity is a vast army advancing to the conquest of lands unknown, against enemies both powerful and astute. The peoples are the different corps, the divisions of that army. Each of them has its post assigned to it, and its special operation to execute; and the common victory depends upon the exactitude with which those distinct operations shall be fulfilled. Disturb not the order of battle. Forsake not the banner given to you by God. Wheresoever you may be, in the centre of whatsoever people circumstances may have placed you, be ever ready to combat for the liberty of that people should it be necessary, but combat in such wise that the blood you shed may reflect glory, not on yourselves alone, but on your country. Say not *I*, but *we*. Let each man among you strive to incarnate his country in himself. Let each man among you regard himself as a guarantee, responsible for his fellow-countrymen, and learn so to govern his actions as to cause his country to be loved and respected through him.

Your country is the sign of the mission God has given you to fulfil towards humanity. The faculties and forces of *all* her sons should be associated in the accomplishment of that mission.

The true country is a community of free men and equals, bound together in fraternal concord to labour towards a common aim. You are bound to make it and to maintain it such.

The country is not an *aggregation*, but an *association*.

There is therefore no true country without an uniform Right. There is no true country where the uniformity of that Right is violated by the existence of castes, privilege, and inequality.

Where the activity of a portion of the powers and faculties of the individual is either cancelled or dormant; where there is not a common Principle, recognised, accepted, and developed by all, there is no true Nation, no People; but only a multitude, a fortuitous agglomeration of men whom circumstances have called together, and whom circumstances may again divide.

In the name of the love you bear your country you must peacefully but untiringly combat the existence of privilege and inequality in the land that gave you life.

There is but one sole legitimate privilege, the privilege of Genius when it reveals itself united with virtue. But this is a privilege given by God, and when you acknowledge it and follow its inspiration, you do so freely, exercising your own reason and your own choice.

Every privilege which demands submission from you in virtue of power, inheritance, or any other right than the Right common to all, is an usurpation and a tyranny which you are bound to resist and destroy.

Be your country your Temple. God at the summit; a people of equals at the base.

Accept no other formula, no other moral law, if you would not dishonour alike your country and yourselves. Let all secondary laws be but the gradual regulation of your existence by the progressive application of this supreme law.

And in order that they may be such, it is necessary that *all* of you should aid in framing them. Laws framed only by a single fraction of the citizens, can never, in the very nature of things, be other than the mere expression of the thoughts, aspirations, and desires of that fraction; the representation, not of the Country, but of a third or fourth part, of a class or zone of the Country.

The laws should be the expression of the *universal* aspiration, and promote the universal good. They should be a pulsation of the heart of the Nation. The entire Nation should, either directly or indirectly, legislate.

By yielding up this mission into the hands of a few, you substitute the egotism of one class for the Country, which is the Union of all classes.

Country is not a mere zone of territory. The true Country is the Idea to which it gives birth; it is the Thought of love, the sense of communion which unites in one all the sons of that territory.

So long as a single one amongst your brothers has no vote to represent him in the development of the National life, so long as there is one left to vegetate in ignorance where others are educated, so long as a single man, able and willing to work, languishes in poverty through want of work to do, you have no Country in the sense in which Country ought to exist—the Country of all and for all.

Education, labour, and the franchise, are the three main pillars of the Nation. Rest not until you have built them strongly up with your own labour and exertions.

Never deny your sister Nations. Be it yours to evolve the life of your Country in loveliness and strength; free from all servile fears or sceptical doubts; maintaining as its basis the People; as its guide the consequences of the principles of its Religious Faith, logically and energetically applied; its strength, the united strength of all; its aim the fulfilment of the mission given to it by God.

And so long as you are ready to die for Humanity, the Life of your Country will be immortal.

15. *THE GROWTH OF NATIONS** / *KARL W. DEUTSCH*

. . . While peoples are found at almost any period in history, nationalism and nations have occurred during only a few periods. A nation is the result of the transformation of a people, or of several ethnic elements, in the process of social mobilization. Thus far, however, the processes of social mobilization and communication have at no time included all mankind. The "universal states" listed by A. J. Toynbee as stages in the disintegration of particular civilizations[4] were superficial short-cuts, rather than solutions to the problem of the unity of mankind.

* Karl W. Deutsch, "The Growth of Nations: Some Recurrent Patterns of Political and Social Integration," *World Politics*, Vol. 5, No. 2 (January 1953), pp. 169–72, 189–94. Reprinted by permission.
    [4] *A Study of History*, London, 1939, IV, pp. 2–3.

Periods of "universal states" have left behind them, however, a number of widespread languages, such as Latin, Greek, or Arabic; and a measure of cultural assimilation among certain social groups such as the nobility, town population, or the clergy of some "universal church."[5] The results have somewhat resembled a *layer-cake pattern*, with a high degree of cultural assimilation and participation in extended social communication among the top layers of society; a lesser degree on the intermediate levels; and little or no assimilation or participation among the mass of the population at the bottom.[6]

In several parts of the world, the cycle—from local isolation to "universal" empire and back to a new age of localism[7]—has been traversed more than once. Yet the cycle has usually shown a net gain, in the sense that there has been a gain in man's technological and scientific command over nature,[8] and that some of the most important cultural, intellectual, moral, and spiritual traditions of the earlier civilization have tended to survive that civilization in which they arose, and continue, often as a "universal church" or religion, to influence the development of new peoples and new regions.[9]

As a result, much of world history has consisted of recurrent "feudal ages" in various parts of the world, though such periods in most cases were "feudal" only in the loose sense of the word. They were characterized by intense localism and dispersion of agriculture and settlement, as well as of military and judicial power, and by sharp distinctions between the class of scattered power-holders and the mass of the peasant population. At the same time, these "feudal" periods were marked by a certain universalism of political and cultural traditions, by memories of a past universal state, or by the

[5] For examples of such limited assimilation during and after the expanding phase of certain civilizations or universal states, see *ibid.*, Vols. i–vi, *passim*, and the appendix on "Lingue Franche" in Vol. v, pp. 483–526. Cf. also A. C. Woolner, *Languages in History and Politics*, London, 1938; and H. A. Innis, *Empire and Communication*, Oxford, 1950, and *The Bias of Communications*, Toronto, 1952. On particular languages, see Woolner, *op. cit.*, pp. 109–48, 156–67; H. A. R. Gibb, *The Arabs*, Oxford, 1940; George Antonius, *The Arab Awakening*, Philadelphia, 1939, p. 16; P. K. Hitti, *History of Syria Including Lebanon and Palestine*, New York, 1951, pp. 483–89.

[6] Cf. Royal Institute of International Affairs, *Nationalism*, London, 1939, p. 9; A. P. Usher, *Economic History of England*, Boston, 1920, pp. 20–21.

[7] For a discussion of the chances of linguistic disintegration following upon the dissolution of a universal empire, see Ramón Menéndez Pidal, *Castilla, la tradición, el idioma*, Buenos Aires, 1945, pp. 191–94.

[8] For the Graeco-Roman and medieval civilizations, this point has been stressed by Gordon Childe, *What Happened in History*, Harmondsworth, Eng., Penguin Books, 1950, pp. 279–82.

[9] Toynbee, *op. cit.*, v, p. 79, and *passim*.

knowledge of a highly developed civilization in some other area.[10] Such unifying memories or traditions were no mere disembodied thoughts: they were carried and disseminated by the institutions of organized churches and monastic orders, by a thin but far-flung network of trade relations and routes of pilgrimage, and sometimes by the movement and resettlement of small numbers of persons with special skills, industrial or military, over considerable distances.

From the point of view of nationality, all these were variations of the common layer-cake pattern. Assimilation to a common standard among the upper classes might be feeble, as during the "dark ages" in Western Europe; it might be somewhat more strongly developed, as among the European nobility at the time of the Crusades; or it might be almost complete, as in a universal state, as it had been in that of Imperial Rome. In any case, it would touch the masses of the people in the villages only indirectly and slowly. And even where it did touch and assimilate them in the course of centuries, there their continued passivity and lack of direct participation in affairs of wider import seemed to make it irrelevant for long periods of time whether the underlying population in the villages had been assimilated at least imperfectly to a common standard as in Italy, or whether they had remained as sharply differentiated as Czechs and Germans in Bohemia, or as Malays and Chinese in Malaya.[11] Only when this relatively passive population was mobilized in the processes of economic growth and political organization, did its cultural and social characteristics acquire in each case a new and crucial importance in the process of nation-building.

The processes of partial social mobilization and of nation-building have been recurrent phenomena in history, at least in certain general characteristics. What uniformities can we find in this growth of nations in the past? And in what ways is our own age

[10] A Conference on Feudalism was held on October 31 and November 1, 1950, at Princeton University under the auspices of the Committee on Uniformities of the American Council of Learned Societies. For the point made in the text, see the papers submitted to the Conference and the abridged report on its proceedings issued by the Council (Washington, D.C., multigraphed). A volume on *Feudalism in History*, containing these papers, with an analytical essay by the editor, Professor Rushton Coulborn, is in process of publication.

[11] Cf. Elizabeth Wiskemann, *Czechs and Germans*, London, 1938; Victor Purcell, *The Chinese in Malaya*, London, 1948; Rupert Emerson, L. A. Mills, and V. Thompson, *Government and Nationalism in Southeast Asia*, New York, 1942; etc.

different in respect to the growth of nations from any age that has gone before?

Some Possible Specific Uniformities

Uniformities which have been found in the growth of nations include the following:

1. The shift from subsistence agriculture to *exchange economies*.

2. The social mobilization of rural populations in *core areas* of denser settlement and more intensive exchange.

3. The growth of *towns*, and the growth of social mobility within them, and between town and country.

4. The growth of *basic communication grids*, linking important rivers, towns, and trade routes in a flow of transport, travel, and migration.

5. The differential accumulation and *concentration of capital* and skills, and sometimes of social institutions, and their *"lift-pump"* *effect* on other areas and populations, with the successive entry of different social strata into the nationalistic phase.

6. The rise of the concept of *"interest"* for both individuals and groups in unequal but fluid situations, and the growth of *individual self-awareness* and awareness of one's predispositions to join a particular group united by language and communications habits.

7. The awakening of *ethnic awareness* and the acceptance of *national symbols*, intentional or unintentional. . . .

What does this process accomplish, and what does it aim at? When a nation has been built up, and when it has been reinforced finally by the full compulsive power of the state, then four things have been accomplished.

(1) A relatively large community of human beings has been brought into existence who can communicate effectively with each other, and who have command over sufficient economic resources to maintain themselves and to transmit this ability for mutual communication to their children as well. In other words, there has been brought into being a large, comprehensive, and very stable human network of communication, capable of maintaining, reproducing, and further developing its channels.

(2) There has been both an effective accumulation of eco-

nomic resources and a sufficient social mobilization of manpower to permit the social division of labor necessary for this process and to permit its continuation.

(3) There has been a social accumulation and integration of memories and symbols and of individual and social facilities for their preservation, transmission, and recombination, corresponding to the level of mobilization and integration of material and human resources, or even pointing beyond it.

(4) There has been at least some development of the capacity to redirect, re-allocate, or form a new combination of economic, social, and human resources as well as of symbols and items of knowledge, habit, or thought—that is to say, of the capacity to learn. Some of the social *learning capacity* is developed invisibly in the minds of individuals; some of it can be observed in the habits and patterns of culture prevailing among them; some of it finally is embodied in tangible facilities and specific institutions. Together, all these constitute the community's capacity to produce and accept new knowledge or new goals, and to take the corresponding action.

On all four counts, it should be evident, the nation represents a more effective organization than the supra-national but largely passive layer-cake society or the feudal or tribal localisms that preceded it.

On all these counts, there may be considerable contrasts between different nations. The social models accepted for imitation, the established institutions, the economic practices, and the methods of compulsion within each nation are all intimately connected with the cultural traditions and leading social classes currently prevailing there. Whether a leading class of businessmen or farmers or wage earners will prove more hospitable to accumulation of resources and to efficient dynamic innovation in their use may depend not merely on the general outlook to be found prevailing in each particular stratum, but also—and perhaps sometimes crucially—on the particular cultural goals and traditions which have become accepted by that particular class in that particular nation.[35] Yet, the

[35] For some problems of conservative aristocratic leadership in undeveloped nations, cf., for the Arabs, the writings of H. A. R. Gibb; for an example from Tibet, Nicholas Mansergh, "The Asian Conference, 1947," in *The Commonwealth and the Nations*, London, 1948, pp. 115–16; and for Southeast Asia, Cora Du Bois, *Social Forces in Southeast Asia*, Minneapolis, Minn., 1949, pp. 33–36, 59. On the contrast, e.g., between French and American business investment policies, cf. David S. Landes, "French Entrepreneurship and Industrial Growth in the Nineteenth Century," *Journal of Economic History*, IX (May 1949), pp. 45–61.

impression remains that even the worst-led nation represents, relative to its numbers of population, a greater amount of social communication facilities, of economic resources, and of social learning capacity than any pattern of ethnic or social organization preceding it.

Where does this process aim? The nation has been valued as a means of social advancement. In a world of extreme differences between living standards, men have tended to use the nation as an instrument to improve their own standards relative to those of their neighbors. The intrinsic bias of this process has been, where the opportunity offered itself, to produce in the temporarily most successful nation a sociological pattern reminiscent of a *mushroom cloud*. The stem of this social mushroom was formed by the "national solidarity" between the poorest and the lower-middle strata of the nation; the poorest strata, both rural and urban, however, tended to be somewhat less in relative numbers, and offered their members greater chances for "vertical mobility" than was the case in other less "successful" nations. The middle and upper strata, on the other hand, tended to form the crown of the mushroom; they tended to be somewhat larger in number than the corresponding group in other nations, with a greater propensity to spread out horizontally into new positions of privilege or control over new territories, populations, or capital resources, and correspondingly with at least somewhat greater opportunities to accept in their midst newcomers from the less favored strata of their own nation.

It is perhaps this sociological explosion into a mushroom cloud that has been at the heart of the transitory popularity of empire-building. Nationalism typically has led to attempts at empire or at least at establishing privileges over other peoples. The essence of this empire-building has been perhaps the attempt at ruling without sharing, just as the essence of nationalism has been the attempt at improving the position of one's "own" group without any sharing with "outsiders." To the extent that this process was successful it could only tend ultimately to transform the whole nation into a privileged class, a *Herrenvolk* lording it over servant peoples, as the Nazis dreamed of it, or a small, select population monopolizing vast natural resources or accumulations of technological equipment regardless of the fate of the rest of mankind. In reality, this state has probably never been achieved; and where it was even partially approximated, the results in the long-run were anything but lasting. Invariably, thus far, the same nation-building process which had permitted one nation to get temporarily on top of its neighbors subsequently raised up other nations to weaken or destroy it.

From this it might seem at first glance that the whole process of the rise and decline of nations has been cyclical, with only the names of the actors changing in an endlessly repeated drama. Closer scrutiny may show that this is not the case, and that some tentative inferences may be drawn from the events and processes surveyed.

The Uniqueness of the Present Period

Our survey offers no support for the belief of many nationalists that nations are the natural and universal form of social organization for mankind. But neither does it confirm entirely the opposite view held by many thoughtful and distinguished observers—the view that nations are exclusively the product of the modern period and of Western civilization.[36] Perhaps the impression that remains might be summed up by saying that the West has gone much farther on a road which all the world's great civilizations have traveled to some extent.

At this moment we might well pause to question the ease with which we accept the designation of our present-day civilization as exclusively "Western." By Western civilization we mean a civilization which arose from the mingling of the Graeco-Roman tradition with the Celtic, Teutonic, and Slavic barbarian cultures north of the Mediterranean; but this Western civilization was Semiticized and Orientalized by the twin influences of Judaism and Christianity, even if we allow for the very appreciable element of Greek tradition in the latter.[37]

Subsequently, this Hellenic-Barbarian-Judaeo-Christian civilization was partially Arabized during more than five hundred years of culture contact from the seventh to the thirteenth century. During the thirteenth and fourteenth centuries, this Arabized Western civilization was then Mongolized and Sinicized. The details of the origin and acquisition of almost all of these innovations offer room for controversy, but there should be little controversy about the cumulative picture. Nor should there be much controversy

[36] Cf. Toynbee, *op. cit., passim;* Hans Kohn, *The Idea of Nationalism,* New York, 1944, *passim;* Carlton H. Hayes, "Nationalism," *Encyclopedia of the Social Sciences;* etc.

[37] For this tradition of the poorest strata of the Hellenic world, see the intriguing case presented by Toynbee, "Christus Patiens," *op. cit.,* VI, pp. 376–539.

about the massive "Amerindianization" of that Western-Arabic-Mongolian world from the sixteenth century onward, once the Indian culture plants of corn and potatoes permitted an entirely new balance of populations on the land, and once the availability of plentiful sugar, cotton, and tobacco transformed man's food, clothing, and consumption habits. What we call today Western civilization is in a very real sense a World civilization, not merely in what it brought to other countries, but also very significantly in what it received from them. Perhaps its "Western" peculiarities lie, then, not only in its ability to originate, but also in its ability to innovate, that is, to learn actively from others.

All these traits of creativity and of the ability to learn are present in all great civilizations of the world, and the West here, too, has perhaps gone faster and farther on a road traveled to some extent by all. In a real sense, Western civilization is carrying on some—though certainly not all—of the traditions of all other civilizations, and its crisis in the world today is also their crisis, and not merely in externals.

It is this universal aspect that also characterizees the growth of nations in the present. During the last fifty years, there seems to have been growth in all the important regions of the world. Everywhere there has been growth in population, in gross economic wealth, and in national awareness. In no region has there been a decline to compensate for an advance elsewhere. Many of these advances in widely different areas have been the continuation of long-standing trends, which have been helped and speeded by the new resources and possibilities offered by the diffusion of science and technology during those last fifty years.

The result is that today all peoples are involved in the growth of national awareness, and that soon there will be no peoples left to play the role of submerged nationalities or underlying populations, or passive bystanders of history, or drawers of water and hewers of wood for their better organized neighbors.

The process has gone further. Within each people, all social strata have been mobilized, socially, economically, and politically, or are in the process of being so mobilized before our eyes. Wherever this social mobilization has progressed, it has undermined the patterns of authority and privilege inherited from an earlier day. The time can be envisioned now when the majority of all mankind will have shifted to non-agricultural occupations. There has never been a period like this in the history of the world. . . .

6
NATIONAL POWER

The measurement of a state's power or capability in international politics is both a very fundamental and a most complicated matter. The selections in this chapter deal with only a few of its aspects. The first selection is Machiavelli's view of the calculation of state power—Chapter 10 of his *The Prince*. His principal, but not exclusive, emphasis is on military factors.

The second selection is concerned with the influence of different governmental systems on national power. Can a democracy pursue a successful foreign policy? Alexis de Tocqueville (1805–59) gives a pessimistic answer to this question in his famous work *Democracy in America*.

The third selection is Stephen B. Jones' discussion of "Global Strategic Views." The author is Professor of Geography at Yale University. He has also written *Geography and World Affairs* and other works.

The final selection in this chapter presents a different kind of global strategic view, based on the criterion of economic development: Lin Piao's argument that a fundamental cleavage exists between the "cities of the world" and the "rural areas of the world." A noteworthy element of his theory is that he emphasizes the relative impotence of nuclear weapons in the struggle between the two forces. Lin Piao is Communist China's Minister of Defense and Vice-Chairman of the Communist Party. His address "Long Live the Victory of People's War" was first published in the Peking *People's Daily* on September 3, 1965.

16. HOW TO MEASURE THE POWER OF STATES*/
NICCOLO MACHIAVELLI

It is also important in the study of governments to examine whether the prince, in time of need, be powerful enough to defend himself by his own forces, without having recourse to the assistance of his allies. To place this point in the clearest view, I may observe that those only can so defend themselves who have men and money enough to bring an army into the field, and give battle to whoever shall attack them. But wretched indeed is the situation of that prince who is reduced to the necessity of shutting himself up in his native city, there to await the enemy's approach. I have already discussed the first point, and shall have occasion to return to it again.

As to the second, I cannot but warn princes of the necessity they are under to fortify and provision the place of their residence, without troubling themselves about the rest of the country; for it, as I have already observed, and shall again have occasion in the sequel to repeat, they have in addition to this precaution learned the art of gaining their people's affection, they will be secure from all danger. Men are naturally cautious of engaging in difficult enterprises without some appearance of success, and it is never prudent to attack a prince whose capital is in a good state of defense and who is on good terms with his subjects.

The cities of Germany enjoy a very extensive liberty; they possess a territory of inconsiderable extent, and obey the Emperor when they please, under no apprehension of being attacked either by him or by others, for the towns are defended by strong walls and deep ditches, and are provided with artillery and provisions for a

* Niccolo Machiavelli, *The Prince* (New York: The National Alumni, 1907), Chap. 10, slightly revised by the editor.

year, so that the siege of these cities would be both long and painful. Moreover, they are always provided with the means of employing the people during the same space of time, so as to support them without the assistance of the public purse. Their troops are exercised regularly, and their rules in that respect are wise and well observed.

A prince, therefore, who possesses a well-fortified city, and is respected by his people, can hardly be attacked with advantage, because the affairs of this world are so liable to change that it would be almost impossible for an enemy to keep the field for a year before a place so defended.

It may perhaps be objected that the people who possess property in the country, and who see their lands ravaged, will lose their patience, and that their attachment to their prince will not long continue against the inconveniences of a long siege, and the desire of preserving their property. I answer, that a prudent and spirited prince will easily surmount these obstacles, by inspiring the people either with hopes that their sufferings will soon be over, or with a dread of the resentment and cruelty of the conqueror, or by taking other proper means to appease those that are clamorous.

To this may be added, that the enemy begins his ravage of the country as soon as he enters it, and at that time the besieged are most animated and disposed to defend themselves; in which case the prince has still less to apprehend, because, before their ardor has cooled, the inhabitants, perceiving that all the mischief has been accomplished, and the loss is irretrievable, will evince the more attachment to their prince in proportion as their sacrifices are greater. For such is the nature of mankind that they become as strongly attached to others by the benefits they render as by the favors they receive.

All these considerations persuade me that a wise and provident prince may, without difficulty, succeed in sustaining the courage of his people under the distress of a siege, if he take care that they are well provided with the means necessary for their sustenance and defense.

17. DEMOCRACY AND FOREIGN POLICY*/

ALEXIS DE TOCQUEVILLE

. . . As the Union [the United States] takes no part in the affairs of

* Alexis de Tocqueville, *Democracy in America*, trans. Henry Reeve, rev. by Francis Bowen (Cambridge, Mass.: Sever and Francis, 1863), Vol. I, Chap. 13.

Europe, it has, properly speaking, no foreign interests to discuss, since it has, as yet, no powerful neighbors on the American continent. The country is as much removed from the passions of the Old World by its position as by its wishes, and it is neither called upon to repudiate nor to espouse them; whilst the dissensions of the New World are still concealed within the bosom of the future.

The Union is free from all pre-existing obligations; it can profit by the experience of the old nations of Europe, without being obliged, as they are, to make the best of the past, and to adapt it to their present circumstances. It is not, like them, compelled to accept an immense inheritance bequeathed by their forefathers,—an inheritance of glory mingled with calamities, and of alliances conflicting with national antipathies. The foreign policy of the United States is eminently expectant; it consists more in abstaining than in acting.

It is therefore very difficult to ascertain, at present, what degree of sagacity the American democracy will display in the conduct of the foreign policy of the country; upon this point, its adversaries as well as its friends must suspend their judgment. As for myself, I do not hesitate to say that it is especially in the conduct of their foreign relations that democracies appear to me decidedly inferior to other governments. Experience, instruction, and habit almost always succeed in creating in a democracy a homely species of practical wisdom, and that science of the petty occurrences of life which is called good sense. Good sense may suffice to direct the ordinary course of society; and amongst a people whose education is completed, the advantages of democratic liberty in the internal affairs of the country may more than compensate for the evils inherent in a democratic government. But it is not always so in the relations with foreign nations.

Foreign politics demand scarcely any of those qualities which are peculiar to a democracy; they require, on the contrary, the perfect use of almost all those in which it is deficient. Democracy is favorable to the increase of the internal resources of a state; it diffuses wealth and comfort, promotes public spirit, and fortifies the respect for law in all classes of society: all these are advantages which have only an indirect influence over the relations which one people bears to another. But a democracy can only with great difficulty regulate the details of an important undertaking, persevere in a fixed design, and work out its execution in spite of serious obstacles. It cannot combine its measures with secrecy, or await their consequences with patience. These are qualities which more especially belong to an individual or an aristocracy; and they are precisely the qualities by which a nation, like an individual, attains a dominant position.

If, on the contrary, we observe the natural defects of aristocracy, we shall find that, comparatively speaking, they do not injure the direction of the external affairs of the state. The capital fault of which aristocracies may be accused is, that they work for themselves, and not for the people. In foreign politics, it is rare for the interest of the aristocracy to be distinct from that of the people.

The propensity which induces democracies to obey impulse rather than prudence, and to abandon a mature design for the gratification of a momentary passion, was clearly seen in America on the breaking out of the French Revolution. It was then as evident to the simplest capacity, as it is at the present time, that the interest of the Americans forbade them to take any part in the contest which was about to deluge Europe with blood, but which could not injure their own country. But the sympathies of the people declared themselves with so much violence in favor of France, that nothing but the inflexible character of Washington, and the immense popularity which he enjoyed, could have prevented the Americans from declaring war against England. And even then, the exertions which the austere reason of that great man made to repress the generous but imprudent passions of his fellow-citizens nearly deprived him of the sole recompense which he ever claimed,—that of his country's love. The majority reprobated his policy, but it was afterwards approved by the whole nation.*

If the Constitution and the favor of the public had not intrusted the direction of the foreign affairs of the country to Washington, it is certain that the American nation would at that time have adopted the very measures which it now condemns.

* See the fifth volume of Marshall's "Life of Washington." "In a government constituted like that of the United States," he says, "it is impossible for the chief magistrate, however firm he may be, to oppose for any length of time the torrent of popular opinion; and the prevalent opinion of that day seemed to incline to war. In fact, in the session of Congress held at the time, it was frequently seen that Washington had lost the majority in the House of Representatives." The violence of the language used against him in public was extreme, and, in a political meeting, they did not scruple to compare him indirectly with the traitor Arnold. "By the opposition," says Marshall, "the friends of the administration were declared to be an aristocratic and corrupt faction, who, from a desire to introduce monarchy, were hostile to France, and under the influence of Britain; that they were a paper nobility, whose extreme sensibility at every measure which threatened the funds induced a tame submission to injuries and insults which the interests and honor of the nation required them to resist."

Almost all the nations which have exercised a powerful influence upon the destinies of the world, by conceiving, following out, and executing vast designs, from the Romans to the English, have been governed by aristocratic institutions. Nor will this be a subject of wonder, when we recollect that nothing in the world has so absolute a fixity of purpose as an aristocracy. The mass of the people may be led astray by ignorance or passion; the mind of a king may be biassed, and made to vacillate in his designs, and, besides, a king is not immortal. But an aristocratic body is too numerous to be led astray by intrigue; and yet not numerous enough to yield readily to the intoxication of unreflecting passion. An aristocracy is a firm and enlightened individual that never dies.

18. *GLOBAL STRATEGIC VIEWS*/ *STEPHEN B. JONES*

. . . "Strategy" in the broad sense can be defined as the art of using power. "Global strategy" implies this art viewed in relation to the whole world. The "global strategic views" of our title are geographical patterns related to global strategic ideas. . . .

The focus is on certain major ideas about the world, their relationships and their consequences. We begin with one of the first men to write of strategy in global terms, Mahan.

Mahan's View

The name of Mahan immediately evokes images of gray ships and blue water. However, as all students of his works know, he was concerned not so much with naval operations (though he described many battles) as with sea power, and sea power is as much of the land as of the sea. In his most famous book[3] Mahan listed six fundamental factors affecting the development of sea power: geographical position, physical conformation, extent of territory, number of population, national character, and governmental character. Merely to read this list is to understand the importance of the land base.

Mahan devoted most of his attention to European and North Atlantic naval history, including offshoot campaigns in the Indian

* Stephen B. Jones, "Global Strategic Views," *The Geographical Review*, Vol. 45, No. 4 (October 1955), pp. 492–508. Reprinted by permission.
  [3] A. T. Mahan: The Influence of Sea Power upon History, 1660–1783 (Boston, 1890), Chap. I.

Ocean. However, in one of his less well-known books we find a global view, somewhat crudely outlined, that adumbrates the views of Mackinder, Fairgrieve, and Spykman. Here Mahan describes Russia in terms that fit Mackinder's Heartland—a "vast, uninterrupted mass" whose "centre cannot be broken."[4] He emphasizes Russia's landlocked position and its dominance in Central Asia. He points to the latitudinal belt of 30° to 40° N. in Asia as the unstable zone between British sea power and Russian land power.[5] This resembles, roughly, the Asiatic part of Fairgrieve's "crush zone."[6] Mahan also adumbrates Fairgrieve's "northern belt of settlement and movement," pointing out that Suez and Panama would mark the southern limit of most active commerce and politics.[7]

Mahan thought that Russian expansion in Asia could be opposed by sea-transported power—a sort of containment policy. Somewhat surprisingly, he advocated giving Russia access to the sea through China[8]—a premonition of Yalta, one might say. He believed this would satisfy Russian aspirations for warm-water ports, though it is hard to see how that could be the case with the bulk of the Russian population in Europe.[9] Mahan also predicted that Britain, Germany, Japan, and the United States would find a common interest in containing Russia and controlling China.[10] This prediction is less startling in 1955 than it seemed 10 years ago, when the present writer first read it. Like Mackinder after him, Mahan probably overestimated the influence of navigable rivers. He refers repeatedly to the navigability of the Yangtze. During the years of China's weakness, when foreign gunboats patrolled the river, it did serve as an avenue for sea power. But adequate land or air forces could make the Yangtze untenable for foreign ships, as happened when the Japanese bombed the *Panay* and the Chinese Communists attacked the *Amethyst*.

Looking back, one may question whether "sea power" was a really happy phrase. It emphasized one medium of power transmission, rather than the whole picture of national power and the places and purposes of its use. A lingering effect of a too literal

[4] *Idem:* The Problem of Asia (Boston, 1900), pp. 24 and 26.
[5] *Ibid.*, pp. 21 ff.
[6] James Fairgrieve: Geography and World Power (8th edit., New York, 1941), p. 334.
[7] Mahan, The Problem of Asia, pp. 84–86.
[8] *Ibid.*, pp. 117–120.
[9] For an interesting related discussion, see J. A. Morrison: Russia and Warm Water, *U. S. Naval Inst. Proc.*, Vol. 78, 1952, pp. 1169–1179.
[10] Mahan, The Problem of Asia [see footnote 4 above], pp. 63–65.

interpretation of the sea-power doctrine is an American belief that might be called "naval isolationism." This is to be distinguished from "continental isolationism," which would defend America at its shores. Naval isolationism is the belief that superior sea power can keep an enemy off the oceans and hence that American shores are safe without sending armies to lands overseas. The basic thesis is doubtful in this age of the airplane and the submarine, and the need to maintain a balance of power in Eurasia is ignored. Mahan's own views on Asia do not support the naval isolationist position, and Mackinder and Spykman, to whom we now turn, regarded it as definitely unsound.

Mackinder's View

It is not surprising that the United States, painfully land-minded since the opening of the West and the decline of sailing ships, should have produced Mahan, while Britain, most maritime of great powers, should have produced Mackinder. Prophets traditionally are voices crying in the wilderness. However, as we have already indicated, the basic views of Mahan and Mackinder are not as far apart as is commonly believed. Mahan outlined in a rough way the Heartland concept. Both men understood that sea power is land-based and that the size, population, and productivity of the land base have much to do wtih the magnitude of the resulting sea power. Mahan recognized the peculiar virtues of Britain's position, a large island off the European shore, and one of Mackinder's most scholarly works is called "Britain and the British Seas."[11] It was in their forecasts that they drew apart. Mahan continued to believe in the greater capacity and flexibility of movement by sea; Mackinder thought the great improvements in land transportation put the shoe on the other foot.

In his famous paper of 1904,[12] Mackinder designated as the "Pivot Area" that part of Eurasia which has interior drainage or drains to the icebound Arctic. The word "heart-land" appears only once in this paper, but in the 1919 book[13] it is capitalized and

[11] H. J. Mackinder: Britain and the British Seas (Oxford, 1902).
[12] *Idem:* The Geographical Pivot of History, *Geogr. Journ.*, Vol. 23, 1904, pp. 421–444.
[13] *Idem:* Democratic Ideals and Reality (New York, 1919 and 1942).

dehyphenated and supersedes "Pivot Area." The rest of Eurasia was called by Mackinder in 1904 "the Inner or Marginal Crescent." In 1919 parts of this crescent were called Coastlands. (Spykman later coined the felicitous term "rimland" for the Inner Crescent.) The Americas, Africa south of the Sahara, Australia, and the large islands off the Eurasian shores, such as the British Isles and Japan, were called in 1904 "the Outer or Insular Crescent." In 1919, Eurasia and Africa together were named the "World Island," Africa south of the Sahara "the Southern Heartland," and the other lands of the Outer Crescent "satellites" of the World Island.[14]

Mackinder's recognition of central Eurasia as the source of powerful forces that have affected Europe, South Asia, and the Far East was of course soundly based and was a needed corrective to the egocentricity of maritime Europe. But the original definition of the Pivot Area was the extreme of hydrographic literalness. It assumed that maritime states could move their forces up rivers—though current would favor the continental power—but would be unable to cross divides, however low. Actually, most transport systems work both ways. This statement applies not only to rivers but to the modern means of land transport that Mackinder especially stressed. In 1940 the Germans pushed the British off the continent. In 1945 the armies of the maritime powers swept into Germany along *Autobahnen* built to serve German troops. It is really a question of which side has the most power and makes the best use of it. It is true that improvements in land and air transportation have increased the burdens of the maritime states. But their burdens are increased primarily because they can no longer put so many of their eggs in the naval basket and because they must advance their strategic frontier as deeply into the Rimland as possible, not because the rivers of central Eurasia fail to reach an open sea.

In "Democratic Ideals and Reality" Mackinder made some alterations in the boundaries of the Heartland. "The Heartland, for the purposes of strategical thinking, includes the Baltic Sea, the navigable Middle and Lower Danube, the Black Sea, Asia Minor, Armenia, Persia, Tibet, and Mongolia."[15] Thus Mackinder now thought that the Baltic and Black Seas were closed to the maritime powers, as they had been during the First World War. This again

---

[14] *Ibid.*, pp. 79–82 and 98–99 (1919 edit.).
[15] *Ibid.*, pp. 135–136 (1919 edit.). The headwaters of the great Indian and Chinese rivers were also included in the Heartland in 1919 (map on p. 94).

seems a highly literal view. If land-based forces can close the Danish and Turkish straits, they can also keep them open to friendly ships. It is a question of who has the power, the initiative, the speed, and of who is allied to whom.

On a small-scale map the central position of the Heartland, or of the Soviet Union, in Eurasia looks terrifying. The Rimland seems such a narrow margin that it might be overwhelmed in a night. It is true that the Soviet position is strong, and that improvements in land and air transportation make it easier to exploit its advantages. Mahan believed that the sea lanes around Eurasia were really the interior lines, strategically.[16] This may no longer be true. But the speed and size of ships have greatly increased since Mahan's day. A modern freighter can cover as great a distance in a day as a truck convoy, carrying far more cargo, and is fueled for thousands of miles. Fast ships are worthy rivals of railway trains. Only the airplane is clearly superior in speed. We shall see below that this does not necessarily give the Heartland an overwhelming positional advantage. The great advantages of the Soviet Union have been political, especially its ability to follow a planned strategy persistently. The shift of China from the non-Communist to the Communist side was not so much a victory of land power over sea power as of a persistent, planned strategy over an inconsistent and blundering one.

Haushofer and his school adopted the main features of the Mackinder global view as part of the mélange of Geopolitik. They hoped that the first term of the famous dictum could be brought about by a partnership of Germany and the Soviet Union,[17] a hope which proved as illusory as Hitler's belief that Britain would agree to his terms.

Spykman's View

Spykman adopted Mackinder's basic geography but gave it a different interpretation. He rejected the apparent fatalism of the land-power doctrine and offered his own formula: "Who controls the rimland rules Eurasia; who rules Eurasia controls the destinies of the

[16] Mahan, The Problem of Asia [see footnote 4 above], pp. 124 ff.
[17] Derwent Whittlesey: Haushofer: The Geopoliticians, *in* Makers of Modern Strategy, edited by E. M. Earle (Princeton, 1943), pp. 388–411, reference on p. 405.

world."[18] Spykman hoped that the Soviet Union, the United Kingdom, and the United States would realize their common stake in controlling the Rimland. He knew, however, that "it may be that the pressure of Russia outward toward the rimland will constitute one important aspect of the post-war settlement."[19]

Mackinder's view has often been twisted into a fatalistic doctrine of "Herzland über alles."[20] Spykman seems to imply such a doctrine when he says that Mackinder emphasized "an inevitable historical opposition between Russian land power and British sea power." But, says Spykman, "there has never really been a simple land power–sea power opposition. The historical alignment has always been in terms of some members of the rimland with Great Britain against some members of the rimland with Russia, or Great Britain and Russia together against a dominating rimland power."[21] Actually, Mackinder knew this, and said so. The Heartland, in its limited sense of the interior and Arctic drainage area, menaced the maritime states only in conjunction with part of the Rimland. In the 1904 paper Mackinder[22] spoke of the peril to the marginal lands if Germany were to ally itself with Russia and of the possibility that China, organized by Japan, might conquer the Russian Empire. In the 1919 book it was the domination of the Heartland by East Europe that would lead to command of the world.

Looked at broadly, the Mahan, Mackinder, and Spykman strategic geographies have much in common. They also have much in common with Kennan's containment policy,[23] which was conceived independently.[24] Containment primarily means preventing extensions of Soviet control in the Rimland. Kennan, it might be noted, does not speak of either land power or sea power, avoiding the confusion that those terms are likely to engender.

---

[18] N. J. Spykman: The Geography of the Peace (New York, 1944), p. 43.
[19] *Ibid.*, p. 53.
[20] J. D. Hayes discusses this in his comments on Miller's "Must We Live in Fear?" *U. S. Naval Inst. Proc.*, Vol. 79, 1953, pp. 759–766; in the *United States Naval Institute Proceedings*, Vol. 80, 1954, pp. 91–93.
[21] Spykman, *loc. cit.* [see footnote 18 above]. "Always," in this quotation, means considerably less than that.
[22] The Geographical Pivot of History [see footnote 12 above], pp. 436–437.
[23] X [G. F. Kennan]: The Sources of Soviet Conduct, *Foreign Affairs*, Vol. 25, 1946–1947, pp. 566–582. Reprinted in G. F. Kennan: American Diplomacy, 1900–1950 (Chicago, 1951), pp. 107–128.
[24] Personal communication from Mr. Kennan.

The Heartland Concept

Mackinder's first term for central Eurasia, the "Pivot Area," implies uniqueness as he uses it. "The Heartland," with the definite article, implies at least primacy among heartlands. In his 1919 book Mackinder[25] called Africa south of the Sahara the "Southern Heartland." Since then other regions have been nominated for heartland status. Cressey writes: "If there is anywhere a world citadel or Heartland, it may well lie in North America rather than in Eurasia. The American continent has adequate size, compact shape, internal accessibility, a central location, good boundaries, access to two oceans, favorable topography, rich minerals, excellent climate, and a dynamic spirit in its people."[26] The relative proximity of the Eurasian and North American heartlands, if there are two heartlands, across the Arctic has often been pointed out.[27] Renner goes on to say that, as a result of air transportation, "the natural world fortress, or heartland, has been expanded to include the interior parts of all the land masses which form a ring around the Arctic Mediterranean—Europe, Asia, and North America."[28] The United States Air Force has given still another meaning to "heartland." Every great power, perhaps every state, has one. "There are two broad aspects of air operations, heartland and peripheral actions. . . . Heartland actions involve attacks against the vital elements of a nation's war sustaining resources. . . ."[29] This definition, it will be noted, does not specifically require an interior location for heartlands.

This proliferation of heartlands suggests that we try to define "heartland" in terms of *what* it is rather than *where* it is. Cressey, we have just read, defines a heartland as "a world citadel" and lists a number of factors of power as criteria, including the unheartlandish one of access to the oceans. Mackinder thought of the Pivot Area as

[25] Democratic Ideals and Reality [see footnote 13 above], p. 100 (1919 edit.). This is criticized by Spykman in "The Geography of the Peace" [see footnote 18 above], p. 41.

[26] G. B. Cressey: The Basis of Soviet Strength (New York and London, 1945), p. 245.

[27] For example, R. E. Harrison and H. W. Weigert: World View and Strategy, *in* Compass of the World, edited by H. W. Weigert and Vilhjalmur Stefansson (New York, 1944), pp. 74–88, reference on p. 79 (map).

[28] G. T. Renner: Peace by the Map, *Collier's*, Vol. 113, 1944, pp. 44–47.

[29] "Basic Doctrine," *U. S. Air Force Manual AFM 1–2*, April, 1954, p. 11.

primarily a region of mobility for land forces, impenetrable by sea power: "we have in this immense area all the conditions for the maintenance of a sparse, but in the aggregate considerable, population of horse-riding and camel-riding nomads"[30]—hardly the description of a great power base. In the 1919 book "Heartland" appears first as a synonym for "Pivot Area" but is extended, as we have seen, to include much of Eastern Europe. Mackinder used the word "citadel" for his Heartland, but he expected the citadel to be supplied and garrisoned chiefly from Eastern Europe, not from the original Pivot Area. By 1943, Mackinder had further shifted his definition. He wrote that "it is sufficiently accurate to say that the territory of the U.S.S.R. is equivalent to the Heartland, except in one direction." This exception is "Lenaland," or Siberia east of the Yenisei. "West of the Yenisei lies what I shall describe as Heartland Russia . . . It contains four and a quarter million square miles and a population of more than one hundred seventy millions."[31] The Heartland concept was thus shifted to conform to a national power base—one of the many things remodeled by the Five-Year Plans.

Renner's proposed transpolar heartland combines the interior power bases of Eurasia and North America with the region of aerial mobility in the high latitudes. Perhaps we might revive "pivot area" for an area where mobility is the chief strategic factor and confine "heartland" to interior power bases. Conceivably the Arctic region could play a role in the age of flight similar to that of central Eurasia in the age of nomadic horsemen. But such are the connotations of "pivot" and "heart" that it may be wiser to drop the terms altogether.[32]

The Wide Blue Yonder

When Mackinder's "The Geographical Pivot of History" was printed in the *Geographical Journal*, the comments made by members of the audience were, according to the usual practice, printed

[30] Mackinder, The Geographical Pivot of History [see footnote 12 above], p. 429.

[31] H. J. Mackinder: The Round World and the Winning of the Peace, *in* Compass of the World [see footnote 27 above], pp. 161–173, reference on pp. 164–165.

[32] Miller, in his "Must We Live in Fear?" [see footnote 20 above], p. 763, says that "the Mediterranean basin was the true heartland, the true power center of the ancient world." In the usage suggested above, the Mediterranean *Sea* might be called the pivot area of the ancient world.

also. Many readers have noted that one auditor, Amery, called
attention to the airplane as possibly upsetting the assumptions on
which Mackinder's theory was based[33]—this in 1904, only a few
weeks after the Wright brothers had made their first flight.

Mackinder, we have seen, wrote of the seaman's and the
landsman's points of view. The basic pattern of the physical world
was of course the same for both, but the strategic forecast hinged on
the belief that land transportation was overtaking sea transportation
as a vehicle of power. We have also seen that putting, or seeming to
put, seaman and landsman in strong contrast may have been a
disservice to clear thinking. Now we have the airman. Must we add
the airman's point of view? Or would that only increase the
confusion?

For one thing, there is a wide range of thought about air
power. Experience with air power is limited, and the pace of
technological change has been extraordinary. We find variation
from the "all-out" school, exemplified by such men as Douhet and
Seversky, through moderate but firmly "air-first" men to the con-
servatives who hold that the main function of air power is to assist
surface operations.

The conservative group holds that the surface battlefield remains the locus of decision. Sea power is vital to the supply of the
battle front. Air power is vital to the security of sea routes, for
observation and rapid transportation, and as long-range artillery to
interdict enemy movements. Strategic bombardment, to this group,
should be related to surface operations. Such a view of air power
leads to no very new view of the globe. A third dimension has been
added to the Mahan or Mackinder world, but its surface features
have not been erased, and the travel-time scale has not been greatly
altered, since surface movement dominates.

For an example of the air-first moderates, we may take Slessor,
who holds that the strategic air force, with nuclear bombs, is "the
Great Deterrent" which may prevent another general war.[34] But
local wars are still possible, with ground forces bearing much of the
load. Slessor sees a need for armies and navies and even for a special
"semi-static" force or militia for local and civil defense. Slessor does
not describe his global view, as we use that term here, but mani-

[33] Mackinder, The Geographical Pivot of History [see footnote 12 above],
p. 441.
[34] John Slessor: Strategy for the West (New York, 1954), especially Chapters 3 and 4.

festly it must combine something like the Rimland—the locus of
local wars—with a disbelief in heartlands. His views on heartlands
seem like an echo of Amery's, amplified by half a century of
aeronautical development:

> Meanwhile do not let us be distracted by geopolitical talk about
> heartlands, which was all very well in Mackinder's day but ceased
> to be relevant with the advent of the long-range bomber. Russia's
> central position has some tactical advantages, vis-à-vis her neigh-
> bours, but in a world air war she would be at a decisive disadvan-
> tage. Air power has turned the vast spaces that were her prime
> defence against Napoleon and Hindenburg and Hitler into a source
> of weakness. In these days of near-sonic speeds, the depth of pene-
> tration necessary to reach some of her vital centres is offset by the
> size of the area to be defended and the fact that it can be attacked
> from almost all round the compass.[35]

In Slessor's view, the virtues of the Heartland—size, centrality, and
inaccessibility—have become either of no advantage or disadvan-
tageous. Have *Raum und Lage* gone into reverse, so to speak, in the
air age?

In order that the Soviet power base be penetrable "from almost
all round the compass," it is essential that the non-Communist
powers maintain a strong position in the Rimland and in what
Spykman called the "off-shore islands" of Great Britain, Japan,
Africa, and Australia.[36] If these areas come under Communist
domination, it will be the Americas that are penetrable "from almost
all round the compass."

Whether centrality in Eurasia gives the Soviet Union a com-
manding position or only a strong one has been discussed above.
The relative value of land power and sea power in the Rimland was
held undecided. What of air power? It is incomparably fast, of
increasing capacity, and less and less restricted by weather and
surface features. But the very speed of the airplane may offset some
of the advantages of position. At near-sonic speeds, to fly, say, from
Tashkent to Delhi would take less than two hours. But from
Singapore to Delhi would take only four. Would the difference be
critical? Would not what Whittlesey calls "pace"[37]—the average
tempo of operations—and timing be more important than the
velocity of flight, at such speeds? Fuel remains a great problem until

---

[35] *Ibid.,* p. 34.
[36] Spykman, *op. cit.* [see footnote 18 above], p. 38.
[37] Derwent Whittlesey: The Horizon of Geography, *Annals Assn. of
Amer. Geogrs.,* Vol. 35, 1945, pp. 1–36; reference on p. 24.

atomic energy is adapted to aircraft, but could not Singapore be supplied as readily as Tashkent? If one is ready and resolute, need one be despondent over geographical position? For that matter, may not the Battle of the Rimland be decided by politics rather than by war? Was Vietminh lost by war, or by French delay in freeing and arming Vietnam and American unwillingness to enter the fray?

How do nuclear weapons affect these matters? One may readily agree that in an all-out nuclear war, with cities blasted from the face of the earth and even the countryside polluted with radioactive fallout, "Heartland," "Rimland," "land power," and "sea power" are words with little significance. But we hear much of the tactical use of nuclear weapons. Just what "tactical use" means is not clear. Should it be stretched to include use against docks, bridges, and freight yards, it comes perilously close to "strategic bombardment," involving or inviting the destruction of cities. If, however, it is possible to confine nuclear weapons to tactical uses, it is not certain that either land power or sea power is favored or that the Heartland-Rimland relationship is altered. Much depends on the relative improvement in methods of attack and defense and on the alertness of the belligerents and the astuteness of their commanders.

Seversky's View

If there is a unique "airman's global view," it probably is essentially that of Seversky, and the azimuthal equidistant projection centered on the North Pole is its cartographic expression . . .[38] The popularity of North Polar projections has been a valuable corrective to the overuse of the Mercator. The equidistant form, however, has the serious defect of stretching the latitudinal scale in the Southern Hemisphere, and this in turn has the visual effect of greatly exaggerating the width of the southern oceans.

Seversky definitely subordinates the army and navy to the air force. He believes that virtually complete air supremacy, not just local or temporary air superiority, is possible. The side that obtains air supremacy holds the other at its mercy. He does not expect this to come without enormous effort and losses, but he feels that a country such as the United States, with advanced technology but limited manpower, can better pay the price of air supremacy than

[38] A. P. de Seversky: *Air Power: Key to Survival* (New York, 1950).

that of superiority in three media.[39] Since he wishes the United
States to avoid surface, and particularly ground, combat, he regards
overseas bases as undesirable, probably untenable, and, in an age of
intercontinental flight, unnecessary. Besides the Soviet Union and
the United States, Britain alone has the potentialities of great air
power. Only in the vicinity of Bering Strait does orthodox warfare
seem justified.[40] Latin America, within the circle of American air
dominance, becomes the main reserve of American industry. Much
of Africa and all of Southeast Asia are within the ellipse of Soviet
air dominance. The overlap of the American circle and the Soviet
ellipse is the "area of decision," where Seversky thinks the mastery
of the air will be decided. Seversky's global view thus swings us
back to the concept of Western Hemisphere defense, with a north-
south rather than an east-west emphasis.

A number of American habits of mind favor acceptance of "the
airman's view." A sort of "air isolationism" appears possible, the
Western Hemisphere is revived, faith in machines and in American
know-how is a string touched, the all-out air strategy seems economical in dollars and men. On the other hand, the conservatism of
the Army and Navy and their civilian supporters is aroused. Dislike
or disregard for "the frozen north" and habitual east-west thinking
are strong. "The suggestive map" that speaks to most Americans is
still likely to have the equator across the middle.

The choice among the conservative, moderate, and all-out air
views is one of the most critical in the American future. The decision will determine the allocation of manpower and resources, the
location of bases, policies toward Rimland countries and Latin
America, and many other matters. It is beyond the reach of this
paper to settle such weighty affairs. All we can do is to propound a
few questions that bear on the evaluation of "the airman's view."

The first question concerns the reality of the Western Hemisphere and its self-sufficiency and defensibility. A report of a Senate
subcommittee on strategic and critical materials says, as if it were
axiomatic, "We belong in the Western Hemisphere."[41] The report
demonstrates the present American dependence on sources of strategic and critical materials outside the Western Hemisphere but
maintains that through stockpiling, exploration, subsidization, and

39 *Ibid.*, p. 11.
40 *Ibid.*, map facing p. 312.
41 "Report of the Minerals, Materials, and Fuels Economic Subcommittee
of the Committee on Interior and Insular Affairs," *83rd Congr., 2nd Sess.,
Senate Rept. No. 1627, 1954*, p. 12.

scientific research the Americas could be made self-sufficient for a period of war. It is held that sea lanes to South America could hug the shore and be protected from enemy aircraft or submarines. "In the last analysis land transportation can be improved."[42] If we grant, if only for the sake of the argument, that the Americas could be made self-sufficient for a period of war, we must still question their complete defensibility by the strategy envisioned. Soviet planes in Central or even East Africa, beyond the circle of American air dominance, would be approximately as near the most vital parts of South America as planes based on Florida. South American cities, and particularly the influential metropolises of Brazil and Argentina, would be vulnerable unless their defenses were virtually perfect. American ability to retaliate, or to "neutralize" African airfields after a blow had fallen, would offer little solace. If substantial parts of Africa should come under Soviet control, it is not certain that Latin America would remain steadfast in support of the United States. We may thus have to defend large parts of the Rimland in order to protect Latin America, which the Senate subcommittee, possibly influenced by the polar projection, calls "our own backyard."[43]

Another question is that of defense against intercontinental bombardment. Perfect defense on both sides would cancel out the offense. In that case, intercontinental bombardment would not even be "the Great Deterrent." True, perfect defense is improbable, but if defense is less than perfect, retaliation is to be expected, and thus to launch an intercontinental air attack entails great risks. Nevertheless, if a nation places all its defensive bets on this strategy, it must be prepared to use it.

The foregoing questions can be reduced to one: When, and under what circumstances, does a nation that adopts the all-out intercontinental strategy launch its aircraft? One choice would be preventive war, a choice that the United States is unlikely to make. Another would be to use the intercontinental air force in the event of any further aggression across the Iron Curtain. This would be containment by intercontinental means. It might succeed—even the threat might be enough—but it would require unlimited fortitude for an American commander in chief to stand ready to give the signal, risking retaliatory destruction of American cities, to halt, for example, Communist expansion in some country of southern Asia.

42 *Ibid.*, p. 28.
43 *Ibid.*, p. 23.

Third, there is "air isolationism." A defensive perimeter, to use that unhappy term, might be drawn around the Americas, perhaps including some overseas areas considered particularly important. Intercontinental air war would be used or threatened only if this perimeter were crossed. Such a stand would require as much fortitude as the other. In fact, we have seen that large parts of the Rimland might have to be included within the defensive perimeter if Latin America were to be secure. Thus "air isolationism" approaches "containment."

The nub of the matter is that strategy and foreign policy are complementary and inseparable. This is particularly true of the key question of when to resort to armed defense.[44] Moreover, they are continuing processes and cannot be redirected overnight. If a state adopts a rigid strategy keyed to a single kind of war, its foreign policy is made rigid in major ways. This is not necessarily evil if the rigid view is sound, but history does not encourage the belief that man can foresee the precise course of future events. Some flexibility in strategic view seems wise. "Flexibility" should be forward-looking, however, not patterned on the past.

Recipe for a Composite View

We have examined, in this and the preceding article, a series of global views of politics and strategy. None of them, taken singly, is an adequate picture of the world. None can unhesitatingly be called "the best" or even "the best yet." There is no simple system of political geography, no single thought filter through which to strain all geographical information. We need a series of filters, a composite or an eclectic global view.

Many of the men whose writings we have studied have in fact held composite views. For ease of analysis and comparison we have selected single items. Whittlesey's "exploitable world," though shrinking now, is a harmonious part of his historical approach. Taylor's maps and graphs show many environmental factors. Spykman discussed and mapped location, landforms, climate, economic production, and population before he proceeded to modify Mackinder's world.[45] There is, however, no virtue in the composite or

---

[44] Cf. W. W. Kaufmann: The Requirements of Deterrence, *Princeton Univ. Center of Internatl. Studies Memorandum No.* 7, 1954.

[45] Spykman, *op. cit.* [see footnote 18 above], pp. 19–34.

eclectic process per se. Haushofer's views were eclectic. Even if one chooses good ingredients, there is the problem of relative weight. Huntington, in his last book,[46] held climate, kith, and diet to be mainsprings of civilization, but, in a given case, which is the main spring?

There is no easy road out of these difficulties. The "recipe for a composite view" that we give here makes no pretense to completeness or finality, nor does it contain anything that a geographer does not already know. It is merely an attempt to list the elements of a global view based on the concept of national power. No map of it is presented. This may be cowardice, engendered by our own warning, in the first article, that mapping an idea is likely to reveal its fuzziness. But much of the material in our list is already on maps, and for other items data are incomplete.

National power, as has been elaborated elsewhere,[47] has two components that may be called "inventory" and "strategy." The former is what one has, the latter what one does with it. The inventory component can largely be subsumed, we believe, under Mackinder's old term "man settling," the strategic component largely under his "man travelling."[48]

I. Man Settling
  A. Population
  B. Culture
  C. Material Base

II. Man Traveling
  A. The Atmosphere
  B. Oceans and Islands
  C. Continental Interiors and Peripheries
  D. The Northern Region

This list probably needs little explanation. What is left out may be more surprising than what is included. For example, climate, landforms, and mineral resources are not specifically mentioned. They are, however, implied under other headings and would appear in the higher orders of subdivision.

No one is likely to question the place of population or material base in a global view of national power. Population has been mapped many times, and its elements have been carefully outlined by Trewartha.[49] Among the more significant subdivisions are trends, in

---

[46] Ellsworth Huntington: Mainsprings of Civilization (New York and London, 1945).
[47] S. B. Jones: The Power Inventory and National Strategy, *World Politics*, Vol. 6, 1953–1954, pp. 421–452.
[48] H. J. Mackinder: The Physical Basis of Political Geography, *Scottish Geogr. Mag.*, Vol. 6, 1890, pp. 78–84.
[49] G. T. Trewartha: A Case for Population Geography, *Annals Assn. of Amer. Geogrs.*, Vol. 43, 1953, pp. 71–97; reference on pp. 88–89.

relation to total numbers and age groups, and urbanization. Urbanization is an indication of the kind of economy and of the tempting targets for nuclear bombs. The material base of course includes sources of food, energy, and essential raw materials. Although maps of such items have been attempted, adequate and commensurable data for recent years are hard to find.[50]

The inclusion of culture as a major heading in a list based on the concept of national power may require some defense. But one element of culture is government, and the common political map is therefore a cultural map. The political interpretation of general culture is difficult and still in the experimental stage; thus it is perhaps faith that leads us to give culture so prominent a place. Culture has been placed between population and the material base because it is through culture that men make the material base economic, turn sources into resources, so to speak.

In subdividing "Man Traveling" our guiding principle has been that, for the immediate future at least, air, land, and sea movement are all of importance as means of projecting power. This is especially true because "projecting power" includes economic as well as military action. The relative importance of the three media varies for different kinds of action and in different parts of the world. The atmosphere, because of its global spread, its vertical extent, and the speed of the vehicles that use it, is of first and increasing importance. This is true whether or not "heartland operations" by strategic air forces are the pattern of future conflict. Every globe and relatively undistorted map gives an airman's view, but it takes imagination to see on them the useful and fearful canopy of air, so that emphasis is justified.

With the oceans we include the islands found in them. Every island is moated to a certain extent, and the defense of Britain in the Second World War and the delay the Formosa Strait imposed on

[50] M. K. Bennett, in his book "The World's Food" (New York, 1954, Chapters 12 and 13), subjects published data on national diets to considerable criticism. Excellent maps of energy production, consumption (1937, with estimates for 1948), and reserves accompany the study of "Energy Resources of the World", prepared under the direction of N. B. Guyol for the Department of State (*U. S. Dept. of State Publ. 3428*, 1949). The energy data in the *Statistical Yearbook* of the United Nations unfortunately do not include major Communist countries. The pending importance of atomic energy in industry further complicates the picture. Rapid strides in the beneficiation of lean iron ores make unreliable many published studies of the distribution of this basic metal.

the Chinese Communists show that the moating is still of some significance. But air power, and not just ships or water, is needed to make the moat effective. Not all islands or parts of the oceans are of equal importance. The islands and narrow seas off the Eurasian coast are of first importance today, those off the North American coast of second.

It is hardly news that the peripheries of continents differ from the interiors in ease of maritime access. In the age of nuclear weapons, peripheral location carries increased vulnerability from sabotage, ship- or submarine-launched missiles, and underwater explosion. It usually means a greater dependence on sea-borne supplies. But it also means wider economic contacts by the most capacious and economical of carriers. Only in Eurasia does the division into interior and periphery have great political significance, as Mackinder showed long ago. In the Americas the interior has been absorbed by the coastal states, with minor exceptions. Nearly all of Africa today is controlled from the shores, though its future political pattern is obscure.

The final item of our composite view is "the northern region," based on the nature of the Arctic Sea and the northern parts of North America and Eurasia and their relation to the great centers of power that are certain, for a long time at least, to lie in the Northern Hemisphere. In the northern region surface movement meets resistance for much or all of the year whereas air movement is relatively easy. The northern region may be, as we have said, an aerial "pivot area." There are other parts of the world where air movement is much easier than surface movement, such as the rain forests and the deserts, but these either are smaller than the northlands or offer less serious obstacles. The deserts, for instance, are traversed more easily than the northlands by conventional vehicles, and the Amazon and Congo basins have their immense, never-frozen rivers.

The global view just outlined is merely what the mythical German scientist is supposed to have written, *eine Einführung in das Leben des Elephanten*, though measurable in pages rather than in volumes. The whole elephant is too big for us to see in detail, but we are not blind, only myopic, and we can discern its outlines. And we can and do pursue it, though the path of our safari is beset by pitfalls. On one side is the flood of unfiltered information that rushes endlessly. On the other are the quicksands of oversimplification. To remain still is to be stung by the scholar's conscience. But hazards and discomforts are inevitable accompaniments of adventure, and the pursuit of the global view is the geographer's intellectual adventure.

19. *LONG LIVE THE VICTORY OF PEOPLE'S WAR!** /
LIN PIAO

The International Significance of Comrade Mao Tse-Tung's Theory of People's War

The Chinese revolution is a continuation of the great October Revolution. The road of the October Revolution is the common road for all people's revolutions. The Chinese revolution and the October Revolution have in common the following basic characteristics: (1) Both were led by the working class with a Marxist-Leninist party as its nucleus. (2) Both were based on the worker-peasant alliance. (3) In both cases state power was seized through violent revolution and the dictatorship of the proletariat was established. (4) In both cases the socialist system was built after victory in the revolution. (5) Both were component parts of the proletarian world revolution.

Naturally, the Chinese revolution had its own peculiar characteristics. The October Revolution took place in imperialist Russia, but the Chinese revolution broke out in a semi-colonial and semi-feudal country. The former was a proletarian socialist revolution, while the latter developed into a socialist revolution after the complete victory of the new-democratic revolution. The October Revolution began with armed uprisings in the cities and then spread to the countryside, while the Chinese revolution won nation-wide victory through the encirclement of the cities from the rural areas and the final capture of the cities.

Comrade Mao Tse-tung's great merit lies in the fact that he has succeeded in integrating the universal truth of Marxism-Leninism with the concrete practice of the Chinese revolution and has

* Lin Piao, *Long Live the Victory of People's War!* (Peking: Foreign Languages Press, 3rd ed., 1967), pp. 42–49, 53, 56–57.

enriched and developed Marxism-Leninism by his masterly generalization and summation of the experience gained during the Chinese people's protracted revolutionary struggle.

Comrade Mao Tse-tung's theory of people's war has been proved by the long practice of the Chinese revolution to be in accord with the objective laws of such wars and to be invincible. It has not only been valid for China, it is a great contribution to the revolutionary struggles of the oppressed nations and peoples throughout the world.

The people's war led by the Chinese Communist Party, comprising the War of Resistance and the Revolutionary Civil Wars, lasted for twenty-two years. It constitutes the most drawn-out and most complex people's war led by the proletariat in modern history, and it has been the richest in experience.

In the last analysis, the Marxist-Leninist theory of proletarian revolution is the theory of the seizure of state power by revolutionary violence, the theory of countering war against the people by people's war. As Marx so aptly put it, "Force is the midwife of every old society pregnant with a new one."[1]

It was on the basis of the lessons derived from the people's wars in China that Comrade Mao Tse-tung, using the simplest and the most vivid language, advanced the famous thesis that "political power grows out of the barrel of a gun".[2]

He clearly pointed out:

The seizure of power by armed force, the settlement of the issue by war, is the central task and the highest form of revolution. This Marxist-Leninist principle of revolution holds good universally, for China and for all other countries.[3] . . .

The history of people's war in China and other countries provides conclusive evidence that the growth of the people's revolutionary forces from weak and small beginnings into strong and large forces is a universal law of development of class struggle, a universal law of development of people's war. A people's war inevitably meets with many difficulties, with many ups and downs and setbacks in the course of its development, but no force can alter its general trend towards inevitable triumph. . . .

Why can the apparently weak new-born forces always triumph

[1] Karl Marx, *Capital*, Foreign Languages Publishing House, Moscow, 1954, Vol. I, p. 751.

[2] Mao Tse-tung, "Problems of War and Strategy", *Selected Works*, FLP, Peking, 1965, Vol. II, p. 224.

[3] *Ibid.*, p. 219.

over the decadent forces which appear so powerful? The reason is that truth is on their side and that the masses are on their side, while the reactionary classes are always divorced from the masses and set themselves against the masses.

This has been borne out by the victory of the Chinese revolution, by the history of all revolutions, the whole history of class struggle and the entire history of mankind.

The imperialists are extremely afraid of Comrade Mao Tse-tung's thesis that "imperialism and all reactionaries are paper tigers", and the revisionists are extremely hostile to it. They all oppose and attack this thesis and the philistines follow suit by ridiculing it. But all this cannot in the least diminish its importance. The light of truth cannot be dimmed by anybody.

Comrade Mao Tse-tung's theory of people's war solves not only the problem of daring to fight a people's war, but also that of how to wage it.

Comrade Mao Tse-tung is a great statesman and military scientist, proficient at directing war in accordance with its laws. By the line and policies, the strategy and tactics he formulated for the people's war, he led the Chinese people in steering the ship of the people's war past all hidden reefs to the shores of victory in most complicated and difficult conditions.

It must be emphasized that Comrade Mao Tse-tung's theory of the establishment of rural revolutionary base areas and the encirclement of the cities from the countryside is of outstanding and universal practical importance for the present revolutionary struggles of all the oppressed nations and peoples, and particularly for the revolutionary struggles of the oppressed nations and peoples in Asia, Africa and Latin America against imperialism and its lackeys.

Many countries and peoples in Asia, Africa and Latin America are now being subjected to aggression and enslavement on a serious scale by the imperialists headed by the United States and their lackeys. The basic political and economic conditions in many of these countries have many similarities to those that prevailed in old China. As in China, the peasant question is extremely important in these regions. The peasants constitute the main force of the national-democratic revolution against the imperialists and their lackeys. In committing aggression against these countries, the imperialists usually begin by seizing the big cities and the main lines of communication, but they are unable to bring the vast countryside completely under their control. The countryside, and the countryside alone, can provide the broad areas in which the revolutionaries can manoeuvre freely. The countryside, and the countryside alone, can provide the revolutionary bases from which the revolutionaries can go forward to final victory. Precisely for this reason, Comrade Mao Tse-tung's theory of establishing revolutionary base areas in the rural districts and encircling the cities from the countryside is attracting more and more attention among the people in these regions.

Taking the entire globe, if North America and Western Europe can be called "the cities of the world", then Asia, Africa and Latin America constitute "the rural areas of the world". Since World War II, the proletarian revolutionary movement has for various reasons been temporarily held back in the North American and West European capitalist countries, while the people's revolutionary movement in Asia, Africa and Latin America has been growing vigorously. In a sense, the contemporary world revolution also presents a picture of the encirclement of cities by the rural areas. In the final analysis, the whole cause of world revolution hinges on the revolutionary struggles of the Asian, African and Latin American peoples who make up the overwhelming majority of the world's population. The socialist countries should regard it as their internationalist duty to support the people's revolutionary struggles in Asia, Africa and Latin America. . . .

At present, the main battlefield of the fierce struggle between the people of the world on the one side and U.S. imperialism and its lackeys on the other is the vast area of Asia, Africa and Latin America. In the world as a whole, this is the area where the people suffer worst from imperialist oppression and where imperialist rule is most vulnerable. Since World War II, revolutionary storms have been rising in this area, and today they have become the most important force directly pounding U.S. imperialism. The contradiction between the revolutionary peoples of Asia, Africa and Latin America and the imperialists headed by the United States is the principal contradiction in the contemporary world. The development of this contradiction is promoting the struggle of the people of the whole world against U.S. imperialism and its lackeys. . . .

Everything is divisible. And so is this colossus of U.S. imperialism. It can be split up and defeated. The peoples of Asia, Africa, Latin America and other regions can destroy it piece by piece, some striking at its head and others at its feet. That is why the greatest fear of U.S. imperialism is that people's wars will be launched in different parts of the world, and particularly in Asia, Africa and Latin America, and why it regards people's war as a mortal danger.

U.S. imperialism relies solely on its nuclear weapons to intimidate people. But these weapons cannot save U.S. imperialism from its doom. Nuclear weapons cannot be used lightly. U.S. imperialism has been condemned by the people of the whole world for its towering crime of dropping two atom bombs on Japan. If it uses nuclear weapons again, it will become isolated in the extreme. Moreover, the U.S. monopoly of nuclear weapons has long been broken; U.S. imperialism has these weapons, but others have them too. If it threatens other countries with nuclear weapons, U.S. imperialism will expose its own country to the same threat. For this reason, it will meet with strong opposition not only from the people elsewhere but also inevitably from the people in its own country. Even if U.S. imperialism brazenly uses nuclear weapons, it cannot conquer the people, who are indomitable.

However highly developed modern weapons and technical equipment may be and however complicated the methods of modern warfare, in the final analysis the outcome of a war will be decided by the sustained fighting of the ground forces, by the fighting at close quarters on battlefields, by the political consciousness of the men, by their courage and spirit of sacrifice. Here the weak points of U.S. imperialism will be completely laid bare, while the superiority of the revolutionary people will be brought into full play. The reactionary troops of U.S. imperialism cannot possibly be endowed with the courage and the spirit of sacrifice possessed by the revolutionary people. The spiritual atom bomb which the revolutionary people possess is a far more powerful and useful weapon than the physical atom bomb. . . .

7

DIPLOMACY

Diplomacy is of crucial importance in international affairs and several facets of it are highlighted in this chapter. The first selection is the account by Thucydides (471–400 B.C.) of the Melian Conference between the powerful Athenians and the much weaker Melians in 416 B.C. The description is taken from Thucydides' famous work *The Peloponnesian War*.

The second selection is Quincy Wright's discussion of the decline of "classic diplomacy." Quincy Wright, Professor Emeritus of International Law at the University of Chicago, is the author of *A Study of War* and *The Study of International Relations*.

The third selection discusses some of the often misunderstood peculiarities of diplomatic life and the reasons behind them. Michael H. Cardozo is Professor of Law at Cornell University and author of *Diplomats in International Cooperation*.

20. *THE MELIAN CONFERENCE**/ *THUCYDIDES*

. . . The Melians are a colony of Lacedæmon that would not
submit to the Athenians like the other islanders, and at first remained neutral and took no part in the struggle, but afterwards
upon the Athenians using violence and plundering their territory,
assumed an attitude of open hostility. Cleomedes, son of Lycomedes,
and Tisias, son of Tisimachus, the generals, encamping in their
territory with the above armament, before doing any harm to their
land, sent envoys to negotiate. These the Melians did not bring
before the people, but bade them state the object of their mission to
the magistrates and the few; upon which the Athenian envoys spoke
as follows:—

Athenians.—'Since the negotiations are not to go on before the
people, in order that we may not be able to speak straight on
without interruption, and deceive the ears of the multitude by
seductive arguments which would pass without refutation (for we
know that this is the meaning of our being brought before the few),
what if you who sit there were to pursue a method more cautious
still! Make no set speech yourselves, but take us up at whatever you
do not like, and settle that before going any farther. And first tell us
if this proposition of ours suits you.'

The Melian commissioners answered:—

Melians.—'To the fairness of quietly instructing each other as
you propose there is nothing to object; but your military preparations are too far advanced to agree with what you say, as we see you
are come to be judges in your own cause, and that all we can
reasonably expect from this negotiation is war, if we prove to have
right on our side and refuse to submit, and in the contrary case,
slavery.'

Athenians.—'If you have met to reason about presentiments of
the future, or for anything else than to consult for the safety of
your state upon the facts that you see before you, we will give over;
otherwise we will go on.'

Melians.—'It is natural and excusable for men in our position to
turn more ways than one both in thought and utterance. However,

* From the book *The History of the Peloponnesian War* by Thucydides,
translated by Richard Crawley, pp. 330–37. Everyman's Library. Reprinted by
permission of E. P. Dutton & Co. Inc. and J. M. Dent & Sons Ltd.

the question in this conference is, as you say, the safety of our country; and the discussion, if you please, can proceed in the way which you propose.'

Athenians.—'For ourselves, we shall not trouble you with specious pretences—either of how we have a right to our empire because we overthrew the Mede, or are now attacking you because of wrong that you have done us—and make a long speech which would not be believed; and in return we hope that you, instead of thinking to influence us by saying that you did not join the Lacedæmonians, although their colonists, or that you have done us no wrong, will aim at what is feasible, holding in view the real sentiments of us both; since you know as well as we do that right, as the world goes, is only in question between equals in power, while the strong do what they can and the weak suffer what they must.'

Melians.—'As we think, at any rate, it is expedient—we speak as we are obliged, since you enjoin us to let right alone and talk only of interest—that you should not destroy what is our common protection, the privilege of being allowed in danger to invoke what is fair and right, and even to profit by arguments not strictly valid if they can be got to pass current. And you are as much interested in this as any, as your fall would be a signal for the heaviest vengeance and an example for the world to meditate upon.'

Athenians.—'The end of our empire, if end it should, does not frighten us: a rival empire like Lacedæmon, even if Lacedæmon was our real antagonist, is not so terrible to the vanquished as subjects who by themselves attack and overpower their rulers. This, however, is a risk that we are content to take. We will now proceed to show you that we are come here in the interest of our empire, and that we shall say what we are now going to say, for the preservation of your country; as we would fain exercise that empire over you without trouble, and see you preserved for the good of us both.'

Melians.—'And how, pray, could it turn out as good for us to serve as for you to rule?'

Athenians.—'Because you would have the advantage of submitting before suffering the worst, and we should gain by not destroying you.'

Melians.—'So that you would not consent to our being neutral, friends instead of enemies, but allies of neither side.'

Athenians.—'No; for your hostility cannot so much hurt us as your friendship will be an argument to our subjects of our weakness, and your enmity of our power.'

Melians.—'Is that your subjects' idea of equity, to put those who have nothing to do with you in the same category with peoples that are most of them your own colonists, and some conquered rebels?'

Athenians.—'As far as right goes they think one has as much of it as the other, and that if any maintain their independence it is because they are strong, and that if we do not molest them it is because we are afraid; so that besides extending our empire we should gain in security by your subjection; the fact that you are islanders and weaker than others rendering it all the more important that you should not succeed in baffling the masters of the sea.'

Melians.—'But do you consider that there is no security in the policy which we indicate? For here again if you debar us from talking about justice and invite us to obey your interest, we also must explain ours, and try to persuade you, if the two happen to coincide. How can you avoid making enemies of all existing neutrals who shall look at our case and conclude from it that one day or another you will attack them? And what is this but to make greater the enemies that you have already, and to force others to become so who would otherwise have never thought of it?'

Athenians.—'Why, the fact is that continentals generally give us but little alarm; the liberty which they enjoy will long prevent their taking precautions against us; it is rather islanders like yourselves, outside our empire, and subjects smarting under the yoke, who would be the most likely to take a rash step and lead themselves and us into obvious danger.'

Melians.—'Well then, if you risk so much to retain your empire, and your subjects to get rid of it, it were surely great baseness and cowardice in us who are still free not to try everything that can be tried, before submitting to your yoke.'

Athenians.—'Not if you are well advised, the contest not being an equal one, with honour as the prize and shame as the penalty, but a question of self-preservation and of not resisting those who are far stronger than you are.'

Melians.—'But we know that the fortune of war is sometimes more impartial than the disproportion of numbers might lead one to suppose; to submit is to give ourselves over to despair, while action still preserves for us a hope that we may stand erect.'

Athenians.—'Hope, danger's comforter, may be indulged in by those who have abundant resources, if not without loss at all events without ruin; but its nature is to be extravagant, and those who go so far as to put their all upon the venture see it in its true colours only when they are ruined; but so long as the discovery would enable them to guard against it, it is never found wanting. Let not this be the case with you, who are weak and hang on a single turn of the scale; nor be like the vulgar, who, abandoning such security as human means may still afford, when visible hopes fail them in extremity, turn to invisible, to prophecies and oracles, and other such inventions that delude men with hopes to their destruction.'

Melians.—'You may be sure that we are as well aware as you of the difficulty of contending against your power and fortune, unless the terms be equal. But we trust that the gods may grant us fortune as good as yours, since we are just men fighting against unjust, and that what we want in power will be made up by the alliance of the Lacedæmonians, who are bound, if only for very shame, to come to the aid of their kindred. Our confidence, therefore, after all is not so utterly irrational.'

Athenians.—'When you speak of the favour of the gods, we may as fairly hope for that as yourselves; neither our pretensions nor our conduct being in any way contrary to what men believe of the gods, or practise among themselves. Of the gods we believe, and of men we know, that by a necessary law of their nature they rule wherever they can. And it is not as if we were the first to make this law, or to act upon it when made: we found it existing before us, and shall leave it to exist for ever after us; all we do is to make use of it, knowing that you and everybody else, having the same power as we have, would do the same as we do. Thus, as far as the gods are concerned, we have no fear and no reason to fear that we shall be at a disadvantage. But when we come to your notion about the Lacedæmonians, which leads you to believe that shame will make them help you, here we bless your simplicity but do not envy your folly. The Lacedæmonians, when their own interests or their country's laws are in question, are the worthiest men alive; of their conduct towards others much might be said, but no clearer idea of it could be given than by shortly saying that of all the men we know they are most conspicuous in considering what is agreeable honourable, and what is expedient just. Such a way of thinking does not promise much for the safety which you now unreasonably count upon.'

Melians.—'But it is for this very reason that we now trust to their respect for expediency to prevent them from betraying the Melians, their colonists, and thereby losing the confidence of their friends in Hellas and helping their enemies.'

Athenians.—'Then you do not adopt the view that expediency goes with security, while justice and honour cannot be followed without danger; and danger the Lacedæmonians generally court as little as possible.'

Melians.—'But we believe that they would be more likely to face even danger for our sake, and with more confidence than for others, as our nearness to Peloponnese makes it easier for them to act, and our common blood insures our fidelity.'

Athenians.—'Yes, but what an intending ally trusts to, is not the goodwill of those who ask his aid, but a decided superiority of power for action; and the Lacedæmonians look to this even more than others. At least, such is their distrust of their home resources that it is only with numerous allies that they attack a neighbour; now is it likely that while we are masters of the sea they will cross over to an island?'

Melians.—'But they would have others to send. The Cretan sea is a wide one, and it is more difficult for those who command it to intercept others, than for those who wish to elude them to do so safely. And should the Lacedæmonians miscarry in this, they would fall upon your land, and upon those left of your allies whom Brasidas did not reach; and instead of places which are not yours, you will have to fight for your own country and your own confederacy.'

Athenians.—'Some diversion of the kind you speak of you may one day experience, only to learn, as others have done, that the Athenians never once yet withdrew from a siege for fear of any. But we are struck by the fact, that after saying you would consult for the safety of your country, in all this discussion you have mentioned nothing which men might trust in and think to be saved by. Your strongest arguments depend upon hope and the future, and your actual resources are too scanty, as compared with those arrayed against you, for you to come out victorious. You will therefore show great blindness of judgment, unless, after allowing us to retire, you can find some counsel more prudent than this. You will surely not be caught by that idea of disgrace, which in dangers that are disgraceful, and at the same time too plain to be mistaken, proves so fatal to mankind; since in too many cases the very men that have their eyes perfectly open to what they are rushing into, let the thing called disgrace, by the mere influence of a seductive name, lead them on to a point at which they become so enslaved by the phrase as in fact to fall wilfully into hopeless disaster, and incur disgrace more disgraceful as the companion of error, than when it comes as the result of misfortune. This, if you are well advised, you will guard against; and you will not think it dishonourable to submit to the greatest city in Hellas, when it makes you the moderate offer of becoming its tributary ally, without ceasing to enjoy the country that belongs to you; nor when you have the choice given you between war and security, will you be so blinded as to choose the worse. And it is certain that those who do not yield to their equals, who keep terms with their superiors, and are moderate towards their inferiors, on the whole succeed best. Think over the matter, therefore, after our withdrawal, and reflect once and again that it is for your country that you are consulting, that you have not more than one, and that upon this one deliberation depends its prosperity or ruin.'

The Athenians now withdrew from the conference; and the Melians, left to themselves, came to a decision corresponding with what they had maintained in the discussion, and answered, 'Our resolution, Athenians, is the same as it was at first. We will not in a moment deprive of freedom a city that has been inhabited these seven hundred years; but we put our trust in the fortune by which the gods have preserved it until now, and in the help of men, that is, of the Lacedæmonians; and so we will try and save ourselves. Meanwhile we invite you to allow us to be friends to you and foes to neither party, and to retire from our country after making such a treaty as shall seem fit to us both.'

Such was the answer of the Melians. The Athenians now departing from the conference said, 'Well, you alone, as it seems to us, judging from these resolutions, regard what is future as more certain than what is before your eyes, and what is out of sight, in your eagerness, as already coming to pass; and as you have staked most on, and trusted most in, the Lacedæmonians, your fortune, and your hopes, so will you be most completely deceived.'

The Athenian envoys now returned to the army; and the Melians showing no signs of yielding, the generals at once betook themselves to hostilities, and drew a line of circumvallation round the Melians, dividing the work among the different states. Subsequently the Athenians returned with most of their army, leaving behind them a certain number of their own citizens and of the allies to keep guard by land and sea. The force thus left stayed on and besieged the place.

. . . Reinforcements afterwards arriving from Athens in consequence, under the command of Philocrates, son of Demeas, the siege was now pressed vigorously; and some treachery taking place inside, the Melians surrendered at discretion to the Athenians, who put to death all the grown men whom they took, and sold the women and children for slaves, and subsequently sent out five hundred colonists and inhabited the place themselves.

21. *THE DECLINE OF CLASSIC DIPLOMACY**/ *QUINCY WRIGHT*

Following the breakup of Medieval Christendom in the 15th century, classic diplomacy developed in Europe amid conditions of anarchy and continuous hostility among sovereign princes struggling for power by the methods advised by Niccolò Machiavelli early in the 16th century.

Origins of Classic Diplomacy

In the religious struggles of the 16th and 17th centuries which culminated in the Thirty-Years War, the territorial monarchs, having gained general recognition of their sovereignty, accepted the peace of Westphalia in 1648. Central Europe had lost a quarter of its population in a war which saw the Holy Roman Emperor, who had tried to restore the unity of Christendom, defeated by a combination of Protestant princes and Catholic France. The peace of Westphalia was based on the principle first suggested at the Augsburg Conference of 1555, *Cuius Regia Eius Religio* (whoever is the prince, that is the religion), thus relegating the religious struggle to the domestic jurisdiction of each prince. The relations of the princes came to be regulated *theoretically* by a law of nations set forth in 1625 by Hugo Grotius, and *practically* by their military

* Quincy Wright, "The Decline of Classic Diplomacy," *Journal of International Affairs,* Vol. 17, No. 1 (1963), pp. 18–28. Reprinted by permission.

rivalry which tended toward a balance of power maintained through diplomatic intercourse.

This "classic diplomacy" assumed the coexistence of many sovereign states each respecting the territorial integrity and political independence of the others. These states dealt bilaterally with controversies about territorial limits, maritime navigation, commercial intercourse, and other issues by means of the exchange of diplomatic representatives. Diplomats were guaranteed immunity from the jurisdiction of the local sovereign, thus enabling them to conclude treaties under the sole instruction of the prince they represented. Through these treaties, a network of obligations arose which confirmed the sovereignty of states, the immunity of diplomats, the freedom of the seas, the sanctity of treaties, and the rights of belligerents and neutrals in time of war. The system recognized that the rights of princes to initiate war, the *ultima ratio regem*, was implicit in their sovereignty, as was their right to keep out of the wars of others so long as they observed an impartial neutrality. This conception of war as a duel of princes superseded the medieval concept that the right to make war depended on the justice of the cause and that non-belligerents should not be neutral, but should help, or at least not hinder, the just cause and should hinder, or at least not help, the unjust.

The Balance of Power

Although the diplomacy which operated under this concept was basically bilateral, power rivalries and the right to initiate war nevertheless made it clear that if a state conquered a neighbor, it would be likely to attack another neighbor. Thus all states were interested in maintaining the "balance of power" by ganging up against any one who was becoming too powerful. The reconciliation of the precepts of power politics, which urged attack on the overly-powerful prince, and the precepts of international law, which required a non-belligerent to be neutral unless one side violated its own rights under international law, was considered by international jurists such as Gentili and Vattel. They concluded that maintenance of the balance of power was essential to the stability and security of all, but in deference to international law, a threatened state should not attack an overly-powerful state until the latter had violated that law. This contingency, they thought, would occur because the overly-powerful state would soon commit aggression.[1,2]

In times of great emergency, especially after major wars, it was not possible to maintain the bilateralism of international relations, so that, following the precedent of Westphalia, multilateral congresses met to consider the general interests of Europe. But the treaties which emerged were more likely to be bilateral than multilateral. The Treaty of Utrecht in 1713 was based explicitly on the principle of the balance of power. The treaties of Paris in 1763, Vienna in 1815, Paris in 1856, Berlin in 1878 and 1885, Peking in 1901, and Washington in 1922, though less explicit, also sought to maintain the existing balance. The 19th century conferences were products of the Concert of Europe which originated in the post-Napoleonic conferences and which induced the five, later six, great powers to harmonize their efforts to settle European problems such as those which developed from the separation of Belgium from the Netherlands, the independence of the Balkan states from the Ottoman Empire, the colonization of Africa, and rivalries for spheres of interest in China.[3] However, classic diplomacy assumed (a) that the dominant interest of states was the preservation of their independence and territorial integrity, (b) that bilateral diplomatic negotiations or war were the means of maintaining rights or promoting interests, (c) that international law and treaties would be respected, at least verbally, but (d) that wars would recur and threats, subversion, and duplicity would be used within an atmosphere of secrecy. It also assumed, somewhat inconsistently, that stability, peace, and plenty were desirable and possible for considerable periods of time if the balance of power were maintained.[4]

Such maintenance was facilitated by the existence of a balancing state, itself relatively invulnerable and able to shift its support to the weaker side in a crisis, thus preventing the most powerful state from establishing a new Roman empire, the possibility of which was in the mind of each statesman, whether his immediate object was to build such an empire for his prince or to prevent its building by another. Great Britain served as such a balancer after it had aban-

[1] Alberico Gentili, *De Jure Belli* (1585) (London: Milford, 1933), chap. xiv, p. 66.
[2] Emerich Vattel, *Le Droit des Gens* (1758) (Washington: Carnegie Institution, 1916), Bk. III, chap. iii, pp. 248–249.
[3] Sir Charles K. Webster, *The Art and Practice of Diplomacy* (London: Chatto, 1961), pp. 55ff.
[4] Hans J. Morgenthau, *Politics Among Nations* (3d ed. rev.; New York: Knopf, 1960), pp. 178ff.

doned continental conquests and devoted attention to overseas colonization, trade, and the defeat of any power which threatened to unite Western Europe. Britain followed this policy for its own security and was successful for several centuries, because seapower and geography made it relatively safe from invasion, and it could rely on the cooperation of many continental states, equally anxious to frustrate the overly powerful in a given emergency.

Diplomacy in the 20th Century

The late 19th century witnessed changes no less momentous than those of the 15th and 16th centuries. These changes have greatly modified, if not displaced, the practice of classic diplomacy in the 20th century.[5,6] Science and technology have greatly augmented industrial production, transportation, commerce, and the dependence of most states on international trade for raw materials and markets. The range, speed, and destructiveness of weapons have made nations vulnerable to sudden and unbearably destructive attack from the most distant parts of the world. The airplane destroyed the security of Britain, and the missile that of the United States. The speed and destructiveness of a nuclear attack promises to leave no time to mobilize traditional alliances, resources, and counterattacks which in the past assured the eventual defeat of the aggressor even though he was usually better prepared on the opening of hostilities and won the first battles. No state could any longer be an invulnerable and effective diplomatic balancer, and war was not likely to restore a shattered balance.

Science and technology, in addition to shrinking the world and making war suicidal, have accelerated the rate of change, making custom and tradition less useful guides to action, reducing the predictability of the intentions—and the calculability of the offensive, defensive, and deterrent capability—of the powers, and therefore increasing the difficulty of maintaining a stable balance of power.

In the past, power relations have been more stable when there has been a large number of states with relatively equal power. There has, however, always been a tendency for more powerful states to

[5] Webster, *op. cit.*, pp. 13ff.
[6] Quincy Wright, *A Study of War* (Chicago: University of Chicago Press, 1942), pp. 647ff, 760ff.

absorb their weaker neighbors, for permanent alliances to be formed, and for the balance of power to become bipolarized and unstable. Formerly, these tendencies have led to war, as illustrated in the situation before the two World Wars. Once power became bipolarized, each side regarded eventual war as inevitable, and if the course of events seemed to favor one side, the other was likely to start war immediately rather than wait until its relative power position deteriorated further. In a multi-polar balance of power, on the other hand, uncommitted states rapidly shifted their positions by opposing the most powerful state, thus making it possible to maintain the equilibrium by diplomacy for some time. Because of this tendency, the balance of power has usually broken down at intervals of roughly fifty years into general wars, such as those against France in the times of Louis XIV and Napoleon, and against Germany under the Kaiser and Hitler, with lesser wars midway between. However, in the experience of Europe during the past three centuries, equilibrium has been re-established after such wars. The new military, political, and economic conditions arising from the new technology have, however, rendered the balance of power system chronically unstable.

Other factors militating against a stable balance of power have been the rise of great powers outside of Europe, such the United States, Japan, and China, and the break up of empires by defeat in war or by independence of their former colonies. The dismemberment of the Ottoman and Hapsburg Empires in the Near East and in Europe, and of the British, Spanish, Portuguese, French, German, American, Japanese, Dutch, and Belgian Empires overseas, have proceeded since 1776 and at an accelerated rate since World War II. The behavior in times of crisis of non-European states, unfamiliar with the European diplomatic system, is difficult to calculate. The new states of Asia and Africa continue to be suspicious of an international law based on European ethical standards which allowed these states to become victims of European colonialism.[7,8,9]

Finally, the spirit of Westphalia, calling for the coexistence of

[7] R. P. Anand, "Role of the New Asian-African Countries in the Present International Legal Order," *American Journal of International Law (AJIL)*, Vol. LVI (April 1962), pp. 387ff.

[8] Quincy Wright, "The Goa Incident," *AJIL*, Vol. LVI (July 1962), pp. 629ff.

[9] Quincy Wright, "Asian Experience and International Law," *International Studies* (New Delhi: Indian School of International Studies), Vol. I (July 1959), pp. 71ff.

territorial states, each unified by an absolute monarch, was affected by democratic ideals springing from the British, American, and French Revolutions and set forth in the writings of Locke, Jefferson, and Rousseau. The philosophy of free trade, free enterprise, and free communication springing from the British liberalism expounded by Adam Smith and John Stuart Mill was also rooted in these revolutions. Freedom of the nation, however, was never reconciled with freedom of the individual. The ideology of communism, initiated by Marx (who was familiar with the ideas of the British economists, French revolutionists, and German Hegelian philosophers) and developed into a strategy of action by Lenin, was emphasized by the Russian and Chinese Revolutions of the 20th century. These philosophies and ideologies, creating missionary zeal to convert peoples, to emancipate colonies, or to remake boundaries raised serious doubts about the Westphalian principle of coexistence of independent states, each competent to regulate its own political philosophy, economy, and government.

Diplomacy and International Organization

The consequences of these changes have been the incapacity of bilateral diplomacy to maintain a stable balance of power or general respect for international law, the occurrence of two world wars of unparalleled destructiveness, and the emergence of a Cold War in a world tending toward bipolarization where the precipitation of a nuclear holocaust might destroy the human race.

The emergence of these forces was dimly foreseen in the late 19th century when efforts were made to build a new international system. Public international unions were established to administer common interests of all states in such matters as communication, transport, trade, and health. The Hague Conferences of 1899 and 1907 met to prevent war, promote disarmament, codify international law, and establish institutions facilitating arbitration and conciliation of disputes. The League of Nations was established after World War I to promote international cooperation and to prevent hasty resort to war by putting teeth into the Hague System. The Kellogg-Briand Pact of 1929 was initiated by the United States, ratified by nearly all nations, and enforced against individuals by the Nuremburg and other war crimes tribunals. The Pact outlawed war as an instrument of national policy and required the settlement of all international disputes and conflicts by peaceful means. The United Nations was established after World War II to fulfill the purposes of the League and the Pact more effectively.

These instruments and organizations were not designed to supersede classic diplomacy, but to supplement it with permanent multilateral obligations and institutions for collective security and cooperative betterment of human welfare. They were not designed to supersede traditional international law, but to supplement it with principles outlawing war and recognizing the rights of man and of the organized international community. The scope of state sovereignty was, therefore, to be limited by requiring each state to settle its international disputes by peaceful means, to abstain from the threat or use of force in its international relations, to assist the United Nations in ending hostilities, to cooperate in general and regional agencies for social and economic progress, to promote the protection of human rights, and to accept the status and the operative authority of the United Nations and the Specialized Agencies.

These efforts have been only partially successful because of the prevailing sentiment demanding the complete sovereignty of the nation-state and because of the influence of zealous ideologies. The conflict between democracy and communism has led, since World War II, to a situation similar to that of the century of religious wars before Westphalia. The principle of coexistence of sovereign states which ended that period has not been fully re-established among adherents of the new "religions." (It is worth noting that the militancy of these new "religions" appears roughly proportionate to the recency of the national revolutions from which they stemmed.) In spite of the assertion in the Charter of the United Nations of the sovereign equality of states, of the assertion by the Soviet Union of the principle of peaceful coexistence of sovereign states of different ideologies,[10] and of the affirmation by the United States of the right of every state to enjoy security and self-determination within its domestic jurisdiction,[11] each side in the East-West conflict has been convinced that the other is less interested in stabilizing peaceful

[10] Nikita S. Khrushchev, "Peaceful Coexistence," *Foreign Affairs,* Vol. XXXVIII (October 1959), pp. 1–18.

[11] Quincy Wright, "Maintaining Peaceful Coexistence," *Preventing World War III,* ed. Quincy Wright, William M. Evan, and Morton Deutsch (New York: Simon & Schuster, 1962), pp. 414ff.

coexistence in accord with United Nations principles than in establishing its own ideology throughout the world by using deceptive propaganda, subversion, or even military force, if debate in the forum of world opinion proves unsuccessful.

Classic diplomacy cannot deal adequately with the problems of a world with more than 110 states of diverse culture and ideology, militarily dominated by two great alliances competing for superior nuclear power in an unstable balance of terror, and for support of the militarily weak but heavily populated uncommitted half of the world. The complexity of the situation is compounded by small wars erupting sporadically in areas such as China, Vietnam, Korea, Germany, Berlin, Kashmir, Israel, and the Caribbean. Peace is threatened by accident, miscalculation, or escalation, if not by design. All states are militarily vulnerable, most are economically dependent on each other, many have extensive political and military commitments, and few are inapprehensive that border hostilities may escalate into global thermonuclear war.

If there is to be stability under such conditions, the vision of major decision-makers must not be limited to the parties to a conflict or a negotiation; it must not be limited to the parties to a defensive alliance, a regional arrangement, or an ideology; it must be world-wide. Decision-makers must be aware that the security and progress of each state is dependent upon the security and progress of all states. Such decision-makers require contacts and information beyond that which classic diplomacy can provide. They must be able to initiate action for collective security and international cooperation by agencies of more extensive competence than diplomatic negotiation. They must be prepared to subordinate regional and defense organizations and a considerable measure of sovereign initiative to universal institutions guided by international law. Such a world was formally accepted by all United Nations members when they ratified the Charter.

Whether the world will actually develop in accord with the needs of the 20th century cannot be predicted, but if general war can be avoided, it seems probable that technologies will spread, that tensions will be reduced, and that ideologies will converge.[12] While in the past, the immediate effect of increased contact among divergent cultures has been conflict, the long-run effect has been

[12] Pitirim A. Sorokin, *Mutual Convergence of the United States and USSR to the New Mixed Socio-Cultural Type* (Mexico City, 1961).

peaceful competitive coexistence, with increasing cooperation as common values and interests were perceived.[13,14]

The progress toward such a realization should not be minimized. The United Nations has promoted cooperation in many fields and has helped to stop incipient wars in Greece, Indonesia, Kashmir, Palestine, Korea, Suez, Lebanon, and Cuba. Its action in the Congo appears promising at this writing. It has organized United Nations forces and has mediated or otherwise settled more than a score of disputes. Since World War II it has, on the whole, been more successful than has classic diplomacy which has attempted to deal with the problems of Vietnam, China, and Germany. This progress gives hope that classic diplomacy, while operative with considerable success under the conditions of the 17th, 18th, and 19th centuries, will subordinate itself to universal institutions better adapted to the conditions of the 20th century.

Diplomacy and Democracy

Classic diplomacy faces particular difficulties in democracies because of their inherent incapacity to adapt themselves to the secrecy, rapidity of maneuver, and freedom from public opinion regarded as essential for its operation. All governments in the age of absolute monarchy could, and totalitarian dictatorships in the present period can, operate with more secrecy, freedom, and dispatch than can constitutional democracies. For this reason, Alexis de Tocqueville[15] was convinced that the American democracy of which he wrote in the 1830's could not play the game of power politics successfully.

Secret diplomacy was regarded by many as a contributing cause of World War I. President Wilson called for its termination in his Fourteen Points. The League of Nations Covenant and the United Nations Charter called for the publication of treaties. The practice of recent diplomatic conferences, such as that at San Francisco, has been to give much greater facilities to newsmen to

---

[13] Malcomb M. Willey and Stuart A. Rice, "The Agencies of Communications," *Recent Social Trends in the United States,* ed. William F. Ogburn (New York: McGraw-Hill, 1933), Vol. I, p. 217.

[14] Harold D. Lasswell, *World Politics and Personal Insecurity* (New York: McGraw-Hill, 1935), pp. 203ff.

[15] *Democracy in America* (1834) (New York: A. S. Barnes, 1862), Vol. I, p. 254.

broadcast the proceedings than was usual in earlier history. Statesmen have frequently practiced "diplomacy of the housetops," publishing diplomatic communications to the world simultaneously with their delivery to the government addressed.

There has been vigorous criticism of these practices. Walter Lippmann[16] asserted that President Kennedy should have communicated his information about missile bases in Cuba to Soviet Foreign Minister Gromyko, and entered into bilateral diplomatic negotiations before establishing a unilateral quarantine of Cuba on October 22, 1962. There can be no doubt that classic diplomacy still has a role to play. Conflicts can sometimes be resolved at private negotiations in which neither side loses face. Publicity may arouse public opinion within the disputing states, preventing either side from making the concessions necessary for peaceful settlement. Private negotiation is important among party leaders in parliaments and nominating conventions if the processes of election and legislation are to proceed within democratic states. Such negotiation can be no less important in international relations.

It seems unlikely, however, that people who have a voice in the selection of major officials and the processes of domestic government will, unless faced by military necessity, abandon that voice in the making of a foreign policy which involves problems of war and peace more vital to them than domestic legislation. It is true that in England during the 19th century the public understood tacitly that foreign policy should be left to the government and should not become a subject of public agitation in parliament and elections. The concept that politics should end at the water's edge in times of crisis and that the nation should support the government "whether right or wrong" expressed this idea. These prescriptions have never been entirely carried out: in England this concept could not withstand the rise of the Labour Party and of a more egalitarian democracy in the 20th century. The governments of democratic countries have found it necessary to inform and, to some extent, be guided by public opinion in foreign policy. Even modern dictators have found it necessary to gain the support of public opinion, although their control of communications allows them to mold public opinion in support of their policies more easily than can leaders of democracies who must face a free press and free radio and television.

[16] "Blockade Proclaimed," *New York Herald Tribune*, October 25, 1962, p. 20.

All genuine democracies impose constitutional limitations upon the freedom of the executive to conduct foreign policy, usually requiring that major international commitments and major uses of force have the consent of one or both houses of the legislature. Also, consent is required for appropriations which today are a vital element in military preparations, alliance commitments, economic assistance programs, and participation in international organizations.

Noting the frequent misinformation and prejudice of public opinion and legislative bodies, the limitations which obedience to public opinion imposes on the flexibility of governmental response to foreign attitudes and conditions, and governmental inability to initiate action, some students of international relations have urged an abandonment of democratic methods in the conduct of foreign relations and a return to a system of government that would be free to employ secrecy, to act rapidly, to make threats, to utilize deception, and to retreat if necessary without loss of face.[17] However, if governments abandon democracy in making foreign policy decisions, they are likely to abandon it also in other decisions. They will find it necessary to support threats with espionage and military action, to develop defense forces by rapid coordination of national arms, economy, and morale, and to gain allies and foreign bases by concessions and bribery, all by secret executive action.

These tendencies of democracy are to be observed in periods of war and crisis. All democracies in such situations tend to abandon democratic methods, to curb civil liberties, and to exercise wide authority not only in recruiting the population for war but also in controlling the economy and opinion. In times of prolonged international crisis, all states tend to become "garrison" or "warfare" states embracing certain totalitarian principles. Such states have an advantage under the conditions of classic diplomacy as Machiavelli and de Tocqueville observed. The prince, according to Machiavelli, must pay major attention to his arms, must practice duplicity, and must keep his movements secret.[18, 19] For these reasons democracy has developed only in countries which for long periods have felt relatively secure from invasion, as did England and the United States when sheltered by seas and navies, and states of Western

[17] Fred. J. Cook, "The Radical Right," *The Warfare State* (New York: Macmillan, 1962), pp. 260ff, 318.

[18] Niccolò Machiavelli, *The Prince* (1513) (New York: Dutton, 1948), chap. xv.

[19] Harold D. Lasswell, "The Garrison State," *American Journal of Sociology*, Vol. XLVI (January 1941), pp. 455–469.

Europe when protected, as in the 19th century, by a relatively stable multilateral balance of power and a viable international law.

While the functioning of democracy through classic diplomacy may be assisted by better education of the public on the realities of international politics, on the precepts of international law, and on the need for secrecy and freedom of action by governments in many circumstances, its survival in the long run may depend not only on such education but on the creation of conditions in the international community favorable to democracy.

These conditions include publicity for all basic decisions in the international field, universal forums in which representatives of all interested parties can participate in such decisions, elimination of war and threat of war making possible the deliberation and publicity basic to democracy, development of basic rules of order and principles of justice adapted to changing conditions of technology and ideology, and maintenance of these conditions by a world public opinion operating through universal institutions able to organize collective security and enforcement of international court decisions.

Conclusion

Classic diplomacy faces great difficulties because of the instability of the balance of power, because of the vital interests of many states in major decisions, because of the rapidity and pervasiveness of change, because of the enlarged and possibly catastrophic consequences of single decisions,[20, 21, 22] and because of the zeal of crusading ideologies. While useful in limited circumstances, classic diplomacy cannot establish conditions suitable for the functioning of democracy in a world in which the use of force may become an instrument of suicide rather than of policy. Such conditions can spring only from successful efforts to reduce tensions, to eliminate the threat or use of force as an instrument of national policy, to achieve a spirit of tolerance among diverse ideologies, to develop among states a modicum of mutual trust and confidence in agreements, and to develop in the minds of men everywhere the image of

[20] John von Neumann, "Can We Survive Technology?," *Fortune,* Vol. LI (June 1955), pp. 106ff.

[21] Adlai E. Stevenson, "My Faith in Democratic Capitalism," *Fortune,* Vol. LII (October 1955), pp. 126ff.

[22] Quincy Wright, "The Human Spirit in the Atomic Age," *Contributors to Synthetic Jurisprudence,* ed. Minocher J. Sethna (Bombay: Tripath, 1962), pp. 69ff.

a world of peacefully coexisting states, each confident that its territorial integrity and political independence will be respected and that it will be free to experiment with its system of economy, culture, and politics within its own borders.

The changed conditions of today's world call for less emphasis on classic diplomacy and more on international law and on international institutions able to deal with problems not only of nations, but also of Mankind.

22. DIPLOMATIC IMMUNITIES, PROTOCOL, AND THE PUBLIC* / MICHAEL H. CARDOZO

A diplomat is a success when he can influence the nation where he is assigned to see world affairs as his country sees them and to follow policies that his government espouses. In part, of course, his influence depends on the strength of his own nation and the image it projects abroad. His own personality and behavior, however, may prove to be major factors in the success of his mission. Consequently, he is well advised to give attention to the impression his conduct makes, not only on his colleagues in the foreign office, but also on the non-official populace.

In his effort to maintain a favorable image in the eyes of the public, however, the diplomat starts with a serious handicap. It is a widely held popular misconception that a foreign envoy may draw on his diplomatic immunity to let him casually disregard the laws of the host country, and that he wastes much of his time worrying about the rules of protocol at fancy teas, cocktail parties, and banquets. There is little awareness that the public laws do apply to him and that at the teas and the parties he gets most of his work done.

Diplomatic Immunity

All nations acknowledge the principle of international law called

* Michael H. Cardozo, "Diplomatic Immunities, Protocol, and the Public," *Journal of International Affairs*, Vol. 17, No. 1 (1963), pp. 61–69. Reprinted by permission.

"diplomatic immunity." The effect of this immunity, however, is not to free an envoy from the general obligation to obey the law, but to clothe him during his term of duty with a cloak of untouchability. If a robber flees across the nation's border with his loot, no one would say that he is free from the law's restraints just because the police may not, without permission, follow him onto foreign soil and bring him back. Once permission has been granted by the country of refuge, he may be apprehended by the pursuers, generally through extradition procedures, carried back across the border, and tried and punished for his offence.

The diplomat is in a comparable position. While he is in a foreign country as the accredited representative of his government, he is treated as though he is standing on his native soil. This is what is meant by the term "extraterritoriality." He may not be molested or arrested unless he loses his immunity through waiver, resignation, or removal. During World War II, for example, the United States waived the immunity of Tyler Kent, an embassy clerk in England who was accused of spying for the Germans. He was duly tried and convicted in the British courts, and served his sentence.

When a long limousine with diplomatic license plates is parked beside a sign saying "No Parking at Any Time," the law is being violated just as much as if the car belonged to the irate ordinary motorist whose access to his destination is blocked. While it is somewhat cumbersome to bring the diplomat to account, it is entirely proper for the transgression to be reported to the State Department and for the Department to complain to the government whose representative has offended. Repeated violations even of traffic laws can justify a request for recall of the envoy, and such a request cannot be denied. A single serious offence against the law may result in immediate recall. In recent years this has been the result after a first secretary of the Haitian Embassy in Washington was accused of shooting the Minister-Counsellor of the same Embassy, and when the son of the Irish Ambassador was involved in an automobile fatality in Washington. The son of an American diplomat in Ireland was similarly shipped home after a girl reported she had been attacked. A Guatemalan diplomat in New York was stripped of his immunity by his own government and exposed to trial when he was caught by United States officials in the act of smuggling a large amount of heroin into the country.

These instances clearly demonstrate the responsibility of diplomats to respect the laws of the host country. Their immunity is only from jurisdiction, which means the exercise of governmental power. When the Constitution states that all persons born in the United States "and subject to the jurisdiction thereof" are citizens of the United States, diplomats are thereby excluded. A child born in Washington to a foreign diplomat and his wife is not a citizen by birth. This is true whether the birth occurs in a hospital or in the foreign embassy. The latter is not foreign territory; an alien mother will not win United States citizenship for her child by gaining admittance to an American embassy abroad at the crucial moment. The embassy building is within the host country's territory and is subject to all the local laws, such as those respecting sanitation and the use of real property. Its diplomatic immunity means that, for some purposes, it is *treated* as though on foreign territory. The local police, for example, may not enter it without permission, since they may not exercise their powers in places devoted to diplomatic purposes.

These immunities have their roots in the same soil as their parent, sovereign immunity. From earliest times, a host sovereign has refrained from trying to impose his local laws and customs on a visiting sovereign and his entourage. The purpose of this self-restraint was primarily to show friendship. Even today the recipro-cal demonstration of the comity between two nations is of primary significance in diplomatic immunity.

There has always been, however, a highly practical justification for the immunity of diplomatic emissaries from local jurisdiction in the host country. Like the legislative representative of a local community sent to the capital to speak for his constituents, the diplomat must be able to reach his destination, deliver his message, and report back to those who sent him without the hindrance of local rules, customs, and police. In a foreign country he may encounter strange and exotic practices to which he cannot conform without years of habituation. There may be fundamental religious differences, calling for observances that would be impossible for a believer in another faith. Gastronomic tastes may vary so widely that the visitor must carry his own victuals and beverages with him, some of which may, in turn, be highly distasteful to the people of the receiving state. Even local traffic regulations might unduly interfere with a diplomat's access to the head of the host nation or to other high officials. The importance of extending the immunity even to the chauffeur of the visiting emissary can also be easily perceived. Naturally it covers the subordinate officers of an embassy who are needed to assist the chief of mission. Indeed, the logic behind the basic concept of immunity—that it makes possible the accomplishment of the diplomatic mission—leads inexorably to the inclusion in its ambit of clerks and messengers in the embassy, the families of the ambassador and his entire staff, their household servants, and their living and working quarters.

There may seem to be less justification today for the full range of immunities for diplomats sent to the United States than in earlier times when life here was more primitive. For representatives from some countries, however, the high-speed, mechanized, urban civilization here may be the very reason why they must be excused from meticulous observance of all our laws and customs. Endless difficulties would be presented if degrees of immunity, depending on local conditions, were adopted.

Some special conditions, however, are often accepted when local situations require them. It is normal practice, for example, for diplomats today to have their automobiles covered by liability insurance. This removes the need for the plea of diplomatic immunity in case of suit arising from an accident, and the custom is to waive the immunity. In New York City the Fire Department, with the concurrence of the State Department in Washington, has notified the various diplomatic missions to the United Nations that even cars bearing diplomatic license plates will be towed away when parked so close to fire hydrants that the public safety is endangered. Neither law nor comity requires that the activities of diplomats create serious hazards to the public safety.

Espionage cases inevitably touch very sensitive nerves. Some irreverent observers have characterized all diplomatic service as a great program of spying for one's country. Admittedly the line between improper spying and legitimate observing is often blurred, especially when the diplomat in question is a military or naval attaché reporting to the intelligence sections of the service department. Nonetheless there can be clear-cut instances of spying by diplomats, such as the seeking and reporting of information that the host government has classified as secret and for the eyes only of its own designated officials.

The advent of representatives of the Soviet Union in the diplomatic world has greatly increased the number of cases of alleged spying by diplomats and quasi-diplomats. The Kremlin has a habit of using such charges as a means of reciprocating for various forms of asserted offences against any of their interests. Every now and then an officer or member of the staff of the embassy of a Western power will be charged with espionage in Moscow or some other Soviet city. The charges are, of course, duly denied. In these cases, after the first apprehension, the Russians appear to have been scrupulous to observe the demands of diplomatic immunity, merely demanding the prompt recall of the named culprit. There is no alternative to complying, whether or not the diplomat's government believes the charges.

On our own side of the Iron Curtain, however, the problem has been more complicated. In the first place, the charges are not likely to be made unless there has been real evidence of improper activity in the nature of espionage. Certainly Russian diplomats have been convincingly shown more often than ours to have engaged in spying. When the charge is against an accredited diplomat, we follow the traditional practice and demand his recall. Frequently, however, the accused is in a kind of twilight zone of diplomatic status. With the United Nations Headquarters in this country, a large number of people working with and for the Organization have some kind of immunity, ranging from full diplomatic immunity for the chief officers of permanent delegations from member countries to the limited immunity related to the official duties of officers and employees of the Organization itself. A member of the latter group would not be immune from prosecution for espionage, an activity clearly outside the scope of his official duties. The Russians, however, often nominate to positions in this category members of their regular foreign service and send them over with diplomatic passports. When such a person is apprehended on charges of spying, the Soviet Government promptly claims diplomatic immunity. While the United States has not agreed to the claim, it has also found it expedient to refrain from subjecting the accused to a jail sentence. The courts have quite properly acceded to State Department representations that the interests of the nation's foreign relations required release of the defendant, treating him as though entitled to diplomatic immunity but without formally expanding its scope. Such releases are not likely to be very popular in the public's eye, but sometimes the release of one or two American aviators from Soviet custody will occur at about the same time. Reciprocity in restraint may be the greater wisdom when government agents are involved with the law.

Another area calling for judicious restraint appeared during the years of Prohibition in the United States, when it was illegal for anyone to transport liquor within the country. Without violating this law, how was a diplomat to entertain in the manner required by the customs of the general international community where wines are as indispensable to a meal as salt? Acceptable compromises were soon developed by enforcement officers, and the beverages were available for the receptions, banquets, and parties of the *corps diplomatique*.

Protocol

Compromises by law enforcement agencies are necessary where the social affairs of a diplomat are concerned simply because they are such an essential part of his work. At a party a diplomat is not off duty; he is representing his government. When Congressional committees roughly cut down the funds requested for "representation allowances" for the United States Foreign Service, it is as though an industrial concern was being denied money for its advertising program. A Congressman representing a typical U.S. constituency finds it hard to be generous with "whiskey money." But could a Senator do his work if he were not permitted to attend committee meetings? The analogy is fair.

The diplomat abroad has two major functions that require him to mingle as much as possible with the officials of the government to which he is accredited and with other diplomats. One of these functions may be called "negotiation." He is expected to convey to the other officials and diplomats his government's views and to seek to convince them of the correctness of those views. Some of this can, of course, be accomplished in formal sessions in the austere setting of government buildings. Far more, however, will be accomplished in the lighter, more informal conversation of social events. In an atmosphere of friendly intercourse the official strain is removed, and unofficial views can be exchanged. As the diplomats and the officials get better acquainted, more trust and confidence can flourish in a way that is most unlikely when contact is limited to office calls.

Social affairs are perhaps even more important to the accomplishment of the diplomat's other vital function, that of reporting to his government the general views of the foreign officials and their attitude toward all the problems of concern to his country. Far more than the officially expressed and publicly announced position is needed. The personal reactions of government officials are much more valuable. These can be learned only with difficulty in the cold atmosphere of the typical office or meeting room, but in the warmth of a comfortable residence, with fine food and wine to foster a companionable feeling, the sought-for opinions will more likely reveal themselves. Any diplomat whose government parsimoniously denies him the means of playing his reciprocal part to maintain this social intercourse is being deprived of an essential tool of his trade. An American Foreign Service officer who is unable to afford to serve bourbon whiskey and dry martinis to his opposite numbers in the foreign office and other embassies will be like a politician denied funds for travel, radio, and television during an election campaign. If he cannot communicate with the right people, he cannot accomplish his mission effectively.

Related to doubts about the importance of the diplomatic reception, cocktail party, or banquet in the skeptical mind of the general public is the whole subject of protocol. The average American is likely to be contemptuous of people who pay close attention to who shakes hands first with a dignitary at an official reception, who sits closest to the host at a lunch or dinner, and who has "DPL 1" or "2" on his car's license plate.

The significance of who has the lowest license number, however, is a matter that the man in the street can understand. He has seen the magic effect of a distinguished plate on the local police. This, however, should give him a clue to the reason for the diplomat's insistence on the proper place in the handshaking line or at the banquet table: these are the indicia of rank, not just of the man, but of the country he represents.

Before the statesmen who gathered at the Congress of Vienna in 1815 agreed that precedence among diplomats sent to a nation's capital would depend on the date of their arrival at the post, each ambassador had to elbow his way to the front of the line at diplomatic gatherings in order to maintain the dignity of his country. It would be unseemly for the representative of a great power to follow behind an envoy from a less significant nation. As a result, there were instances of physical violence among diplomats, each trying to prevent an affront to his country. Sometimes this concern is still expressed in diplomatic correspondence. At one capital, during World War II, there was a shortage of ladies in the diplomatic set because wartime conditions required many diplomats to leave their families at home. At a certain party given by the foreign minister, there was seen an attractive young lady without diplomatic rank. She was the secretary of one of the ambassadors, one of the few ladies available for such a gathering. The next day the foreign minister received a formal note from the government of another country, protesting the presence of a "clerk" from one embassy at a party to which "the Counsellor of our embassy was not invited." This was a violation of protocol.

Diplomats with New Functions

While there is now a generally accepted and very rigid protocol for determining precedence among those performing the normal functions of the diplomatic corps, there are still some serious problems to be solved. The growing number of people concerned with multilateral diplomacy, in international organizations, and in the diplomacy of international cooperation, through which various mutual aid programs are operated, has called for new rules respecting immunities and new solutions from the chiefs of protocol. Many of these people are outside the ranks of the traditional foreign service. The United States, for example, now sends to Brussels and to Paris envoys with the top rank of ambassador who are not part of our embassies in those capitals. They head the missions to the international organizations whose headquarters are also in those cities. Which ambassador in Brussels, under the rules of protocol, has the higher rank: the new Chief of the United States Mission to the European Communities or the holder of the venerable title of United States Ambassador to Belgium?

Before World War II the State Department seldom had to cope with the problem of ranking people who were not in the regular order of the Foreign Service. During the war, however, representatives of all kinds of unusual agencies were scattered about the world, and suddenly the question of their status and rank began to press for an answer. Lend-lease and economic warfare specialists needed as much access to officials of the other governments as did the regular embassy officers, but how could they be included in diplomatic functions if they were not in the foreign service and so not really diplomats? Furthermore, how could they be considered diplomats by the host government if they did not even carry diplomatic passports, which were the exclusive privilege of employees of the Department of State?

One of the greatest huddles the State Department had to cross before it could place these new emissaries in their proper slots was the passport question. It was common for the chief lend-lease representative, with responsibilities commensurate with a multi-billion dollar program, to carry a passport that connoted a non-diplomatic status, while a code clerk or stenographer sent to work in the same embassy would carry the magic diplomatic passport. This distinction can be crucial in the success of a special envoy's mission. If the officials in the other countries see that his own government ranks him below the salt and gives him credentials importing minor stature, why should they give much heed to his pleas for prompt acquiescence in his proposals?

During the long period while the functional diplomacy of international cooperation has been maturing as a fixed part of United States foreign relations, the passport question has arisen recurrently as a symbol of the conflict between traditional foreign service and the special missions required for modern programs such as relief and rehabilitation, economic recovery, technical assistance, and military aid. It has been as hard for a specialist in these areas to gain admittance to the diplomatic club house as for the camel to pass through the needle's eye. The march of events, however, has eroded some of the resistance. Missions to NATO and the OEEC from the beginning were almost always headed by persons of such eminence that their stature was not dependent on their title or passport. When Averell Harriman acted as lend-lease representative in London early in the war, Winston Churchill did not have to hear him addressed by subordinates as "Your Excellency" to know that he was the man to listen and talk to. His pipeline to the White House was known to be better than the holder of the formal title of United States Ambassador to the Court of St. James. Harriman carried the same weight when he headed the first European mission in the Marshall Plan, with headquarters in Paris.

Heads of lesser special missions and the officers on their staffs, however, need the support of recognized rank to assure them the power to function effectively. This means the assignment by their own government of titles and other indicia commensurate with their responsibilities. In diplomatic circles, as we have seen, protocol is likely to be inexorable, and insufficient rank can be a serious obstacle to success. A special envoy sent abroad to negotiate on an important subject will fume in vain as he sits at the foot of a table while the people he is supposed to be convincing converse gaily at the head with higher ranked Foreign Service officers who have none of the special knowledge required under the circumstances. No matter how unseemly and undignified it may appear to insist, before departure on a mission, that the necessary rank, immunities, and passport be assigned, the specialist from outside the Department of State is wise if he raises the issue before he encounters the frustrations of the innocent official abroad.

During the past decade there has been a gradual return to the State Department of various responsibilities in the field of international cooperation that started out under separate administration. While this development calls for a vigor and imagination that has not always characterized that venerable department, it is nonetheless highly desirable because it concentrates under one authority the various aspects of foreign relations. Today even the miscellaneous aid programs, although administered by separate staffs, are still within the State Department and under the Secretary of State. A similar trend has appeared abroad where the special missions are being placed under embassy control. Even in Paris, the United States Mission to the European Regional Organization—NATO and OECD—is in the State Department, unlike its predecessor, the Special Representative for Europe, which was part of the independent Economic Cooperation Administration and its renamed successors.

While this concentration within the foreign affairs department removes one of the problems that has created protocol difficulties, the way is not yet all smooth sailing. Suspicion still exists that functional specialists sent abroad to work on the programs in international cooperation are not really considered diplomats, entitled to all the privileges, immunities, and recognition that go with that characterization. Perhaps, as in the case of the United Nations staff, there will have to be degrees of immunities so as not to create too large a body of people who can claim the special treatment that is needed for diplomatic service. The distinction, however, should not be based on the identity of the government agency or bureau that employs the emissary, but the importance of his mission. With responsibility should go whatever rank, passport, and immunities are required by the traditions and demands of diplomatic service.

part **III**
INTERNATIONAL
CONFLICT

8

CAUSES OF CONFLICT

In one form or another, war is an almost permanent condition of the world. It is therefore of great importance to diagnose its causes. Professor Kenneth N. Waltz of Brandeis University does a masterful job in his book *Man, the State and War* of classifying and analyzing the various origins to which war has been attributed. The first chapter of this book is reprinted here.

Waltz distinguishes three "images" of international relations and the origin of conflict. The first image which locates the source of war in man himself, is exemplified by the other selections in this chapter. Plato (427–347 B.C.) ascribes war to a first-image cause in his *The Republic*. The principal concern of Desiderius Erasmus (1466–1536) is the moral condemnation of war and the persuasion of the rulers of his time to avoid war as much as possible, rather than the dis-

covery of the causes of wars. His arguments, however, also show
that he is primarily a first-image thinker.

A different form of the first-image concept of war is the
UNESCO approach, criticized by Frederick S. Dunn in his book
War and the Minds of Men. Dunn was Professor of Politics at
Princeton University and founder of the journal *World Politics.*

Examples of the second and third images of the origins of war
may be found in other chapters. For instance, Lenin is a second-
image theorist (selection 28), and the discussions of sovereignty,
international anarchy, and world-government in Chapters III and
IV are directly relevant to the third image.

23. MAN, THE STATE, AND WAR*/
KENNETH N. WALTZ

Asking who won a given war, someone has said, is like asking who
won the San Francisco earthquake. That in wars there is no victory
but only varying degrees of defeat is a proposition that has gained
increasing acceptance in the twentieth century. But are wars also
akin to earthquakes in being natural occurrences whose control or
elimination is beyond the wit of man? Few would admit that they
are, yet attempts to eliminate war, however nobly inspired and
assiduously pursued, have brought little more than fleeting moments
of peace among states. There is an apparent disproportion between
effort and product, between desire and result. The peace wish, we
are told, runs strong and deep among the Russian people; and we are
convinced that the same can be said of Americans. From these
statements there is some comfort to be derived, but in the light of
history and of current events as well it is difficult to believe that the
wish will father the condition desired.

Social scientists, realizing from their studies how firmly the
present is tied to the past and how intimately the parts of a system
depend upon each other, are inclined to be conservative in estimating the possibilities of achieving a radically better world. If one asks
whether we can now have peace where in the past there has been

* Kenneth N. Waltz, *Man, the State and War: A Theoretical Analysis*
(New York and London: Columbia University Press, 1959), Chap. 1. Copyright © 1954, 1959 Columbia University Press. Reprinted by permission.

war, the answers are most often pessimistic. Perhaps this is the wrong question. And indeed the answers will be somewhat less discouraging if instead the following questions are put: Are there ways of decreasing the incidence of war, of increasing the chances of peace? Can we have peace more often in the future than in the past?

Peace is one among a number of ends simultaneously entertained. The means by which peace can be sought are many. The end is pursued and the means are applied under varying conditions. Even though one may find it hard to believe that there are ways to peace not yet tried by statesmen or advocated by publicists, the very complexity of the problem suggests the possibility of combining activities in different ways in the hope that some combination will lead us closer to the goal. Is one then led to conclude that the wisdom of the statesman lies in trying first one policy and then another, in doing what the moment seems to require? An affirmative reply would suggest that the hope for improvement lies in policy divorced from analysis, in action removed from thought. Yet each attempt to alleviate a condition implies some idea of its causes: to explain how peace can be more readily achieved requires an understanding of the causes of war. . . .

Why does God, if he is all-knowing and all-powerful, permit the existence of evil? So asks the simple Huron in Voltaire's tale, and thereby confounds the learned men of the church. The theodicy problem in its secular version—man's explanation to himself of the existence of evil—is as intriguing and as perplexing. Disease and pestilence, bigotry and rape, theft and murder, pillage and war, appear as constants in world history. Why is this so? Can one explain war and malevolence in the same way? Is war simply mass malevolence, and thus an explanation of malevolence an explanation of the evils to which men in society are prey? Many have thought so.

> For though it were granted us by divine indulgence to be exempt from all that can be harmful to us from without [writes John Milton], yet the perverseness of our folly is so bent, that we should never cease hammering out of our own hearts, as it were out of a flint, the seeds and sparkles of new misery to ourselves, till all were in a blaze again.[1]

Our miseries are ineluctably the product of our natures. The root of all evil is man, and thus he is himself the root of the specific evil, war. This estimate of cause, widespread and firmly held by many as an article of faith, has been immensely influential. It is the convic-

[1] Milton, "The Doctrine and Discipline of Divorce," in *Works*, III, 180.

tion of St. Augustine and Luther, of Malthus and Jonathan Swift, of Dean Inge and Reinhold Niebuhr. In secular terms, with men defined as beings of intermixed reason and passion in whom passion repeatedly triumphs, the belief has informed the philosophy, including the political philosophy, of Spinoza. One might argue that it was as influential in the activities of Bismarck, with his low opinion of his fellow man, as it was in the rigorous and austere writings of Spinoza. If one's beliefs condition his expectations and his expectations condition his acts, acceptance or rejection of Milton's statement becomes important in the affairs of men. And, of course, Milton might be right even if no one believed him. If so, attempts to explain the recurrence of war in terms of, let us say, economic factors, might still be interesting games, but they would be games of little consequence. If it is true, as Dean Swift once said, that "the very same principle that influences a bully to break the windows of a whore who has jilted him, naturally stirs up a great prince to raise mighty armies, and dream of nothing but sieges, battles, and victories,"[2] then the reasons given by princes for the wars they have waged are mere rationalizations covering a motivation they may not themselves have perceived and could not afford to state openly if they had. It would follow as well that the schemes of the statesman Sully, if seriously intended to produce a greater peace in the world, were as idle as the dreams of the French monk Crucé—idle, that is, unless one can strike at the roots, the pride and petulance that have produced the wars as they have the other ills that plague mankind.

There are many who have agreed with Milton that men must look to man in order to understand social and political events, but who differ on what man's nature is, or can become. There are many others who, in effect, quarrel with the major premise. Does man make society in his image or does his society make him? It was to be expected, in a time when philosophy was little more than a branch of theology, that the theologian-philosophers would attribute to human agency what many philosophers before and since have described as the effects of the polity itself. Rousseau, among many who could be mentioned, makes a clean break with the view that, man being a social animal, one can explain his behavior in society by pointing to his animal passion and/or his human reason. Man is born and in his natural condition remains neither good nor bad. It is society that is the degrading force in men's lives, but it is the moralizing agency as well. And this latter effect Rousseau was unwilling to surrender even had he thought it possible for men to

[2] Swift, *A Tale of a Tub*.

retreat to the state of nature. This is his position, consistently reflected in his various works, though the myth persists that he believed the savage noble and lamented the advent of society.[3] Man's behavior, his very nature, which some have taken as cause, is, according to Rousseau, in great part a product of the society in which he lives. And society, he avers, is inseparable from political organization. In the absence of an organized power, which as a minimum must serve as the adjudicating authority, it is impossible for men to live together with even a modicum of peace. The study of society cannot be separated from the study of government, or the study of man from either. Rousseau, like Plato, believes that a bad polity makes men bad, and a good polity makes them good. This is not to say that the state is the potter and man a lump of clay posing no resistance to the shape the artist would impart. There are, as Rousseau recognized, similarities among men wherever they may live. There are also differences, and the search for causes is an attempt to explain these differences. The explanation of consequence—whether one is worried about the recurrence of theft or of war—is to be found in studying the varying social relations of men, and this in turn requires the study of politics.

Can man in society best be understood by studying man or by studying society? The most satisfactory reply would seem to be given by striking the word "or" and answering "both." But where one begins his explanation of events makes a difference. The Reverend Thomas Malthus once wrote that, "though human institutions appear to be the obvious and obtrusive causes of much mischief to mankind; yet, in reality, they are light and superficial, they are mere feathers that float on the surface, in comparison with those deeper seated causes of impurity that corrupt the springs, and render turbid the whole stream of human life."[4] Rousseau looked at the same world, the same range of events, but found the locus of major causes in a different ambit.

Following Rousseau's lead in turn raises questions. As men live in states, so states exist in a world of states. If we now confine our attention to the question of why wars occur, shall we emphasize the role of the state, with its social and economic content as well as its political form, or shall we concentrate primarily on what is sometimes called the society of states? Again one may say strike the word "or" and worry about both, but many have emphasized either

[3] For further discussion of Rousseau, see ch. vi, of *Man, the State and War*.

[4] Malthus, *An Essay on the Principle of Population*, pp. 47–48 (ch. x of the 1798 ed.).

the first or the second, which helps to explain the discrepant conclusions reached. Those who emphasize the first in a sense run parallel to Milton. He explains the ills of the world by the evil in man; they explain the great ill of war by the evil qualities of some or of all states. The statement is then often reversed: If bad states make wars, good states would live at peace with one another. With varying degrees of justification this view can be attributed to Plato and Kant, to nineteenth-century liberals and revisionist socialists. They agree on the principle involved, though they differ in their descriptions of good states as well as on the problem of bringing about their existence.

Where Marxists throw the liberals' picture of the world into partial eclipse, others blot it out entirely. Rousseau himself finds the major causes of war neither in men nor in states but in the state system itself. Of men in a state of nature, he had pointed out that one man cannot begin to behave decently unless he has some assurance that others will not be able to ruin him. This thought Rousseau develops and applies to states existing in a condition of anarchy in his fragmentary essay on "The State of War" and in his commentaries on the works of the Abbé de Saint-Pierre. Though a state may want to remain at peace, it may have to consider undertaking a preventive war; for if it does not strike when the moment is favorable it may be struck later when the advantage has shifted to the other side. This view forms the analytic basis for many balance-of-power approaches to international relations and for the world-federalist program as well. Implicit in Thucydides and Alexander Hamilton, made explicit by Machiavelli, Hobbes, and Rousseau, it is at once a generalized explanation of states' behavior and a critical *point d'appui* against those who look to the internal structure of states to explain their external behavior. While some believe that peace will follow from the improvement of states, others assert that what the state will be like depends on its relation to others. The latter thesis Leopold Ranke derived from, or applied to, the history of the states of modern Europe. It has been used to explain the internal ordering of other states as well.[5]

Statesmen, as well as philosophers and historians, have attempted to account for the behavior of states in peace and in war. Woodrow Wilson, in the draft of a note written in November of

[5] Ranke, "The Great Powers," tr. H. H. Von Laue, in Theodore H. Von Laue, *Leopold Ranke*. And see, e.g., Homo, *Roman Political Institutions*, tr. Dobie, especially pp. 146, 364–69.

1916, remarked that the causes of the war then being fought were obscure, that neutral nations did not know why it had begun and, if drawn in, would not know for what ends they would be fighting.[6] But often to act we must convince ourselves that we do know the answers to such questions. Wilson, to his own satisfaction, soon did. He appears in history as one of the many who, drawing a sharp distinction between peaceful and aggressive states, have assigned to democracies all the attributes of the first, to authoritarian states all the attributes of the second. To an extent that varies with the author considered, the incidence of war is then thought to depend upon the type of national government. Thus Cobden in a speech at Leeds in December of 1849:

> Where do we look for the black gathering cloud of war? Where do we see it rising? Why, from the despotism of the north, where one man wields the destinies of 40,000,000 of serfs. If we want to know where is the second danger of war and disturbance, it is in that province of Russia—that miserable and degraded country, Austria—next in the stage of despotism and barbarism, and there you see again the greatest danger of war; but in proportion as you find the population governing themselves—as in England, in France, or in America—there you will find that war is not the disposition of the people, and that if Government desire it, the people would put a check upon it.[7]

The constant interest of the people is in peace; no government controlled by the people will fight unless set upon. But only a few years later, England, though not set upon, did fight against Russia; and Cobden lost his seat in 1857 as a result of his opposition to the war. The experience is shattering, but not fatal to the belief; for it relives in the words of Wilson, for example, and again in those of the late Senator Robert Taft. In the manner of Cobden but in the year 1951, Taft writes: "History shows that when the people have the opportunity to speak they as a rule decide for peace if possible. It shows that arbitrary rulers are more inclined to favor war than are the people at any time."[8] Is it true, one wonders, that there is a uniquely peaceful form of the state? If it were true, how much would it matter? Would it enable some states to know which other states they could trust? Should the states that are already good seek ways of making other states better, and thus make it possible for all

---

[6] Link, *Woodrow Wilson and the Progressive Era*, p. 257n.
[7] Cobden, *Speeches*, ed. Bright and Rogers, I, 432–33.
[8] Robert A. Taft, *A Foreign Policy for Americans*, p. 23.

men to enjoy the pleasures of peace? Wilson believed it morally imperative to aid in the political regeneration of others; Cobden thought it not even justifiable. Agreeing on where the causes are to be found, they differ in their policy conclusions.

But what of those who incline to a different estimate of major causes? "Now people," President Dwight Eisenhower has said, "don't want conflict—people in general. It is only, I think, mistaken leaders that grow too belligerent and believe that people really want to fight."[9] Though apparently not all people want peace badly enough, for, on a different occasion, he had this to say: "If the mothers in every land could teach their children to understand the homes and hopes of children in every other land—in America, in Europe, in the Near East, in Asia—the cause of peace in the world would indeed be nobly served."[10] Here the President seems to agree with Milton on where cause is to be found, but without Milton's pessimism—or realism, depending on one's preconceptions. Aggressive tendencies may be inherent, but is their misdirection inevitable? War begins in the minds and emotions of men, as all acts do; but can minds and emotions be changed? And, if one agrees that they can be, how much and how fast can whose minds and feelings be changed? And, if other factors are relevant as well, how much difference would the changes make? The answers to these questions and to those of the preceding paragraph are not obvious, but they are important. How can they best be sought?

Some would suggest taking possible answers as hypotheses to be investigated and tested empirically. This is difficult. Most English liberals at the time of the First World War argued, as did Wilson, that the militarist and authoritarian character of the German state prompted Germany to seek the war that soon spread to most of the world. At the same time some liberals, most notably G. Lowes Dickinson, argued that no single state could be held guilty. Only by understanding the international system, or lack of system, by which the leaders of states were often forced to act with slight regard for conventional morality, could one understand and justly assess the processes by which the war was produced.[11] Dickinson was blasted by liberals and socialists alike for reversing the dominant inside-out explanation. Acceptance or rejection of explanatory theses in

[9] Quoted by Robert J. Donovan, "Eisenhower Will Cable Secret Geneva Reports," in New York *Herald Tribune*, July 13, 1955, p. 1.

[10] Eisenhower, address to a meeting of the National Council of Catholic Women. Text in New York *Times*, November 9, 1954, p. 14.

[11] Dickinson, *The European Anarchy, passim.*

matters such as this most often depends on the skill of the pleaders and the mood of the audience. These are obviously not fit criteria, yet it would be foolish to argue that simply by taking a more intensive look at the data a compelling case could be built for one or the other explanatory theory. Staring at the same set of data, the parties to the debate came to sharply different conclusions, for the images they entertained led them to select and interpret the data in different ways. In order to make sense of the liberals' hypothesis we need somehow to acquire an idea of the interrelation of many possibly relevant factors, and these interrelations are not given in the data we study. We establish or, rather, assert them ourselves. To say "establish" would be dangerous; for, whether or not we label them as such, we cannot escape from philosophic assumptions. The idea we entertain becomes a filter through which we pass our data. If the data are selected carefully, they will pass like milk through cheesecloth. The recalcitrance of the data may cause us to change one filter for another, to modify or scrap the theory we hold—or it may produce ever more ingenious selection and inter-pretation of data, as has happened with many Marxists trying to salvage the thesis that with the development of capitalism the masses become increasingly impoverished.

If empirical investigations vary in incidence and in result with the ideas the empiricists entertain, it is worth asking ourselves if the ideas themselves can be subjected to scrutiny. Obviously they can be. The study of politics is distinguished from other social studies by concentration upon the institutions and processes of government. This focuses the political scientists' concern without constituting a self-denying ordinance against the use of materials and techniques of other social scientists.[12] On the latter point there is no difficulty for the student of international relations; there is considerable difficulty on the former, for international relations are characterized by the absence of truly governmental institutions, which in turn gives a radically different twist to the relevant processes. Yet there is a large and important sense in which traditional political philosophy, concentrating as it does upon domestic politics, is relevant for the student of international relations. Peace, it is often said, is the problem of the twentieth century. It is also one of the continuing concerns of political philosophers. In times of relative quiescence

[12] Cf. David B. Truman, "The Impact on Political Science of the Revolu-tion in the Behavioral Sciences," in Bailey *et al.*, *Research Frontiers in Politics and Government*, pp. 202–31.

the question men put is likely to be: What good is life without justice and freedom? Better to die than live a slave. In times of domestic troubles, of hunger and civil war, of pressing insecurity, however, many will ask: Of what use is freedom without a power sufficient to establish and maintain conditions of security? That life takes priority over justice and freedom is taken to be a self-evident truth by St. Augustine and Luther, by Machiavelli, Bodin, and Hobbes. If the alternative to tyranny is chaos and if chaos means a war of all against all, then the willingness to endure tyranny becomes understandable. In the absence of order there can be no enjoyment of liberty. The problem of identifying and achieving the conditions of peace, a problem that plagues man and bedevils the student of international relations, has, especially in periods of crisis, bedeviled political philosophers as well.

R. G. Collingwood once suggested that the best way to understand the writings of philosophers is to seek out the questions they were attempting to answer. It is here suggested that the best way to examine the problems of international political theory is to pose a central question and identify the answers that can be given to it. One may seek in political philosophy answers to the question: Where are the major causes of war to be found? The answers are bewildering in their variety and in their contradictory qualities. To make this variety manageable, the answers can be ordered under the following three headings: within man, within the structure of the separate states, within the state system. The basis of this ordering, as well as its relevance in the world of affairs, is suggested in the preceding pages. These three estimates of cause will subsequently be referred to as images of international relations, numbered in the order given, with each image defined according to where one locates the nexus of important causes.

Previous comments indicate that the views comprised by any one image may in some senses by as contradictory as are the different images *inter se*. The argument that war is inevitable because men are irrevocably bad, and the argument that wars can be ended because men can be changed, are contradictory; but since in each of them individuals are taken to be the locus of cause, both are included in the first image. Similarly, acceptance of a third-image analysis may lead to the false optimism of the world federalists or to the often falsely defined pessimism of a *Realpolitik* position. Since in all respects but one there may be variety of opinion within images and since prescription is related to goal as well as to analysis, there is no one prescription for each image. There are, however, in relation to each image-goal pairing, logical and illogical prescriptions.

One can say that a prescription is wrong if he can show that following it does not bring about the predicted result. But can one ever show that a prescription was actually followed? One often hears statements like this: "The League of Nations didn't fail; it was never tried." And such statements are irrefutable. But even if empirical disproof were possible, the problem of proving a prescription valid would remain to be solved. A patient who in one period of illness tries ten different medications may wonder just which pill produced the cure. The apportioning of credit is often more difficult than the assigning of blame. If a historical study were to show that in country A increases in national prosperity always followed increases in tariffs, to some observers this might seem to prove that high tariffs are a cause of prosperity; to others, that both of these factors are dependent on a third; and to still others, nothing at all. The empirical approach, though necessary, is not sufficient. The correlation of events means nothing, or at least should not be taken to mean anything, apart from the analysis that accompanies it.

If there is no empirical solution to the problem of prescription verification, what solution is there? Prescription is logically impossible apart from analysis. Every prescription for greater peace in the world is then related to one of our three images of international relations, or to some combination of them. An understanding of the analytical terms of each of the images will open up two additional possibilities for accepting or rejecting prescriptions. (1) A prescription based on a faulty analysis would be unlikely to produce the desired consequences. The assumption that to improve men in a prescribed way will serve to promote peace rests on the further assumption that in some form the first image of international relations is valid. The latter assumption should be examined before the former is made. (2) A prescription would be unacceptable if it were not logically related to its analysis. One who suffers from infected tonsils profits little from a skillfully performed appendectomy. If violence among states is caused by the evilness of man, to aim at the internal reform of states will not do much good. And if violence among states is the product of international anarchy, to aim at the conversion of individuals can accomplish little. One man's prognosis confounds the other man's prescription. If the validity of the images themselves can be ascertained, the critical relating of prescription to image becomes a check on the validity of prescriptions. There is, however, an additional complicating factor. Some combination of our three images, rather than any one of them, may be required for an accurate understanding of international relations. We may not be in a situation where one can consider just the patient's tonsils or his appendix. Both may be infected but removing either may kill the patient. In other words, understanding the likely consequences of any one cause may depend on understanding its relation to other causes. The possible interrelation of causes makes the problem of estimating the merit of various prescriptions more difficult still.

What are the criteria of merit? Suppose we consider again the person who argues that "bad" states produce war, that "good" states would live peacefully together, that therefore we must bring states into accord with a prescribed pattern. To estimate the merit of such a series of propositions requires asking the following questions: (1) Can the final proposition be implemented, and if so, how? (2) Is there a logical relation between prescription and image? In other words, does the prescription attack the assigned causes? (3) Is the image adequate, or has the analyst simply seized upon the most spectacular cause or the one he thinks most susceptible to manipulation and ignored other causes of equal or greater importance? (4) How will attempts to fill the prescription affect other goals? This last question is necessary since peace is not the only goal of even the most peacefully inclined men or states. One may, for example, believe that world government and perpetual peace are synonymous, but one may also be convinced that a world state would be a world tyranny and therefore prefer a system of nation-states with a perpetual danger of war to a world state with a promise of perpetual peace. . . .

24. *THE ORIGIN OF WAR* * / *PLATO*

A State, I said, arises, as I conceive, out of the needs of mankind; no one is self-sufficing, but all of us have many wants. Can any other origin of a State be imagined?

There can be no other.

* Plato, *The Republic*, trans. Benjamin Jowett, rev. ed. (New York: Willey Book Co., 1901), pp. 47–53.

Then, as we have many wants, and many persons are needed to supply them, one takes a helper for one purpose and another for another; and when these partners and helpers are gathered together in one habitation the body of inhabitants is termed a State.

True, he said.

And they exchange with one another, and one gives, and another receives, under the idea that the exchange will be for their good.

Very true.

Then, I said, let us begin and create in idea a State; and yet the true creator is necessity, who is the mother of our invention.

Of course, he replied.

Now the first and greatest of necessities is food, which is the condition of life and existence.

Certainly.

The second is a dwelling, and the third clothing and the like.

True.

And now let us see how our city will be able to supply this great demand: We may suppose that one man is a husbandman, another a builder, someone else a weaver—shall we add to them a shoemaker, or perhaps some other purveyor to our bodily wants?

Quite right.

The barest notion of a State must include four or five men.

Clearly.

And how will they proceed? Will each bring the result of his labors into a common stock?—the individual husbandman, for example, producing for four, and laboring four times as long and as much as he need in the provision of food with which he supplies others as well as himself; or will he have nothing to do with others and not be at the trouble of producing for them, but provide for himself alone a fourth of the food in a fourth of the time, and in the remaining three-fourths of his time be employed in making a house or a coat or a pair of shoes, having no partnership with others, but supplying himself all his own wants?

Adeimantus thought that he should aim at producing food only and not at producing everything.

Probably, I replied, that would be the better way; and when I hear you say this, I am myself reminded that we are not all alike; there are diversities of natures among us which are adapted to different occupations.

Very true.

And will you have a work better done when the workman has many occupations, or when he has only one?

When he has only one.

Further, there can be no doubt that a work is spoilt when not done at the right time?

No doubt.

For business is not disposed to wait until the doer of the business is at leisure; but the doer must follow up what he is doing, and make the business his first object.

He must.

And if so, we must infer that all things are produced more plentifully and easily and of a better quality when one man does one thing which is natural to him and does it at the right time, and leaves other things.

Undoubtedly.

Then more than four citizens will be required; for the husbandman will not make his own plough or mattock, or other implements of agriculture, if they are to be good for anything. Neither will the builder make his tools—and he, too, needs many; and in like manner the weaver and shoemaker.

True.

Then carpenters and smiths and many other artisans will be sharers in our little State, which is already beginning to grow?

True.

Yet even if we add neatherds, shepherds, and other herdsmen, in order that our husbandmen may have oxen to plough with, and builders as well as husbandmen may have draught cattle, and curriers and weavers fleeces and hides—still our State will not be very large.

That is true; yet neither will it be a very small State which contains all these.

Then, again, there is the situation of the city—to find a place where nothing need be imported is well-nigh impossible.

Impossible.

Then there must be another class of citizens who will bring the required supply from another city?

There must.

But if the trader goes empty-handed, having nothing which they require who would supply his need, he will come back empty-handed.

That is certain.

And therefore what they produce at home must be not only enough for themselves, but such both in quantity and quality as to accommodate those from whom their wants are supplied.

Very true.

Then more husbandmen and more artisans will be required?

They will.

Not to mention the importers and exporters, who are called merchants?

Yes.

Then we shall want merchants?

We shall.

And if merchandise is to be carried over the sea, skilful sailors will also be needed, and in considerable numbers?

Yes, in considerable numbers.

Then, again, within the city, how will they exchange their productions? To secure such an exchange was, as you will remember, one of our principal objects when we formed them into a society and constituted a State.

Clearly they will buy and sell.

Then they will need a market-place, and a money-token for purposes of exchange.

Certainly.

Suppose now that a husbandman or an artisan brings some production to market, and he comes at a time when there is no one to exchange with him—is he to leave his calling and sit idle in the market-place?

Not at all; he will find people there who, seeing the want, undertake the office of salesmen. In well-ordered States they are commonly those who are the weakest in bodily strength, and therefore of little use for any other purpose; their duty is to be in the market, and to give money in exchange for goods to those who desire to sell, and to take money from those who desire to buy.

This want, then, creates a class of retail-traders in our State. Is not "retailer" the term which is applied to those who sit in the market-place engaged in buying and selling, while those who wander from one city to another are called merchants?

Yes, he said.

And there is another class of servants, who are intellectually hardly on the level of companionship; still they have plenty of bodily strength for labor, which accordingly they sell, and are called, if I do not mistake, hirelings, "hire" being the name which is given to the price of their labor.

True.

Then hirelings will help to make up our population?

Yes.

And now, Adeimantus, is our State matured and perfected?

I think so.

Where, then, is justice, and where is injustice, and in what part of the State did they spring up?

Probably in the dealings of these citizens with one another. I cannot imagine that they are more likely to be found anywhere else.

I dare say that you are right in your suggestion, I said; we had better think the matter out, and not shrink from the inquiry.

Let us then consider, first of all, what will be their way of life, now that we have thus established them. Will they not produce corn and wine and clothes and shoes, and build houses for themselves? And when they are housed, they will work, in summer, commonly, stripped and barefoot, but in winter substantially clothed and shod. They will feed on barley-meal and flour of wheat, baking and kneading them, making noble cakes and loaves; these they will serve up on a mat of reeds or on clean leaves, themselves reclining the while upon beds strewn with yew or myrtle. And they and their children will feast, drinking of the wine which they have made, wearing garlands on their heads, and hymning the praises of the gods, in happy converse with one another. And they will take care that their families do not exceed their means; having an eye to poverty or war.

But, said Glaucon, interposing, you have not given them a relish to their meal.

True, I replied, I had forgotten; of course they must have a relish—salt and olives and cheese—and they will boil roots and herbs such as country people prepare; for a dessert we shall give them figs and peas and beans; and they will roast myrtle-berries and acorns at the fire, drinking in moderation. And with such a diet they may be expected to live in peace and health to a good old age, and bequeath a similar life to their children after them.

Yes, Socrates, he said, and if you were providing for a city of pigs, how else would you feed the beasts?

But what would you have, Glaucon? I replied.

Why, he said, you should give them the ordinary conveniences of life. People who are to be comfortable are accustomed to lie on sofas, and dine off tables, and they should have sauces and sweets in the modern style.

Yes, I said, now I understand: the question which you would have me consider is, not only how a State, but how a luxurious State is created; and possibly there is no harm in this, for in such a State we shall be more likely to see how justice and injustice originate. In my opinion the true and healthy constitution of the State is the one which I have described. But if you wish also to see a State at fever-heat, I have no objection. For I suspect that many will not be satisfied with the simpler way of life. They will be for adding sofas and tables and other furniture; also dainties and perfumes and incense and courtesans and cakes, all these not of one sort only, but in every variety. We must go beyond the necessaries of which I was at first speaking, such as houses and clothes and shoes; the arts of the painter and the embroiderer will have to be set in motion, and gold and ivory and all sorts of materials must be procured.

True, he said.

Then we must enlarge our borders; for the original healthy State is no longer sufficient. Now will the city have to fill and swell with a multitude of callings which are not required by any natural want; such as the whole tribe of hunters and actors, of whom one large class have to do with forms and colors; another will be the votaries of music—poets and their attendant train of rhapsodists, players, dancers, contractors; also makers of divers kinds of articles, including women's dresses. And we shall want more servants. Will not tutors be also in request, and nurses wet and dry, tirewomen and barbers, as well as confectioners and cooks; and swineherds, too, who were not needed and therefore had no place in the former edition of our State, but are needed now? They must not be forgotten: and there will be animals of many other kinds, if people eat them.

Certainly.

And living in this way we shall have much greater need of physicians than before?

Much greater.

And the country which was enough to support the original inhabitants will be too small now, and not enough?

Quite true.

Then a slice of our neighbors' land will be wanted by us for

pasture and tillage, and they will want a slice of ours, if, like ourselves, they exceed the limit of necessity, and give themselves up to
the unlimited accumulation of wealth?

That, Socrates, will be inevitable.

And so we shall go to war, Glaucon. Shall we not?

Most certainly, he replied.

Then, without determining as yet whether war does good or
harm, thus much we may affirm, that now we have discovered war
to be derived from causes which are also the causes of almost all the
evils in States, private as well as public.

Undoubtedly.

25. *ON GOING TO WAR* / *DESIDERIUS ERASMUS*

A good prince will never go to war unless he has first made every
possible effort to avoid it. If every ruler should follow this principle,
there would hardly ever be war among us. But if the prince cannot
avoid such a calamity, his first duty shall be to carry on the struggle
with as little suffering for his people and as little shedding of
Christian blood as possible, and to end it as quickly as possible.

The prince who is truly Christian will first consider the
difference between men, born for peace and good will, and beasts,
born for war and plunder; and then, the difference between man
and Christian man. He will further contemplate the beauty, desirability, and salutary effects of peace, and in contrast the destructiveness and viciousness of war. He will also reflect on the many
sufferings caused by war, even when it is a very just war (if any
war can be called just). Finally, he will set aside his sentiments, and
rely on his reason to calculate exactly how much the war will cost
and whether the aim for which the war is fought is worth so much—
assuming that victory is certain, which is not always the case even
with the best cause. He must consider the anxiety, the expense, the
danger, the laborious and long preparation. The prince must assemble mercenary soldiers, who are the barbarous and infamous
dregs of mankind. He must bribe and coax this most abject and exe-
crable class of the human race in order to appear more generous
than his opponent.

* Desiderius Erasmus, *Principis Christiani Institutio* (Leyden: J. Maire,
1641), pp. 212–219. Translated by Eva Tamm Lijphart and Arend Lijphart.

Nothing is dearer to the good prince than to have subjects of the highest quality. But is there a greater and more immediate corruptor of morals than war? His strongest desire is to see his people secure and prosperous. But when he wages war, he has to expose his young men to innumerable dangers, and often in an hour makes multitudes of orphans, widows, childless old people, beggars, and mourners. . . .

Some princes deceive themselves by thinking that war is entirely just and that they have a just cause to go to war. Leaving unsettled the question whether war is ever just, who does not regard his own cause as just? And among all the changes and vicissitudes of human affairs, with so many convenants and treaties now concluded, now rescinded, who can lack a cause, if any reason whatsoever is a sufficient cause to go to war?

The pontifical laws do not condemn all wars. Augustine, too, approves of war in some instances. Saint Bernard also praises some soldiers. But Christ himself as well as Peter and Paul everywhere teach the contrary. Why is their authority less valid with us than that of Augustine or Bernard? Augustine, in one or two places, does not disapprove of war, but the whole philosophy of Christ teaches that it is evil. The apostles everywhere condemn it. Moreover, the same holy teachers whose approval of war in one or two passages is cited, condemn and detest it in many more places. Why do we ignore all these, and seize upon that which condones our sins? Finally, if we examine the matter carefully, we find that no one has approved of the kind of war in which we now commonly engage.

Certain arts are forbidden by the laws, because they are closely related to imposture and are frequently practiced with deceit: for instance, astrology and alchemy (although it is possible that they are sometimes practiced honestly). Wars should be treated in a similar way. Although some wars may perhaps be just, I do not know whether in the present state of human affairs I could find a single one of which the cause has not been ambition, wrath, ferocity, lust, or avarice. It often happens that leaders spend more than their private means allow, and that they deliberately stir up war in order to increase their own resources by despoiling their subjects. It also often happens that princes conspire together, and devise fictitious reasons for going to war in order to diminish the power of their peoples and to strengthen themselves at the expense of the public interest. Therefore, the good and Christian prince should look upon every war, however just, with suspicion.

It is often said, however, that one must not abandon one's rights. But any right deriving from a family relationship concerns chiefly the prince's private affairs. How unjust it would be to enforce this right at the cost of such terrible suffering of the people, and, in order to make some small territorial gains, to plunder the entire kingdom and plunge it into a death struggle. If one prince offends another with regard to some trivial and private matter of hereditary right or some similar issue, how does this concern the people as a whole?

A good prince measures everything in terms of the public welfare; otherwise he would not even be a prince. The right over men is not the same as the right over cattle. An important part of government is the consent of the people, which was the origin of kings. If a dispute arises between princes, why do they not resort to arbiters? There are so many bishops, abbots, learned men, and eminent magistrates, whose judgment, rather than carnage, plunder, and universal calamity, should settle the dispute.

26. POLITICS, CULTURE, AND PEACE*/
FREDERICK S. DUNN

Most government documents make deplorably dull reading and only on rare occasions are they illumined by new ideas or a fresh turn of phrase. An exception is to be found in the opening lines of the Constitution of the United Nations Educational, Scientific and Cultural Organization (UNESCO). With disarming candor and an easy poetic rhythm, the preamble discusses the eternal problem of war and peace in terms somewhat different from those which governments normally use in their relations with each other. It suggests that the origin of wars is to be found not, as had generally been supposed, in the formal acts of sovereign states, but rather in the minds of the masses of men, and it is accordingly in the minds of men that the defenses of peace must be constructed. The preamble further argues that ignorance among nations of each other's ways and lives leads to suspicion and mistrust which in turn lead to war,

* Frederick S. Dunn, *War and the Minds of Men* (New York: Harper & Brothers, for the Council on Foreign Relations, 1950), Chap. 1. Reprinted by permission.

and hence the way to peace is to remove such ignorance. On the whole, it takes a distinctly skeptical view of the durability of a peace based principally upon the usual political and economic arrangements of governments, and places its faith instead on the removal from men's minds of the attitudes and predispositions that lead them to entertain the idea of war with each other.

The deceptive simplicity of this statement might give the impression that it is intended merely as melodious preamble music, to be repeated on solemn public occasions but not to be taken seriously as an expression of empirical truth about the source of political conflicts. There is in fact some reason to suppose that the drafters themselves were not in full agreement as to the precise significance of the theory they were offering as the basis for the operations of UNESCO. But whatever may have been the original intention, there can be no doubt that the phrase about the "minds of men" has caught hold of the imagination of a great many people in a number of countries and has come to symbolize a distinctive and somewhat optimistic approach to the whole problem of how to lessen the threat of war in the present age.

1. Peace by Changing Men's Attitudes

There are some obvious reasons why this idea of constructing the defenses of peace in the minds of men should have attracted so much attention.

In the first place, it is quite clear that there has been a general loss of confidence in existing notions about how to avoid war in the current world crisis. While most governments are proceeding on traditional assumptions about the sources of war and are endeavoring to construct the defenses of peace in an expanded national strength and in useful alliances, there is a strong undercurrent of despair arising from the belief that in the end this method is just not going to work. The ancient dilemma of trying to achieve security in a world of sovereign states seems to have become vastly more baffling in an atomic age. The prospect of maintaining a lasting equilibrium in a bipolar world appears more doubtful than ever.

Now the threat of the hydrogen bomb, with its fantastic capacity for destruction, has come along to sharpen the dilemma a hundredfold. At the moment, it does not appear that armed forces of any size could insure the great industrial centers from instant incineration at the hands of a determined enemy possessing even a small supply of these bombs. Mighty ships and well-equipped divisions can no longer provide even a minimum of that comfortable feeling of safety which they used to be able to give. A trial by battle involving the use of all the newest weapons of mass destruction can appear only as the final madness of men. Hence great numbers of people have anxiously turned to this doctrine which seems to open up a whole new method of attack on the problem of war and peace.

A second reason why the minds-of-men theory has attracted so much attention is the realization that the masses of men are now exerting a great and apparently expanding influence on the making of policy decisions in international affairs. As the interests of people have spread outward, a greater concern with the way in which those interests are fostered has likewise begun to penetrate the international level. Everywhere outside the Soviet orbit there has been a definite tendency toward wider popular control of foreign policy. In the colonial empires of the world, the native populations have surged forward to enforce their demands for a direct voice in the determination of their status in the international community. In all save the dictator countries, legislative bodies seem to have won an increased share in the making of foreign policy. Hence, a theory which proposes to construct the defenses of peace in the minds of men appears to make much more sense today than it would have made when the management of foreign affairs was the exclusive province of a small group of officials.

A third reason why the minds-of-men doctrine has seemed to offer a ray of hope in the current crisis is the growing belief that we are at last coming into the possession of knowledge and techniques that will enable us to influence men's political behavior in desired directions and so exercise a greater control over international events. We seem to be traveling along the edge of a new and engrossing experience in the long and difficult enterprise of learning about the forces that influence social action. There is excitement in the air and a feeling that we are breaking out into new and fertile territory in the understanding of social behavior. Spectacular improvements in the technical means of communication with the masses of men have added to the hope that we are acquiring new power as well as new insights in the control of international events.

For these reasons, there has been a ready audience for the theory that the conflicts of nations arise in the minds of men and might be controlled by changing men's attitudes. On the surface there seems to be much in favor of the idea. It is easy enough to see that widespread feelings of hostility and misunderstanding provide fertile soil for the seeds of war. It is also obvious that conflicts among nations can grow fat on a diet of ignorance and bias. Presumably a state of peace and order is what nearly everybody wants, and if its achievement is really a matter of influencing men's minds, one would be hard pressed to say why massive efforts should not be made in this field.

2. *Large Hopes and Small Results*

However, when it comes to the actual effort to put this doctrine into effect, the difficulties seem mountainous. . . .

Everyone knows in general what is meant by "mutual understanding" and everyone approves of it as a sentiment, but little effort seems to have been made to translate it into categories of observable data about which hypotheses can be made and tested by objective methods. The result is that no two people who use the term can ever be sure that they are talking about the same thing or that what they say has any basis in reality. The language and the conceptual systems used in the halls of UNESCO are for the most part of a traditional character, and reveal little appreciation of what has been taking place recently in the way of systematic analysis of social action.

Some people who are genuinely convinced of the essential validity of the minds-of-men doctrine have nevertheless raised serious questions about the premises on which this doctrine is being put into effect. Thus the belief that men go to war because they are ignorant of each other's ways of life or have incorrect views of each other's motives has been strongly challenged on the basis of past history. It is pointed out that the nations which go to war most frequently are not those in which ignorance of other people is most common, but are instead the more advanced nations with the highest educational standards. For example, the people of France and Germany have had abundant opportunity to get to know each other well; yet this has not prevented them from engaging in wars of spectacular dimensions.

Even in everyday human affairs, the connection between

knowledge of others and peaceful relations with them is not always evident. Thus on the family level the bitterest of controversies frequently take place between the closest of relatives. Civil wars, which are between peoples of the same civilization who presumably possess a good understanding of each other, are notoriously sharp and cruel. On the other hand, isolated nations have managed to live both in ignorance of, and in harmony with, other nations for long periods of time.

It is persistently asked whether the differences between Soviet Russia and the United States today are really due to a lack of understanding of their respective positions, or whether these differences do not in fact arise out of a clear realization that the two countries have fundamental goals which are to a large extent incompatible. One recalls the case of the European monarch who, when urged by his advisers to settle a boundary war with a neighboring sovereign, replied that there was really no dispute at all between them—they both wanted the same thing. Their mutual understanding was perfect.

Will full knowledge of what nations want in fact bring peace among them, or is it not more likely that, under certain circumstances, such knowledge might even increase the tendency to go to war? Those who raise this question are quite ready to concede that, where means can be found for giving both contestants substantially what they desire, a full exploration of the possible alternatives would undoubtedly contribute to the avoidance of hostilities. But when such inquiry reveals that the goals of the two sides are incompatible and there is no way in which they can be harmonized, it is a serious question whether public revelation of that fact would increase the chances for peace.

Past experience affords some ground for skepticism as to whether extensive cultural interchange has had much effect upon the underlying causes of wars. Does freedom of communication across national boundaries necessarily lead to the development of common conceptions of justice among nations? Is it even true that nations possessing similar conceptions of justice will therefore refrain from going to war against each other? Cultural interchange is freely conceded to be a good thing in itself. But some scholars have asked whether, in the light of historical instances, one can expect such interchange to have much effect in preventing wars.[1]

[1] See Hans J. Morgenthau, *Politics Among Nations*, New York, Alfred A. Knopf, 1948, pp. 407–412; also Reinhold Niebuhr, "The Theory and Practice of UNESCO," *International Organization*, February 1950, pp. 3–11.

Finally, there is little reason, it is said, for supposing that governments are really serious in wanting to take action that would reduce the nationalistic attitudes of their citizens. Such attitudes may be a useful source of support for a government that is engaged in a power competition with a rival nation. Under such circumstances, it would be too much to expect that any government would seriously want its own citizens to become more internationally minded. Thus in the present contest between the Soviet Union and the United States, a program of education for international understanding on one side of the line but not on the other would merely strengthen the side that relies on the fostering of nationalistic attitudes among its people.

The upshot of all these criticisms is that a good many people who would normally be well disposed toward the idea that the defenses of peace should be built in the minds of men nevertheless feel that the doctrine really has no particular relevancy to the present world crisis. They believe that UNESCO's activities in improving standards of education, science and culture in various countries may be excellent in themselves, but that aside from the infinitely slow building up of the tissues of a world community, there is little that UNESCO can contribute to the maintenance of peace in the years ahead.

It would be difficult to deny the strength of many of the points made above. However, they could all be admitted, and it might still be a perfectly good working proposition that wars begin in the minds of men and that the defenses of peace must be constructed there. What is valid in these criticisms is directed not so much at the idea itself as at the way in which people have sought to apply it.

Where else, one might ask, could wars begin save in the minds of men? Even the greenest tyro in the halls of world politics is now aware that, although we talk about states acting and making decisions, only human beings can act. The state, being an abstraction of thought, cannot have a will of its own apart from human wills. It is in one sense just a name to describe the process whereby politically organized people arrive at decisions and take action which is accepted as the action of the collectivity.

But having said this, one is still a long way from knowing what to do about it, or even whether anything can be done about it at all. Having identified the source of our troubles, it is still a highly perplexing business to discover reliable ways of freeing men's minds from the impulses and attitudes that lead to wars. Yet it is obvious that, if there is a grain of truth in the minds-of-men doctrine, one must examine it with sympathetic care to see what guidance it can offer for more intelligent policy-making in the future.

In order to do this with any hope of success, it will be necessary to break out of the traditional framework of thinking about foreign affairs and to use a new focus for our analysis. This is always a difficult thing to do, but there is no other way of getting a fresh view of the problem and of arriving at an objective evaluation of the steps that are being taken to solve it.

At any rate it is time that the case for approaching the problem of war and peace through the minds-of-men doctrine should be placed on some other ground than that of stirring appeals to the sentiments. If the phrase has any useful meaning as a signpost to effective action, that meaning will be discovered only by a realistic analysis that will reveal its connection with the actual world of events and suggest hypotheses which can be tested by observation and concrete experience.

To a crusader in a cause, a realistic appraisal of the premises on which his beliefs are founded can appear only as rank heresy. Many people today have a sacred-cow attitude toward UNESCO that prevents them from looking at it with a detached eye. But if a movement or doctrine cannot stand up under a realistic examination, then it does not deserve the support of intelligent men; if it can, it is doubly strong.

3. *A Problem of Communication*

The most important thing to be observed about the minds-of-men theory is that it is primarily a theory of communication and learning. It asserts that, if only the right things are communicated by some people to some other people, a change can be effected in the attitudes of nations toward each other that will make a durable peace possible. This is a technical proposition which rests upon our knowledge of the processes of using ideas or symbols to modify the behavior of men. . . .

In the present state of the world, this is a very complicated business indeed. Because of the prodigious revolutionary changes taking place in various parts of the world, it is no easy matter to identify either the proper communicators or the appropriate audiences, or even the correct aims of communication policies. One cannot simply say that the purpose of such policies is to avoid open warfare, since that kind of peace might be purchased, at least temporarily, by making men submissive to tyrants. One would have to assume that the purpose is to achieve a peace based on those attitudes which make for the full development of the capacities of free men in a free society. Instead of merely seeking to deprive men of the will to resist those whose aim is to enslave them, the goal of the minds-of-men theory might even be to strengthen their resistance in the face of threats of violence. Certainly a peace of subservience based on the deterioration of human society and the breakdown of individual personality is not what is desired by those who embrace the theory. Such a peace could end finally only in the jungle warfare of barbarians. In the complex society of today, no enduring peace is possible that is not based on the continuing development of human potentialities. . . .

9

IMPERIALISM AND COLONIALISM

Why do some states seek to expand beyond their own boundaries? What is their justification? And what are the effects of expansionism? In the first selection, Theodore Roosevelt (1858–1919), 26th President of the United States, presents an enthusiastic defense of American empire building. He delivered his speech "The Strenuous Life" before the Hamilton Club in Chicago on April 10, 1899.

The second selection consists of excerpts from V. I. Lenin's *Imperialism.* Lenin (1870–1924), the leader of the Bolshevik Revolution of 1917 and the first ruler of the Soviet Union, argued that imperialism was a product of specific economic forces. In one form or another, this economic explanation of imperialism has had great appeal in the twentieth century in spite of its obvious shortcomings.

The third selection is by William L. Langer, who is eminently qualified to review the history of imperialism. He is Professor of Modern History at Harvard University and author of *The Diplomacy of Imperialism.*

27. *THE STRENUOUS LIFE** / *THEODORE ROOSEVELT*

In speaking to you, men of the greatest city of the West, men of the State which gave to the country Lincoln and Grant, men who preëminently and distinctly embody all that is most American in the American character, I wish to preach, not the doctrine of ignoble ease, but the doctrine of the strenuous life, the life of toil and effort, of labor and strife; to preach that highest form of success which comes, not to the man who desires mere easy peace, but to the man who does not shrink from danger, from hardship, or from bitter toil, and who out of these wins the splendid ultimate triumph.

A life of slothful ease, a life of that peace which springs merely from lack either of desire or of power to strive after great things, is as little worthy of a nation as of an individual. I ask only that what every self-respecting American demands from himself and from his sons shall be demanded of the American nation as a whole. Who among you would teach your boys that ease, that peace, is to be the first consideration in their eyes—to be the ultimate goal after which they strive? You men of Chicago have made this city great, you men of Illinois have done your share, and more than your share, in making America great, because you neither preach nor practise such a doctrine. You work yourselves, and you bring up your sons to work. If you are rich and are worth your salt, you will teach your sons that though they may have leisure, it is not to be spent in idleness; for wisely used leisure merely means that those who possess it, being free from the necessity of working for their livelihood, are all the more bound to carry on some kind of non-remunerative work in science, in letters, in art, in exploration, in historical research—work of the type we most need in this country, the successful carrying out of which reflects most honor upon the nation. We do not admire the man of timid peace. We admire the man

---

* Theodore Roosevelt, *The Strenuous Life: Essays and Addresses* (New York: The Century Co., 1905), pp. 1–10, 16–21.

who embodies victorious effort; the man who never wrongs his
neighbor, who is prompt to help a friend, but who has those virile
qualities necessary to win in the stern strife of actual life. It is hard
to fail, but it is worse never to have tried to succeed. In this life we
get nothing save by effort. Freedom from effort in the present
merely means that there has been stored up effort in the past. A man
can be freed from the necessity of work only by the fact that he or
his fathers before him have worked to good purpose. If the freedom
thus purchased is used aright, and the man still does actual work,
though of a different kind, whether as a writer or a general, whether
in the field of politics or in the field of exploration and adventure,
he shows he deserves his good fortune. But if he treats this period of
freedom from the need of actual labor as a period, not of preparation, but of mere enjoyment, even though perhaps not of vicious
enjoyment, he shows that he is simply a cumberer of the earth's
surface, and he surely unfits himself to hold his own with his fellows
if the need to do so should again arise. A mere life of ease is not in
the end a very satisfactory life, and, above all, it is a life which
ultimately unfits those who follow it for serious work in the world.

In the last analysis a healthy state can exist only when the men
and women who make it up lead clean, vigorous, healthy lives; when
the children are so trained that they shall endeavor, not to shirk
difficulties, but to overcome them; not to seek ease, but to know
how to wrest triumph from toil and risk. The man must be glad to
do a man's work, to dare and endure and to labor; to keep himself,
and to keep those dependent upon him. The woman must be the
housewife, the helpmeet of the homemaker, the wise and fearless
mother of many healthy children. In one of Daudet's powerful and
melancholy books he speaks of "the fear of maternity, the haunting
terror of the young wife of the present day." When such words can
be truthfully written of a nation, that nation is rotten to the heart's
core. When men fear work or fear righteous war, when women fear
motherhood, they tremble on the brink of doom; and well it is that
they should vanish from the earth, where they are fit subjects for
the scorn of all men and women who are themselves strong and
brave and high-minded.

As it is with the individual, so it is with the nation. It is a base
untruth to say that happy is the nation that has no history. Thrice
happy is the nation that has a glorious history. Far better it is to dare
mighty things, to win glorious triumphs, even though checkered

by failure, than to take rank with those poor spirits who neither enjoy much nor suffer much, because they live in the gray twilight that knows not victory nor defeat. If in 1861 the men who loved the Union had believed that peace was the end of all things, and war and strife the worst of all things, and had acted up to their belief, we would have saved hundreds of thousands of lives, we would have saved hundreds of millions of dollars. Moreover, besides saving all the blood and treasure we then lavished, we would have prevented the heartbreak of many women, the dissolution of many homes, and we would have spared the country those months of gloom and shame when it seemed as if our armies marched only to defeat. We could have avoided all this suffering simply by shrinking from strife. And if we had thus avoided it, we would have shown that we were weaklings, and that we were unfit to stand among the great nations of the earth. Thank God for the iron in the blood of our fathers, the men who upheld the wisdom of Lincoln, and bore sword or rifle in the armies of Grant! Let us, the children of the men who proved themselves equal to the mighty days, let us, the children of the men who carried the great Civil War to a triumphant conclusion, praise the God of our fathers that the ignoble counsels of peace were rejected; that the suffering and loss, the blackness of sorrow and despair, were unflinchingly faced, and the years of strife endured; for in the end the slave was freed, the Union restored, and the mighty American republic placed once more as a helmeted queen among nations.

We of this generation do not have to face a task such as that our fathers faced, but we have our tasks, and woe to us if we fail to perform them! We cannot, if we would, play the part of China, and be content to rot by inches in ignoble ease within our borders, taking no interest in what goes on beyond them, sunk in a scrambling commercialism; heedless of the higher life, the life of aspiration, of toil and risk, busying ourselves only with the wants of our bodies for the day, until suddenly we should find, beyond a shadow of question, what China has already found, that in this world the nation that has trained itself to a career of unwarlike and isolated ease is bound, in the end, to go down before other nations which have not lost the manly and adventurous qualities. If we are to be a really great people, we must strive in good faith to play a great part in the world. We cannot avoid meeting great issues. All that we can determine for ourselves is whether we shall meet them well or ill. In

1898 we could not help being brought face to face with the problem of war with Spain. All we could decide was whether we should shrink like cowards from the contest, or enter into it as beseemed a brave and high-spirited people; and, once in, whether failure or success should crown our banners. So it is now. We cannot avoid the responsibilities that confront us in Hawaii, Cuba, Porto Rico, and the Philippines. All we can decide is whether we shall meet them in a way that will redound to the national credit, or whether we shall make of our dealings with these new problems a dark and shameful page in our history. To refuse to deal with them at all merely amounts to dealing with them badly. We have a given problem to solve. If we undertake the solution, there is, of course, always danger that we may not solve it aright; but to refuse to undertake the solution simply renders it certain that we cannot possibly solve it aright. The timid man, the lazy man, the man who distrusts his country, the over-civilized man, who has lost the great fighting, masterful virtues, the ignorant man, and the man of dull mind, whose soul is incapable of feeling the mighty lift that thrills "stern men with empires in their brains"—all these, of course, shrink from seeing the nation undertake its new duties; shrink from seeing us build a navy and an army adequate to our needs; shrink from seeing us do our share of the world's work, by bringing order out of chaos in the great, fair tropic islands from which the valor of our soldiers and sailors has driven the Spanish flag. These are the men who fear the strenuous life, who fear the only national life which is really worth leading. They believe in that cloistered life which saps the hardy virtues in a nation, as it saps them in the individual; or else they are wedded to that base spirit of gain and greed which recognizes in commercialism the be-all and end-all of national life, instead of realizing that, though an indispensable element, it is, after all, but one of the many elements that go to make up true national greatness. No country can long endure if its foundations are not laid deep in the material prosperity which comes from thrift, from business energy and enterprise, from hard, unsparing effort in the fields of industrial activity; but neither was any nation ever yet truly great if it relied upon material prosperity alone. All honor must be paid to the architects of our material prosperity, to the great captains of industry who have built our factories and our railroads, to the strong men who toil for wealth with brain or hand; for great is the debt of the nation to these and their kind. But our debt is yet greater to the men whose highest type is to be found in a statesman like Lincoln, a soldier like Grant. They showed by their lives that they recognized the law of work, the law of strife; they toiled to win a competence for themselves and those dependent upon them; but they recognized that there were yet other and even loftier duties—duties to the nation and duties to the race.

We cannot sit huddled within our own borders and avow ourselves merely an assemblage of well-to-do hucksters who care nothing for what happens beyond. Such a policy would defeat even its own end; for as the nations grow to have ever wider and wider interests, and are brought into closer and closer contact, if we are to hold our own in the struggle for naval and commercial supremacy, we must build up our power without our own borders. We must build the isthmian canal, and we must grasp the points of vantage which will enable us to have our say in deciding the destiny of the oceans of the East and the West.

So much for the commercial side. From the standpoint of international honor the argument is even stronger. The guns that thundered off Manila and Santiago left us echoes of glory, but they also left us a legacy of duty. If we drove out a medieval tyranny only to make room for savage anarchy, we had better not have begun the task at all. It is worse than idle to say that we have no duty to perform, and can leave to their fates the islands we have conquered. Such a course would be the course of infamy. It would be followed at once by utter chaos in the wretched islands themselves. Some stronger, manlier power would have to step in and do the work, and we would have shown ourselves weaklings, unable to carry to successful completion the labors that great and high-spirited nations are eager to undertake. . . .

In the West Indies and the Philippines alike we are confronted by most difficult problems. It is cowardly to shrink from solving them in the proper way; for solved they must be, if not by us, then by some stronger and more manful race. If we are too weak, too selfish, or too foolish to solve them, some bolder and abler people must undertake the solution. Personally, I am far too firm a believer in the greatness of my country and the power of my countrymen to admit for one moment that we shall ever be driven to the ignoble alternative.

The problems are different for the different islands. Porto Rico is not large enough to stand alone. We must govern it wisely and well, primarily in the interest of its own people. Cuba is, in my judgment, entitled ultimately to settle for itself whether it shall be an independent state or an integral portion of the mightiest of republics. But until order and stable liberty are secured, we must remain in the island to insure them, and infinite tact, judgment, moderation, and courage must be shown by our military and civil representatives in keeping the island pacified, in relentlessly stamping out brigandage, in protecting all alike, and yet in showing proper recognition to the men who have fought for Cuban liberty. The Philippines offer a yet graver problem. Their population includes half-caste and native Christians, warlike Moslems, and wild pagans. Many of their people are utterly unfit for self-government, and show no signs of becoming fit. Others may in time become fit but at present can only take part in self-government under a wise supervision, at once firm and beneficent. We have driven Spanish tyranny from the islands. If we now let it be replaced by savage anarchy, our work has been for harm and not for good. I have scant patience with those who fear to undertake the task of governing the Philippines, and who openly avow that they do fear to undertake it, or that they shrink from it because of the expense and trouble; but I have even scanter patience with those who make a pretense of humanitarianism to hide and cover their timidity, and who cant about "liberty" and the "consent of the governed," in order to excuse themselves for their unwillingness to play the part of men. Their doctrines, if carried out, would make it incumbent upon us to leave the Apaches of Arizona to work out their own salvation, and to decline to interfere in a single Indian reservation. Their doctrines condemn your forefathers and mine for ever having settled in these United States.

England's rule in India and Egypt has been of great benefit to England, for it has trained up generations of men accustomed to look at the larger and loftier side of public life. It has been of even greater benefit to India and Egypt. And finally, and most of all, it has advanced the cause of civilization. So, if we do our duty aright in the Philippines, we will add to that national renown which is the highest and finest part of national life, will greatly benefit the people of the Philippine Islands, and, above all, we will play our part well in the great work of uplifting mankind. But to do this work, keep ever in mind that we must show in a very high degree the qualities of courage, of honesty, and of good judgment. Resistance must be stamped out. The first and all-important work to be done is to establish the supremacy of our flag. We must put down armed resistance before we can accomplish anything else, and there should be no parleying, no faltering, in dealing with our foe. As for those in our own country who encourage the foe, we can afford contemptuously to disregard them; but it must be remembered that their utterances are not saved from being treasonable merely by the fact that they are despicable.

When once we have put down armed resistance, when once our rule is acknowledged, then an even more difficult task will begin, for then we must see to it that the islands are administered with absolute honesty and with good judgment. If we let the public service of the islands be turned into the prey of the spoils politician, we shall have begun to tread the path which Spain trod to her own destruction. We must send out there only good and able men, chosen for their fitness, and not because of their partisan service, and these men must not only administer impartial justice to the natives and serve their own government with honesty and fidelity, but must show the utmost tact and firmness, remembering that, with such people as those with whom we are to deal, weakness is the greatest of crimes, and that next to weakness comes lack of consideration for their principles and prejudices.

I preach to you, then, my countrymen, that our country calls not for the life of ease but for the life of strenuous endeavor. The twentieth century looms before us big with the fate of many nations. If we stand idly by, if we seek merely swollen, slothful ease and ignoble peace, if we shrink from the hard contests where men must win at hazard of their lives and at the risk of all they hold dear, then the bolder and stronger peoples will pass us by, and will win for themselves the domination of the world. Let us therefore boldly face the life of strife, resolute to do our duty well and manfully; resolute to uphold righteousness by deed and by word; resolute to be both honest and brave, to serve high ideals, yet to use practical methods. Above all, let us shrink from no strife, moral or physical, within or without the nation, provided we are certain that the strife is justified, for it is only through strife, through hard and dangerous endeavor, that we shall ultimately win the goal of true national greatness.

28. IMPERIALISM: THE HIGHEST STAGE OF CAPITALISM* / V. I. LENIN

Under the old capitalism, when free competition prevailed, the export of *goods* was the most typical feature. Under modern capitalism, when monopolies prevail, the export of *capital* has become the typical feature.

Capitalism is commodity production at the highest stage of development, when labour power itself becomes a commodity. The growth of internal exchange, and particularly of international exchange, is the characteristic distinguishing feature of capitalism. The uneven and spasmodic character of the development of individual enterprises, of individual branches of industry and individual countries, is inevitable under the capitalist system. England became a capitalist country before any other, and in the middle of the nineteenth century, having adopted free trade, claimed to be the "workshop of the world," the great purveyor of manufactured goods to all countries, which in exchange were to keep her supplied with raw materials. But in the last quarter of the nineteenth century, *this* monopoly was already undermined. Other countries, protecting themselves by tariff walls, had developed into independent capitalist states. On the threshold of the twentieth century, we see a new type of monopoly coming into existence. Firstly, there are monopolist capitalist combines in all advanced capitalist countries; secondly, a few rich countries, in which the accumulation of capital reaches gigantic proportions, occupy a monopolist position. An enormous "superabundance of capital" has accumulated in the advanced countries.

It goes without saying that if capitalism could develop agriculture, which today lags far behind industry everywhere, if it could raise the standard of living of the masses, who are everywhere still poverty-stricken and underfed, in spite of the amazing advance in technical knowledge, there could be no talk of a superabundance of capital. This "argument" the petty-bourgeois critics of capitalism advance on every occasion. But if capitalism did these things it

* V. I. Lenin, *Imperialism: The Highest Stage of Capitalism* (New York: International Publishers, 1939), Chap. 4, 7, 10. By permission of International Publishers Co., Inc.

would not be capitalism; for uneven development and wretched conditions of the masses are fundamental and inevitable conditions and premises of this mode of production. As long as capitalism remains what it is, surplus capital will never be utilised for the purpose of raising the standard of living of the masses in a given country, for this would mean a decline in profits for the capitalists; it will be used for the purpose of increasing those profits by exporting capital abroad to the backward countries. In these backward countries profits are usually high, for capital is scarce, the price of land is relatively low, wages are low, raw materials are cheap. The possibility of exporting capital is created by the fact that numerous backward countries have been drawn into international capitalist intercourse; main railways have either been built or are being built there; the elementary conditions for industrial development have been created, etc. The necessity for exporting capital arises from the fact that in a few countries capitalism has become "over-ripe" and (owing to the backward state of agriculture and the impoverished state of the masses) capital cannot find "profitable" investment. . . .

We must now try to sum up and put together what has been said above on the subject of imperialism. Imperialism emerged as the development and direct continuation of the fundamental attributes of capitalism in general. But capitalism only became capitalist imperialism at a definite and very high stage of its development, when certain of its fundamental attributes began to be transformed into their opposites, when the features of a period of transition from capitalism to a higher social and economic system began to take shape and reveal themselves all along the line. Economically, the main thing in this process is the substitution of capitalist monopolies for capitalist free competition. Free competition is the fundamental attribute of capitalism, and of commodity production generally. Monopoly is exactly the opposite of free competition; but we have seen the latter being transformed into monopoly before our very eyes, creating large-scale industry and eliminating small industry, replacing large-scale industry by still larger-scale industry, finally leading to such a concentration of production and capital that monopoly has been and is the result: cartels, syndicates and trusts, and merging with them, the capital of a dozen or so banks manipulating thousands of millions. At the same time monopoly, which has grown out of free competition, does not abolish the latter, but exists over it and alongside of it, and thereby gives rise to a number of very acute, intense antagonisms, friction and conflicts. Monopoly is the transition from capitalism to a higher system.

If it were necessary to give the briefest possible definition of imperialism we should have to say that imperialism is the monopoly stage of capitalism. Such a definition would include what is most important, for, on the one hand, finance capital is the bank capital of a few big monopolist banks, merged with the capital of the monopolist combines of manufacturers; and, on the other hand, the division of the world is the transition from a colonial policy which has extended without hindrance to territories unoccupied by any capitalist power, to a colonial policy of monopolistic possession of the territory of the world which has been completely divided up.

But very brief definitions, although convenient, for they sum up the main points, are nevertheless inadequate, because very important features of the phenomenon that has to be defined have to be especially deduced. And so, without forgetting the conditional and relative value of all definitions, which can never include all the concatenations of a phenomenon in its complete development, we must give a definition of imperialism that will embrace the following five essential features:

1) The concentration of production and capital developed to such a high stage that it created monopolies which play a decisive role in economic life.

2) The merging of bank capital with industrial capital, and the creation, on the basis of this "finance capital," of a "financial oligarchy."

3) The export of capital, which has become extremely important, as distinguished from the export of commodities.

4) The formation of international capitalist monopolies which share the world among themselves.

5) The territorial division of the whole world among the greatest capitalist powers is completed.

Imperialism is capitalism in that stage of development in which the dominance of monopolies and finance capital has established itself; in which the export of capital has acquired pronounced importance; in which the division of the world among the international trusts has begun; in which the division of all territories of the globe among the great capitalist powers has been completed.

. . . We have seen that the economic quintessence of imperialism is monopoly capitalism. This very fact determines its place in history, for monopoly that grew up on the basis of free competition, and precisely out of free competition, is the transition from the capitalist system to a higher social-economic order. We must take special note of the four principal forms of monopoly, or the four principal manifestations of monopoly capitalism, which are characteristic of the epoch under review.

Firstly, monopoly arose out of the concentration of production at a very advanced stage of development. This refers to the monopolist capitalist combines, cartels, syndicates and trusts. We have seen the important part that these play in modern economic life. At the beginning of the twentieth century, monopolies acquired complete supremacy in the advanced countries. And although the first steps towards the formation of the cartels were first taken by countries enjoying the protection of high tariffs (Germany, America), Great Britain, with her system of free trade, was not far behind in revealing the same basic phenomenon, namely, the birth of monopoly out of the concentration of production.

Secondly, monopolies have accelerated the capture of the most important sources of raw materials, especially for the coal and iron industries, which are the basic and most highly cartelised industries in capitalist society. The monopoly of the most important sources of raw materials has enormously increased the power of big capital, and has sharpened the antagonism between cartelised and non-cartelised industry.

Thirdly, monopoly has sprung from the banks. The banks have developed from modest intermediary enterprises into the monopolists of finance capital. Some three or five of the biggest banks in each of the foremost capitalist countries have achieved the "personal union" of industrial and bank capital, and have concentrated in their hands the disposal of thousands upon thousands of millions which form the greater part of the capital and income of entire countries. A financial oligarchy, which throws a close net of relations of dependence over all the economic and political institutions of contemporary bourgeois society without exception—such is the most striking manifestation of this monopoly.

Fourthly, monopoly has grown out of colonial policy. To the numerous "old" motives of colonial policy, finance capital has added the struggle for the sources of raw materials, for the export of capital, for "spheres of influence," *i.e.*, for spheres for profitable deals, concessions, monopolist profits and so on; in fine, for economic territory in general. When the colonies of the European powers in Africa, for instance, comprised only one-tenth of that territory (as was the case in 1876), colonial policy was able to develop by methods other than those of monopoly—by the "free grabbing" of territories, so to speak. But when nine-tenths of Africa had been seized (approximately by 1900), when the whole world had been divided up, there was inevitably ushered in a period of colonial monopoly and, consequently, a period of particularly intense struggle for the division and the redivision of the world.

The extent to which monopolist capital has intensified all the contradictions of capitalism is generally known. It is sufficient to mention the high cost of living and the oppression of the cartels. This intensification of contradictions constitutes the most powerful driving force of the transitional period of history, which began from the time of the definite victory of world finance capital.

Monopolies, oligarchy, the striving for domination instead of the striving for liberty, the exploitation of an increasing number of small or weak nations by an extremely small group of the richest or most powerful nations—all these have given birth to those distinctive characteristics of imperialism which compel us to define it as parasitic or decaying capitalism. More and more prominently there emerges, as one of the tendencies of imperialism, the creation of the "bondholding" (rentier) state, the usurer state, in which the bourgeoisie lives on the proceeds of capital exports and by "clipping coupons." It would be a mistake to believe that this tendency to decay precludes the possibility of the rapid growth of capitalism. It does not. In the epoch of imperialism, certain branches of industry, certain strata of the bourgeoisie and certain countries betray, to a more or less degree, one or other of these tendencies. On the whole, capitalism is growing far more rapidly than before. But this growth is not only becoming more and more uneven in general; its unevenness also manifests itself, in particular, in the decay of the countries which are richest in capital (such as England). . . .

From all that has been said in this book on the economic nature of imperialism, it follows that we must define it as capitalism in transition, or, more precisely, as moribund capitalism. It is very instructive in this respect to note that the bourgeois economists, in describing modern capitalism, frequently employ terms like "interlocking," "absence of isolation," etc.; "in conformity with their functions and course of development," banks are "not purely private business enterprises; they are more and more outgrowing the sphere of purely private business regulation." And this very Riesser, who uttered the words just quoted, declares with all seriousness that the "prophecy" of the Marxists concerning "socialisation" has "not come true"!

What then does this word "interlocking" express? It merely expresses the most striking feature of the process going on before our eyes. It shows that the observer counts the separate trees, but cannot see the wood. It slavishly copies the superficial, the fortuitous, the chaotic. It reveals the observer as one who is overwhelmed by the mass of raw material and is utterly incapable of appreciating its meaning and importance. Ownership of shares and relations between owners of private property "interlock in a haphazard way." But the underlying factor of this interlocking, its very base, is the changing social relations of production. When a big enterprise assumes gigantic proportions, and, on the basis of exact computation of mass data, organises according to plan the supply of primary raw materials to the extent of two-thirds, or three-fourths of all that is necessary for tens of millions of people; when the raw materials are transported to the most suitable place of production, sometimes hundreds or thousands of miles away, in a systematic and organised manner; when a single centre directs all the successive stages of work right up to the manufacture of numerous varieties of finished articles; when these products are distributed according to a single plan among tens and hundreds of millions of consumers (as in the case of the distribution of oil in America and Germany by the American "oil trust")—then it becomes evident that we have socialisation of production, and not mere "interlocking"; that private economic relations and private property relations constitute a shell which is no longer suitable for its contents, a shell which must inevitably begin to decay if its destruction be delayed by artificial means; a shell which may continue in a state of decay for a fairly long period (particularly if the cure of the opportunist abscess is protracted), but which will inevitably be removed. . . .

29. *FAREWELL TO EMPIRE* */ WILLIAM L. LANGER*

Now that the liquidation of Europe's overseas empires is all but complete, the world is in travail, beset by problems of readjustment and groping for new relationships that may make possible the peace-

*William L. Langer, "Farewell to Empire," *Foreign Affairs*, Vol. 41, No. 1 (October 1962), pp. 115–30. Copyright by the Council on Foreign Relations, Inc., New York. Reprinted by permission.

ful and prosperous coexistence of more than a hundred states of widely differing characters and needs. The age-old expansion of Europe in terms of military power, settlement, trade, proselytism, territorial rule and, finally, social dominance has come to an abrupt end. Thoughtful people, particularly in the Western world, are bound to reflect on this epochal upheaval, and to realize that one of the very great revolutions in human affairs has taken place. They must be impressed, not to say awed, by the thought that the political and social structure of our planet has undergone such fundamental alterations at the very time when science and technology are opening to view the vast possibilities as well as the dangers of the space age.

Historians and political scientists have for some time been grappling with the problems of expansion, without, however, having come to anything like generally accepted conclusions. Political controversy has seriously beclouded the meaning of the terms *imperialism* and *colonialism,* while scholarly analysis has revealed ever more clearly how loose and unmanageable these words and concepts really are. I take it that, in its broadest sense, imperialism means domination or control of one nation or people over another, recognizing that there may be many forms and degrees of control. But there is probably no hope of ever constructing a generalized theory of imperialism. Indeed, the most violent differences of opinion persist with regard to the causes and character even of modern European expansion, with little if any prospect of reconciling the Communist doctrine, so positively formulated by Lenin, with the manifold theories advanced by Western "bourgeois" writers.

However, among non-Communist critics and students substantial progress is being made in the evaluation of European imperialism. The initial phase of expansion, consequent to the great discoveries of the fifteenth and sixteenth centuries, involved large-scale settlement of Europeans in sparsely populated areas of the world. This in turn led to the gradual conquest of vast territories, along with complete subjection and at least partial extermination of the natives. But this earlier stage of imperialism, while it certainly remade much of the globe in the European image, had relatively little bearing on recent and contemporary problems of expansion. For in the late eighteenth and early nineteenth centuries most of the American colonies of Britain, Spain and Portugal attained their complete independence of European rule. In the sequel Canada,

Australia, New Zealand and eventually South Africa became British dominions, independent of the mother country in all but name. Meanwhile Siberia, which was overrun and partially settled by Russians in the seventeenth century, became an integral part of the contiguous Tsarist state.

This process of settlement and territorial extension occasionally brought in its train the destruction of highly developed cultures like those of the Inca, Maya and Javanese. But in general it touched only primitive, thinly populated regions, which previously had been outside the main stream of history. Such was the case also with the trading posts and military establishments acquired in the East by the Portuguese, Dutch, British and French in the seventeenth and eighteenth centuries. Only with the military victories of the British over local potentates and the repeated extension of their territorial domination in India did modern imperialism, in the sense of the rule or control of one state or nation over an alien people or culture, become a reality. Even so, India remained a rather special case, an almost unique instance of a private company over a long period of time ruling a huge area of highly developed cultures and constantly expanding its territorial control even at times when the home government was opposed to any extension of its responsibilities. For the European powers had, by the early nineteenth century, become highly skeptical about overseas commitments. It is true that both the British and the French made substantial territorial acquisitions in these years, but they resulted largely from the efforts of local officials to safeguard existing establishments and further trade. Only in Russia, where the government engaged in systematic encroachment and eventually in the conquest of the Transcaucasian principalities, was there anything like purposeful expansionism, though on this side of the Atlantic the war against Mexico was certainly a comparable demonstration of imperial acquisitiveness.

Imperialism revived only in the period after 1870 when, however, it developed to such a degree that most of Africa was quickly partitioned among a few European powers and some form of domination or control was established over many Asian peoples. Concurrently Russia, operating against adjoining countries, imposed its rule upon most of Central Asia and, having earlier acquired the Maritime Province on the Pacific, inaugurated a policy of peaceful penetration of Manchuria and Korea.

To account for this phenomenal spread of European authority is certainly a fascinating and challenging assignment for the historian. Innumerable theories, both general and special, have been advanced in the search for an adequate explanation. They run the gamut from the hard-hitting, straightforward propaganda of Lenin's "Imperialism, the Highest Stage of Capitalism" to the highly sophisticated and daringly original speculation of Schumpeter's "Sociology of Imperialism." But the one conclusion to be safely drawn from all this ratiocination is that modern imperialism constituted a most complicated episode of recent history, that it was the expression of many and varied forces and motives, and that the economic explanation, so cogently argued by Hobson in his "Imperialism: A Study" (1902), and so fondly cherished by Lenin, is as inadequate as it is popular. Humanitarian, religious and psychological factors were clearly important, to say nothing of considerations of national power and pride. It should never be forgotten that the present condemnation and rejection of imperialism by the Western world is a very recent development. Prior to 1920, if not even later, European rule of overseas colonies was considered honorable and altruistic—definitely in the best interest of the "backward" peoples. It has been pointed out with complete justice that the campaign against the slave trade and the effort to propagate Christianity were among the prime motive forces behind modern expansion, and that the imperial powers as well as their agents were moved, with some exceptions, by a desire to play a beneficent role in the world, to fulfill a noble, national mission.

Recent monographic studies of various aspects of modern imperialism suggest also that certain elusive, not to say irrational, forces contributed to the dynamism of expansion. Schumpeter, and indeed both Kautsky and Hobson before him, gave emphasis to the atavistic feature of imperialism. That is to say, they saw it as a survival in modern society of an outworn, feudal-militaristic mentality, devoted to conquest for its own sake, without specific objective or limit. One might underline also the importance of basic human traits such as aggressiveness and acquisitiveness, along with the urge to dominate, as fundamental to any analysis of imperialism. To do so would leave open, however, many instances in which powerful states with dynamic populations showed no inclination to express these drives in terms of expansion and domination. The American people's rejection of imperialism almost as soon as it was tried, in the wake of the war with Spain, would be a case in point.

Yet it does seem that there was something feudal or at least aristocratic about imperialism, even in its modern phase. It was, in fact, frequently criticized on this score. Colonies, it was said, were desired by the ruling classes in order to provide for their "clamorous and needy dependents." They were, according to James Mill, "a vast system of outdoor relief for the upper classes," and, in the words of Richard Cobden, a "costly appendage of an aristocratic government."[1] And much later, in 1903, Henry Labouchere referred to imperialists as magpies: "They steal for the love of stealing." Certainly the men who made the decisions for expansion were, in England, peers and great landowners, and on the Continent aristocrats, notables and soldiers. Bismarck, than whom no statesman of modern times had a keener sense of the requirements of power politics, reckoned at all times with the dynamism of the traditional military castes. He encouraged Russian expansion in Central Asia on the theory that it was better to have the military engaged there than on the European front. In the same spirit he attempted to divert the attention of the French from the blue line of the Vosges by supporting their activities in North Africa. And a particularly clear demonstration of the operation of feudal-military forces is provided by the history of modern Japan. The Genyosha Society, which was the driving power behind Japan's expansion, represented primarily the samurai elements which had been eclipsed by the Restoration.[2]

It may be argued that the above theory is at least in part invalidated by the fact that imperialism enjoyed great popular acclaim. But actually this proves very little, for it was more true of England than of other countries, and in England, it will be conceded, the lower classes were traditionally interested in the doings of the aristocracy and readily applauded its achievements. Actually the common man, in England as elsewhere, knew little of the issues and policies involved in imperialism. Colonial affairs, like foreign affairs, remained the preserve of the ruling class. As for continental countries, it is perfectly clear that popular interest in and support for colonial enterprise were never widespread or sustained. Explorers, missionaries, publicists, professors and certain business interests were the prime movers in the cause of overseas undertakings.

With further reference to the economic interpretation of imperialism, I would say that recent studies of specific cases reinforce the proposition that business interests were much less important

[1] Klaus Knorr, "British Colonial Theories, 1570–1850." Toronto: University of Toronto Press, 1944, p. 356 ff.
[2] E. H. Norman, "The Genyosha: A Study in the Origins of Japanese Imperialism," *Pacific Affairs*, XVII, 1944, p. 261–284.

than considerations of national power and prestige, to say nothing of national security. A new analysis of the partition of Africa[3] contends convincingly that Britain, concerned by the disturbance of the European balance of power by the German victories of 1870–1871, was driven primarily by concern for its communications with India to assume control of Egypt, and that this move in turn had such repercussions on international relations as to precipitate the "scramble for Africa." It certainly becomes increasingly clear that much of modern imperialism reflected problems of power in Europe itself during a period when the alliance systems had produced a temporary deadlock.

The competition for markets and for sources of raw materials as well as the search for new fields for capital investment were much talked of in the heyday of imperialism and underlay the argumentation of a host of writers on economic imperialism. But it is well known now that in actual fact the colonies played a distinctly subordinate role in the foreign economic activities of the major imperial powers. These powers at all times remained each others' best customers. At the height of the colonial age, in the early twentieth century, less than a third of Britain's exports went to the dominions and colonies, and less than one-half of British foreign investment was in the Empire. The major European investments in this period were in the United States, Russia, the Ottoman Empire and Latin America, where there could hardly be any question of true imperial domination.

If in fact the European governments in the 1880s and 1890s plunged headlong into the scramble for colonies, they were evidently acting in panic. Confronted with the entirely novel problems arising from progressive industrialization, and alarmed by the depression that set in in 1873, as well as by the strong tendency on the Continent to abandon free trade in favor of protection, they sought to safeguard their overseas economic interests by acquiring actual control of as much territory as possible. They hoped thereby to ensure themselves against unknown eventualities. Failure to act seemed improvident and dangerous. I would call this "preclusive imperialism," and would describe it as obviously a concomitant of the onrushing industrial revolution. A misguided effort, this reaction to hypothetical dangers, as we can now recognize; but in the late

[3] Ronald Robinson and John Gallagher, "Africa and the Victorians." New York: St. Martin's, 1961.

nineteenth century it evidently was so compelling that most statesmen, even the skeptical Bismarck, were carried away by it.

III

The final accounting suggests that the colonies brought their
masters but indifferent returns. It has been frequently argued that
even though the European governments may have spent more on
their overseas possessions—especially in terms of defense, police,
administration and public health—than they ever received in return,
private interests made huge profits through the ruthless exploitation
of native labor and natural resources. Bookkeeping in these matters
is extremely difficult, because it is impossible to isolate and allocate
specific items of expense. The best recent studies indicate that the
governments, and so the home countries, did in fact make large and
continuing outlays, in many ways anticipating more recent policies
of aid to underdeveloped nations. An admirable analysis of the
finances of the Congo[4] arrives at the conclusion that that colony,
unusually rich in raw materials such as ivory, rubber and copper,
was indeed a source of considerable enrichment for Belgium as a
country, but that between 1908 (when the Belgian government took
over the colony from King Leopold II) and 1950 the Brussels
government spent 260 million gold francs on the Congo in return
for only 25 million francs in taxes and other income. In like manner
an eminent French authority[5] has estimated that even in the period
prior to 1914 the Paris government spent two billion gold francs on
the French colonial empire.

In the large, the profits taken by private interests seem to have
been anything but exorbitant—indeed, little above the average
returns of home investments. Of course there were instances of
huge profits made through forced labor and other forms of ruthless
exploitation, as in the Congo of King Leopold, in German South-
west Africa and in British South Africa. No one would excuse or
condone such practices, but again it is important to retain a proper
sense of proportion. The mercantilist idea that colonies existed
solely for the purpose of enriching the mother country persisted for

[4] Jean Stengers, "Combien le Congo a-t-il coûté à la Belgique?" Brussels:
Académie royale des sciences coloniales, 1957.

[5] Henri Brunschwig, "Mythes et réalités de l'impérialisme colonial français."
Paris: A. Colin, 1960.

a long time. Leopold II of Belgium, for example, was an ardent admirer of the Dutch "culture system" as enforced in the East Indies, and was interested in the Congo exclusively for the revenue it might bring. As for the treatment of the natives, it may be doubted whether it was any worse than that meted out to Russian serfs and American Negro slaves until past the middle of the nineteenth century. Sad though it may be, the fact is that the human race became sensitive to suffering only at a very late date. When one considers the heartless attitude taken toward the miseries of the early factory workers or even toward the Irish peasantry in the days before the great famine, one is bound to marvel at the callousness of human nature, obviously not restricted to the brutalities of Hitler's Nazi régime.

Students of the problem have of late devoted much attention to the advantages which accrued to the colonies from European rule. They included defense and public order, suppression of tribal warfare and restriction of patriarchal tyranny, the establishment of adequate administration and justice, the furtherance of public health and, in many cases, substantial contributions to the development of communications.

No doubt the price paid by the colonies was a high one: the subversion of traditional institutions and social forms, not necessarily intentionally, but none the less effectively. To some Europeans as well as to many natives this has been a matter of real regret. But if in fact European expansion was the ineluctable expression of a dynamism generated by the economic and social revolution of the nineteenth century, then it follows that the progressive destruction of static, traditional societies was inevitable under the impact of outside forces. Thinkers and statesmen of the Ottoman Empire, of Japan and of China recognized this feature of the situation at an early date. They saw that the only hope of survival lay in the adoption of Western technology and institutions, however distasteful they might be. The remaking of the world in the Western image began long before the tide of imperialism came to the flood.

IV

The South African War (1899–1902) not only drained imperialism of much of its emotional content but also induced the British and other imperial governments to reconsider their relations to the colonies. Far more thought was given to the welfare of the colonial peoples, and far more effort was made in the direction of development and improvement. The more liberal régimes encouraged the education of the natives and their participation at the lower levels of the administration. Thereby they fostered the growth of the native élite, members of which presently began to apply the lessons learned from the West to the task of getting rid of Western control. The imperial powers, having themselves inculcated the ideas of equality, self-determination, independence and nationalism, thereby prepared the way for the destruction of their own dominion. For it would hardly seem possible, in historical retrospect, that Western rule could have long withstood the weight of the arguments drawn from its own intellectual armory. Imperialism was bound to lose its moral basis as soon as the principle of equality was recognized and the notions of responsibility and trusteeship were generally accepted. The reaction of British liberals, radicals and socialists to the war in South Africa was in itself irrefutable proof of the incompatibility of democracy and imperialism. Without doubt the anti-colonialist movement that developed in Europe and in the United States following the war with Spain contributed heavily to the growth of nationalism in various colonies during the early twentieth century. So also did the defeat of the Russians by Japan in 1904–1905, for that defeat broke the spell of European superiority and invincibility.

The First World War then set the stage for the actual breakdown of imperialism. The fratricidal conflict within the European master race deflated whatever prestige the ruling nations may still have had, while the employment of hundreds of thousands of colonial troops and laborers in the great war opened the eyes of multitudes of natives to conditions in the more advanced countries of the world. It is generally recognized that in 1919, while the victorious powers were busily applying the principle of self-determination to European peoples and as consistently ignoring it as regards the colonial peoples, imperialism had already received the mortal blow. The subsequent inter-war period then witnessed the rapid development of nationalist movements in many additional areas, despite the drastic measures of repression employed by some of the imperial governments. It took only the Second World War, fought as it was in many of the most remote places of the world, to loose the impounded flood-waters of colonial nationalism. The European nations were now so weakened and discredited that they could no longer offer effective resistance. Those which, like France, attempted to hold their possessions found themselves involved in long and costly wars, ending invariably in colonial triumph. In less than 20 years, millions of subject peoples attained their independence and more than 50 new states appeared on the international scene.

V

Ever since its advent to power in Russia, the Soviet Government has proclaimed the right of self-determination and has given all possible encouragement and support to the national movements aimed at liberation of the European overseas colonies from imperial rule. Soviet propaganda has to a large extent succeeded in restricting the definition of "imperialism" and "colonialism" to these overseas territories and in fostering the idea that Russia, having no such colonies, has had no part in imperial domination. Actually, it is impossible to draw a valid distinction between the expansion of Russia and that of other European states. The conquest of Central Asia was basically equivalent to the extension of British power in India. It began with trade interests, followed by conquest and annexation for reasons for security and prestige. And at the end of the nineteenth century Russian penetration of Manchuria and Korea was an integral part of the European effort to "partition" the Celestial Empire. Eminent Russian historians like Kliuchevski and Miliukov were just as bitterly critical of Russian expansion as were the anti-colonialists of the West with reference to the overseas empires.

The Russian-Japanese War put an early end to Tsarist aspirations in China, while the First World War, by precipitating the revolution in Russia, brought on a premature struggle for independence or autonomy on the part of almost all the subject peoples of the old empire. In this extremity Lenin and Stalin proclaimed the most conciliatory policy, even going so far as to recognize the right of any people to cast off all ties to Russia. It soon turned out, however, that these moves were purely tactical. Self-determination was to be restricted to the "workers" of the subject nations, which were warned by Stalin that if they seceded, they would surely fall victim to world imperialism. It was inconceivable, he added, that these peoples should abandon the Soviet Union, which was so dependent on them for food and raw materials. They clearly had an important contribution to make to the victory of socialism. In order to forestall "treason" on their part, the Soviet Government proceeded to suppress liberation movements, by force if necessary, carrying on a protracted war against even the avowedly Communist leaders of the various Turkic peoples.

For geographical reasons it is much easier for Soviet Russia to hold adjacent peoples in subjection than it was for countries like Britain and France to maintain their hold on distant overseas possessions. For a time following Hitler's attack in 1941, Soviet rule was, nevertheless, again seriously jeopardized. In revenge, the Kremlin in its hour of victory meted out the most ferocious treatment to the disaffected peoples and furthermore set up on its western borders a system of satellites reminiscent of the client system through which the great Napoleon controlled so much of the Continent. Whether for ideological or for security reasons, the Soviet Government now exercises effective control over adjoining states all the way from Finland in the north to Bulgaria in the south. To safeguard that control it will, if necessary, resort to military force, as was demonstrated so clearly in the case of Hungary.

In short, the Soviet Government has taken advantage of its contiguity to hold in subjection not only the ancient states of Eastern Europe, but also Armenians, Georgians and other Caucasian peoples, as well as some millions of Turkic peoples in Central Asia. Under the old régime, spasmodic attempts were made at Russification and at forced conversion to orthodoxy. In Central Asia much of the best land was appropriated by the conquerors, while the natives were subjected to heavy taxation. On the other hand, the nomadic tribes were left largely to themselves and the well-developed khanates of Khiva and Bokhara enjoyed a large measure of autonomy. The Soviet Government, especially in Stalin's time, was much more repressive. The status of the subject nationalities as federated republics was altogether misleading, for all important political and economic posts were held by Russians or by carefully selected native Communists. Besides, the economic life of these puppet republics was regulated entirely by the needs of the Kremlin. For a time the Soviet Government carried on propaganda directed even at the language, religion and culture of the subject peoples.

In some respects this policy is still in effect. In any event, the subject nationalities have been deprived of all hope of freedom. Their leaders disappear before they can become dangerous. Unobtrusively, Russians are being settled among the native populations, so that by now some six or seven million Europeans are established in Central Asia. In Kazakhstan it has been reported that fully half of the population is now European. Furthermore, the Russian language is an obligatory subject in all schools and a Cyrillic-type alphabet has been introduced for the Turkic languages. While there is no concerted attack on non-Russian cultures, it has been made abundantly clear that the chances of success in life depend largely on identification with Russianism as well as with Communism.

In view of the realities of Russian imperialism, it is surprising that the Soviets have been so successful in their efforts at concealment and have managed so well to exploit the issue of "colonialism" to the detriment of the West. It is likely, however, that the effectiveness of their propaganda has already passed its peak. After all, the world cannot ignore the fact that the overseas empires have now been largely liquidated. Besides, the experience of some of the new states with Soviet guidance and aid has been disillusioning and disquieting. Already at the Bandung Conference (1955) there were round denunciations of Soviet imperialism, accompanied by pointed warnings against Communist designs on the freedom of colonial peoples.

It is unrealistic to suppose that either the European satellites or the subject nationalities of the Soviet Union can obtain their independence so long as the Soviet Government remains what it is and its objectives are unaltered. How long that may be is certainly a debatable question. The Soviet régime, having itself become outspokenly nationalistic and having systematically supported nationalist movements in the overseas colonies, can no longer condemn nationalism among its own subjects as a reactionary deviation. Furthermore, Soviet society is steadily evolving along lines familiar to us from Western history. It is at least not inconceivable that its transformation under the impact of industrialization may become accelerated and that, with the growth of representative institutions and the development of a more democratic mentality, there will come a change of attitude toward the imperialism that is now so basic to Russian policy. At the same time the economic evolution of the satellites and subject nationalities is speeding their westernization and strengthening forces which in the long run the Kremlin may find it difficult to hold in check.

The Soviet Government, with its prodigious military and economic power, can for the present certainly hold in subjection the adjacent nationalities of Europe and Asia. It may, indeed, succeed in exploiting the nationalist theme to the point of luring some of the newly liberated peoples into the Communist camp and thereby bending the anti-colonialist sentiment of the entire world to the purposes of the world revolution. But the subjection of weaker peoples by the stronger runs counter to the democratic sentiments characteristic of modern industrial societies. There may be serious lapses, such as the Nazi interlude in Germany. But the example of Western nations suggests that industrial populations are basically peace-loving and definitely averse to the subjugation and exploitation of other peoples. In the later nineteenth century the imperial aspirations of the French Government met their strongest obstacle in the opposition of democratic and socialist elements. It is most unlikely, therefore, that the Soviet Union, simply by denying its imperialism, will be able, in the long term, to shield itself from the forces inherent in modern society.

In this context, some reference to the forces of Chinese Communist expansion and indeed to the entire problem of world Communist domination is perhaps unavoidable. Communist China's imperialist aspirations permit of no doubt. They appear, however, to derive from traditional notions of universal or at least Asian empire as well as from more immediate considerations of national security or ideological zeal. The Chinese thus interpret their efforts to establish control over Korea, Taiwan and the countries of south-eastern Asia as a gathering-in of the *membra disjecta* of the millenary Celestial Empire, less as the conquest of new than the recovery of ancient domains.

As for the world revolution and the new world of Communism, it would seem that whatever validity this program might have would depend on its ideological content. If neither Napoleon nor Hitler could dominate Europe, it can hardly be supposed that Soviet leaders—on the whole a sober and realistic lot—imagine it possible for the U.S.S.R. to control the entire world. The developments of recent years must suggest to them the difficulties of managing even the present Communist domain. No doubt the Soviet Union would feel more secure in an all-Communist world, just as the United States would in a world made safe for democracy. But as the Soviet Union grows in strength this consideration is bound to lose some of its importance. It is quite possible, in fact, that Marxism, already so largely overtaken by events, may in time lose not only its revolutionary fervor but also its incentive to world domination.

VI

The end of European political domination in Africa and Asia does not alter the fact that the stamp of European ideas and institutions has now been put upon the whole world. Even the Soviet and Chinese Communists rely for their power upon Western technology and to a considerable extent upon the imitation of Western institutions. As for the newly liberated peoples, they have set themselves the same course. No doubt there are in all of them conservative and even reactionary elements which would like, if possible, to return to their traditional society. But in most countries the ruling group consists of men educated in Western schools and convinced that the future lies with the adoption of Western techniques. They have no intention whatever of reverting to pre-imperialist days. On the contrary, they want more and more of what imperialism brought them: great productivity and a higher standard of living through industrialization; social improvements of every kind, and especially more and better education as a basis for democracy.

Their problems are many, and by no means exclusively economic. The transformation of assorted tribes into modern nations is in itself a stupendous undertaking. Besides, these new states are for the most part too weak militarily as well as economically to stand on their own feet. Their political independence therefore does not by any means imply complete independence. Because of their almost unlimited need for economic and technical assistance they are certainly in some danger of falling again under the influence if not the control of powerful advanced nations, be they Western or Communist.

They can find some insurance against such threats in the antagonism between the free world and Communism, which enables their leaders to play off one side against the other. They are bound to derive some protection also from the strong anti-imperialism that has come to pervade the entire free world and will probably become ever more deeply enrooted. Indeed, the new underdeveloped states will be fortunate if Western disillusionment with empire does not reach the point where it will obstruct seriously the aid programs without which many of the former colonies cannot hope to survive. Happily some progress is being made in the coördination of the economic efforts of the free world through the Organization for

Economic Coöperation and Development. The Western world has so much greater an aid potential that it should be possible, with even a modicum of statesmanship, to maintain the connection of Europe and the United States with the erstwhile colonial world.

It is truly noteworthy that, for all the heat and rancor generated by anti-colonialism, so many liberated colonies have chosen to remain members of the British Commonwealth or the French Community. The enthusiastic reception accorded to Queen Elizabeth in India and Ghana provided occasions for the expression, on the part of their governments, of appreciation for the important contribution made by imperial rule. No doubt considerations of security have a significant bearing on the attitude of the former colonies, but it would seem that in the world at large the old—shall we say atavistic, aristocratic?—notion of domination and exploitation has given way to the concept of association and collaboration. Even in the Communist world it has become fashionable to speak of the "Socialist Commonwealth."

VII

In bidding farewell to empire we cannot and must not suppose that human nature has undergone a sudden, radical change—that basic aggressive urges will disappear completely and that sweetness and light will soon prevail. The argument of this essay has been that fundamental drives lay behind imperial expansion; that European dynamism, combined with technological superiority, enabled the European nations to settle the largely unoccupied continents and to found European communities all over the globe. It permitted them also, in the sequel, to impose their rule over many peoples of old and highly developed, as well as of primitive, cultures. So marked was Europe's material power and so alluring its political and economic institutions that within a comparatively short span of time the stamp of European civilization was put upon the whole earth.

Europe's political domination is gone. Its cultural influence remains, and there is no likelihood that it will be supplanted in the foreseeable future. The new states, while still vociferously denouncing "colonialism," may genuinely fear that cultural influence will eventually change to economic control and so to some new form of political domination. The Soviet Government is already accusing the Common Market of being a new device by which the Western powers will attempt to keep the colonial world in an economically subordinate and undeveloped state. In this connection the importance of the erstwhile colonial areas as sources of raw materials for the industrialized nations remains a prominent consideration. But imperialism provided no real solution for this problem, while for the future more, it would seem, is to be hoped from coöperation than from domination and exploitation.

It is highly unlikely that the modern world will revert to the imperialism of the past. History has shown that the nameless fears which in the late nineteenth century led to the most violent outburst of expansionism were largely unwarranted. The Scandinavian states and Germany since Versailles have demonstrated that economic prosperity and social well-being are not dependent on the exploitation of other peoples, while better distribution of wealth in the advanced countries has reduced if not obviated whatever need there may have been to seek abroad a safety-valve for the pressures building up at home. Even in the field of defense, the old need for overseas bases or for the control of adjacent territories is rapidly being outrun.

It is often said that human nature does not change, but it is none the less true that it does undergo changes of attitude. With reference to imperialism it is certainly true that there has been over the past century a marked alteration of mood, reflecting greater sensitivity to human suffering and a greater readiness to assume responsibility for the weak and helpless. In our day, anti-imperialism runs as strong in the West as did imperialism a couple of generations ago. Domination and exploitation of weaker peoples by the stronger, which seemed altogether natural in the past, is now felt to be incompatible with the principles of freedom, equality and self-determination so generally accepted in modern societies. Imperialism has been on its way out since the beginning of the century and particularly since the First World War. Writing on imperialism in this very journal in the days when Mussolini was embarking on the conquest of Ethiopia, I ventured to disparage his undertaking and to describe him as being behind the times. The world, I opined, had outgrown the mentality of imperialism. I could not, of course, foresee that the edifice of colonialism would collapse so suddenly and so completely after the Second World War, but I suggested that if the tide of native resistance continued to rise, the abandonment of the colonies would soon become inevitable. To make this forecast did not require any particular prescience, but only recognition of the forces at work in modern society. At the present day the Soviet Union may still pose as the doughty opponent of a system that is already done for, but by maintaining its own imperial sway it is appearing more and more in the role of champion of an outworn and discredited system.

Imperialism's one great achievement was to open up all parts of the world and to set all humanity on the high road to eventual association and collaboration. In the process much has been lost of cultural value, but much also has been gained in the suppression of abuses, in the alleviation of suffering, and above all in the raising of the standard of living. The seamy sides of industrial society are familiar to us all, but it should never be overlooked that the machine age for the first time in history provided the common man with more than the requirements of the barest subsistence. This in itself has given human life a new dimension. It was perhaps the greatest of Europe's contributions to the world. Without the imperialist interlude it is difficult to see how the static, secluded, backward peoples of the globe could possibly have come to share in it. So much at least seems certain: without the period of European rule none of these peoples or states, not even India, would today be embarked on the course leading to a better and richer life.

10
WAR

The classic definition of war is that of Carl von Clausewitz. It is most appropriate therefore that we begin this chapter with an excerpt from his principal work, *On War*. Von Clausewitz (1780–1831) wrote it during the 1820s, and it was published after his death. Although the book is nearly a century and a half old, his forceful observations on war and particularly on the relationship between war and politics are still very relevant today.

Since the Second World War, two kinds of warfare have become particularly important for international politics: nuclear war and guerrilla war. The second selection in this chapter, on guerrilla war, consists of excerpts from a long article by an outstanding practitioner of this kind of warfare: Mao Tse-tung, Chairman of the Chinese Communist Party. He wrote the article in

May 1938, during the early phase of the war of resistance against Japan.

The nature of nuclear warfare is discussed by Herman Kahn, the foremost contemporary expert on this subject. As the title of the book, from which the third selection is drawn, indicates, he attempts to show how one must think dispassionately about the "unthinkable," i.e., the unpleasant question of what nuclear war will be like. Kahn is also the author of *On Thermonuclear War* and co-author of *The Year 2000*.

The nature of total war in the nuclear era is also discussed by General Douglas MacArthur, who needs no introduction as a military expert. Partly because he is much more pessimistic about the consequences of nuclear war than Kahn, he reaches some provocative and unexpected conclusions about this subject. He delivered his speech at a civic banquet sponsored by the Los Angeles County Council of the American Legion on the dedication of a monument to General MacArthur on January 26, 1955.

30. *WHAT IS WAR?** / *CARL VON CLAUSEWITZ*

Definition

We do not want to give a ponderous and tedious definition of war, but concentrate on its basic element: the duel. War is nothing but an expanded duel. To conceive as a unit the countless number of separate duels of which a war consists, we should envisage two wrestlers. By means of physical force each attempts to bring his opponent completely under his control. His aim is to overpower his opponent and thus render him incapable of any further resistance.

War is, therefore, an act of violence to compel our opponent to do our will.

Violence arms itself with the inventions of art and science in order to contend against violence. The restrictions imposed by

* Carl von Clausewitz, *Vom Kriege* (Potsdam, 1832), Book I, Chap. 1, par. 2, 3, 11, 23, 24. Translated by Eva Tamm Lijphart and Arend Lijphart.

international law and custom are insignificant and hardly worth mentioning, and do not really weaken its power. Violence, that is to say, physical force (for there is no moral force apart from the conception of state and law), is therefore the *means;* the *end* is to impose our will on the enemy. In order to ensure the achievement of this goal, we must render the enemy defenseless. This is the real purpose of the war act. It takes the place of the final object, and to a certain extent pushes it aside as something not belonging to war itself.

Utmost Use of Violence

A humanitarian might easily imagine the existence of a skillful way of disarming or defeating the enemy without causing too many wounds, and that this is the proper function of the art of warfare. No matter how good this may appear, it is an error and must be extirpated. Because war is such a dangerous enterprise, the mistakes arising from kindness and compassion are exactly the worst. Because the utmost use of physical force in no way excludes the cooperation of the intelligence, it follows that he who uses this force ruthlessly and without regard to the bloodshed involved must gain the upper hand if his opponent does not do the same. Thereby the former forces the latter's hand, and they push each other to extremes only limited by each side's counter-acting power.

That is how one must look at the matter, and it is to no avail and completely wrong to disregard its real nature because of one's aversion to its horrors. . . .

We therefore repeat our statement: War is an act of violence and there are no limits to its use. Each party forces its opponent's hand, and a reciprocal action arises which logically must lead to an extreme. . . .

The Political Object of War

Now *the political object of war* again enters the picture. . . . The smaller the sacrifice we demand from our opponent, the smaller may we expect his efforts to be to resist us. But the smaller his efforts, the smaller need our own be. Furthermore, the smaller our political object is, the less will be the value we attach to it and the sooner shall we be ready to give it up altogether. Likewise, the smaller will our efforts be.

Hence, the political object, as the original motive for war, will be the standard both for the goal of the military action and for the efforts required. However, it will not be an absolute standard but a standard relative to the two belligerent states, since we are dealing with realities rather than abstract concepts. One and the same political object may produce entirely different effects on different peoples or even on the same people at different times. We can only use the political object as the standard, therefore, if we take into consideration its influence on the masses. Hence the nature of these masses must also be considered. It is easy to realize that the result varies according to the strengthening or weakening of the action by the feelings of the masses. In two peoples and states such tensions and such animosities may exist that a very minor motive for war may produce an effect completely out of proportion—a veritable explosion.

This applies to the efforts that the political object calls forth in both states, and to the aim it prescribes for the military action. At times it may itself become this aim, for instance, in the case of the conquest of a certain province. At other times the political object itself will not be suited to provide the aim for military action. In that case, an equivalent aim must be found to substitute for it in the conclusion of peace. But here also due attention to the special characteristics of the states involved is always assumed. There are circumstances where the equivalent must be much greater than the political object if this object is to be attained. The more indifferent the attitude of the masses and the less the tensions stemming from other causes in both states and their relations, the more will the political object be the dominant and decisive standard. There are also cases where the political object almost alone will be the decisive factor.

Now if the aim of the military action is an equivalent of the political object, they will usually decrease together, especially the more the political object dominates. That is why, without self-contradiction, there may be wars of all degrees of importance and energy, ranging from a war of annihilation to mere armed observation. . . .

War Is a Serious Means to a Serious End

. . . war is no pastime, no mere delight in daring and winning, no work of a free enthusiasm. It is a serious means to a serious end. All the glamor of fortune, passion, courage, imagination, and enthusiasm, are only the special characteristics of this means.

The war of a community—of whole nations and particularly of civilized nations—always stems from a political condition and is called forth by a political motive. Hence it is a political act. If it were a complete, unrestrained, and absolute expression of violence, as we had to deduce from its mere conception, it would, from the moment it is called forth by policy, take the place of policy as a quite independent factor, push it aside and only follow its own laws, just as an exploding mine can take no other direction than the one originally prepared for it. This is how the matter has really been viewed up to now, whenever a lack of harmony between policy and the conduct of war has led to such theoretical distinctions. But this is not so, and this idea is basically false. War in the real world, as we have seen, is not of such an extreme nature that its tension is released in a single explosion; it is the operation of powers which do not develop exactly in the same way and to the same extent, but which sometimes expand enough to overcome the resistance caused by inertia and friction, while at another moment they are too weak to have any effect. Hence, war is, to a certain extent, a pulsation of violence more or less vehement, and consequently releasing its tensions and exhausting its powers more or less quickly. In other words, it leads more or less quickly to its goal, but it always lasts long enough to be influenced in this or that direction. In short, it remains subject to a guiding intelligence. Now if we keep in mind that war arises from a political object, then it follows that this first motive which called it into being also remains the first and foremost consideration in its conduct. But the political object is no despotic lawgiver; it must adapt itself to the nature of the means which may even change it completely, but it always has to be considered first. Policy, therefore, will permeate the entire military action, and exert a continuous influence on it to the extent its inherent explosive powers will permit.

War Is a Mere Continuation of Policy by Other Means

So we see that war is not merely a political act but a real political instrument, a continuation of political relations, a carrying out of the same by other means. What remains peculiar to war is only the peculiar nature of its means. The art of war in general and the commander in each particular case can demand that the directions and intentions of policy do not conflict with these means, and this claim is certainly no minor one. But no matter how strongly this may affect the political intentions in isolated cases, it always has to be regarded as only a modification of the intentions. For the political aim is the end, while war is the means, and the means can never be considered apart from the end.

31. *PROBLEMS OF STRATEGY IN GUERRILLA WAR**/ *MAO TSE-TUNG*

Now let us see what policies or principles have to be adopted in guerrilla operations against Japan before we can attain the object of preserving ourselves and destroying the enemy. Since the guerrilla units in the War of Resistance (and in all other revolutionary wars) generally grow out of nothing and expand from a small to a large force, they must preserve themselves and, moreover, they must expand. Hence the question is, what policies or principles have to be adopted before we can attain the object of preserving and expanding ourselves and destroying the enemy? . . .

If we take the War of Resistance as a whole, the fact that Japan is a strong country and is attacking while China is a weak country and is defending herself makes our war strategically a defensive and protracted war. As far as the operational lines are concerned, the Japanese are operating on exterior and we on interior lines. This is one aspect of the situation. But there is another aspect which is just the reverse. The enemy forces, though strong (in arms, in certain

* Mao Tse-tung, "Problems of Strategy in Guerrilla War Against Japan," *Selected Works* (Peking: Foreign Languages Press, 1965), Vol. II, pp. 82–91.

qualities of their men, and certain other factors), are numerically small, whereas our forces, though weak (likewise, in arms, in certain qualities of our men, and certain other factors), are numerically very large. Added to the fact that the enemy is an alien nation invading our country while we are resisting his invasion on our own soil, this determines the following strategy. It is possible and necessary to use tactical offensives within the strategic defensive, to fight campaigns and battles of quick decision within a strategically protracted war and to fight campaigns and battles on exterior lines within strategically interior lines. Such is the strategy to be adopted in the War of Resistance as a whole. It holds true both for regular and for guerrilla warfare. Guerrilla warfare is different only in degree and form. Offensives in guerrilla warfare generally take the form of surprise attacks. Although surprise attacks can and should be employed in regular warfare too, the degree of surprise is less. In guerrilla warfare, the need to bring operations to a quick decision is very great, and our exterior-line ring of encirclement of the enemy in campaigns and battles is very small. All these distinguish it from regular warfare.

Thus it can be seen that in their operations guerrilla units have to concentrate the maximum forces, act secretly and swiftly, attack the enemy by surprise and bring battles to a quick decision, and that they must strictly avoid passive defence, procrastination and the dispersal of forces before engagements. Of course, guerrilla warfare includes not only the strategic but also the tactical defensive. The latter embraces, among other things, containing and outpost actions during battles; the disposition of forces for resistance at narrow passes, strategic points, rivers or villages in order to deplete and exhaust the enemy; and action to cover withdrawal. But the basic principle of guerrilla warfare must be the offensive, and guerrilla warfare is more offensive in its character than regular warfare. The offensive, moreover, must take the form of surprise attacks, and to expose ourselves by ostentatiously parading our forces is even less permissible in guerrilla warfare than in regular warfare. From the fact that the enemy is strong and we are weak it necessarily follows that, in guerrilla operations in general even more than in regular warfare, battles must be decided quickly, though on some occasions guerrilla fighting may be kept up for several days, as in an assault on a small and isolated enemy force cut off from help. Because of its dispersed character, guerrilla warfare can spread everywhere, and in many of its tasks, as in harassing, containing and disrupting the enemy and in mass work, its principle is dispersal of forces; but a guerrilla unit, or a guerrilla formation, must concentrate its main forces when it is engaged in destroying the enemy, and especially when it is striving to smash an enemy attack. "Concentrate a big force to strike at a small section of the enemy force" remains a principle of field operations in guerrilla warfare. . . .

What is initiative in guerrilla warfare?

In any war, the opponents contend for the initiative, whether on a battlefield, in a battle area, in a war zone or in the whole war, for the initiative means freedom of action for an army. Any army which, losing the initiative, is forced into a passive position and ceases to have freedom of action, faces the danger of defeat or extermination. . . .

The question of the initiative is even more vital in guerrilla warfare. For most guerrilla units operate in very difficult circumstances, fighting without a rear, with their own weak forces facing the enemy's strong forces, lacking experience (when the units are newly organized), being separated, etc. Nevertheless, it is possible to build up the initiative in guerrilla warfare, the essential condition being to seize on the enemy's three weaknesses. Taking advantage of the enemy's shortage of troops (from the viewpoint of the war as a whole), the guerrilla units can boldly use vast areas as their fields of operation; taking advantage of the fact that the enemy is an alien invader and is pursuing a most barbarous policy, the guerrilla units can boldly enlist the support of millions upon millions of people; and taking advantage of the stupidities in the enemy's command, the guerrilla units can give full scope to their resourcefulness. While the regular army must seize on all these weaknesses of the enemy and turn them to good account in order to defeat him, it is even more important for the guerrilla units to do so. As for the guerrilla units' own weaknesses, they can be gradually reduced in the course of the struggle. Moreover, these weaknesses sometimes constitute the very condition for gaining the initiative. For example, it is precisely because the guerrilla units are small that they can mysteriously appear and disappear in their operations behind enemy lines, without the enemy's being able to do anything about them, and thus enjoy a freedom of action such as massive regular armies never can.

When the enemy is making a converging attack from several directions, a guerrilla unit can exercise initiative only with difficulty and can lose it all too easily. In such a case, if its appraisals and dispositions are wrong, it is liable to get into a passive position and consequently fail to smash the converging enemy attack. This may occur even when the enemy is on the defensive and we are on the offensive. For the initiative results from making a correct appraisal of the situation (both our own and that of the enemy) and from making the correct military and political dispositions. A pessimistic appraisal out of accord with the objective conditions and the passive dispositions ensuing from it will undoubtedly result in the loss of the initiative and throw one into a passive position. On the other hand, an over-optimistic appraisal out of accord with the objective conditions and the risky (unjustifiably risky) dispositions ensuing from it will also result in the loss of the initiative and eventually land one in a position similar to that of the pessimists. The initiative is not an innate attribute of genius, but is something an intelligent leader attains through open-minded study and correct appraisal of the objective conditions and through correct military and political dispositions. It follows that the initiative is not ready-made but is something that requires conscious effort.

When forced into a passive position through some incorrect appraisal and disposition or through overwhelming pressure, a guerrilla unit must strive to extricate itself. How this can be done depends on the circumstances. In many cases it is necessary to "move away." The ability to move is the distinctive feature of a guerrilla unit. To move away is the principal method for getting out of a passive position and regaining the initiative. But it is not the sole method. The moment when the enemy is most energetic and we are in the greatest difficulties is often the very moment when things begin to turn against him and in our favour. Frequently a favourable situation recurs and the initiative is regained as a result of "holding out a little longer".

Next, let us deal with flexibility.

Flexibility is a concrete expression of the initiative. The flexible employment of forces is more essential in guerrilla warfare than in regular warfare.

A guerrilla commander must understand that the flexible employment of his forces is the most important means of changing the situation as between the enemy and ourselves and of gaining the initiative. The nature of guerrilla warfare is such that guerrilla forces must be employed flexibly in accordance with the task in hand and with such circumstances as the state of the enemy, the terrain and the local population, and the chief ways of employing the forces are dispersal, concentration and shifting of position. In employing his forces, a guerrilla commander is like a fisherman casting his net, which he should be able to spread wide as well as draw in tight. When casting his net, the fisherman has to ascertain the depth of the water, the speed of the current and the presence or absence of obstructions; similarly, when dispersing his units, a guerrilla commander must take care not to incur losses through ignorance of the situation or through miscalculated action. Just as the fisherman must keep a grip on the cord in order to draw his net in tight, so the guerrilla commander must maintain liaison and communication with all his forces and keep enough of his main forces at hand. Just as a frequent change of position is necessary in fishing, so a frequent shift of position is necessary for a guerrilla unit. Dispersal, concentration and shifting of position are the three ways of flexibly employing forces in guerrilla warfare.

Generally speaking, the dispersal of guerrilla units, or "breaking up the whole into parts", is employed chiefly: (1) when we want to threaten the enemy with a wide frontal attack because he is on the defensive, and there is temporarily no chance to mass our forces for action; (2) when we want to harass and disrupt the enemy throughout an area where his forces are weak; (3) when we are unable to break through the enemy's encirclement and try to slip away by making ourselves less conspicuous; (4) when we are restricted by terrain or supplies; or (5) when we are carrying on mass work over a wide area. But whatever the circumstances, when dispersing for action we should pay attention to the following: (1) we should never make an absolutely even dispersal of forces, but should keep a fairly large part in an area convenient for manoeuvre, so that any possible exigency can be met and there is a centre of gravity for the task being carried out in dispersion; and (2) we should assign to the dispersed units clearly defined tasks, fields of operation, time limits for actions, places for reassembly and ways and means of liaison.

Concentration of forces, or "assembling the parts into a whole", is the method usually applied to destroy an enemy when he is on the offensive and sometimes to destroy some of his stationary forces when he is on the defensive. Concentration of forces does not mean absolute concentration, but the massing of the main forces for use in one important direction while retaining or dispatching part of the forces for use in other directions to contain, harass or disrupt the enemy, or to carry on mass work.

Although the flexible dispersal or concentration of forces according to circumstances is the principal method in guerrilla warfare, we must also know how to shift (or transfer) our forces flexibly. When the enemy feels seriously threatened by guerrillas, he will send troops to attack or suppress them. Hence the guerrilla units will have to take stock of the situation. If advisable, they should fight where they are; if not, they should lose no time in shifting elsewhere. Sometimes, in order to crush the enemy units one by one, guerrilla units which have destroyed an enemy force in one place may immediately shift to another so as to wipe out a second enemy force; sometimes, finding it inadvisable to fight in one place, they may have to disengage quickly and fight the enemy elsewhere. If the enemy's forces in a certain place present a particularly serious threat, the guerrilla units should not linger, but should move off with lightning speed. In general, shifts of position should be made with secrecy and speed. In order to mislead, decoy and confuse the enemy, they should constantly use stratagems, such as making a feint to the east but attacking in the west, appearing now in the south and now in the north, hit-and-run attacks, and night actions.

Flexibility in dispersal, concentration and shifts of position is a concrete expression of the initiative in guerrilla warfare, whereas rigidity and inertia inevitably lead to passivity and cause unnecessary losses. But a commander proves himself wise not just by recognition of the importance of employing his forces flexibly but by skill in dispersing, concentrating or shifting them in good time according to the specific circumstances. This wisdom in sensing changes and choosing the right moment to act is not easily acquired; it can be gained only by those who study with a receptive mind and investigate and ponder diligently. Prudent consideration of the circumstances is essential to prevent flexibility from turning into impulsive action.

Lastly, we come to planning.

Without planning, victories in guerrilla warfare are impossible. Any idea that guerrilla warfare can be conducted in haphazard fashion indicates either a flippant attitude or ignorance of guerrilla warfare. The operations in a guerrilla zone as a whole, or those of a guerrilla unit or formation, must be preceded by as thorough planning as possible, by preparation in advance for every action. Grasping the situation, setting the tasks, disposing the forces, giving military and political training, securing supplies, putting the equipment in good order, making proper use of the people's help, etc.—all these are part of the work of the guerrilla commanders, which they must carefully consider and conscientiously perform and check up on. There can be no initiative, no flexibility, and no offensive unless they do so. True, guerrilla conditions do not allow as high a degree of planning as do those of regular warfare, and it would be a mistake to attempt very thorough planning in guerrilla warfare. But it is necessary to plan as thoroughly as the objective conditions permit, for it should be understood that fighting the enemy is no joke.

The above points serve to explain the first of the strategic principles of guerrilla warfare, the principle of using initiative, flexibility and planning in conducting offensives within the defensive, battles of quick decision within protracted war, and exterior-line operations within interior-line operations. It is the key problem in the strategy of guerrilla warfare. The solution of this problem provides the major guarantee of victory in guerrilla warfare so far as military command is concerned.

Although a variety of matters have been dealt with here, they all revolve around the offensive in campaigns and battles. The initiative can be decisively grasped only after victory in an offensive. Every offensive operation must be organized on our initiative and not launched under compulsion. Flexibility in the employment of forces revolves around the effort to take the offensive, and planning likewise is necessary chiefly in order to ensure success in offensive operations. Measures of tactical defence are meaningless if they are divorced from their role of giving either direct or indirect support to an offensive. Quick decision refers to the tempo of an offensive, and exterior lines refer to its scope. The offensive is the only means of destroying the enemy and is also the principal means of self-preservation, while pure defence and retreat can play only a temporary and partial role in self-preservation and are quite useless for destroying the enemy.

The principle stated above is basically the same for both regular and guerrilla war; it differs to some degree only in its form of expression. But in guerrilla war it is both important and necessary to note this difference. It is precisely this difference in form which distinguishes the operational methods of guerrilla war from those of regular war. If we confuse the two different forms in which the principle is expressed, victory in guerrilla war will be impossible. . . .

32. *SOME POSSIBLE SIZES AND SHAPES OF THERMONUCLEAR WAR*/ HERMAN KAHN*

How a War Might Be Fought

If we believe a war to be possible (not probable—possible), then we must for several reasons consider how a war might be fought. In the first place if there are more and less destructive ways of fighting a war, humanitarian considerations alone require that we make some investigation of the possibilities of limiting destruction and death. The morality of refusing to think seriously about the unthinkable is for this reason alone at least open to question. Second, careful consideration of the ways in which a war might be fought sheds additional light on the possible ways in which a war might start. We must learn all we can about this, both to help us avoid starting a war inadvertently or by miscalculation, and to allow us to contribute to preventing a war being started by others. Third, as will appear in the next chapter, the more thought one gives to these problems the more possible it becomes to mitigate some of the disastrous effects of thermonuclear war and to protect our values, both from the holocaust and from the more subtle politico-military forces in the world. And, last, it might prove essential to the preservation of these values, whether we like it or not, to be able to "fight, survive and win" a thermonuclear war.

The usual image of war today held by many experts as well as most laymen can be summed up in the phrase "orgiastic spasm of destruction," or, "spasm war." Many believe that if one single button is pressed all the buttons will be pressed, and that some 30 minutes or so later missiles will rain enough destruction to terminate the defender's existence as a nation; subsequently, some minutes or hours later, a similar rain of death and destruction will anihilate the attacking nation. Within perhaps an hour or two the war will be effectively over—both combatants having received death blows— with only one question left: "How bad will the radioactivity be for the rest of the world?" . . . However, even if the offensive forces grow quite large, and counterbalancing active and passive defenses

---

* Herman Kahn, *Thinking About the Unthinkable*, pp. 58–69. Reprinted by permission of the publisher, Horizon Press. Copyright 1962.

are not procured, it is by no means inevitable that quick mutual annihilation will actually result from the use of thermonuclear weapons.

To orient the reader as to the possible outcomes of a war today, I shall first consider the possible targeting objectives a warring nation might choose, and comment briefly upon the strategic implications of each attack. I shall then describe and analyze several special situations in which an ability to fight, survive, and terminate a war would be especially feasible or especially necessary to us or to the Soviet Union.

Targeting Objectives

There are at least five different possible types of attack, each with different targeting objectives:

1. Countervalue (Population-property damage)
2. Counterforce + Countervalue (Population-property-military)
3. Straight Counterforce (Narrow military considerations only)
4. Counterforce + Bonus (Population and property as a bonus)
5. Counterforce + Avoidance (Population and property actively spared)

1. *The Countervalue Attack.* The attacker may try to destroy those things which the defender prizes most highly regardless of whether such destruction helps the attacker to achieve an immediate or essential military objective. Presumably, nations prize people and property most highly.[1] Therefore, the most likely Countervalue attack would be made against the cities which contain the greatest concentrations of people and property in a manner designed to cause the greatest possible number of deaths and injuries and handicaps to recuperation. For example, an attacker might deliberately attempt to achieve massive blast and thermal effects with missiles and warheads of the highest megatonnage available.

Attacks concentrated upon people and property are likely to be based only upon a Countervalue motivation. Massive destruction of

[1] It is possible, of course, that a particular nation might value military power more highly than people and property. Some observers believe that such a priority of values is plausible in the case of the Soviet Union and China.

people and property is not likely to achieve any immediate or essential military objective. It would be more important militarily, for example, for an attacker to try to destroy forces which can hurt him in immediate retaliation. Most experts agree that, unlike World Wars I and II, any future wars are likely to be short and fought only by military forces in being. If this be true, populations and production lines are of doubtful value at best as a military mobilization base. Moreover, since the number of usable delivery vehicles—bombers and missiles—may be limited, any vehicles "wasted" on cities will be unavailable for their primary mission of destroying the defender's retaliatory forces.

It is generally easy for laymen to believe that a city-busting attack would be the most likely beginning to a thermonuclear war. Visualizing themselves as the defenders, they naturally think of the attacker as vindictive or malevolent, and interested primarily in hurting them. But it is irrational for an attacker to ignore his own priority of interests in order to hurt the defender. The attacker is usually not nearly so interested in hurting the defender as he is in the dual objects of achieving his military objective and escaping destruction himself. If later he decides that the defender must be completely eradicated, he will be in a much better position to achieve it after the defender has been disarmed or badly weakened by the loss of the war. Hence, most experts now doubt that a surprise attack is likely to involve an all-out concentration on people and cities.

However, an exclusively Countervalue attack could occur, as a result of doctrinal lag or irrationality. In the early sixties the Soviets might be able, by devoting all their striking power to such an attack, to inflict as many as 50 to 100 million casualties upon the United States. If we do not acquire elaborate and expensive systems of active and passive defense, it will no doubt be technically and economically feasible for them to kill between 75 and 100 per cent of our population by the mid- or late sixties; even if we develop and install elaborate and expensive systems of defense there would be considerable uncertainty as to the effectiveness of such systems if the Soviets are vigorous in developing offensive techniques and systems. Many experts believe that by the mid- or late sixties there will be no practicable defensive measures which would enable us to save most of our population in the event of an all-out attack solely upon it, other than a permanent and disciplined alert status for all—civilians and military—and even more elaborate and expensive physical preparations.

Fortunately, an all-out surprise attack in which all resources are devoted to Countervalue targets would be so irrational that, barring an incredible lack of sophistication or actual insanity among Soviet decision makers, such an attack is highly unlikely. Small Countervalue attacks, initiated by us or by the Soviets, are not as highly unlikely, however, as moves in the international game of chicken, or as desperate alternatives to all-out thermonuclear war.

Consider as an example the following extremely hypothetical situation: Imagine that both sides had achieved such an enormous potential that it was actually possible for each, using only one per cent of its strategic forces, to destroy totally the other's civilians and its economy (but not its strategic forces). Then, if either side used all of its forces in a Countervalue attack, it could totally destroy its opponent's society 100 times over. Imagine also that the forces on both sides were invulnerable enough so that an attack directed at the opponent's strategic forces could at most destroy 50 per cent of such strategic forces. This means that the opponent who had been struck would still be able to "over-kill" his attacker. In fact, he would have the ability to destroy his attacker's society fifty times over. If, therefore, the attack on the defender's strategic forces touched off an all-out Countervalue retaliation it would not have accomplished anything except national suicide, although it had destroyed 50 per cent of the defender's strategic force. An all-out attack on the defender's cities would also be senseless, since it too could only cause the opponent to retaliate with an all-out destructive attack. In these circumstances, there should be a firm balance of terror between the two nations.[2]

In order to understand some of the possible impacts of this firm balance of terror upon policy in the real world, it is well to consider an extreme situation. Suppose for a moment that the Soviets were to drop nuclear bombs on several West European cities and were to couple this action with a demand for the European nations to surrender. The Soviets could then, of course, point out quite persuasively that no American action would result in the protection of Europe. Even if we were to launch an all-out Counterforce attack on the Soviets, they would still have more than enough weapons surviving the attack to destroy both the United States and Europe

[2] In terms of this balance of terror each side does not have a factor of safety of 100 but only of 2. If either side reduced its deterrent by 50 per cent that deterrent could, by hypothesis, be destroyed completely by the opponent's attack. Some simple models of this sort will be considered further in Chapter Five.

in retaliation. The Soviet argument would, under these hypothetical assumptions, be correct. The all-out attack would be senseless.

This does not mean there would be no checks upon Soviet action. Aside from the ever-present fear that calculations, however rationally made, might prove wrong, there would remain another deterrent. We might take a leaf from the Soviet book and destroy some Soviet cities, coupling this with a demand that the Soviets desist from further violence. The Soviets could retaliate by destroying some of our cities, pointing out that since they had the greater resolve they were unlikely to back down first, and we had therefore better acquiesce in the surrender of Europe. At this point both nations would be engaging in a super-destructive game of chicken.

As stupid and bizarre as this game of chicken may seem, under the assumptions of mutual Countervalue over-kill, it would be less stupid and bizarre than initiating an all-out Countervalue exchange. Obviously, the "controlled" city exchange might escalate into an all-out spasm war as a result of anger or miscalculation or some other event. Such drastic action is obviously inappropriate for minor provocations. It is, in fact, hard to imagine a "controlled" city exchange or similar limited Countervalue attack being used more than once in two generations. If used once, the shock might be sufficient to cause drastic and irreversible changes in the international order which would make repetitions unlikely. At the least it would provide a powerful impetus toward a satisfactory arms control plan.

I will refer to the limited Countervalue attack as a Controlled Reprisal or a nuclear show of force, depending on whether the nation using the operation is defending or attacking. In a Controlled Reprisal or nuclear show of force one would be trying not so much to destroy the enemy's military capability or people or property as to force one's will on him by threatening destruction of Countervalue targets. The operations would be chosen so as to demonstrate resolve, commitment, and/or recklessness, and to frighten and harass the enemy, but not to destroy him or provoke him to suicidal desperation. A Controlled Reprisal or nuclear show of force need not be designed to kill many people. It could even be a spectacular fireworks display (such as exploding a megaton bomb at 200,000 feet over Moscow or Washington), or it could involve the destruction of such targets as isolated military bases, dams, factories, and so on. Such targets would not result in the severe human casualties or psychological aftermath of an attack on major cities.

Many experts (notably Kaplan, Schelling, and Szilard) have

advocated that we replace our policy of deterring extreme provocation by the threat of massive retaliation with some variation of a policy of Controlled Reprisal. These experts point out that the threat of a Controlled Reprisal is more credible than the threat of mutual annihilation, and that it may therefore be more deterring though less potentially destructive. Most of the experts who have advocated the use of Controlled Reprisal as a punishment for some provocation assume that if we initiate a Controlled Reprisal to punish the Soviets for some act we will have to allow them to do a certain amount of damage to ourselves in return. While the damage that the Soviets do to us will not compensate them for the cities or other valuable things they have lost, allowing them to return the blow in a tit-for-tat fashion introduces an element of stability into the situation by giving the exchange an appearance of "equity" and by making it clear that no principle or custom has been established that would lead to the expectation that we would lightly initiate a Controlled Reprisal. The side using a type of Controlled Reprisal requiring the sacrifice of whole cities of its own will no doubt experience enormous political problems at home and among the uncommitted countries, most of which prefer any "peaceful" resolution of East-West difficulties to the use of nuclear force. Moreover the "controlled" city exchange is a device that the Soviets or Chinese, both of which have control of internal information and fewer problems with public opinion, must be able to use far more effectively than we could.

I have mentioned only a few of the many serious difficulties with the idea of Controlled Reprisal. There will also be serious difficulties in any other policy that tries to restrain an aggressor in a world in which there is a firm balance of terror based on a reliable mutual over-kill capability and no effective rule of law, reason, or ritual to substitute for the threat or use of force.

2. *Counterforce Plus Countervalue.* The next kind of attack to be examined is a mixed attack against both our strategic forces and the things we value most highly. The objects of such an attack might be divided approximately 50-50, or possibly less symmetrically. This type of attack corresponds to the picture most experts had of war until quite recently. This was not because historically most wars have been fought this way (historically they have not), but because World War I and World War II were fought this way. The possibility of such an attack must not be discounted. If either side refuses to "think about the unthinkable," "old-fashioned" ideas may prevail.

In the previously described hypothetical situation in which each side can over-kill by a factor of 100, the mixed attack is as senseless as the all-out Countervalue attack. It seems to make sense to some planners only because it is more in accord with intuitions gained from the irrelevant experience in World Wars I and II.

As we have previously pointed out, unless the attacker has an over-kill capability as to the defender's strategic forces, the mixed attack is likely to be a great mistake. If the attacker lacks the capability to destroy totally the other side's strategic forces, he should not waste resources attacking his opponent's cities. If, on the other hand, he wishes only to punish the other side, there is probably no reason for hitting the other side's military forces in addition to his cities unless such destruction of forces contributes in some desirable way to the peace negotiations, the state of the postwar world, or some other useful objective.

3. *Straight Counterforce.* In the third kind of attack, the attacker ignores the things which the defenders particularly value, and concentrates on those targets which may be used to hurt him most immediately in retaliation. Reverting to fundamental and historical military principles, and reversing the trend of the most recent years, the "modern" attacker should realize that destroying the defenders' cities, factories, and population cannot help his war effort or do much harm to that of the defenders. Unlike World Wars I and II, and in a war lasting between a few hours and a month, the defenders today are not going to manufacture anything of importance, or draft any soldiers, or even hold elections. Moreover, the potential fallout which would force the surviving civilian population to seek shelter in any event, makes it more unlikely that problems of civilian morale would worry the defenders during the war. Lastly, and probably most important, the surviving civilian population may be valuable hostages in deterring retaliation and in achieving political objectives, including the enforcement of peace terms without further mass violence. If fewer cities were destroyed more hostages would be available for this purpose, and the likelihood of irrational and self-destructive responses caused by anger and a desire for revenge would be diminished.

Adding all this up, why should an attacker waste bombs on cities, particularly in the initial attack? A Straight Counterforce attack is a reasonable tactic and quite likely to be chosen if the planning is determined by narrow military considerations. There are also strong political considerations in its favor. Whoever launches a surprise nuclear attack will have to justify it to his own people and to future generations. Since the probable justification would be that they had to beat the other side to the punch a relatively humane attack might help to reinforce the argument. In the early sixties a Straight Counterforce attack by the Soviets might well result in 1 to 20 million dead, with a vigorous civil-defense program; or 5 or 30 million dead, if we had even a modest civil-defense program; or perhaps 10 to 50 million if we had no program at all. In the middle and late sixties, if the Soviets increase their force and we disperse hard missile bases throughout the country these estimates might be multiplied by as much as five.

4. *Counterforce and Bonus.* In the fourth kind of attack the attacker has basically the same attitude toward the military importance of cities that he had in the third; however, he feels it desirable to destroy as much of the other side's civilian population and property as he can, though not at the cost of decreasing significantly the military efficiency of an attack concentrated upon the defender's strategic forces. An attacker might want to obtain a "bonus" to foreclose any possibility of a long war, to prevent or lessen postwar competition, to be revenged, or simply to be malevolent. He might also have an obsolete doctrine, or even some reasons which he could not articulate, but which might still seem sufficient to make him accept a modest decrease in military efficiency over the Straight Counterforce attack. To obtain a "bonus" the attacker could move the designated ground zeros slightly, use the largest workable weapons, and in other ways greatly increase bonus damage to civilians and property without materially decreasing the efficiency of the Counterforce operation. This attack can be combined with "post-attack coercion" by deliberately sparing some, but not all, of the hostages.

Such an attack would result in quite different casualties and damage from that of the straightforward Counterforce attack, though the primary targets would be much the same. Depending upon the details of the capabilities and tactics used in pursuing a Counterforce Plus Bonus attack over that of a Straight Counterforce attack, the casualties might be increased by factors of 5 to 10 in the lower ranges (1-10), and by factors of 2 to 5 in the higher ranges (10-50).

5. *Counterforce Plus Avoidance.* In this last type of attack the attacker's attitude and objectives with respect to Countervalue targets are the opposite of his objectives in the Counterforce Plus

Bonus Attack. The attacker actively wishes to avoid destroying the defender's population. He may be motivated by moral or political reasons, because he wishes to hold hostage as many as possible, or because he wishes to avoid unnecessary provocation. If an avoidance objective is pursued vigorously, an attacker might accept some relatively large potential military disadvantages. For example, should there be a SAC base near a major U.S. City, then, rather than drop a 20 megaton bomb on it, he might avoid the base completely or he might compromise and drop only 100 kilotons. (In most circumstances 100 kilotons are likely to be almost as effective in destroying the SAC base as a 20 megaton bomb and far less damaging to the nearby city.) It has been estimated that a Counterforce Plus Avoidance attack on the United States in the early sixties might result in as "few" as one million casualties. It would almost certainly be less than five million so long as the attacker is careful, no weapons go disastrously astray, and we have a modest civil-defense capability.

In an actual war, which of these five types of attacks might we most reasonably expect? I have no idea. There is nothing in law or logic that says we or an enemy have to be reasonable. However, for the side which strikes first, only the third and fifth attacks—the Straight Counterforce and the Counterforce Plus Avoidance—seem to me to make sense, and in most cases the last it to be preferred. The other three types of attacks involve either a waste of resources or an unnecessary and likely self-defeating brutality. The side which strikes second (the side presumably trying to deter the war), might in fact wish to appear committed to an all-out Countervalue response. It might best deter the attack by this *appearance* of irrationally inexorable commitment. If deterrence fails, however, it would then be irrational to carry through the commitment. In most people's value system, revenge will have a lower priority than survival. One would wish, if one could, to revoke the commitment after the first attack, and use whatever force has survived the aggressor's strike to prevent further strikes and to terminate the war on the best terms possible. This implies that the defender should rationally concentrate his attack on Counterforce targets, perhaps withholding some forces to increase his future negotiating strength. Alternatively, he might attack Countervalue targets according to the previously outlined principles of Controlled Reprisal.[3]

[3] See pp. 179–87 of Herman Kahn, *On Thermonuclear War* (Princeton: Princeton University Press, 1960) for a discussion on possible objectives of the defender.

There is also some advantage in not using too extreme a "rationality of irrationality" strategy. If the enemy suspects that one may not reply with an all-out Countervalue retaliation, the original attack might be made carefully (Counterforce Plus Avoidance) and combined with a reasonable peace offer. Such care would not cost the attacker much, and might buy him a great deal if it were to induce the defender also to be careful. This knowledge or expectation, even if weak or uncertain, might motivate the attacker to adhere to a Counterforce and Avoidance objective. While this expectation on the part of the attacker might weaken the defender's deterrence, it might not weaken it much. It is unlikely that an attacker would be so willing to rely on these expectations as to be induced, in normal circumstances, to attack. . . .

33. *THE ABOLITION OF WAR* /*
DOUGLAS MACARTHUR

War's History

. . . Many in this brilliant audience were my comrades-in-arms in the days of used-to-be. They have known war in all its horror and, as veterans, hope against its recurrence. How, we ask ourselves, did such an institution become so integrated with man's life and civilization? How has it grown to be the most vital factor in our existence? It started in a modest enough way as a sort of gladiatorial method of settling disputes between conflicting tribes. One of the oldest and most classical examples is the biblical story of David and Goliath. Each of the two contesting groups selected its champion. They fought and based upon the outcome an agreement resulted. Then, as time went on, small professional groups . . . known as armies replaced the individual champions. And these groups fought in some obscure corner of the world and victory or defeat was accepted as the basis of an ensuing peace. And from then on, down through the ages, the constant record is an increase in the character and strength

* Douglas MacArthur, "The Abolition of War: Triumph of Scientific Annihilation," *Vital Speeches of the Day*, Vol. 21, No. 9 (February 15, 1955), pp. 1041–43. Reprinted by permission.

of the forces with the rate of increase always accelerating. From a small percentage of the populace it finally engulfed all. It is now the nation in arms.

Within the span of my own life I have witnessed this evolution. At the turn of the century, when I entered the Army, the target was one enemy casualty at the end of a rifle or bayonet or sword. Then came the machine gun designed to kill by the dozens. After that, the heavy artillery raining death upon hundreds. Then the aerial bomb to strike by the thousands—followed by the atom explosion to reach the hundreds of thousands. Now electronics and other processes of science have raised the destructive potential to encompass millions. And with restless hands we work feverishly in dark laboratories to find the means to destroy all at one blow.

But, this very triumph of scientific annihilation—this very success of invention—has destroyed the possibility of war being a medium of practical settlement of international differences. The enormous destruction to both sides of closely matched opponents makes it impossible for the winner to translate it into anything but his own disaster.

The second World War, even with the now antiquated armaments, clearly demonstrated that the victor had to bear in large part the very injuries inflicted on his foe. Our own country spent billions of dollars and untold energies to heal the wounds of Germany and Japan. War has become a Frankenstein to destroy both sides. No longer is it the weapon of adventure whereby a short cut to international power and wealth—a place in the sun—can be gained. If you lose, you are annihilated. If you win, you stand only to lose. No longer does it possess the chance of the winner of duel—it contains rather the germs of double suicide. Science has clearly outmoded it as a feasible arbiter. The great question is—does this mean that war can now be outlawed from the world? If so, it would mark the greatest advance in civilization since the Sermon on the Mount. It would lift at one stroke the darkest shadow which has engulfed mankind from the beginning. It would not only remove fear and bring security—it would not only create new moral and spiritual values—it would produce an economic wave of prosperity that would raise the world's standard of living beyond anything ever dreamed of by man. The hundreds of billions of dollars now spent in mutual preparedness could conceivably abolish poverty from the face of the globe. It would accomplish even more than this; it would at one stroke reduce the international tensions that seem so insurmountable now to matters of more probable solution. For instance, the complex problems of German rearmament, of preventive war, of satellite dominance by major powers, of Universal Military Service, of unconscionable taxation, of nuclear development for industry, of freer exchange of goods and people, of foreign aid and indeed of all issues involving the application of armed force. It would have equally potent political effects. It would reduce immeasurably the power of leaders of Government and thus render more precarious totalitarian or autocratic rule. The growing and dangerous control by an individual over the masses—the socialistic and paternal trends resulting therefrom—is largely by virtue of his influence to induce war or to maintain peace. Abolish this threat and the position of chief magistrate falls into a more proper civic perspective.

Abolition Possible

You will say at once that although the abolition of war has been the dream of man for centuries every proposition to that end has been promptly discarded as impossible and fantastic. Every cynic, every pessimist, every adventurer, every swashbuckler in the world has always disclaimed its feasibility. But that was before the science of the past decade made mass destruction a reality. The argument then was that human character has never reached a theological development which would permit the application of pure idealism. In the last two thousand years its rate of change has been deplorably slow, compared to that of the arts and sciences. But now the tremendous and present evolution of nuclear and other potentials of destruction has suddenly taken the problem away from its primary consideration as a moral and spiritual question and brought it abreast of scientific realism. It is no longer an ethical equation to be pondered solely by learned philosophers and ecclesiastics but a hard core one for the decision of the masses whose survival is the issue. This is as true of the Soviet side of the world as of the free side—as true behind the Iron Curtain as in front of it. The ordinary people of the world, whether free or slave, are all in agreement on this solution; and this perhaps is the only thing in the world they do agree upon. But it is the most vital and determinate of all. The leaders are the laggards. The disease of power seems to confuse and befuddle them. They have not even approached the basic problem, much less evolved a working formula to implement this public demand. They debate and turmoil over a hundred issues—they bring us to the verge of despair or raise our hopes to Utopian heights over the corollary misunderstandings that stem from the threat of war—but never in the chancelleries of the world or the halls of the United Nations is the real problem raised. Never do they dare to state the bald truth, that the next great advance in the evolution of civilization cannot take place until war is abolished. It may take another cataclysm of destruction to prove to them this simple truth. But, strange as it may seem, it is known now by all common men. It is the one issue upon which both sides can agree, for it is the one issue upon which both sides will profit equally. It is the one issue—and the only decisive one—in which the interests of both are completely parallel. It is the one issue which, if settled, might settle all others.

Both Must Profit

Time has shown that agreements between modern nations are generally no longer honored as valid unless both profit therefrom. But both sides can be trusted when both do profit. It becomes then no longer a problem based upon relative integrity. It is now no longer convincing to argue, whether true or not, that we cannot trust the other side—that one maverick can destroy the herd. It would no longer be a matter depending upon trust—the self-interest of each nation outlawing war would keep it true to itself. And there is no influence so potent and powerful as self-interest. It would not necessarily require international inspection of relative armaments— the public opinion of every part of the world would be the great denominator which would insure the issue—each nation would so profit that it could not fail eventually to comply. This would not, of course, mean the abandonment of all armed forces, but it would reduce them to the simpler problems of internal order and international police. It would not mean utopia at one fell stroke, but it would mean that the great roadblock now existing to development of the human race would have been cleared.

The present tensions with their threat of national annihilation are kept alive by two great illusions. The one, a complete belief on the part of the Soviet world that the capitalist countries are preparing to attack them; that sooner or later we intend to strike. And the other, a complete belief on the part of the capitalistic countries that the Soviets are preparing to attack us; that sooner or later they intend to strike. Both are wrong. Each side, so far as masses are concerned, is equally desirous of peace. For either side war with the other would mean nothing but disaster. Both equally dread it. But the constant acceleration of preparation may well, without specific intent, ultimately produce a spontaneous combustion.

I am sure that every pundit in the world, every cynic and hypocrite, every paid brainwasher, every egotist, every trouble-maker, and many other of entirely different mold will tell you with mockery and ridicule that this can be only a dream—that it is but the vague imaginings of a visionary. But, as David Lloyd George once said in Commons at the crisis of the First World War, "We must go on or all will go under." And the great criticism we can make of the world's leaders is their lack of a plan which will enable us "to go on." All they propose merely gravitates around but dares not face the real problem. They increase preparedness by alliances, by distributing resources throughout the world, by feverish activity in developing new and deadlier weapons, by applying conscription in times of peace—all of which is instantly matched by the prospective opponent. We are told that this increases the chances of peace—which is doubtful—and increases the chances of victory if war comes—which would be incontestable if the other side did not increase in like proportion. Actually, the truth is that the relative strengths of the two change little with the years. Action by one is promptly matched by reaction from the other.

Dangerous Doctrines

We are told we must go on indefinitely as at present—some say fifty years or more. With what at the end? None say—there is no definite objective. They but pass along to those that follow the search for a final solution. And, at the end, the problem will be exactly the same, as that which we face now. Must we live for generations under the killing punishment of accelerating preparedness without an announced final purpose or, as an alternative, suicidal war; and trifle in the meanwhile with corollary and indeterminate theses—such as limitation of armament, restriction on the use of nuclear power, adoption of new legal standards as propounded at Nuremberg—all of which are but palliatives and all of which in varying form have been tried in the past with negligible results?

Dangerous doctrines, too, appear—doctrines which might result in actual defeat; such doctrines as a limited war, of enemy sanctuary, of failure to protect our fighting men when captured, of national subversive and sabotage agencies, of a substitute for victory on the battlefield—all in the name of peace. Peace, indeed, can be obtained at least temporarily by any nation if it is prepared to yield its freedom principles. But peace at any price—peace with appeasement—peace which passes the dreadful finality to future generations—is a peace of sham and shame which can end only in war or slavery.

I recall so vividly this problem when it faced the Japanese in their new Constitution. They are realists; and they are the only ones that know by dread experience the fearful effect of mass annihilation. They realize in their limited geographical area, caught up as a sort of no man's land between two great ideologies, that to engage in another war, whether on the winning or the losing side, would spell the probable doom of their race. And their wise old Prime Minister, Shidehara, came to me and urged that to save themselves they should abolish war as an international instrument. When I agreed, he turned to me and said, "The world will laugh and mock us as impractical visionaries, but a hundred years from now we will be called prophets."

Sooner or later the world, if it is to survive, must reach this decision. The only question is, when? Must we fight again before we learn? When will some great figure in power have sufficient imagination and moral courage to translate this universal wish—which is rapidly becoming a universal necessity—into actuality? We are in a new era. The old methods and solutions no longer suffice. We must have new thoughts, new ideas, new concepts, just as did our venerated forefathers when they faced a new world. We must break out of the straitjacket of the past. There must always be one to lead, and we should be that one. We should now proclaim our readiness to abolish war in concert with the great powers of the world. The result would be magical. . . .

part IV
THE SEARCH FOR ORDER AND PEACE

11
BALANCE OF POWER

The balance of power is of vital importance in contemporary international relations and a central analytical concept in the study of world affairs, in spite of all its weaknesses and ambiguities. One of the earliest thorough discussions of the balance of power is the famous essay by David Hume (1711–76), which is included here as the first selection.

The second selection is Ernst B. Haas' careful analysis of the various meanings of the term "balance of power." Haas is Professor of Political Science at the University of California at Berkeley. He has written *The Uniting of Europe, Beyond the Nation-State*, and many other books and articles.

The balance of power in the age of nuclear weapons and ballistic missiles is discussed by Glenn H. Snyder of the State

University of New York at Buffalo, an expert on military strategy
and security policy. He has written *Deterrence by Denial and Punishment, Deterrence and Defense*, and other works.

34. *OF THE BALANCE OF POWER* / DAVID HUME

It is a question, whether the *idea* of the balance of power be owing
entirely to modern policy, or whether the *phrase* only has been
invented in the later ages? It is certain that Xenophon[a], in his
Institution of Cyrus, represents the combination of the Asiatic
powers to have arisen from a jealousy of the increasing force of the
Medes and Persians; and though that elegant composition should be
supposed altogether a romance, this sentiment, ascribed by the
author to the Eastern princes, is at least a proof of the prevailing
notion of ancient times.

In all the politics of Greece, the anxiety, with regard to the
balance of power, is apparent, and is expressly pointed out to us,
even by the ancient historians. Thucydides[b] represents the league
which was formed against Athens, and which produced the Peloponnesian war, as entirely owing to this principle. And after the
decline of Athens, when the Thebans and Lacedemonians disputed
for sovereignty, we find that the Athenians (as well as many other
republics) always threw themselves into the lighter scale, and
endeavoured to preserve the balance. They supported Thebes
against Sparta, till the great victory gained by Epaminondas at
Leuctra; after which they immediately went over to the conquered,
from generosity, as they pretended, but in reality from their
jealousy of the conquerors[c].

Whoever will read Demosthenes's oration for the Megalopoli-
tans, may see the utmost refinements on this principle that ever
entered into the head of a Venetian or English speculatist. And upon
the first rise of the Macedonian power, this orator immediately
discovered the danger, sounded the alarm throughout all Greece,

* David Hume, *Essays and Treatises on Several Subjects* (Edinburgh:
Bell & Bradfute, and W. Blackwood, 1825), Vol. I, pp. 331-39.
  a Lib. i.
  b Lib. i.
  c Xenoph. Hist. Græc. lib. vi. and vii.

and at last assembled that confederacy under the banners of Athens which fought the great and decisive battle of Chaeronea.

It is true, the Grecian wars are regarded by historians as wars of emulation rather than of politics; and each state seems to have had more in view the honour of leading the rest, than any well-grounded hopes of authority and dominion. If we consider, indeed, the small number of inhabitants in any one republic, compared to the whole, the great difficulty of forming sieges in those times, and the extraordinary bravery and discipline of every freeman among that noble people; we shall conclude, that the balance of power was, of itself, sufficiently secured in Greece, and need not to have been guarded with that caution which may be requisite in other ages. But whether we ascribe the shifting of sides in all the Grecian republics to *jealous emulation* or *cautious politics*, the effects were alike, and every prevailing power was sure to meet with a confederacy against it, and that often composed of its former friends and allies.

The same principle, call it envy or prudence, which produced the *Ostracism* of Athens, and *Petalism* of Syracuse, and expelled every citizen whose fame or power over-topped the rest; the same principle, I say, naturally discovered itself to foreign politics, and soon raised enemies to the leading state, however moderate in the exercise of its authority.

The Persian monarch was really, in his force, a petty prince compared to the Grecian republics; and therefore, it behoved him, from views of safety more than from emulation, to interest himself in their quarrels, and to support the weaker side in every contest. This was the advice given by Alcibiades to Tissaphernes[a], and it prolonged, near a century, the date of the Persian empire; till the neglect of it for a moment, after the first appearance of the aspiring genius of Philip, brought that lofty and frail edifice to the ground, with a rapidity of which there are few instances in the history of mankind.

The successors of Alexander showed great jealousy of the balance of power; a jealousy founded on true politics and prudence, and which preserved distinct for several ages the partition made after the death of that famous conqueror. The fortune and ambition of Antigonus[b] threatened them anew with a universal monarchy; but their combination, and their victory at Ipsus, saved them. And in subsequent times, we find, that, as the Eastern princes considered

[a] Thucyd. lib. viii.
[b] Diod. Sic. lib. xx.

the Greeks and Macedonians as the only real military force with whom they had any intercourse, they kept always a watchful eye over that part of the world. The Ptolemies, in particular, supported first Aratus and the Achæans, and then Cleomenes king of Sparta, from no other view than as a counterbalance to the Macedonian monarchs. For this is the account which Polybius gives of the Egyptian politics[a].

The reason why it is supposed that the ancients were entirely ignorant of the *balance of power*, seems to be drawn from the Roman history more than the Grecian; and as the transactions of the former are generally more familiar to us, we have thence formed all our conclusions. It must be owned, that the Romans never met with any such general combination or confederacy against them, as might naturally have been expected for their rapid conquests and declared ambition, but were allowed peaceably to subdue their neighbours, one after another, till they extended their dominion over the whole known world. Not to mention the fabulous history of the Italic wars, there was, upon Hannibal's invasion of the Roman state, a remarkable crisis, which ought to have called up the attention of all civilized nations. It appeared afterwards (nor was it difficult to be observed at the time)[b] that this was a contest for universal empire; yet no prince or state seems to have been in the least alarmed about the event or issue of the quarrel. Philip of Macedon remained neuter, till he saw the victories of Hannibal; and then most imprudently formed an alliance with the conqueror, upon terms still more imprudent. He stipulated, that he was to assist the Carthaginian state in their conquest of Italy; after which they engaged to send over forces into Greece, to assist him in subduing the Grecian commonwealth[c].

The Rhodian and Achæan republics are much celebrated by ancient historians for their wisdom and sound policy; yet both of them assisted the Romans in their wars against Philip and Antiochus. And what may be esteemed still a stronger proof, that this maxim was not generally known in those ages, no ancient author has remarked the imprudence of these measures, nor has even blamed that absurd treaty above mentioned, made by Philip with the Carthaginians. Princes and statesmen, in all ages, may, beforehand,

[a] Lib. ii. cap. 51.
[b] It was observed by some, as appears by the speech of Agesilaus of Naupactum, in the general congress of Greece. See Polyb. lib. v. cap. 104.
[c] Tit. Livii, lib. xxiii. cap. 33.

be blinded in their reasonings with regard to events: But it is somewhat extraordinary, that historians, afterwards, should not form a sounder judgment of them.

Massinissa, Attalus, Prusias, in gratifying their private passions, were all of them the instruments of the Roman greatness, and never seem to have suspected, that they were forging their own chains, while they advanced the conquests of their ally. A simple treaty and agreement between Massinissa and the Carthaginians, so much required by mutual interest, barred the Romans from all entrance into Africa, and preserved liberty to mankind.

The only prince we meet with in the Roman history, who seems to have understood the balance of power, is Hiero, king of Syracuse. Though the ally of Rome, he sent assistance to the Carthaginians during the war of the auxiliaries; "Esteeming it requisite," says Polybius[a], "both in order to retain his dominions in Sicily, and to preserve the Roman friendship, that Carthage should be safe; lest by its fall the remaining power should be able, without control or opposition, to execute every purpose and undertaking. And here he acted with great wisdom and prudence: For that is never, on any account, to be overlooked; nor ought such a force ever to be thrown into one hand, as to incapacitate the neighbouring states from defending their rights against it." Here is the aim of modern politics pointed out in express terms.

In short, the maxim of preserving the balance of power is founded so much on common sense and obvious reasoning, that it is impossible it could altogether have escaped antiquity, where we find, in other particulars, so many marks of deep penetration and discernment. If it was not so generally known and acknowledged as at present, it had at least an influence on all the wiser and more experienced princes and politicians. And indeed, even at present, however generally known and acknowledged among speculative reasoners, it has not, in practice, an authority much more extensive among those who govern the world.

After the fall of the Roman empire, the form of government, established by the northern conquerors, incapacitated them, in a great measure, for farther conquests, and long maintained each state in its proper boundaries. But when vassalage and the feudal militia were abolished, mankind were anew alarmed by the danger of universal monarchy, from the union of so many kingdoms and principalities in the person of the Emperor Charles. But the power

[a] Lib. i. cap. 83.

of the house of Austria, founded on extensive but divided dominions; and their riches, derived chiefly from mines of gold and silver, were more likely to decay, of themselves, from internal defects, than to overthrow all the bulwarks raised against them. In less than a century, the force of that violent and haughty race was shattered, their opulence dissipated, their splendour eclipsed. A new power succeeded, more formidable to the liberties of Europe, possessing all the advantages of the former, and labouring under none of its defects, except a share of that spirit of bigotry and persecution, with which the house of Austria was so long, and still is so much infatuated.

In the general wars maintained against this ambitious power, Great Britain has stood foremost, and she still maintains her station. Beside her advantages of riches and situation, her people are animated with such a national spirit, and are so fully sensible of the blessings of their government, that we may hope their vigour never will languish in so necessary and so just a cause. On the contrary, if we may judge by the past, their passionate ardour seems rather to require some moderation; and they have oftener erred from a laudable excess than from a blameable deficiency.

In the *first* place, we seem to have been more possessed with the ancient Greek spirit of jealous emulation, than actuated by the prudent views of modern politics. Our wars with France have been begun with justice, and even perhaps from necessity, but have always been too far pushed, from obstinacy and passion. The same peace, which was afterwards made at Ryswick in 1697, was offered so early as the year ninety-two; that concluded at Utrecht in 1712 might have been finished on as good conditions at Gertruytenberg in the year eight; and we might have given at Frankfort, in 1743, the same terms which we were glad to accept of at Aix-la-Chapelle in the year forty-eight. Here then we see, that above half of our wars with France, and all our public debts, are owing more to our own imprudent vehemence, than to the ambition of our neighbours.

In the *second* place, we are so declared in our opposition to French power, and so alert in defence of our allies, that they always reckon upon our force as upon their own; and expecting to carry on war at our expence, refuse all reasonable terms of accommodation. *Habent subjectos, tanquam suos; viles, ut alienos.* All the world knows, that the factious vote of the House of Commons, in the beginning of the last parliament, with the professed humour of the nation, made the Queen of Hungary inflexible in her terms, and prevented that agreement with Prussia, which would immediately have restored the general tranquillity of Europe.

In the *third* place, we are such true combatants, that, when once engaged, we lose all concern for ourselves and our posterity, and consider only how we may best annoy the enemy. To mortgage our revenues at so deep a rate in wars where we were only accessaries, was surely the most fatal delusion that a nation, which had any pretensions to politics and prudence, has ever yet been guilty of. That remedy of funding, if it be a remedy, and not rather a poison, ought, in all reason, to be reserved to the last extremity; and no evil, but the greatest and most urgent, should ever induce us to embrace so dangerous an expedient.

These excesses, to which we have been carried, are prejudicial, and may, perhaps, in time, become still more prejudicial another way, by begetting, as is usual, the opposite extreme, and rendering us totally careless and supine with regard to the fate of Europe. The Athenians, from the most bustling, intriguing, warlike, people of Greece, finding their error in thrusting themselves into every quarrel, abandoned all attention to foreign affairs; and in no contest ever took part on either side, except by their flatteries and complaisance to the victor.

Enormous monarchies are probably destructive to human nature in their progress, in their continuance[a], and even in their downfall, which never can be very distant from their establishment. The military genius, which aggrandized the monarchy, soon leaves the court, the capital, and the centre of such a government, while the wars are carried on at a great distance, and interest so small a part of the state. The ancient nobility, whose affections attach them to their sovereign, live all at court, and never will accept of military employments, which would carry them to remote and barbarous frontiers, where they are distant both from their pleasures and their fortune. The arms of the state must therefore be entrusted to mercenary strangers, without zeal, without attachment, without honour, ready on every occasion to turn them against the prince, and join each desperate malcontent who offers pay and plunder. This is the necessary progress of human affairs. Thus human nature checks itself in its airy elevation; thus ambition blindly labours for the destruction of the conqueror, of his family, and of every thing

___

[a] If the Roman empire was of advantage, it could only proceed from this, that mankind were generally in a very disorderly, uncivilized condition, before its establishment.

near and dear to him. The Bourbons, trusting to the support of their brave, faithful, and affectionate nobility, would push their advantage without reserve or limitation. These, while fired with glory and emulation, can bear the fatigues and dangers of war; but never would submit to languish in the garrisons of Hungary or Lithuania, forgot at court, and sacrificed to the intrigues of every minion or mistress who approaches the prince. The troops are filled with Cravates and Tartars, Hussars and Cossacs, intermingled, perhaps, with a few soldiers of fortune from the better provinces; and the melancholy fate of the Roman emperors, from the same cause, is renewed over and over again, till the final dissolution of the monarchy.

35. THE BALANCE OF POWER: PRESCRIPTION, CONCEPT, OR PROPAGANDA?* / ERNST B. HAAS

Balance of Power as Description

Forswearing any theoretical or analytical purpose, writers commonly have recourse to the term "balance of power" in discussing international affairs. Current references to the balance of power by journalists and radio commentators most frequently fall into this category. And in most instances the meaning to be conveyed to the audience merely implies "distribution" of power, rather than "balance" in anything like the literal sense. . . .

On other occasions, however, the descriptive use of the term implies more than a mere distribution of power. It may then come to mean "equilibrium" or even "hegemony" or "preponderance" of power, still without implying more than a descriptive intent. It is quite possible that the political motivations of the particular user may make their entrance at this point. Thus Lisola, writing in the seventeenth century, saw in the balance of power the equilibrium between Habsburg and Bourbon interests. But he used his description to counsel war on France in order to maintain that very

* Ernst B. Haas, "The Balance of Power: Prescription, Concept, or Propaganda?" *World Politics*, Vol. 5, No. 4 (July 1953), pp. 459-74. Reprinted by permission. Footnotes follow original sequence.

equilibrium. Austrian writers again invoked the balance of power principle during the wars of the Polish and Austrian Succession in order to secure allies against France and Prussia, represented as seeking hegemony. During the preceding century, French writers had used the equilibrium connotation of the term to demand war on Austria. And it might be pointed out parenthetically that during the Seven Years' War British officials frowned on the use of balance of power terms to justify British aid to Prussia, since it was Frederick II who had "disturbed the balance" with his attack on Austria.[41] In all these writings and statements the term "balance of power" is used and abused as a descriptive phrase, connoting the existence or non-existence of equilibrium and the actual or threatened hegemony of some state or alliance. The same easy transition in meaning from "distribution" to "equilibrium" and finally to "hegemony" can sometimes be detected in contemporary references to the balance of power. These usages are rarely kept in their separate compartments. And, when the users' intentions go beyond that of mere description, clarity of thought and purpose may be seriously jeopardized.

Balance of Power as Propaganda and "Ideology"

A precise understanding of the verbal meaning of the term "balance of power" becomes especially important when it is used as a propagandistic slogan or as an ideological phrase, in the Mannheimian sense. The meanings of "balance" as being identical with either "peace" or "war" fall into this category. Obviously, while it might be correct to speak of a state of balance or imbalance *implying* or *engendering* either war or peace, the balance as such cannot logically be equated with conditions which might arise as a consequence of the balance, i.e., war or peace. In the cases in which the authors employed it to mean "peace" or "war," "balance of power" then became no more than a convenient catchword to focus individual aspirations into a generally acceptable mold; and there can be no doubt that at certain times the concept of balance was an extremely popular one, whether it was used for policy-making or not. If used in a patently forced manner, the term becomes indistin-

[41] For examples, see E. Kaeber, *Die Idee des Europäischen Gleichgewichts in der publizistischen Literatur vom 16. bis zur Mitte des 18. Jahrhunderts*, Berlin, 1906, pp. 44–47.

guishable from plain propaganda. Of this particular usage some striking examples may be cited.

Thus, the anonymous author of the *Relative State of Great Britain in 1813* saw fit to make the phrase cover the total complex of his social, economic, moral, and political predilections:

> The French revolution being founded in the principle of depraving and reversing the human heart and feeling (as the American Republic is built upon frigid indifference and calculation of gain), it is not difficult to perceive how everything which tended to preserve the bond of sacredness of national contracts, and the reciprocity of benefits and engagements—how history, and memory itself, became objects of hatred and jealousy, and organized assault and hostility—and how the balance of power, in particular, opposed and threatened the views of France, which were to ruin and destroy everything, and the views of America to make profit and percentage upon the ruin and destruction of everything. Nor is it easy to pronounce a juster or more happy panegyric upon that system, than what evidently and immediately results from the forced and unnatural coalition of such powers as these (the very worst extremes of democracy and despotism), and the common interest their leaders conceive themselves to have discovered in extinguishing it.

The depraved ideology of France and the United States seemed here to be identified with the upsetting of the balance of power. And the re-establishment of the balance would be the means to end this deplorable state of morality:

> For my part, I shall never blush to confess, that I am able to form no conception of any security in any peace that shall have no guarantees—any effectual guarantee, without a distribution and partition of force, adjusted by political alliance and combination—of any defense or protection for that distribution without a permanent and recognized system of public law, and a real or reputed balance of power amongst the several states it embraces.[42]

This treatment, then, identifies the balance of power with the kind of world conditions, in their totality, which the author desires. The fact that domestic, moral, and ideological factors are haphazardly mixed up with considerations of pure power seems not to have made any difference.

This invocation of the balance of power was no more propagandistic, however, than the use made of it by Friedrich Wilhelm II

---

[42] Anon., *Considerations on the Relative State of Great Britain in 1813,* London, 1813, pp. 3–4.

in the Declaration of Pillnitz, June 25, 1792, which constituted the manifesto of the allied monarchs attacking France:

> There was no power interested in maintaining the European balance which could be indifferent when the Kingdom of France, which formed such a considerable weight in that great balance, was delivered for long periods of time to internal agitation and to the horrors of disorder and anarchy, which, so to speak, have nullified its political existence.[43]

But the era of the Revolution and the Empire by no means provided the only examples of this type of application. It enjoyed a renaissance during World War I. Then F. J. Schmidt, for instance, asserted that "Germany has the historical call to realize the idea of the balance of power in all its territorial and maritime consequences."[44] And as detached a scholar as Friedrich Meinecke argued that the peace treaty should establish a "new balance of power" instead of depriving Germany of all her conquests.[45] Nor was the invocation of the balance by Louis XIV much different when he used it to justify the accession of his grandson to the throne of Spain, nor Fleury's use of it when he called upon its absolving force to explain France's attack on the Pragmatic Sanction in 1740.[46]

It is apparent that in all these cases the balance of power was invoked in such a way as to serve as the justification for policies not *ipso facto* related to balancing anything. In some instances it was used to cloak ideological conflicts, in others to sanctify the search for hegemony over Europe, and in still others to "justify" the continued strength and size of a defeated state. The significance of this invocation, then, lies not in any theoretical belief but in the fact that the users of the term felt so convinced of its popularity as to

[43] Cited in A. de Stieglitz, *De l'équilibre politique, du légitimisme et du principe des nationalités*, Paris, 1893–1897, I, p. 51. See also the facile use of the doctrine made by Bonald in (1) justifying Napoleonic expansion and (2) asking for a lenient peace in 1815 (Moulinié, *De Bonald*, Paris, 1915, pp. 390–97).

[44] F. J. Schmidt, in *Preussische Jahrbücher*, CLVIII (1914), pp. 1–15; also H. Oncken, *Das alte und das neue Mitteleuropa*, Gotha, 1917, passim.

[45] F. Meinecke, *Probleme des Weltkriegs*, Munich, 1917, p. 134. In his important *Die Idee der Staatsräson in der neueren Geschichte*, in which he claims to be analyzing the doctrine and philosophical meaning of the *raison d'état* idea completely dispassionately, the same argument shows up rather prominently in the last chapter dressed up in terms of historical necessity.

[46] K. Jacob, "Die Chimäre des Gleichgewichts," *Archiv für Urkundenforschung*, VI (1918), pp. 349, 351, 354–55.

make its conversion into a symbol of proper policy propagandistically profitable.

Propaganda assumes the dishonest use of facts and the distortion of concepts devised on intellectually sincere grounds. It implies conscious and deliberate falsification.[47] Ideology, as defined by Mannheim, however, postulates belief in a set of symbols which, even though they may be "false" objectively, still characterize the total myth system of social groups and are essential to the spiritual cohesion of a ruling group which would lose its sense of control if it were conscious of the "real" state of affairs. It is therefore possible to raise the hypothesis that the balance of power may have served such "ideological" purposes. It may have been used to explain policies in terms of natural laws, in terms of moral rightness, or in terms of historical necessity if the symbol chosen to "put it over" was a sufficiently widely accepted one; indeed, if it was a symbol— even a metaphorical one—which the ruling groups themselves tended to accept. In this sense, the term "balance of power" would not serve a strictly propagandistic purpose, since the element of falsification yields to the element of self-deception.[48]

In a remarkable eighteenth-century essay the whole concept of the balance of power was criticized in these very terms. In his *Die Chimäre des Gleichgewichts von Europa,* Justi concluded that the balance of power theory is nothing but the ideological justification adopted by statesmen eager to hide their real motives, motives usually described by the term "aggression." As he put it:

> We regard the dependence of a free state upon another and more powerful state, the latter trying to prevent the former from adopting the proper measures for its happiness, as the greatest misfor-

[47] My conception of propaganda may be expressed in Leonard W. Doob's definition: "Intentional propaganda is a systematic attempt by an interested individual (or individuals) to control the attitudes of groups of individuals through the use of suggestion and, consequently, to control their actions" (*Propaganda,* New York, 1935, p. 89). It is clear that this postulation does not assume that the propagandist himself accepts the material or shares the attitudes he attempts to disseminate. I cannot accept the definition of propaganda offered by Doob in *Public Opinion and Propaganda* (New York, 1948, p. 240), since it seems almost indistinguishable from the more general concept of ideology.

[48] For a masterful analysis of this aspect of the balance of power, see Alfred Vagts, "The Balance of Power: Growth of an Idea," *World Politics,* I (October 1948), pp. 88–89, 100 ff. I have explored the ideological significance of the concept with respect to European diplomacy in the 1830's in my doctoral dissertation, *Belgium and the Balance of Power,* Columbia University Library.

tune of a people, which should be avoided through the system of the balance of power. Yet such a coarse idea of universal monarchy which aims at reducing all states to provinces of its own state can scarcely ever be realized; however, the means proposed to avoid it are far more to be feared than the evil itself. If a balance of power were to exist in actuality then no slavery would be as hard, since each state would oppose every other state. Upon each new domestic arrangement, each internal improvement, the other states would be compelled to protest and interfere in order to prevent the first state from growing too powerful because of its domestic perfection. And the mutual dependence of such states would be far worse slavery than dependence upon one powerful neighbor. One state would object to one feature and the second to another feature of the internal improvement, and each state would concern itself more with the domestic business of its neighbors than with its own perfection.

All this, Justi argues, means that the whole concept is impossible.[49] And again, he urges what he considers the real *raison d'être* of the usage, thus, incidentally, coming perilously close to characterizing the balance of power as a purely propagandistic device:

> When a state which has grown more powerful internally is attacked . . . in order to weaken it, such action is motivated least of all by the balance of power. This would be a war which is waged by the several states against the strong state for specific interests, and the rules of the balance of power will only be camouflage under which these interests are hidden. . . . States, like private persons, are guided by nothing but their private interests, real or imaginary, and they are far from being guided by a chimerical balance of power. Name one state which has participated in a war contrary to its interests or without a specific interest, only to maintain the balance of power.[50]

The distinction between the propagandistic and ideological uses is thus a tenuous one. The "camouflage" is ideological only if the actors on the international stage are themselves convinced, to some extent, of the identity of "private interest" with a general need for balancing power *qua* power.

[49] J. H. G. von Justi, *Die Chimäre des Gleichgewichts von Europa*, Altona, 1758, p. 60.

[50] *Ibid.*, p. 65. Albert Sorel's estimate of the invocation of balancing terminology by statesmen is a similar one. Since he denies that balancing policies are deliberately chosen by diplomats and since he urges that only the search for unilateral hegemony motivates policy, he argues in fact that the use of the term by statesmen implies a disguised hankering for superiority and no more (*L'Europe et la Révolution francaise*, Paris, 1908, I, p. 34).

Balance of Power as Analytical Concept

At the opposite pole of the propaganda-oriented application of the term "balance of power" lies the user's intention to employ the term as a tool of analysis. It is in this area of intentions that the term rose to the status of a theory of international relations during the eighteenth and nineteenth centuries, no less than it has in our own era. It is also true, however, that in this area as well as in the other fields of intentions analyzed so far not one but several of the verbal meanings of the term find application. Even as a tool of scholarly analysis the term has been used to mean "power politics," "equilibrium," "hegemony" and, finally, a "universal law" of state conduct.

"The basic principle of the balance of power," wrote Réal de Curban, "is incontestable: the power of one ruler, in the last analysis, is nothing but the ruin and diminution of that of his neighbors, and his power is nothing but the weakness of the others."[51] And in a Hobbesian state of nature which was presupposed to exist among sovereign states no other conclusion seemed possible. This reasoning has led numerous writers to equate the balance of power with power politics or *Realpolitik* generally. The struggle for self-preservation in the state of nature implies the formation of alliances and mutually antagonistic blocs which in turn make negotiations in "good faith" a contradiction in terms. Power politics are the only discernible pattern in which balancing is an inherent process. As such, it is not separate from but identical with competitive power struggles. Consequently, in dispassionate analyses of international affairs the "balance" of power carries no significance other than that usually associated with "power politics," unrefined by any conception of equilibrium or deliberate balancing measures.[52]

Furthermore, the concept of evenly balanced power, or "equilibrium," finds frequent application as a tool of analysis. In the preceding discussion the equilibrium concept found application merely as a descriptive phrase implying no generalized behavior pattern in international relations. In the present context the reverse

---

[51] Réal de Curban, *La science du gouvernement*, Paris, 1764, VI, p. 442.
[52] See, e.g., H. N. Brailsford and G. Lowes Dickinson, as quoted in Georg Schwarzenberger, *Power Politics*, London, 1940, p. 123, and also the author's own comments, which also tend to equate power politics with power balance.

is true. Lasswell, in speaking of the "balancing process," for instance, assumes that under conditions of expected future violence—domestic as well as international—any increase in the coercion potential of one power unit will lead to a compensatory increase in the competing unit or units. Further increases on the part of one side will always bring corresponding increases on the part of its competitors, so that in effect a rough equality of power potential will always prevail, a factor which may make for either open conflict or induce fear of refraining from hostilities, depending on circumstances, the nature of the elites in question, and the accuracy of intelligence reports concerning the degree of "balancing." The analytical application of the equilibrium-meaning of the balance of power, in short, generalizes the basic assumption of the absence of international consensus and the consequent inherent presence of conflict into a pattern of balancing.

Carrying the equilibrium-meaning one step further results in the application of the balance of power concept as implying the search for hegemony. This application again finds its counterpart in the intentions of detached analysts striving for a generalized understanding of phenomena rather than for description. Spykman, as demonstrated above, clearly sets forth the assumptions of this approach. His argument is that the search for power by sovereign states is an end in itself, since conflict—actual or potential—is the only consistent pattern in relations between state units. While the search for power originally implied the desire for self-preservation, a generalized desire for power-seeking over a long period of time converts this process into an end in itself. On this level, the discussion of the balance of power is identical with power politics generally. As in the case of Lasswell's balancing process, however, the generalized process of competitive power-seeking must result in equilibrium if war is avoided—temporarily. But statesmen, as indicated above, seek a margin of safety in superiority of power and not in equality of power. Hence the search for equilibrium in effect is the search for hegemony, and the balance of power as an analytical concept becomes another term for the simultaneous search for preponderance of power by all the sovereign participants. No wonder Spykman exclaims that

He who plays the balance of power can have no permanent friends. His devotion can be to no specific state but only to balanced power. The ally of today is the enemy of tomorrow. One of the charms of power politics is that it offers no opportunity to grow weary of one's friends. England's reputation as *perfide Albion* is the inevitable result of her preoccupation with the balance of power.[53]

In this refined analysis, the balance of power comes to be considered as a special case—either in its equilibrium or its hegemony connotation—in the general pattern of power politics, though Spykman in the passage just cited again tends to use the two terms interchangeably.

The supreme attempt to use the balance of power as an analytical concept arises in the case of those writers who make the balance the essence of a theory of international relations. It is here that the balance attains the quality of a "law of history," as indeed Rousseau and Donnadieu implied by their very choice of words, and many contemporary writers by their emphasis on the "naturalness" of state behavior in accordance with the dictates of balanced power. The universal law connotation of the balance of power presupposes state conduct in no way different from the assumptions of Spykman and Lasswell. But Professors Morgenthau and Schuman, for instance, in giving the balance of power this extended meaning, go beyond the characterization of equilibrium and hegemony. They develop the thesis that it is inherent in the nature of a multi-state system based on sovereignty to engage in mutually hostile policies, for whatever motives. In this process the search for balanced power, the need to form blocs and counterblocs to prevent the feared attainment of hegemony by one or the other of the participants in the conflict is a natural, if not instinctive, choice of policy. A group of revisionist states always lines up against a group of states devoted to the maintenance of the status quo in such a way that approximate balance results. So general is this pattern that it attains the quality of a historical law. And the characteristic feature of this law is that it does not necessarily assume a conscious intention on the part of statesmen to "balance power with power" in a sense which would imply the official acceptance of a balance of power theory by governments. Statesmen, to be sure, may be consciously motivated by balancing notions. But, if they are not, the policies which they would most logically adopt would be those consistent with the balance of power. As Professor Morgenthau indicates, if they fail to do so, they do not make "logical" policy and thereby violate historically proven and generalized modes of conduct. The distinc-

[53] N. Spykman, *America's Strategy in World Politics*, New York, 1942, pp. 1–21, 103–4.

tive feature about the balance of power applied as a tool of analysis, then, is its possible separation from the motivations of governments.

Balance of Power as Prescription

While the analytical application of the term does not imply conscious acceptance of balancing rules by governments, there is a large body of thought—historical and contemporary—which does insist that the balance of power is—or should be—a guiding principle for decision-making on the part of governments. It is this application of the term which makes use of the meaning defined above as "guide-and-system." Once more international relations are pictured, in one version, as being in the Hobbesian state of nature, so that survival dictates the formation of alliances among those states committed to "preserving the balance" against the onslaught of the state(s) allegedly seeking world or regional domination or, as the eighteenth-century writers put it, "universal monarchy." In this sense, the balance is a conscious guide dictating the rules of survival. In another sense, however, the world (or Europe, in the earlier writing) is represented as a "system" of states tied together by mutual interdependence, common institutions, and a common system of law (the law of nations), and the search for hegemony of a single member of this "system" was then represented as an attack upon the whole organic unit.[54] The system was based on the continued independence of all members and their common will to resist the search for hegemony by any one of their number. The balance of power was inherent in the very system itself and also acted as a body of rules dictating the proper policies for preventing the attainment of hegemony, i.e., it acted as a "guide."

That Metternich subscribed in principle and in considerable detail to the theory of the balance of power as a guide to foreign policy-making is beyond any doubt. Consistent with his overall political philosophy of the value of historically sanctioned social and political traditions, of the need for preserving what the historical process had created and for protecting it against the fanaticism and stupidity of misguided men, i.e., the liberals, Metternich considered

[54] The extreme example of this body of thought is represented by Wolff with his concept of the *civitas maxima* and the role of the balance of power in preventing its destruction (*Ius Gentium Methoda Scientifica Pertractantum*, pars. 642–43, 646, 651. *Classics of International Law*, no. 13, 1934). Also Pufendorf, *Ius Naturae et Gentium*. Book viii, ch. 6, *ibid.*, no. 17, 1934.

the balance of power as another of these time-hallowed doctrines, and as an international institution vital to the preservation of the total institutional status quo which he so cherished. As he wrote:

> Politics is the science of the life of the state, on its highest level. Since isolated states no longer exist . . . it is the society of states, this important condition of the contemporary world, which has to be watched carefully. Thus each state, in addition to its particular interests, has certain common interests, either with the totality of the other states or with certain groups among them. The great axioms of political science derive from the understanding of real political interests, of all states; the guarantee for their existence rests in these general interests, whereas particular interests . . . only possess a relative and secondary value. History teaches that whenever the particular interests of one state are in contradiction with the general interest and whenever the latter is neglected or misunderstood, this condition . . . is to be regarded as exceptional and pathological. . . . The modern world is characterized, in distinction to the old world, by a tendency of states to approach one another and to enter into the bonds of society in some manner; so that the resulting bond rests on the same foundations as the great society which developed in the shadow of Christianity. This foundation consists of the command of the Book of Books: "Do not do unto others what you would not have others do unto you." Applying this basic rule of all human associations to the state, the result is reciprocity, politically speaking, and its effect is. . . : mutual respect and honest conduct. In the ancient world, politics sought pure isolation and practiced absolute egoism, without any control save common sense. . . . Modern history, however, shows us the application of the principle of solidarity and the balance of power offers us the drama of the unified efforts of several states in restraining the hegemony of a single state and limiting the expansion of its influence, and thus forcing it to return to public law.[55]

This formulation of international relations in general as necessary and close rapport between the states of Europe, which he regarded in the then customary manner as so many atoms in a universe held together by Christian moral rules and the dictates of international law, and of the balance of power as the *ad hoc* regulating mechanism of this system, is in almost all respects identical with the formulation of Ancillon, of Castlereagh, of Brougham, and of Gentz. Thus Ancillon, Prussian court chaplain in the 1820's, tutor to Frederick William IV, and State Secretary for Foreign Affairs from 1832 until 1835, argued:

[55] Metternich, *Aus Metternichs Nachgelassenen Papieren*, Vienna, 1882, I, pp. 32ff., a section entitled, "Maxims on Which the Actions of My Political Career Have Been Based."

All forces are similar to the nature of expanding bodies; thus, in the society of large states in which law does not enjoy an external guarantee, we take as our point of departure the possible or even probable misuse of force. What will be the result? Mutual distrust, fear and restlessness, always recurring and always effective. Each state can have no other maxims in its external relations than these: whoever can do us damage through an excessive balance of power in his favor, or through his geographical position, is our natural enemy, but whoever in view of his position and forces is able to harm our enemy, is our natural friend. These simple maxims which the need for self-preservation has given to man, are and have been at all times the anchors on which all of politics rests.[56]

Nor was Castlereagh's understanding of the balance of power much different, even though he indicated that "my real and only object was to create a permanent counterpoise to the power of France in peace as well as in war." The Concert of Europe through its regular conferences was merely to be the consultative mechanism whereby the *ad hoc* balance could be maintained through timely negotiations.[57] However, the likelihood of the guide-and-system version of the balance implying different "rules" for different states is here betrayed.

Gentz's theory of the balance of power was stated in his *Fragmente aus der neusten Geschichte des politischen Gleichgewichts in Europa* (1806), the purpose of which was to give the Austrian and British governments an excuse for unleashing a new war on Napoleon without having been attacked first. Gentz, it might be added, was in the pay of the British cabinet to produce writings of this type. He rejected the arguments that an exact equilibrium is impossible and that power cannot be measured as irrelevant to the system, since all the system requires is eternal vigilance that no state acquires enough power to overawe all of Europe.[58] Also, he thought that the certainty of a strong counterforce being mustered against the hegemony-seeker was a sufficient deterrent and that actual war would usually be unnecessary. And

[56] Paul Haake, *J. P. F. Ancillon and Kronprinz Friedrich Wilhelm IV. von Preussen*, Munich, 1920, p. 40. Of Ancillon's own works, see his *Ueber den Geist der Staatsverfassungen und dessen Einfluss auf die Gesetzgebung*, Berlin, 1825, pp. 16–19, 313–14, 317–31, and *Tableau des révolutions du système de l'Europe*, Paris, 1806, iv, pp. 5–19.

[57] Sir Charles Webster, *British Diplomacy, 1813–1815*, London, 1921, pp. 62, 218; and Castlereagh's memorandum of October 30, 1814, for Alexander I, cited in Angeberg, *Les traités de Vienne*, Paris, 1864, pp. 399–401.

[58] Gentz, *Fragmente aus der neutsten Geschichte des politischen Gleichgewichts in Europa*, St. Petersburg, 1806, pp. 1–8.

Only when one or the other state, with open violence, invented pretexts, or artificially concocted legal titles, undertakes enterprises which, directly or in their inevitable consequences, lead to the enslavement of its weaker neighbors, or to the constant endangering, gradual weakening and eventual demise of its stronger neighbors, only then there will come about a breach of the balance, according to the sound conceptions of the collective interest of a system of states; only then will the several states combine in order to prevent the hegemony of a single state, through a timely contrived counterweight.[59]

Yet Gentz opposed policies of partition and compensation as violating the true conservative character of the theory. Moreover, there could be no such thing as indifference to a given issue, since under the power rules all issues had to be of equal interest to all states in the system.[60] His comments on the right to intervene in the domestic affairs of other states are of the highest interest. Gentz urged that ideological distastes for internal changes elsewhere did not in themselves constitute a ground for balance of power intervention and war. But as soon as such changes had the necessary consequence of upsetting the balance of power, i.e., as soon as the new ideology seemed to suggest the search for hegemony, then the right to intervene existed, as in 1793.[61]

The case of Lord Brougham is a fascinating one for the study of the theory of the balance of power. In his essay on "The Balance of Power," written in 1803, he urged that the balance was the only tenable theory of international relations. He defined it in the same terms as Gentz and Ancillon and added:

Had it not been for that wholesome jealousy of rival neighbors, which modern politicians have learned to cherish, how many conquests and changes of dominion would have taken place, instead of wars, in which some lives were lost, not perhaps the most valuable in the community, and some superfluous million were squandered! How many fair portions of the globe might have been deluged in blood, instead of some hundreds of sailors fighting harmlessly on the barren plains of the ocean, and some thousands of soldiers carrying on a scientific and regular and quiet system of warfare in countries set apart for the purpose, and resorted to as the arena where the disputes of nations might be determined.

The old argument of the tacit federation of Europe, the common system of law and morals, and the need for the regulating mechanism of the balance to keep one of the "federated" states from

59 *Ibid.*, pp. 10–14.
60 *Ibid.*, ch. ii.
61 *Ibid.*, ch. iv.

absorbing the others is restated in full.[62] The principle, as well as the detailed application of the theory in its guide-and-system form, were stated by the young Brougham in the classical manner, and with unsurpassed and brief lucidity:

> It is not then in the mere plan for forming offensive or defensive alliances; or in the principles of attacking a neighbor in order to weaken his power, before he has betrayed hostile views; or in the policy of defending a rival, in order to stay, in proper time, the progress of a common enemy; it is not in these simple maxims that the modern system consists. These are indeed the elements, the great and leading parts of the theory; they are the maxims dictated by the plainest and coarsest views of political expediency: but they do not form the whole system; nor does the knowledge of them . . . comprehend an acquaintance with the profounder and more subtile parts of modern policy. The grand and distinguishing feature of the balancing theory, is the systematic form to which it reduces those plain and obvious principles of national conduct; the perpetual attention to foreign affairs which it inculcates; the constant watchfulness which it prescribes over every movement in all parts of the system; the subjection in which it tends to place all national passions and antipathies to the views of remote expediency; the unceasing care which it dictates of national concerns most remotely situated, and apparently unconnected with ourselves; the general union, which it has effected, of all the European powers in one connecting system—obeying certain laws and actuated, for the most part, by a common principle; in fine, as a consequence of the whole, the right of mutual inspection, now universally recognized among civilized states, in the appointment of public envoys and residents [sic]. This is the balancing theory.[63]

Intervention in domestic developments of other states, of course, is legal if the balance of power is really and truly threatened by these changes. The superiority of the balance to all ideological considerations, so plainly stated here, is especially striking. This principle he repeated in his "General Principles of Foreign Policy" (1843) in most emphatic terms:

> But the mere circumstance of our preferring a democratic to an aristocratic or a monarchical to a republican scheme of government, can never afford any good ground for uniting with others who have the same preference, against a community or a league of states, whose views of national polity are of a contrary description.[64]

[62] Brougham, *Works*, London, 1872, viii, pp. 4–12.
[63] *Ibid.*, pp. 12–13, 33–38.
[64] *Ibid.*, pp. 70–71, 77, 79–80, 80–83.

Hence the Holy Alliance—or the Western bloc against it after 1832—was not consistent with the rules of the balance. Not only is ideological intervention condemned, but Brougham urged that

> it is the bounden duty of all rulers to discourage sentiments in their subjects leading to national enmities; and when a popular cry arises against any foreign people, a general clamor for war, there is no more sacred duty on the part of the government than to resist such a clamor and keep the peace in spite of it.[65]

In short, any manifestations of public opinion had to be rigorously excluded from policy-making under balancing rules, a sentiment heard more and more frequently in our present epoch.

Whether the balance of power is regarded merely as a set of rules to be applied to the preservation of the state or whether it is expanded into the defensive mechanism of some "system"—and by analogy the United Nations system might today be considered the successor to the European system postulated by the earlier writers—the rules laid down by Gentz and Brougham remain the same. The statesman who is anxious to preserve his state must have recourse to balancing principles in averting the hegemony of his rival. The perusal of the contemporary literature on this subject confirms this conclusion. George F. Kennan's *American Diplomacy* is merely the latest and best-known example of the continuing importance ascribed to balancing rules in international relations. And the fact that the examples cited concerned statesmen conscious of the balance as a motivating force underlines the possible importance of the concept as prescription. . . .

36. *THE BALANCE OF POWER AND THE BALANCE OF TERROR* / GLENN H. SNYDER*

It is now rather widely believed that the balance of power has been overtaken by technology; that nuclear weapons and missiles have brought the balancing process to a halt and substituted a new and

* Glenn H. Snyder, "The Balance of Power and the Balance of Terror," in Paul Seabury, ed., *Balance of Power* (San Francisco: Chandler Publishing Company, 1965), pp. 185–201. Reprinted by permission of the International Textbook Company.

quite different regulator—that of nuclear deterrence.[1] This article will challenge this view. The balance of power theory is still generally valid and still a useful model of at least certain important aspects of contemporary world politics. The new military technology has not terminated but only modified the balance of power process. It has superimposed a new system of equilibrium (the phrase "balance of terror" will serve) upon the old system which was based on nonnuclear capabilities. The two systems operate according to different tendencies and principles and can be separated analytically, but in practice they are inextricably mixed in a new balance of power in which elements of the old coexist with the new. I will attempt to compare the two subprocesses at certain salient points and then describe the nature of their interaction in an integrated process.

The Balance of Terror

There are naïve and sophisticated versions of the "balance of terror" or the nuclear strategic balance. The naïve view, the image held by relatively uninformed laymen, is simply that both sides are deterred from using nuclear weapons against the other by the fear of devastating retaliation. In this image, the targets of the nuclear strikes are cities. To initiate nuclear war would be to commit national suicide; hence a "balance" or "stalemate" exists.

The sophisticated version focuses on "counterforce" rather than "countervalue" (city) targeting. One or both sides could eliminate or drastically reduce the other side's retaliatory capacity by directing the first strike at the opponent's nuclear striking forces rather than at his cities. There are circumstances, theoretically at least, in which thermonuclear war initiated in this manner would be a rational act. According to this version, a "balance of terror" exists when neither side can, by executing a counterforce first-strike, reduce the opponent's retaliation to "acceptable" proportions. Or, to use the jargon of the trade, neither side has a "full first-strike capability," or (what amounts to virtually the same thing) both sides possess at least a "minimum strike-back capability"—i.e., a residual capacity which after suffering the attrition of the attacker's first

---

[1] For an early statement of this view, see Arthur Lee Burns, "From Balance to Deterrence," *World Politics*, Vol. IX (1957), pp. 494-529.

blow, could still inflict intolerable damage on the attacker's cities, population and economic assets in a retaliatory blow.

But the "sophisticated" version, as here defined, is not sophisticated enough. What, for example, is the criterion for defining the degree of retaliation that is "acceptable"? What purpose does the victim serve by retaliation against the attacker's cities, other than revenge? What motivates the attacker to strike in the first place; what purpose of political goal is served by a counterforce first strike? Eliminating or reducing the victim's capacity to retaliate is not a purpose but a precaution. How is the war terminated after the initial strike and reprisal? What then determines the terms of settlement? What constitutes "victory" or "defeat"?

To make use of the sophisticated version for our purposes, it is necesaary to return part way to the naïve image. I shall assert, somewhat heretically, that the *ultimate* function of nuclear weapons (especially the "strategic" variety) is either to destroy the enemy's cities and conventional war potential, or to support a threat to do so for purposes of blackmail or deterrence. To make this clear it is convenient to start with a model of the balance of terror in its "pure" form. Assume two states, A and B armed only with nuclear strategic missiles. Assume that both states are expansionist—i.e., that they both would like to subjugate all or part of the other if they could do so at acceptable cost.

In this model, the only means of subjugation is by nuclear blackmail. Blackmail, of course, cannot succeed as long as the opponent can make a "deterrent" counterthreat of devastating retaliation. But A, for example, may be able to blackmail B successfully if it can ment two requirements. First, it must be able to disarm B by a counterforce "first strike" or at least destroy enough of B's forces to restrict its retaliation to "acceptable" proportions. The criterion of "acceptability" is the amount of retaliatory damage to A which is just equivalent to the value which A places on B's capitulation to its demands. The demand may be for B's total capitulation or for some lesser concession. Secondly, A must maintain in reserve a force sufficient to blackmail B into conceding by the threat of "countervalue" or population destruction. Roughly, the necessary size of this force is measured by the value which A thinks B places on the things he is being asked to concede. If A fires all its forces in attempting to disarm B, it dissipates its blackmail or bargaining power and cannot achieve its political goal.

If A (or B, or both) can meet both of these requirements the balance of terror is in disequilibrium. If both sides fall short of one or both requirements, an attack by either side is either futile or too costly and the balance of terror is in a state of equilibrium.

Note that A's initial counterforce strike is merely preliminary, undertaken only to put itself in a position to blackmail B. Counterforce strikes do not contribute *directly* to "winning the war," as is suggested in some of the current literature; they contribute only indirectly by improving the attacker's relative bargaining power— i.e., his power to coerce the victim by the threat to strike cities. And they contribute to this end *with high confidence* only if they are sufficient to reduce the victim's retaliatory capacity to below A's "acceptable" level. If B is left with residual forces higher than this level, he may be able to resist A's postattack blackmail.

In the "real world," of course, A will have conventional forces; a combination of counterforce and countervalue strikes against B may so prostrate B as to make physical conquest possible and blackmail unnecessary. But such conquest would be the result of A's preponderance in the conventional balance after the nuclear exchange, and therefore falls under the heading of "interaction" between the two balances, which is discussed below.

Differences between the Conventional Balance and the Nuclear Balance

To compare and then integrate the two balancing systems, the first questions to be asked are: What is the nature of the "power" being balanced? What is the nature of "equilibrium" in each case? In traditional theory of (conventional) balance of power, the kind of power involved was the physical capability to take or hold territory. Equilibrium was said to obtain when military capabilities and war potential on each side were roughly equal, so that neither side had the capacity to defeat the other in war and by so doing to change the territorial status quo. The preceding discussion shows that this is not the case in the nuclear "balance of terror." Nuclear weapons cannot, when employed, in and of themselves, take or hold territory. Physical conquest during or after a nuclear exchange requires the intervention of conventional forces. In the "pure" balance of terror, the political status quo can be changed only by political coercion—that is, by a process of blackmail supported by the threat of severe punishment. The status quo is preserved by "deterrence" supported by a similar threat. Thus the power that is balanced in the balance of terror is essentially "political power" rather than physical capabilities; capabilities enter in only as the threatened sanction supporting the political demand; not as an instrument for the direct physical achievement of political goals as is usually the case in the traditional or conventional balance of power.

The balance of terror is more subjective in nature than the old balance of power. Whether "equilibrium" exists depends at least as much on factors "within the minds" of the opponents as upon an objective comparison of military capabilities. Subjectivity is obvious in the fact that equilibrium is defined in terms of "acceptability" of damage for both sides; what is acceptable depends on the values attached to the political stakes. Thus, in contrast to the old balance of power, in which the state of the equilibrium could be objectively —if roughly—determined by the uninvolved observer, such an observer can only intuitively guess at equilibrium in the balance of terror, since it depends principally on whether the gains to be made or losses to be avoided by striking first are less than the costs to be incurred—all as subjectively valued in the minds of the decision-makers.

The balance of terror is subjective in still another sense. The participants themselves, while presumably they can judge what is unacceptable damage for themselves, cannot be certain what is unacceptable for the opponent. Thus the determination of whether equilibrium exists is ultimately reduced to a guessing game about the opponent's values and intentions. There is therefore vast scope for disagreement or asymmetrical perceptions about the state of the balance and about the degree of political, military or technological change which would throw it "out of balance." For example, the balance may actually be in equilibrium, but one side may fear the other side *may* possess a full first-strike capability. Then the latter may achieve its political aims by bluff, whether these aims are of a deterrent or blackmail nature. In the obverse case—when the balance is in disequilibrium because one side can be provoked to strike first, but its opponent doesn't perceive this—the outcome could be war by "miscalculation."

Subjective considerations determine the "location" or "boundaries" of equilibrium within the spectrum of possible force ratios, but a comparison of relative capabilities is obviously still necessary for estimating whether equilibrium actually exists at any given time. However, in sharp contrast to the traditional balance of power, the notion of quantitative equality between striking forces is totally irrelevant as a criterion for "balance." Equilibrium can exist when one side's offensive forces are far inferior to the other's, provided the inferior side's forces are relatively invulnerable to a counterforce strike and provided the forces surviving such a strike can penetrate the attacker's air defenses in sufficient numbers to inflict unacceptable damage. Or equilibrium might require having more striking forces than the opponent if one's own forces are highly vulnerable, and the enemy has a very good air defense and civil defense system. The essential criterion for equilibrium is a mutual capacity to inflict intolerable damage n retaliation, and this depends on a variety of technological factors in addition to numbers of delivery vehicles.

A corollary of this distinction is that, while a balance of conventional power can be said to exist only within a rather narrow range of relative capabilities on either side of strict equality, a balance of terror can exist within a wide range of force ratios. To illustrate: assuming relatively invulnerable offensive forces and rather impotent air-missile defense systems on both sides, side A, with 100 missiles, might be in a state of equilibrium against side B with 500 missiles; equilibrium might still obtain if side A were to increase its force to 1,000 missiles. In other words, even a ten-fold increase by one side might not overturn the balance. The "range of equilibrium" would be the difference between the forces which A needs for a "minimum strike-back capability" and the forces it needs for a "full first-strike capability." This consideration has important implications for the *stability* of the balance of terror, to be discussed below.

Another important contrast between the two systems lies in the relative weight given to the functions of *deterrence* and *defense*. Both were functions of the prenuclear balance (and still are in today's conventional balance of power); but deterrence was secondary in the sense that it was an incidental consequence of an obvious capacity to defend territory successfully. It was also secondary in the sense that the primary purpose of balancing techniques—armaments, alliances, etc.—was to be ready to frustrate an expansionist state rather than to influence the intentions of that state. If deterrence failed, defensive war was considered to be a normal technique of the balancing process, a continuation of the process by violent means.

By contrast, the balance of terror centers heavily on the function of deterrence. Deterrence is achieved by the threat of devastating punishment or damage, not as a simple by-product of a capacity to defend territory or otherwise to frustrate the aggressor's aims. If deterrence fails, the system will have broken down completely; nuclear war cannot be considered a normal "technique" for adjusting or restoring the balance. This does not mean that it is not useful or wise to take measures in advance of war to mitigate the dreadful consequences of nuclear war, or even to "win the war" in some sense. In particular, it may be desirable (as the United States has done) to develop a "surplus" of offensive striking forces far beyond the amount needed for a deterrent equilibrium, in order to be able to destroy a maximum amount of the attacker's postattack residual forces, while holding in reserve a powerful force for bargaining purposes. Such additional forces do not essentially disturb the equilibrium, unless they create a degree of preponderance which begins to approach a full first-strike capability.

Interactions in the "Mixed" Balance of Power

Nuclear and conventional balancing processes do not operate independently; they impinge on each other in various ways. The contemporary balancing process, in an overall sense, is a mixture of the two. Generally speaking, the entire system is in overall "balance" when either of two conditions exist. One is when each of the two subprocesses is "out of balance" but in different directions—i.e., when one side preponderates in one component and the other side in the other. The other condition is when both conventional and nuclear balances are separately in equilibrium. If one is in balance and the other is not, the entire system is in a state of disequilibrium, at least with respect to any particular political issue. This is also the case when both processes are unbalanced in favor of one side.

To illuminate these somewhat cryptic remarks, let us turn away from our abstract model to the world of reality. We see a world of two nuclear powers (the Soviet Union, and the United States–Great Britain as a unit) which also have conventional forces; we also see two incipient nuclear powers and many nonnuclear powers. All possess conventional forces; some of them enjoy the protection of one or the other of the nuclear great powers.

That the latter enjoy the protection of the nuclear great powers means that the political function of nuclear weapons has been extended from strictly bilateral deterrence and blackmail between nuclear powers to that of deterring aggression against other (nonnuclear) countries. This function may require the nuclear protector to create an actual or apparent nuclear disequilibrium in his favor to make credible a determination to strike first if provoked by an attack on his allies. Short of this, or concurrent with it, he can threaten the *limited* use of nuclear weapons in either a "tactical" or "strategic" manner.

The best example of interaction is the balance of power in Europe. Here, the Soviets preponderate in the conventional balance (although not so greatly as we thought a few years ago); while the United States, as West Europe's protector, remains superior in nuclear forces. Yet it is doubtful whether the United States superiority, while quantitatively great, really constitutes a "full first-strike capability." If it did in its maximum sense—i.e., if we could completely eliminate the Soviet nuclear forces in a first strike—it would be possible, theoretically at least, to dispense with conventional forces in Western Europe. Total and obvious strategic nuclear disequilibrium would remove any need to even partially balance the Soviets at the conventional level. Conversely, if it were true that the United States obviously lacked a first-strike capability (meaning that we were clearly not willing to strike first in any circumstances), then this might reinstate the conventional balancing process in Europe in its full prenuclear dimensions—i.e., it might well stimulate a build-up of conventional forces sufficient to hold successfully against a Red Army invasion.

That this has not occurred, is due in part to the uncertainty of Soviet leadership as to whether equilibrium exists or whether the United States nuclear preponderance really amounts to disequilibrium. In other words, the Soviets may suspect that the United States has a full first-strike capability which could be activated if sufficiently provoked. Or they may believe that we are irrational enough to strike even when our force does not meet the objective requirements of such a capability. For in the case of deterrence (or blackmail) it is what the opponent thinks or fears that counts, and the United States nuclear superiority is great enough that the Soviet leadership no doubt fears some probability of a United States first strike in particularly tense or provocative circumstances. Considering the very great damage they would suffer if we did strike, a quite low probability in their calculations may be sufficient to deter.

Any remaining doubts which the Russians might have about our implicit threat of a strategic first strike are offset by the presence of tactical nuclear weapons in the hands of the NATO forces on the "central front" in West Germany. The American resolve in NATO to use these weapons if necessary to stop a Soviet invasion has been firmly declared and implemented by the rather thorough incorporation of their use into NATO's military plans and organization. It is no doubt highly credible to the Soviets that these weapons would be used if necessary and considering their own apparent belief that a tactical nuclear war in Europe could not remain limited, our tactical nuclear posture constitutes, in effect, a very credible threat of all-out nuclear war. Even if they were to assume that the *strategic* nuclear balance by itself was in a state of equilibrium, the tactical nuclear weapons would make it a rather unstable equilibrium. This instability is a potent deterrent of Soviet conventional provocations and reduces the need for balancing at the conventional level.

The function of the conventional NATO forces on the central front—apart from turning back small and medium-scale incursions—is further to enhance the credibility of nuclear deterrence by forcing the Soviets to undertake a major attack provocative enough to exceed the United States' "threshold of nuclear response." Thus the overall balance of power in Western Europe is a function of three factors: the U.S. first-strike capability at the strategic level; the tactical nuclear threat; and the defense and deterrent effects of conventional forces. Each probably would be inadequate by itself, but the three together have created a mixed conventional-nuclear equilibrium which effectively deters Soviet aggression. The primary function of the tactical nuclear weapons is to form a "bridge" between a nonexistent conventional balance and a *possibly* extant strategic nuclear equilibrium. In other words, they assure the Soviets, in case they might otherwise have doubts, that a combined tactical-strategical nuclear imbalance in favor of the United States does exist.

We may turn the point around and note that during the period of the United States nuclear monopoly (strategic nuclear disequilibrium in our favor) we were deterred from capitalizing on this imbalance at least partly by the obvious Soviet superiority in the conventional balance which potentially enabled them to resist our nuclear pressure by credibly threatening to overrun Western Europe. An overall equilibrium obtained precisely because of a sharp disequilibrium in opposite directions in each of the two subcomponents.

Whereas in Europe conventional forces serve as auxiliary to the nuclear deterrent, in Asia the reverse is probably true. The obvious disequilibrium in the strategic nuclear balance between the United States and Communist China serves to deter the Chinese from openly committing their own conventional forces in internal wars (e.g., South Vietnam) and thus tends to create a conventional balance of power in Southeast Asia which might not otherwise exist. Alternatively, should the Chinese become involved with the United States in an overt conventional conflict, they probably would be deterred from committing enough forces to defeat the United States forces in fear of a United States nuclear response. Nuclear disequilibrium favoring the United States tends to limit our Communist opponents in Asia to a commitment of conventional forces which the U.S. and our allies can deal with successfully at the conventional level. In short, nuclear disequilibrium tends to promote conventional equilibrium or operational conventional preponderance for the United States.

When nuclear deterrence is extended to the protection of allies, the element of mutual assessment of *intentions* becomes critically important, much more so than in simple bilateral deterrence where the "credibility" of retaliation can more or less be taken for granted. In such "extended deterrence," the deterring side tries to create the impression that the balance of terror is out of balance in its favor or could be thrown into disequilibrium by sufficient provocation. He attempts to establish the "credibility" of his threat to strike first "all-out" or to initiate limited nuclear action. Estimates of relative capability are not irrelevant, but because of the essential subjectivity and hence uncertainty (in the opponent's mind) about what actually constitutes a "first-strike capability" for the deterrer, or about his willingness to run the risk of escalation, capability comparisons tend to be overshadowed by appraisals of the deterrer's apparent "resolve," "nerve," irrationality, gambling propensities and other subjective factors that bear upon his intentions. Paradoxically, it would seem that intent-perception has become more crucial in today's balance of power than in the prenuclear balance, even though (or perhaps, *because*) the physical capabilities have become many orders of magnitude more destructive.

Appraisals of intent not only are now more important, but important in a different way than in the old balance of power. In the latter, the relevant intentions were largely political in nature, centering on the question of *which* countries were likely to fight on either the offensive or the defensive side. It could reasonably be assumed that the countries which did participate in a war would do so to the full extent of their capabilities, but there was often considerable uncertainty about who would participate. With the emergence of bipolarity, the uncertainty about alliance partners drastically declined, but nuclear technology introduced a new form of intent-perception and a new form of uncertainty—that concerning what types of military capability the opponent was likely to use and what degree of violence he was willing to risk or accept.

One might say that this new kind of uncertainty has replaced the former uncertainty about alliance partners as a major source of stability in the balance of power. Or, to put it slightly differently, the implicit or explicit threat to "raise the ante" in order to avoid defeat has taken the place of the threat to recruit additional states to the defending alliance. Such a threat is more or less analogous to the practice of "holding the ring" in the old balance—when a state promised to be neutral if its ally were attacked by one country, but to come to its aid if it were attacked by two or more powers. In short, technology has to some extent provided a substitute for the political flexibility and stability which was lost to the balancing process when it shifted to a bipolar structure after World War II.

Stability

A careful distinction should be made between "equilibrium" and "stability" in both the conventional balance of power and the nuclear balance. The two terms often are erroneously used interchangeably. Equilibria in both balances can have varying degrees of stability; and it is even possible to have disequilibrium with relatively high stability, if the dominant side is not aggressively inclined and this fact is recognized by other members of the system.

In the traditional balance of power theory, the idea of stability usually referred generally to a supposed perpetual tendency of the system to maintain itself at or near a state of equilibrium. Deviations from equilibrium generated "feedback" forces which moved the balance back in the direction of equilibrium. Within this general notion, stability had at least three subdimensions which, so far as I know, were never precisely delineated. These were: the tendency or lack of tendency toward an arms race, tendencies either to stimulate or inhibit war, and the tendency of the process to preserve the independence of the major actors. Theorists tended to emphasize the third dimension; in fact, armament and warfare often were treated not as types of instability but as *methods* for preserving stability in the third sense, along with alliances and other techniques.

By contrast, the dimension of stability which receives most attention in the balance of terror, and by extension, in the contemporary balancing process as a whole, is the propensity of the system to produce war, the obvious reason being the possibility of *nuclear* war, the horrifying nature of which seems to outweigh all other considerations. How stable is the contemporary balance of power in this sense?

The basic criterion of stability in the balance of terror is the "distance" which both sides are from possessing a full first-strike capability. If neither side has forces which even approach this capacity—i.e., if both have a very strong "strike-back" capability—the balance of terror is very stable. If one or both are very close to having a first-strike capability, or actually do have it, the balance can be very unstable. It might be only moderately unstable if only one side possessed such a capability if that side were benevolent; but if both sides had it, fears of a first strike by the other, and consequent incentives to preempt, would be strong, even despite intrinsic benevolence on both sides.

Stability can be defined alternatively as the degree of economic, technological, or politicomilitary "shock" which the system can sustain without creating for one side or the other a capability and willingness to strike first. Economic shock (or degree of instability) refers to the amount of resource expenditure required for one or the other to acquire the *quantity* of forces required for a successful first strike—assuming a given technology, if neither side has the economic resources to produce such a capability, the balance is stable in this sense. Technological instability refers to magnitude of the technological breakthrough (e.g., the degree of efficiency of an antimissile defense) which would create a sufficient first-strike force for either side. Politicomilitary instability means the extent of "provocation" by either side which would touch off a first strike by the other. The word "provocation" includes a wide variety of contingencies: being "backed into a corner" in a confrontation of threats and counterthreats, becoming involved in a limited conventional war which one is in danger of losing, suffering a limited nuclear strike by the opponent, becoming involved in an escalating nuclear war, and many others. Any of these events may drastically increase the potential cost and risk of *not* striking first and thereby potentially create a state of disequilibrium in the strategic nuclear balance. As noted earlier, whether equilibrium exists depends on the context of events; the "acceptability" of damage is calculated not only against the gains to be made by striking first but also against the *losses to be avoided,* in any particular set of circumstances.

Although these three criteria of stability-instability interact, it is my judgment that the balance of terror is currently most stable in the "economic" or resource sense, somewhat less stable technologically, and least stable according to the "politicomilitary" criterion. The apparently firm United States commitment to use nuclear weapons in the defense of Western Europe, if necessary, indicates that there are types of Soviet provocation at the lower levels of violence which could touch off a United States strategic first strike, or more likely, a tactical nuclear response, from which the war could escalate. It is hoped, of course, that the Soviets' recognition of the U.S. commitment will deter the provocation; that instability in this dimension will preserve a stable equilibrium in the overall balance of power. However, the risks of Soviet miscalculation and subsequent escalation which this commitment creates should not be underestimated and probably are the most serious potential sources of instability in the contemporary balance.

The point is often made in the strategic literature that the greater the stability of the "strategic" balance of terror, the lower the stability of the overall balance at its lower levels of violence. The reasoning is that if neither side has a "full first-strike capability," and both know it, they will be less inhibited about initiating conventional war, and about the limited use of nuclear weapons, than if the strategic balance were unstable. Thus firm stability in the strategic nuclear balance tends to destabilize the conventional balance and also to activate the lesser nuclear "links" between the latter and the former. But one *could* argue precisely the opposite— that the greater likelihood of gradual escalation due to a stable strategic equilibrium tends to deter both conventional provocation and tactical nuclear strikes—thus stabilizing the overall balance. The first hypothesis probably is dominant, but it must be heavily qualified by the second, since nations probably fear the possibility of escalation "all the way" nearly as much as they fear the possibility of an "all-out" first strike.

There is another stability hypothesis which is just the reverse—

although not contradictory to—the one just described: a stable conventional equilibrium tends to increase the stability of the nuclear component of the balance. When both sides can defend themselves successfully at the conventional level, conventional aggression is likely to be deterred, and if it is not, there is little pressure on the defender to resort to nuclear action. But this one also has its obverse: it is sometimes argued that when the *status quo* side attempts to create a conventional equilibrium, the credibility of its nuclear threats is undermined since it might thereby indicate an unwillingness to initiate nuclear war by seeking to create an alternative to it. The potential aggressor might be then more willing to attack when he believes (perhaps mistakenly) that he has achieved a margin of conventional superiority. The first hypothesis tends to stress the effect of conventional balance in reducing the probability of escalation if war occurs; the second stresses the increased chances of the outbreak of war due to the apparently lower risk incurred by starting it.

When a great nuclear power places smaller nonnuclear countries under its nuclear protection (as a substitute for creation of a conventional equilibrium), one effect may be to reduce the stability of the strategic nuclear balance in the sense of stimulating an arms race. Nuclear deterrence of attacks on "third parties" theoretically requires a strategic nuclear capability approaching first strike dimensions. Forces of this size may raise fears of an aggressive surprise first strike in the opponent's mind and therefore place psychological pressure on him to increase his nuclear force in order to strengthen his deterrence, perhaps to strengthen his chances of winning the war should his fears materialize, and, at the extreme, to develop a first-strike force himself to be in a position to preempt. This type of instability would be much weaker if the great nuclear powers were to limit themselves to bilateral mutual deterrence.

The nature of the "balance of power" process in a world of many nuclear powers is a challenging speculative problem which can only be touched upon here in connection with the question of stability. It is rather remarkable that the balance of terror is generally believed to be most stable when it is bipolar and least stable when it is multipolar, whereas the exact reverse was said to be true in the traditional theory of the balance of power. In the latter, bipolarity was said to be unstable because of the absence of a strong unattached power center (a "holder of the balance"), or several centers, which could be recruited to block one of the "poles" which had developed marginal preponderance of capabilities and apparently aggressive intentions. A multiplicity of power centers would provide such balancing material and create uncertainty for an incipient aggressor as to the amount of power which would oppose his designs. A bipolar balance of terror is said to be relatively stable because only two power centers have the capacity to initiate nuclear war and because they are likely to be cautious in conflict situations which involve the danger of nuclear war. The major powers in the contemporary bipolar balance are said to be relatively "responsible" powers.

Many specific arguments have been advanced in support of the hypothesis that nuclear diffusion would greatly increase instability, but two in particular are probably the most influential. One is the "statistical argument": the notion that the more countries that have nuclear weapons, the more likely it is that some of these weapons will be fired, accidentally or otherwise, and the firing of nuclear weapons anywhere in the world may trigger a global holocaust. The other is the "irresponsibility argument": the idea that some of the countries which may acquire nuclear power will lack the caution and restraint which seems to characterize the nuclear great powers; they may threaten to use their nuclear weapons recklessly, perhaps because of domestic instability or simply a lack of concern for, or lack of comprehension of, the broader consequences of their actions.

The point is raised merely to note the striking difference between the two sets of stability hypotheses, not to analyze either, which would be far beyond the scope of this paper.

In Lieu of Conclusion

International relations theory and military-strategic analysis have been ignoring each other for too long. This essay has attempted to introduce a measure of integration, focusing on an idea which is common to both fields—that of equilibrium. Balance of power theory cannot embrace all phenomena of international politics, not even all military phenomena. Yet it has enjoyed a rather high degree of historical validation, as political theories go, and deserves to be rehabilitated, refined and renovated.

Ancient ideas die hard; the notion that military preponderance means superior strength and that this means superior political power is so deeply ingrained that it continues to be believed and acted upon by both sides even though, in the strategic nuclear balance, it has little objective or logical basis. Further research would surely uncover many additional deviations which would serve to qualify and thus to enrich the logical analysis presented here.

12

COLLECTIVE SECURITY

Collective security is the key element of the peace and security systems contained in both the League of Nations Covenant and the United Nations Charter. Based on the idea of "all for one and one for all," it seeks to counter or, better yet, deter any breach of the peace by marshaling overwhelming strength against any aggressor.

The first selection is the second of the three Definitive Articles for a Perpetual Peace proposed by Immanuel Kant (1724–1804) in his essay *Perpetual Peace*. Although Kant uses such terms as "federation" and "state of nations," he does not propose the establishment of a single world-state. Instead he proposes a less far-reaching arrangement that is yet superior to the anarchy of unrestrained sovereignties: an "alliance of peace" or an "alliance for the prevention of war."

The name most prominently associated with collective security is that of Woodrow Wilson (1856–1924), 28th President of the United States. Though the idea of using collective force to maintain or achieve peace can be traced far back, it was not fully elaborated and envisaged on a worldwide scale until the early years of the twentieth century. During the First World War, the establishment of a collective security system following the war's end was advocated by an international association with headquarters in neutral The Hague. In the United States, the League to Enforce Peace was in the forefront of the propaganda effort. The second selection is President Wilson's speech to the first annual meeting of this League to Enforce Peace in Washington, D.C., on May 27, 1916. It embodies his first endorsement of the collective security approach to peace.

The theory of collective security seems appealingly simple and foolproof, but it has not been very successful in practice. What is wrong with the idea? And what is right? The second selection is a slightly abridged version of the trenchant analysis of collective security by Kenneth W. Thompson. The author taught at the University of Chicago and Northwestern University, and is now Vice-President of the Rockefeller Foundation.

The theory of collective security seems appealingly simple and foolproof, but it has not been very successful in practice. What is wrong with the idea? And what is right? The third selection is a slightly abridged version of the trenchant analysis of collective security by Kenneth W. Thompson. The author taught at the University of Chicago and Northwestern University, and is now vice-president of the Rockefeller Foundation.

After the Korean War, the United Nations has not taken collective security measures again, but there have been a number of important collective peace forces such as the U.N. Emergency Force in the Middle East (UNEF), the peacekeeping force in the Congo (ONUC), and the U.N. force in Cyprus (UNFICYP). These collective actions are usually referred to as instances of "preventive diplomacy." The differences between the new concept of preventive diplomacy and the older concept of collective security are discussed in the fourth selection by Inis L. Claude, Jr. Professor Claude is the author of *Swords into Plowshares, Power and International Relations,* and other works on international politics and organization.

37. SECOND DEFINITIVE ARTICLE OF PERPETUAL PEACE* / IMMANUEL KANT

The law of nations must be founded on a federation of free states.

Nations, as states, may be judged like single individuals, who in their natural condition (that is, independent of external laws) injure each other merely because they live side by side. For his own safety's sake, each can and ought to enter into a constitution with his neighbor by which everyone's rights are guaranteed. This would be an alliance of nations, but not necessarily a state of nations. A "state of nations" would be self-contradictory, because a state entails a relationship of a sovereign lawgiver to the subject people and many nations in one state would constitute only one nation. This contradicts our premise, since we are considering the rights of nations in their mutual relations insofar as they remain separate states and will not merge into one.

We despise and regard as crude, barbaric, and a brutal degradation of humanity the attachment of savages to their lawless freedom and their preference for constant fighting rather than for submission to a legal constraint to be established by themselves, that is, their preference for chaotic freedom rather than reasonable liberty. Likewise one might imagine that civilized nations (each constituting a state by itself) would hasten to emerge from such a depraved condition as soon as possible. But instead each state thinks that its majesty (the term "majesty" applied to a nation is ridiculous) means precisely that it is not subject to any external force and that the glory of its ruler is based on the fact that thousands of people are at his command, ready to sacrifice themselves for a cause which does not even concern them without any risk to the ruler's own safety. The difference between the European savages and those in America lies mainly in this, that whereas several tribes among the latter have been completely devoured by their enemies, the former know a better way of using their captives: they prefer to add them to their subjects, and thus also increase the number of tools available to them for even more widespread wars.

* Immanuel Kant, *Zum ewigen Frieden: Ein philosophischer Entwurf,* 9th ed. (Königsberg, 1796). Translated by Eva Tamm Lijphart and Arend Lijphart.

The vicious element in human nature appears openly in the unrestrained relations among nations, whereas much of it remains hidden within the state as a result of governmental compulsion. It is therefore remarkable that the term "right" has not yet been completely banished from the politics of war as pedantic, and that no state has yet dared to declare itself publicly in support of this opinion. For Hugo Grotius, Puffendorf, Vattel, and others (all poor comforters) are still faithfully quoted in justification of a military attack, even though their code is no more than a philosophical or diplomatic one, and does not and cannot have the slightest legal force, because states as such are not subject to a common external authority. No example can be given of a state being moved to refrain from its intention by arguments supported by the testimony of such eminent men. This homage rendered to the concept of justice by each state, at least in words, does prove the existence of a higher, although at times dormant, moral tendency in man which will one day overcome his undeniably evil inclinations. And this hope he also holds for others. Otherwise, states wishing to fight against each other would not make use of the word "right," except in derision like the Gallic prince who stated: "The prerogative nature has given to the stronger is that the weaker should obey him."

The means by which states pursue their rights can never be a legal process as in an external court of justice, but only war. But the question of right is not settled by war and victory. A peace treaty may put an end to a particular war, but not to the conditions of war for which new pretexts can always be found; one cannot even dismiss this as completely unjust, as each one is his own judge under these circumstances. The law of nature charges individuals living in a lawless condition to "emerge from this condition." But according to the law of nations, not quite the same rule holds good for states. The reason is that, as states, they already have a legal constitution established within themselves, and consequently cannot be forced by others, according to their sense of right, to enter into an expanded legal constitution. Nevertheless, reason from the throne of the highest moral lawgiving power absolutely condemns war as a rightful procedure and makes a state of peace an immediate duty. But this peace cannot be established or guaranteed without a treaty among nations. A special kind of alliance must be formed which we may call an alliance of peace (*foedus pacificum*) different from a peace treaty (*pactum pacis*) in that the latter only seeks to end one war whereas the alliance of peace seeks to end all wars forever. This alliance does not seek to deprive the state of any of its power, but merely strives to maintain and secure the freedom of the state and of all other allied states, without compelling them to submit, like men in a state of nature, to public laws and coercion. The practicability (objective reality) of this idea of a federation which will gradually extend to all states and so lead to perpetual peace, can be demonstrated. If fortune directs that a powerful and enlightened people should form a republic (which is by nature inclined to perpetual peace), this state would serve as a center for the federal union. Other states would join it and thus the freedom of all states would be secured in accordance with the idea of the law of nations. And the alliance would gradually extend further and further.

If a people should say: "There shall be no war among us, for we shall organize ourselves into a state, that is, set up a supreme legislative, administrative, and judicial power which shall settle our differences peaceably," their decision is a logical one. But if this state says: "There shall be no war between me and other states although I recognize no supreme lawgiving power which shall guarantee my rights and whose rights I shall guarantee," then it is not clear at all on what it bases its confidence in having its rights guaranteed. The only solid basis for such a confidence would be an alliance of societies, namely a free federation, which reason must necessarily link with the idea of the law of nations, if that idea is to have any meaning at all.

The idea of the law of nations as giving the right to make war is really meaningless, for this right can only be a power of deciding what is just not according to universally valid external laws limiting the freedom of each individual, but according to one-sided application of force. Unless it means that people so inclined get their just reward when they exterminate each other, and thus find perpetual peace in the wide grave which covers them together with their atrocities. It stands to reason that there is no other remedy for the lawless and warlike condition of international relations than that states give up their wild, lawless freedom, just like individuals within the state, and accept the compulsion of public laws. Thus they can form a continually growing state of nations (*civitas gentium*) which would eventually include all the peoples of the earth. But states, according to their idea of international law, are absolutely opposed to this, and therefore reject in practice what is correct in theory. Hence, instead of the positive idea of a world-republic, if all is not to be lost, only a negative substitute may be feasible: a permanent and ever expanding alliance for the prevention of war. This alliance may stem the tide of lawless and warlike propensities, although there will always be the risk of war breaking out.

38. *A LEAGUE TO ENFORCE PEACE* / WOODROW WILSON*

When the invitation to be here to-night came to me, I was glad to accept it,—not because it offered me an opportunity to discuss the program of the League,—that you will, I am sure, not expect of me,—but because the desire of the whole world now turns eagerly, more and more eagerly, towards the hope of peace, and there is just reason why we should take our part in counsel upon this great theme. It is right that I, as spokesman of our Government, should attempt to give expression to what I believe to be the thought and purpose of the people of the United States in this vital matter.

This great war that broke so suddenly upon the world two years ago, and which has swept within its flame so great a part of the civilized world, has affected us very profoundly, and we are not only at liberty, it is perhaps our duty, to speak very frankly of it and of the great interests of civilization which it affects.

With its causes and its objects we are not concerned. The obscure fountains from which its stupendous flood has burst forth we are not interested to search for or explore. But so great a flood, spread far and wide to every quarter of the globe, has of necessity engulfed many a fair province of right that lies very near to us. Our own rights as a Nation, the liberties, the privileges, and the property of our people have been profoundly affected. We are not mere disconnected lookers-on. The longer the war lasts, the more deeply do we become concerned that it should be brought to an end and the world be permitted to resume its normal life and course again. And when it does come to an end we shall be as much concerned as the nations at war to see peace assume an aspect of permanence, give

* James Brown Scott, ed., *President Wilson's Foreign Policy: Messages, Addresses, Papers* (New York: Oxford University Press, 1918), pp. 189–95.

promise of days from which the anxiety of uncertainty shall be lifted, bring some assurance that peace and war shall always hereafter be reckoned part of the common interest of mankind. We are participants, whether we would or not, in the life of the world. The interests of all nations are our own also. We are partners with the rest. What affects mankind is inevitably our affair as well as the affair of the nations of Europe and of Asia.

One observation on the causes of the present war we are at liberty to make, and to make it may throw some light forward upon the future, as well as backward upon the past. It is plain that this war could have come only as it did, suddenly and out of secret counsels, without warning to the world, without discussion, without any of the deliberate movements of counsel with which it would seem natural to approach so stupendous a contest. It is probable that if it had been foreseen just what would happen, just what alliances would be formed, just what forces arrayed against one another, those who brought the great contest on would have been glad to substitute conference for force. If we ourselves had been afforded some opportunity to apprise the belligerents of the attitude which it would be our duty to take, of the policies and practices against which we would feel bound to use all our moral and economic strength, and in certain circumstances even our physical strength also, our own contribution to the counsel which might have averted the struggle would have been considered worth weighing and regarding.

And the lesson which the shock of being taken by surprise in a matter so deeply vital to all the nations of the world has made poignantly clear is, that the peace of the world must henceforth depend upon a new and more wholesome diplomacy. Only when the great nations of the world have reached some sort of agreement as to what they hold to be fundamental to their common interest, and as to some feasible method of acting in concert when any nation or group of nations seeks to disturb those fundamental things, can we feel that civilization is at last in a way of justifying its existence and claiming to be finally established. It is clear that nations must in the future be governed by the same high code of honor that we demand of individuals.

We must, indeed, in the very same breath with which we avow this conviction admit that we have ourselves upon occasion in the past been offenders against the law of diplomacy which we thus forecast; but our conviction is not the less clear, but rather the more clear, on that account. If this war has accomplished nothing else for the benefit of the world, it has at least disclosed a great moral necessity and set forward the thinking of the statesmen of the world by a whole age. Repeated utterances of the leading statesmen of most of the great nations now engaged in war have made it plain that their thought has come to this, that the principle of public right must henceforth take precedence over the individual interests of particular nations, and that the nations of the world must in some way band themselves together to see that that right prevails as against any sort of selfish aggression; that henceforth alliance must not be set up against alliance, understanding against understanding, but that there must be a common agreement for a common object, and that at the heart of that common object must lie the inviolable rights of peoples and of mankind. The nations of the world have become each other's neighbors. It is to their interest that they should understand each other. In order that they may understand each other, it is imperative that they should agree to co-operate in a common cause, and that they should so act that the guiding principle of that common cause shall be even-handed and impartial justice.

This is undoubtedly the thought of America. This is what we ourselves will say when there comes proper occasion to say it. In the dealings of nations with one another arbitrary force must be rejected and we must move forward to the thought of the modern world, the thought of which peace is the very atmosphere. That thought constitutes a chief part of the passionate conviction of America.

We believe these fundamental things: First, that every people has a right to choose the sovereignty under which they shall live. Like other nations, we have ourselves no doubt once and again offended against that principle when for a little while controlled by selfish passion, as our franker historians have been honorable enough to admit; but it has become more and more our rule of life and action. Second, that the small states of the world have a right to enjoy the same respect for their sovereignty and for their territorial integrity that great and powerful nations expect and insist upon. And, third, that the world has a right to be free from every disturbance of its peace that has its origin in aggression and disregard of the rights of peoples and nations.

So sincerely do we believe in these things that I am sure that I speak the mind and wish of the people of America when I say that the United States is willing to become a partner in any feasible association of nations formed in order to realize these objects and make them secure against violation.

There is nothing that the United States wants for itself that any other nation has. We are willing, on the contrary, to limit ourselves along with them to a prescribed course of duty and respect for the rights of others which will check any selfish passion of our own, as it will check any aggressive impulse of theirs.

If it should ever be our privilege to suggest or initiate a movement for peace among the nations now at war, I am sure that the people of the United States would wish their Government to move along these lines: First, such a settlement with regard to their own immediate interests as the belligerents may agree upon. We have nothing material of any kind to ask for ourselves, and are quite aware that we are in no sense or degree parties to the present quarrel. Our interest is only in peace and its future guarantees. Second, a universal association of the nations to maintain the inviolate security of the highway of the seas for the common and unhindered use of all the nations of the world, and to prevent any war begun either contrary to treaty covenants or without warning and full submission of the causes to the opinion of the world,—a virtual guarantee of territorial integrity and political independence.

But I did not come here, let me repeat, to discuss a program. I came only to avow a creed and give expression to the confidence I feel that the world is even now upon the eve of a great consummation, when some common force will be brought into existence which shall safeguard right as the first and most fundamental interest of all peoples and all governments, when coercion shall be summoned not to the service of political ambition or selfish hostility, but to the service of a common order, a common justice, and a common peace. God grant that the dawn of that day of frank dealing and of settled peace, concord, and co-operation may be near at hand!

39. *COLLECTIVE SECURITY REEXAMINED* * / *KENNETH W. THOMPSON*

* Kenneth W. Thompson, "Collective Security Reexamined," *The American Political Science Review*, Vol. 47, No. 3 (September 1953), pp. 754-55, 757-63, 766-72. Reprinted by permission.

. . . What is collective security in theory? What are its precepts and main tenets? What, in simplest terms, is the philosophy of collective security? The rock bottom principle upon which collective security is founded provides that an attack on any one state will be regarded as an attack on all states. It finds its measure in the simple doctrine of one for all and all for one. War anywhere, in the context of Article 11 of the League of Nations, is the concern of every state.

Self-help and neutrality, it should be obvious, are the exact antithesis of such a theory. States under an order of neutrality are impartial when conflict breaks out, give their blessings to combatants to fight it out, and defer judgment regarding the justice or injustice of the cause involved. Self-help in the past was often "help yourself" so far as the great powers were concerned; they enforced their own rights and more besides. In the eighteenth and nineteenth centuries this system was fashionable and wars, although not eliminated, were localized whenever possible. In a more integrated world environment, a conflict anywhere has some effect on conditions of peace everywhere. A disturbance at one point upsets the equilibrium at all other points, and the adjustment of a single conflict restores the foundations of harmony at other points throughout the world.

This idea of collective security is simple, challenging and novel. It would do for the international society what police action does for the domestic community. If the individual is threatened or endangered in municipal society, he turns to the legitimate agents of law enforcement, the police. The comparatively successful operation of this system has meant relative peace and tolerable harmony for most local communities. Through the action of police or "fire brigades" on a world scale, collective security has as its goal two comparable objectives. It would *prevent* war by providing a deterrent to aggression. It would *defend* the interests of peace-loving states in war if it came, by concentrating a preponderance of power against the aggressor. These two ends have been the goals of both the League and the United Nations. Through power and persuasion, a collective system would seek to deter aggression, as in the case of the Soviet imperialist threat to Titoist Yugoslavia. A potential aggressor must know that Yugoslavia and other United Nations powers stand together under the same protective umbrella. If war comes, the security system by pooling resources defends its interests against any nation which threatens to undermine it by swallowing up one of its members. . . .

This simple picture of the idea of collective security hardly furnishes a useful and realistic perspective on the way such a system operates in practice today. Nor are we helped by comparing the structure of the two historic experiments in collective security. The formal agencies for collective security after World War I were in several important respects unimpressive. Article 16 of the Covenant provided that any member resorting to war contrary to the Covenant had committed *ipso facto* an act of aggression against all other members. It was intended that first economic measures and then overt force should be applied against any offender. But although the international obligations of members were less ambiguous than in the Charter, there was no clear provision for their implementation or organization by a central enforcement agency. Each nation had full freedom to provide what troops it saw fit. The Council could then advise on additional measures. In contrast, Article 39 of the Charter of the United Nations commissions the Security Council to determine the existence of a threat to the peace or act of aggression and Articles 43–47 obligate the members, upon the completion of agreements, to supply troops to the Military Staff Committee. The agencies for partial collective security, as found in the constitutional provisions of the North Atlantic Pact and the practical steps undertaken under NATO, are even more impressive and formidable today.

From the beginning, however, the real issue concerning collective security has had little to do with charters or compacts. The real issue has been the question of why the implementation of a system logically so flawless, and enjoying such impressive official devotion and popular support, should have been accompanied by a period of virtually unprecedented collective insecurity. It is a sobering fact that the nineteenth century was perhaps the most peaceful of modern centuries; the twentieth, by contrast, has been an epoch of unparalleled bloodshed. From 1815 to 1914 a system of old-fashioned balance of power contributed to the achievement of nearly a full century of uninterrupted peace. The past forty years have witnessed in rapid succession two great wars which the historian Arnold J. Toynbee compares to the double wars of the Romans and the Carthaginians and the two struggles of the Peloponnesian War which wrecked Hellenic Civilization. He has observed that quite possibly we have dealt ourselves the same "knockout blows" that these wars represented for the older civilizations. There were only eighteen months in the nineteenth century when France, Russia,

Austria, Prussia, England and Spain found themselves at war with one another (excluding the Crimean War as a colonial struggle). By contrast, our experience thus far with the novel machinery of collective security has hardly warranted the unqualified postwar optimism of men like Mr. Hull that, with the new international organization, power politics and war were being left far behind in our progress toward utopia.

Instead the recent decades have been years of unceasing war or threats of war. What are the causes of this state of affairs? What are the reasons for the enormous gap between the theory and practice, the promise and performance of collective security? The most popular and reassuring answer has been that the radical doctrines of National Socialism and Communism have undermined the ideal system, and that modern technology has shattered the earlier limitations on conflict. Yet an equally dynamic creed challenged peace and order in the nineteenth century and provided a fighting faith for imperialist France.

The serious observer must look more deeply at the substance of political reality. In so doing he will find that collective security yesterday and today has been viewed unrealistically, and that its executors have been asked to perform tasks which could be performed with complete success only if certain objective conditions were realized. The most vital questions regarding collective security have seldom been asked; the real problems have often been evaded. The fundamental issues and problems which should have been boldly and realistically confronted have been concealed and obscured in constitutional verbiage and formal legalistic arguments. The four basic problems responsible for the tragic predicament of collective security include the problem of its basic preconditions, the political problem, the psychological problem and the problem of peaceful change. The first is from one standpoint most basic, for the preconditions of collective security, being frequently misunderstood, have presented the most stubborn obstacle to the maintenance of international peace.

Preconditions of Collective Security. Manifestly, collective enforcement is unattainable in the absence of appropriate international machinery and binding obligations clearly set forth in recognized legal instruments. Yet every informed citizen knows from experience that a legal arrangement imposed upon political and social conditions incompatible with its fulfillment makes successful political action difficult. Therefore it is essential in considering the reality of collective security that we understand fully its assumptions and requirements.

First, collective enforcement assumes a status quo, or situation of peace, on which the nations with predominant strength agree. In practical terms, the peace which a collective system must defend is the territorial status quo existing at the time the system is brought into being. There is nothing in past experience to indicate that all nations, or even a combination sufficiently powerful to defy the rest, will agree on the meaning of a particular status quo. Following every war, the defeated powers who feel they have suffered most by the terms of peace come to oppose the established status quo. In the aftermath of World War II, however, the question of satisfaction or dissatisfaction with the status quo has largely been superseded by an earlier and prior question. Up to the present time, no practical arrangement has been worked out acceptable to the major powers, who in this case are primarily the Soviet Union and the United States, on which the postwar status quo could be founded. The unresolved conflict between East and West has prevented the establishment of peace. Consequently, the latest experiment in collective security presents us with the anomalous picture of a system created to defend a status quo which has not yet been brought into being. . . .

Second, collective security demands that nations subscribing to the status quo be willing and able at all times to muster overwhelming strength for collective defense at successive points of conflict. In theory, the supporters of the status quo might be capable in particular emergencies of mobilizing effective and decisive power against the single aggressor who sought to defy them. Or, by pooling the resources of all the nations in a permanently organized international force, collective enforcement could be made automatic, instantaneous, and preponderant. The former condition, however, is practically impossible of fulfillment, inasmuch as the threat to the status quo comes historically from more than one dissatisfied power or aggressor. The second condition would call for the unprecedented practice of international contingents operating under an international agency empowered to decide conclusively when and how they should be used.

The United Nations Charter seems to take a long step toward this objective by providing that all members are "to make available to the Security Council, on its call and in accordance with a special agreement or agreements, armed forces, assistance and facilities.

. . ." (Article 43, Paragraph 1.) Through this provision, the incurable weakness of decentralized enforcement by which past international systems have been rendered impotent is ostensibly rectified. For the Achilles' heel of the earlier experiments was the decentralized character of the enforcement process; separate nations retained the right to determine whether or not military forces would be made available to meet particular crises. In 1942, Cordell Hull had urged that "some international agency must be created which can—by force, if necessary—keep the peace. . . ."[15] Yet Mr. Hull's proposition and Articles 43ff of the Charter, by which this historic difficulty apparently had been surmounted, in practice have remained a dead letter. No special agreements have been concluded by Members with the Security Council; talks in the Military Staff Committee soon reached an impasse. The Soviet Union has opposed proportionate contributions to an international air and naval force, which would leave it particularly vulnerable to forces overwhelmingly more powerful than its own. The United States has been concerned to make the United Nations Armed Force as strong as possible against the military preponderance of the Soviet Army in Europe and Asia, while the Russians have sought to keep it as weak as possible.[16] The stalemate in the Military Staff Committee is fundamentally a symptom of the struggle between the two great powers and between supporters and opponents of the undefined status quo. In practice, the realization of the second condition of overwhelming strength for collective enforcement has constantly run afoul of special national demands for military security and supremacy.

There is a *third* and final prerequisite of collective security, however, to which we now turn, that was widely assumed to be in existence at the time preparations for the United Nations were first being made. It is essential to collective security in a world of

---

[15] 7 Department of State *Bulletin* (1942), p. 645.

[16] It should be noted that the Russians have no monopoly on opposition to a powerful world police force. Senator Vandenberg declares in his Memoirs: "I am opposed to what is generally understood by the term 'international police force.' So, I believe, are the President, Secretary Hull and most realistic students of this problem. To be adequate, an international police force would have to be larger than the regular army and navy of any other power on earth. I think it is fantastic to believe that the people would long consent to the maintenance of any such enormous concentration of power in the postwar peace; and I also think that the temptation to reach for its ultimate control could become the greatest possible threat to peace in years to come." Vandenberg, *Private Papers*, pp. 120–21.

unequal powers that at least the major powers enjoy a minimum of political solidarity and moral community. On October 13, 1944, Premier Stalin asked himself, in an article appearing in the Soviet *Information Bulletin*, if the world organization could be effective. He predicted that it would "be effective if the Great Powers, which have borne the brunt of the war against Hitler-Germany continue to act in a spirit of unanimity and accord."[17]

The effectiveness of the United Nations and of the Security Council in particular was predicated upon the unanimity of the five great powers. It was an article of political faith in the Roosevelt Administration that trustworthiness and good will on the part of Americans would inspire the same qualities among the Russians. In a particularly revealing memorandum for President Harry S. Truman dated September 11, 1945, Mr. Stimson explained: "The chief lesson I have learned in a long life is that the only way you can make a man trustworthy is to trust him; and the surest way to make him untrustworthy is to distrust him and show your distrust."[18] Unanimity among the great powers which alien ideologies and conflicting interests might otherwise undermine would be secured through the application of a code of social ethics that had in general been effective within the United States.[19]

By October of 1947, Mr. Stimson, writing in *Foreign Affairs*, had cause to reformulate his proposition and to say: "I have often said that the surest way to make a man trustworthy is to trust him. But I must add that this does not always apply to a man who is determined to make you his dupe. Before we can make friends with the Russians, their leaders will have to be convinced that they have nothing to gain, and everything to lose, by acting on the assumption that our society is dying and that our principles are outworn."[20] Thus the preconditions of collective security under the United

---

[17] USSR *Information Bulletin*, Oct. 13, 1944.

[18] Stimson, *On Active Service*, p. 644.

[19] It remained, however, for Premier Stalin in conversation with Harry Hopkins to furnish unwittingly the key to the success or failure of this endeavor. He declared that trust and confidence in international as in national relations is dependent upon the existence of ". . . a minimum moral standard between all nations and without such a minimum moral standard nations could not exist." Premier Stalin continued that the leaders of Nazi Germany "knew no such minimum moral standard [but] . . . without a second's thought would sign a treaty today, break it tomorrow and sign a second one the following day. Nations must fulfill their treaty obligations, he said, or international society could not exist." Nor, it might be added, could collective security survive. Sherwood, *Roosevelt and Hopkins*, Vol. 1, pp. 399–400.

[20] Stimson, *On Active Service*, pp. 649–50.

Nations have either been wanting from the beginning, or have been corroded and destroyed by the all-consuming forces of the "cold war."

The Political Problem. The chief practical obstacle to collective security is the political problem deriving from the conflict of independent foreign policies. The loyalties and interests of nations participating in international organizations and collective security systems are of a different order from those of individuals taking part in the more intimate communities of the family and nation.[21] Both individuals and nations pursue their own interests, but in some areas and on certain occasions the individual may forsake his egotistic motives for loyalty to some higher institution or nobler cause. There are institutions in integrated societies which provide common standards under which the individual can realize his aspirations. There need be no inherent conflict between an individual's private interests and his national loyalties, for the latter can often promote the realization of the former. On the other hand, conflicts are often inevitable between national and supranational loyalties, and when the projected policy of an international organization conflicts with that of a particular nation, at all times and in all places the national interest prevails. . . .

The Psychological Problem. Collective security founders on other shoals. It sometimes breaks down because of collective resentments or hatreds and reactions which express certain features of a particular national character. In 1931, the Japanese spilled over into Manchuria. Why was it that more positive action was not taken? To be sure there were legal, economic, and political obstacles existing. "War" in international relations is a weaselword, and debates which surround it easily become legal quagmires. Japan said it had not declared war, China had not done so, and therefore the bombs were a mere illusion. Behind this legal smokescreen the struggle went on and men were as dead as if they had fought in a legally more respectable war. Economically, the world was deep in a painful depression; politically, Manchuria seemed far away and of little

[21] Some years ago Monsieur Paul Henri Spaak in an address before the Foreign Press Union declared: "There must be a hierarchy in international obligations. The nations of the continent cannot be asked to consider with the same realism and sincerity of judgment affairs which directly concern them and events which are taking place thousands of kilometres away in regions where they have neither interests nor influence. Indivisible peace, mutual assistance, and even collective security are general ideas whose practical effect must be clearly explained and clearly limited." Quoted in *Survey of International Affairs, 1936* (London, 1937), pp. 354–55.

immediate interest of Western nations. There was in addition, however, a psychological factor. Certain groups in the West harbored deep resentments against the victims of Japanese imperialism. In particular, certain elements within the British trading community remembered private scores that had not been settled and the recent ingratitude of the Chinese toward the West. This sector of Western public opinion took a kind of vicarious pleasure in the punishment the Japanese were inflicting upon China which, with India, became a symbol of the heavy toll being taken economically and psychologically in Europe by Asia's revolt. The Japanese action was unconsciously viewed as a retaliation against the whole anti-foreign movement that was sweeping Asia.

Another psychological factor was the attitude of responsible naval and military experts in Britain. One major result of the Washington Treaties of 1921–22 had been to leave Japan supreme on all fronts in the Far East. Its strategic position made it virtually immune from any serious attack. This confronted the newborn collective system with a military and naval problem which was made more acute by the prospects of joint operations by British and American naval forces. To British naval experts, American admirals and naval leaders were a boisterous and unproven lot. They had emerged overnight as the one irresistible threat to British naval supremacy. As youngsters in naval warfare, they would as likely as not prove erratic and unreliable under fire. Therefore, for Britain to commit herself unqualifiedly to a policy of military and naval intervention in an area where the newly acquired American naval supremacy would prevail would be risky and hazardous to British national interests. The disdain in which British naval leaders held their American opposite numbers was a psychological factor of great importance in 1931.[30]

In 1950–51, a new psychological obstacle appeared to block effective universal collective security. The British have had a Far Eastern policy for nearly a century-and-a-half. To them the policy of the United Nations, as influenced by the United States and especially by its spectacular and outspoken general, was from the first based on false assumptions. When General MacArthur's abortive thrust toward the Yalu River was turned back and the one

[30] The psychological turn of mind among certain professional Western soldiers before the Second World War offers a further illustration of this point. Admiration and respect for Germany's amazing rearmament program inspired the opinion that the conquest of England by Germany would prove the inevitable superiority of ground and air over sea power.

action which all Western policy had sought to forestall—the intervention of the Chinese Communists—followed, the British reaction, however restrained, was clearly inevitable. Given the policy, the outcome was inescapable.

Peaceful Change. Collective security, as we have seen, depends upon agreed concepts of justice in international society shared by all or most of its members. In domestic societies this consensus is arrived at by public opinion's availing itself of the instruments of government in registering the majority will. If societies were characterized by ideal justice and perfect equilibrium among contending social groups, the problems of social change would perhaps disappear. Since the demands for social change are continuously asserted in the market place and resolved in legislative and electoral debates, the pursuit of abstract justice assumes less urgency than the claims for justice of particular social groups.

In every society two social forces inevitably exist in basic tension with one another. The one force comprises the groups supporting the status quo as stabilized and perpetuated in the political and legal order of the day. Another force made up of the groups sharing common opposition to the status quo seeks to change or overturn it. In the light of this conflict, the basic problem of government is to provide ways by which continuity is achieved and social change not prevented. Within organized and integrated societies, the courts historically have contributed continuity whereas legislatures have been the faithful agents of change. As Congress was the forum in which the claims and grievances of distressed groups were alleviated by New Deal laws and decrees in the 1930's, the British Parliament in the nineteenth century was the agency in which the middle-class revolt against feudalism was expressed and achieved.

It should be apparent, however, that the process of change in society is made possible by other agencies as well. The executive has provided an instrument through which opinion can be channeled and transformed into effective policy. Peaceful change thus involves the whole of society with its orderly machinery through which social groups seek support for their claims elevated into principles of justice that must be compatible with the society's fundamental values. It is the whole of domestic society, therefore, and not the legislature in isolation, that brings about social change. For while the making of new laws is the formal act of social change, the role of legislatures is essentially the ratification of the choices at which unorganized society has already arrived. This is made possible by the generally accepted framework of justice within which disputes can be settled.

It is obvious that the conditions and institutions which exist within domestic societies are absent or greatly weakened in international society. Legislative bodies with law-making powers capable of fulfilling the functions that Congress or any other legislature performs are conspicuously absent on the international scene. The General Assembly has the power to "make recommendations" on matters prescribed in the Charter; the Security Council may "decide" on measures to be taken and "call upon" members to act. While these powers appear to mark an advance, in practice they have hardly resulted in any especially decisive step toward international law-making. The basic defects in the structure of international society are nowhere more apparent than in connection with peaceful change. . . .

In the face of the problems we have outlined and discussed, two approaches to the idea and the reality of collective security have vied with one another in recent years. The one demands in the name of a principle that all nations at all times resist aggression. Its adherents maintain that only in this way can the national interests of independent states be protected and served. This approach takes its stand on the abstract and uncorruptible ideal of collective security.

Another approach, based primarily on what we have denoted the reality of collective security, reaches other conclusions on the basis of opposing concepts and principles. In the present state of world affairs, we are told, a policy of collective security leads inevitably down the road of general war and universal catastrophe. The Founding Fathers of this Republic knew more clearly than their present day heirs the futility of seeking to coerce sovereign states. At the Constitutional Convention of 1787, it was argued that unless states were united in one sovereign government (which both approaches agree is absent from the international scene today), they could be coerced only through civil war. Alexander Hamilton declared to the New York State Convention, met to ratify the new Constitution: "to coerce the states is one of the maddest projects that was ever devised. A failure of compliance will never be confined to a single state. This being the case can we suppose it wise to hazard a civil war."[34] Writing in the same tradition, Hans J.

[34] Quoted in Harrop Freeman and Theodore Paullin, *Coercion of States in Federal Unions* (Philadelphia, 1943), p. 14. The late Professor Edwin Borchard warned: "There is no element of the proposal of punishing aggressors which is not contested by history and disproved by experience." "The Impracticability of Enforcing Peace," *The Yale Law Journal*, Vol. 55, p. 968 (Aug., 1946).

Morgenthau has maintained: "Under a system of collective security operating under less than ideal conditions, war between A and B or between any other two nations anywhere in the world is of necessity tantamount to war among all or at best most nations of the world."[35] Since ideal conditions are not presently in sight, collective security is tantamount to war.

Thus the West is presented, in theory at least, with a choice between almost equally hopeless and catastrophic alternatives. Through the fact of membership in the United Nations, Western nations are committed to a system of collective security embodied in the Charter. Confronted with reality, however, the staunchest champions of collective security are driven to invoke a dual standard as a guide for action. On the one hand, they must firmly resolve on principle to intervene to arrest aggression at its source. On the other hand, while unable to disavow the principle, in concrete actions they are required to apply it judiciously with immense self-restraint.

The gulf between principles and actions in 1935–36 and again in 1950 illustrates the irony of collective security in the real world for, under its dispensation, Mussolini's aggression in Ethiopia and the North Korean invasion of South Korea made intervention a foregone conclusion. Once aggression is identified, the duty of the nations espousing collective security is unequivocal. Yet since Britain and France were unprepared in 1935, it was doubtful that more could be accomplished than to drive Italy into the camp of Germany. Notwithstanding, the viewpoint prevailed that if the champions of collective security did nothing, other more dangerous acts of aggression would follow.

The perils in pursuing the idea of collective security to its logical conclusion are matched only by the hazards involved in abandoning it. It is tempting to say that since collective security against a great power is unworkable, since psychological and political obstacles exist, and since the requirements for peaceful change are quite frequently at odds with enforcement, the system should be scrapped and replaced. Yet the coalition of the Western nations has been aroused to the threat confronting it by the resolute stand that was taken in Korea, and the whole free world has been animated and inspired by our boldness, courage and, lately, our patience and restraint. In the struggle against Soviet imperialism, it is vital that we have firm friends and willing allies who recognize mutual

[35] Hans J. Morgenthau, *Politics Among Nations* (New York, 1948), p. 335.

interests. We can best assure their cooperation by preserving and strengthening the tenuous ties by which all are bound together within the United Nations.

Perhaps the supreme paradox of American foreign policy today is the necessity placed upon us to seize and employ the essentially utopian instruments of collective security in a brutally realistic power struggle. Its agencies furnish a political framework through which the broad coalition of the free world can be strengthened and a more stable equilibrium of world power be restored. Britain and France and the free powers of Asia are more likely to play their part and contribute to the restoration of a balance of power in Europe and Asia if we assure them of support through mutual guarantees and create confidence by discussions in the halls and anterooms of the United Nations.

Collective security, with its present foundations weakened and enfeebled, can contribute to peace and order if wisely and moderately employed. It has become clear in Korea that policies undertaken in the name of collective security are not necessarily tantamount to world war. Localized struggles are still possible if major powers are not confounded by the ideal or misled by a too absolute interpretation of the meaning of collective enforcement. Moreover, the influence of other nations more skilled in historic diplomacy has served within the United Nations as a kind of built-in restraint on the impulses of American foreign policy. Our partners in utopia have nudged us in the direction of what would appear to be a more realistic foreign policy. Beyond this, with the recent breakup of the simple bi-polar balance of power in the world, the practical uses for collective agencies may be multiplied indefinitely as the prospect of action by coalitions of members against independent if minor centers of power becomes a reality.

The uses of collective security are more modest and limited than its more ardent advocates appreciate. Yet if participants base their policies on enduring political principles and judge and measure each action by the interests and power involved, it need not be an inevitable blind alley. Between the scylla of blind acceptance and the charybdis of logical rejection we must aim to establish the intellectual foundations required for an empirical and pragmatic approach to the modern concept of collective security.

40. *PREVENTIVE DIPLOMACY AS AN APPROACH TO PEACE*/INIS L. CLAUDE, JR.*

If the United Nations has contributed anything new to the list of direct approaches to the problem of peace, it is in the development of the theory and practice of preventive diplomacy. While it would be misleading to treat this phenomenon as an instance of pure innovation, it is nonetheless true that the concept of preventive diplomacy, which is not to be found in the theoretical substructure of the Charter, has emerged from the operating experience of the United Nations to join peaceful settlement, collective security, and disarmament as a major approach to peace through international organization.

This concept is irrevocably associated with the name of the late Dag Hammarskjöld, as collective security is tied to that of Woodrow Wilson. It derives from the practice of international statesmanship by the second Secretary-General of the United Nations, and from his theoretical interpretation of the role which he conceived the organization as playing, actually and potentially, in the cold war era. Preventive diplomacy, so labeled by Hammarskjöld, represents his answer to the question of how the United Nations can be made directly relevant to the crucial struggle between East and West.

In his major exposition of the concept of preventive diplomacy,[1] Hammarskjöld defined it as United Nations intervention in an area of conflict outside of, or marginal to, the sphere dominated by cold war struggles, designed to forestall the competitive intrusion of the rival power blocs into that area. He began with the acknowledgment that "it is extremely difficult for the United Nations to exercise an influence on problems which are clearly and definitely within the orbit of present day conflicts between power blocs." Having thus conceded that the organization could not effectively intervene in the central arena of the cold war, he turned his attention to the periphery, asserting that "the areas which are not committed in the

* From *Swords into Plowshares*, rev. ed., by Inis L. Claude, Jr. Copyright © 1956, 1959, 1964 by Inis L. Claude, Jr. Reprinted by permission of Random House, Inc., and the University of London Press Ltd.

[1] *Introduction to the Annual Report of the Secretary-General on the Work of the Organization, 16 June 1959–15 June 1960*, General Assembly, Official Records: Fifteenth Session, Supplement No. 1 A (A/4390/Add. 1).

major conflicts are still considerable." These areas, he suggested, provided "the main field of useful activity of the United Nations, in its efforts to prevent conflicts or to solve conflicts." He described this activity as the filling of vacuums by the United Nations, or the localization of conflicts in the no-man's-land of the cold war, with the relatively uncommitted members of the organization serving as its agents for this purpose. By undertaking such activity, he believed, the United Nations might prevent the extension and the exacerbation of the cold war. Preventive diplomacy, in short, was conceived by Hammarskjöld as an international version of the policy of containment, designed not to restrict the expansion of one bloc or the other, but to restrict the expansion of the zone permeated by bloc conflicts; it was put forward as a means for containment of the cold war.

In stating the concept of preventive diplomacy, Hammarskjöld was not indulging in armchair speculation. He explicitly related his analysis to a series of cases, including the Middle Eastern crises of 1956 and 1958, the Laos case of 1959, and the Congo crisis of 1960, in which the United Nations had "moved so as to forestall developments which might draw the specific conflict, openly or actively, into the sphere of power bloc differences." Essentially, his theoretical essay was a set of reflections upon recent and continuing experience, and a projection into the future of the role which the United Nations had begun to evolve under his imaginative leadership.

In citing these cases, the Secretary-General stressed the flexibility of the requirements and the variety of the means for United Nations intervention in particular situations. In some instances, largely symbolic manifestations of the United Nations' presence had sufficed—as in Jordan, in 1958, and in Laos, in 1959. The Lebanese crisis in 1958, involving allegations of external intrusion into an unstable domestic situation, had brought about the creation of the United Nations Observation Group in Lebanon (UNOGIL), a substantial body of military personnel provided by more than a score of member states, which undertook for several months to discourage infiltration and illegal arms shipments into that troubled country.

The Middle Eastern and Congo crises of 1956 and 1960 had involved the United Nations in much more elaborate forms of intervention. These two cases were the major elements in the background of experience which inspired Hammarskjöld's formulation of the concept of preventive diplomacy. United Nations activities in the other cases could be construed as variants of well established international methods for dealing with dangerous disputes, modified forms of pacific settlement technique, fitting into a line of evolution which could be traced back through such institutions as the United Nations Truce Supervision Organization in the Palestine area and the United Nations Military Observer Group in India and Pakistan, to the commissions of inquiry and conciliation which the League had utilized. The two major cases, however, called forth United Nations operations which were sufficiently different in scope and nature from other international ventures to be treated as innovations —the first episodes in the development of a new political and military role for the organization. These cases may be regarded as the prototypes of preventive diplomacy. . . .

Preventive Diplomacy and Collective Security

The line betwen preventive diplomacy and collective security may not be obvious to the casual observer, for operations representing the former approach, like those associated with the latter, are likely to involve the formation and utilization of an international military force of more than negligible size, composed—in the absence of a standing force—of units made available from national military establishments. Thus, both UNEF and ONUC may be characterized as collective forces, and, consequently, may readily be mistaken for instrumentalities of collective security—although neither of them approaches the level of size and strength that would be required for any significant collective security operation. Indeed, further experience may confirm the impression derived from UNEF and ONUC that an international military operation designed for preventive diplomacy can be identified as one intermediate in size: two large for the requirements of conventional peaceful settlement, but too small for those of collective security.

Size, however, is chiefly important as a clue to *function;* preventive diplomacy is ultimately differentiated from collective security by the mission assigned to the military forces assembled under international auspices. A collective security force is designed for combat with the military arm of an aggressive state. Its function is to defeat and repel aggression. The tasks of a preventive diplomacy force may be varied—and, as in the case of ONUC, ill-defined —but they emphatically do *not* include that of fighting to frustrate a deliberate and systematically organized campaign of aggression. The contrast may be illustrated by comparing the Korean action of the United Nations with operations in the Middle East and the Congo. The Korean operation—which may be roughly described as a collective security venture undertaken in the absence of a collective security system—involved the use of collective forces to combat a determined aggressor. UNEF and ONUC, on the other hand, moved into the crises for which they were improvised, with the acquiescence or consent of all the states involved in those situations, and without the intent or the assignment of doing battle with any of them. To be sure, forces engaged in preventive diplomacy may encounter a variety of coercive tasks, as vividly illustrated by the vicissitudes of the Congo operation; there can be no guarantee that they will be able to function entirely without gunfire and bloodshed. Nevertheless, armed combat is at most a peripheral aspect of their mission, not its primary element as in the case of a force dispatched to effectuate collective security.

The central objective of preventive diplomacy is to abort the development of situations where the need for the operation of collective security might arise—that is, to prevent the extension of great power confrontations that might produce violent conflict. The emphasis here is not on the frustration of a would-be aggressor, but on the avoidance of intensified rivalry. The aim is not to threaten an expansionist state with defeat, but to offer the promise of assistance to competing states or blocs in limiting the scope of their competition. Helping all states to avoid war, rather than helping some states to resist attack, is the theme of preventive diplomacy.

This is not to say that the *preventive* motif is a monopoly of preventive diplomacy. Collective security, too, aims at preventing war; it is a scheme for deterring aggression. However, the two approaches represent different preventive strategies. Collective security focuses upon aggressive intent, while preventive diplomacy concerns itself with dangerous confrontation. The former assumes a situation in which one power may be tempted to strike, and uses the threat of overwhelming resistance to prevent such action. The latter undertakes preventive measures at an earlier stage, and of a different sort; it represents an attempt to aid both parties engaged in rivalry by inhibiting the development of situations conducive to an explosive showdown, deliberately or inadvertently precipitated. A collective security force in action aims to separate an aggressor, forcibly, from his victim. A preventive diplomacy force in action aims to keep competitive powers, by mutual agreement, separated from each other.

The launching and conduct of the United Nations operation in the Congo provides important evidence that the contrast of preventive diplomacy and collective security is not simply a matter of theoretical distinction, but of political choice as well. When the Security Council first considered the Congo crisis, on July 13 and 14, 1960, a number of states—including the Soviet Union—regarded it as a case of Belgian aggression and insisted that the military forces to be assembled under the United Nations flag be used "to take effective action to halt the aggression."[2] From this point of view, ONUC was to be a collective security operation. The majority, however, led by the United States, held that the crucial problem was the chaotic situation in the Congo which had prompted emergency intervention by Belgium, and that the task of the organization was to remedy that situation so as to eliminate the need and minimize the temptation for states to intervene. This position clearly reflected an urge to exculpate Belgium; moreover, it expressed concern about Belgium's action, not on the ground that such intervention represented the international sin of aggression but that it might stimulate intervention by other states. The objective was not to make the Congo another Korea, but to prevent it from producing a new version of the Spanish Civil War of the 1930s. From this viewpoint, ONUC was to serve the purpose of preventive diplomacy.

Both in words and in action, the Secretary-General gave evidence from the beginning of the Congo operation that he agreed with the conception of its mission that had been stated by the United States and other Western powers. Hammarskjöld made this explicit in the document, signed on August 31, 1960, containing his basic statement of the doctrine of preventive diplomacy:

> The view expressed here as to the special possibilities and responsibilities of the Organization in situations of a vacuum has reached an unusually clear expression in the case of the Congo. There, the main argument presented for United Nations intervention was the breakdown of law and order, the rejection of the attempt to maintain order by foreign troops, and the introduction of the United Nations Force so as to create the basis for the withdrawal of the foreign troops and for the forestalling of initiatives to introduce any other foreign troops into the territory with the obvious risks

[2] See Security Council, *Official Records: 15th Year, 873rd Meeting.* The quotation is from a statement by the Soviet representative, p. 21.

for widening international conflict which would ensue.[3]

The USSR's bitter repudiation of ONUC in the fall of 1960 stemmed in part from the realization that the operation had not acquired the character of a collective security action against Belgium, but had, as an exercise in preventive diplomacy, tended to inhibit Communist moves to transform the Congo into a new arena of the cold war. The ultimate clash of political views as to the purpose of ONUC had been implicit in the original debate in the Security Council as to whether the task should be defined in terms of collective security or of preventive diplomacy.

Preventive Diplomacy and Disarmament

The contrast between preventive diplomacy and the more conventional approaches to peace through international organization is sharpest in the case of disarmament. Preventive diplomacy is compatible with the latter, in that it raises no obstacles to the elimination, reduction, or control of national armaments. On the other hand, disarmament is incompatible with preventive diplomacy, in that the achievement of the former would undermine the basis for the latter. Preventive diplomacy is a phenomenon arising out of the arms race, a response to the emergence of a situation of mutual deterrence. Since the advent of the atomic age, the USSR and the United States have moved inexorably toward the point of decisive mutual vulnerability, where neither can rationally afford to precipitate a showdown with the other. The approach to this point has bred a mood of prudential pacifism—an urge to avoid total war which is rooted fundamentally in good sense rather than in good will, in calculations of the national interest in survival rather than in idealistic aspirations. The cold war is a form of struggle between powers which are not, in Wilsonian terms, too proud to fight, but in terms of present-day reality, too prudent to fight in all-out encounter; a fight to the finish has become too literally possible for rational men to contemplate it as a deliberate policy choice.

This is the setting within which the possibility of United Nations action to implement preventive diplomacy has arisen. Pre-

[3] *Introduction to the Annual Report of the Secretary-General on the Work of the Organization, 16 June 1959–15 June 1960*, General Assembly, Official Records: Fifteenth Session, Supplement No. 1 A, pp. 4–5.

ventive diplomacy is dependent upon the willingness of the major powers to have the United Nations seal off trouble spots, excluding these areas from their competitive intrusion. This willingness is a function of prudential pacifism; the opportunity to exercise preventive diplomacy occurs only when, and to the extent that, each of the primary contestants dreads the implications of a showdown more than it values the possibilities of winning an engagement in the cold war. Clearly, the essential backdrop for this situation is the thermonuclear arms race; without it, the reluctance of the great contenders to risk decisive confrontation would be deprived of much of its strength.

These observations may explain some of the ambiguities in Soviet policy regarding ONUC. As we noted above, the USSR supported the initiation of the Congo operation with the stated intention and apparent expectation that it would be a device for expelling Belgian forces, which it regarded as having committed aggression in the Congo, but turned sharply against the operation when it became evident that ONUC was being used primarily as an instrument of preventive diplomacy. The Soviet polemic against the operation and its executive director, Secretary-General Hammarskjöld, was extraordinarily vigorous for a number of months, beginning in the fall of 1960, and raised a grave threat to the successful continuation of the operation and the survival of the United Nations. Subsequently, the virulence of the attack gradually subsided, and the Soviet position was reduced to one of passive opposition to ONUC. A number of factors may have contributed to this moderation of Soviet opposition—including the death of Hammarskjöld and the adoption of limited concessions to Soviet demands —but it is possible that the USSR was ultimately restrained from pressing its attack by an appreciation, however vehemently disavowed in public, of the value of preventive diplomacy, or, to put it differently, of the peril of entering into a confrontation that might eventuate in thermonuclear conflict.

The arms race has not only given the great powers a strong incentive for keeping the cold war cold, and accepting assistance to that end, but, in establishing the context for the cold war, it has also stimulated the emergence of a substantial group of uncommitted states, thereby providing a source of supply for the indispensable operators of preventive diplomacy, the agents of the United Nations in its efforts to promote the containment of the cold war. Whereas collective security in action postulates a "two world" situation—an aggressive camp and an overwhelmingly powerful set of defenders of the established order—preventive diplomacy requires a "three world" system—two groups of antagonists and an in-between world which both serves as the locale for the operation of preventive diplomacy and provides the personnel for that operation. In the present era, the power struggle between East and West has produced just this sort of tripartitism; the bipolar contest makes preventive diplomacy necessary, while the existence of an uncommitted sector makes it possible. . . .

13

INTERNATIONAL ORGANIZATION

This chapter will be devoted to the two universal multi-purpose international organizations: the League of Nations and the United Nations. Regional and functional organizations will be considered in the next chapter.

An early blueprint for a U.N.-type organization—complete with a charter, an assembly, rules of financing the organization, a collective security agreement, etc.—was outlined by Jean Jacques Rousseau (1712–78) in his *Sketch of a Project for Permanent Peace*. The essay is a summary of and commentary on the peace plan of the Abbé de Saint Pierre written in the early eighteenth century, but Rousseau made several alterations in it and added ideas of his own.

The League and the United Nations are compared in the second selection by U

Thant, the third U.N. Secretary General. Thant delivered this speech at the University of California in Berkeley on April 2, 1964.

The third selection is by Thant's predecessor, Dag Hammar-skjöld, Secretary General from 1953 until 1961. Hammarskjöld's analysis of the two concepts of the U.N.'s proper role were incorporated in his introduction to the last annual report to the General Assembly that he prepared. The introduction is dated August 17, 1961, a short time before his tragic death in Africa.

The final selection in this chapter is by one of the most prominent and outspoken critics of the United Nations: General Charles de Gaulle, first President of the Fifth French Republic. De Gaulle made these remarks at a press conference in the Elysée Palace on April 11, 1961.

41. *SKETCH OF A PROJECT FOR PERMANENT PEACE** / *JEAN JACQUES ROUSSEAU*

. . . From time to time certain general assemblies called congresses are convened among us, to which delegates from all states of Europe proceed solemnly, to return home again; where they assemble to say nothing; where all public affairs are discussed in detail; where they engage in common deliberation whether the conference table shall be round or square, how many doors the conference room shall have, whether one plenipotentiary shall sit with his face or his back to the window, whether another shall be allowed to enter the room as much as two inches on a formal visit; and a thousand questions of equal importance, vainly discussed for three centuries and certainly most worthy of occupying the attention of our statesmen.

It is possible that the members of one of these assemblies may be blessed with common sense some day. It is not even impossible that they will sincerely want to serve the public interest. And, for reasons to be discussed shortly, it is also conceivable that after ironing out many difficulties, they will be instructed by their respective sovereigns to sign the charter of the General Confederation containing the following five articles:

* Jean Jacques Rousseau, *Extrait du Projet de Paix Perpétuelle de M. L'Abbé de Saint-Pierre* (Geneva, 1761). Translated by Eva Tamm Lijphart and Arend Lijphart.

1. The contracting sovereigns shall establish a perpetual and irrevocable alliance, and shall appoint plenipotentiaries to hold in a specified place a permanent diet or congress, in which all disputes between the contracting parties shall be settled and terminated by means of arbitration or adjudication.

2. The second article shall specify: the number of sovereigns whose plenipotentiaries shall have a vote in the diet; those who shall be invited to join the organization; the order, time, and method by which the presidency shall pass from one to another at equal intervals; and finally each member's financial contribution and the method of collecting it, to pay for the common expenses.

3. The Confederation shall guarantee to each of its members the control and government of all its present possessions as well as the rules of succession, elective or hereditary, as established by the fundamental laws of each country. Moreover, in order to eliminate once and for all the source of those constantly recurring territorial disputes, the contracting powers shall agree to regard the status quo and their last treaties as the basis of their mutual rights, and to renounce forever any anterior claim. All future disputed successions and other claims shall be settled by the diet by means of arbitration. Resort to force or taking up arms against each other shall not be permitted under any pretext whatsoever.

4. The fourth article shall specify the cases in which any member state breaking the treaty shall be put to the ban of Europe and proscribed as a public enemy: namely, refusing to execute the judgments of the grand alliance, making preparations for war, negotiating treaties harmful to the Confederation, taking up arms to resist it or to attack any one of the member states.

The same article shall also stipulate that the member states shall take collective military measures, at the common expense, against any state put to the ban of Europe, until this state lays down its arms, executes the judgments and rules of the diet, makes reparations for its wrongs, pays the costs, and makes amends even for preparations for war contrary to the treaty.

5. Finally, the plenipotentiaries of the European states assembled in the diet shall always have the power, on the instruction of their courts, to establish rules which they consider essential for the greatest possible benefit for the Confederation as a whole and for each of its members. Provisional rules shall be adopted by a simple majority of votes; definitive rules (after five years) by a

three-fourths majority. But no change in these five fundamental articles shall ever be made without the unanimous consent of the member states. . . .

42. THE LEAGUE OF NATIONS AND THE UNITED NATIONS*/ U THANT

Next year the United Nations will celebrate the twentieth anniversary of its birth in San Francisco. It will have then been in existence for almost exactly the same number of years as the effective life of the League of Nations, its forerunner. Some comparison of the experience and development of the two organizations is therefore timely.

The word "failure" is often applied to the League of Nations, and the history, especially of its early and successful years, is not much studied now, or even mentioned. And yet in the closing years of World War II the victorious allies hastened to organize and build a new international organization which was, in fact, an improved and strengthened version of the old League. It was not the League, or the ideas behind it, that failed. Rather its members, in the critical years of the 1930's, failed to use and support it, and to rally under its banner against aggression and other dangers. It was thus that they finally had to face these dangers separately and in disarray in the terrible first years of the Second World War.

President Woodrow Wilson laid the first draft of the Covenant of the League before the Paris Conference in 1919 with the words "A living thing is born". Despite disaster and unfulfilled promise, these words have proved to be prophetic, as we can see when we look at the world today as represented in the United Nations. For this first great attempt to move toward a "worldwide political and social order in which the common interests of humanity could be seen and served across the barriers of national tradition, racial differences and geographical separation" (as the League's historian, Mr. Frank Walters, has described it) was a historical event of the very highest importance. The League embodied a concept which has fundamentally altered, in our own century, the entire conduct

* U Thant, "The League of Nations and the United Nations," *UN Monthly Chronicle*, Vol. 1, No. 1 (May 1964), pp. 70–75.

of international relations and even the general convictions which form the basis of public opinion.

Let us look for a moment at the meaning of this change. Before the League of Nations came into being, it was almost universally held that every state was the sole and sovereign judge of its own acts and was immune from criticism or even questioning by other states. The idea—now generally accepted—that the community of nations had a moral or legal right to discuss and judge the international conduct of its members was not embodied in any treaty or institution until the Covenant. From that time also dates the idea, now almost universally accepted, that aggressive war is a crime against humanity and that it is the interest, the duty and the right of every state to join in preventing it. That these ideas now seem commonplace is a measure of the vision of the authors of the Covenant of the League.

The Covenant was based on other ideas no less important or fundamental—a new respect for the rights of small nations, the recognition of the need for cooperation in social and economic affairs, the habit of public debate on even the gravest diplomatic issues, the formation of an international civil service. It is the lasting achievement of the League that such ideas are an essential part of the political thinking of our world. Thus the League, as the embodiment of certain ideals and ideas, is very much alive and with us today.

In its time the Covenant of the League was a tremendous step forward, a radical change in the concept of international order. It was a response to the bitter, futile and appalling experience of the First World War, and in retrospect it may be thought the step was too far-reaching to provide a firm foothold when new and terrible dangers threatened. When its basic ideas were reborn in the closing years of the Second World War, however, they were supported by a far greater public understanding and by an even more compelling necessity for success.

The world has changed so rapidly in the last 20 years that it is hard to remember what it was like in the 1920's and 1930's. Thus we tend to forget how much, in the context of the inter-war world, the League actually did or attempted, or how important were the new models of international organization and action which it devised and developed. Despite its fluctuating fortunes, the central purpose of the League remained constant—to be the constitutional embodiment of man's aspirations for peace and a rationally organized world. We, in our time, owe an immense debt to those who, in far harder times, kept this idea alive and did as much as they could to build upon it.

I have already mentioned their achievement in the realm of political ideas. In the practical sphere also, their efforts made it possible for the United Nations, when it came into being in 1945, to build on firm and already existing foundations. Quite apart from the central political structure, many of the new organizations continued and developed from the old with unbroken continuity. The International Labour Organisation was maintained and the Permanent Court at The Hague re-established as the International Court of Justice. The Economic and Social Council was modelled on plans made by the Bruce Committee in the last days of peace in 1939. The WHO and FAO and UNESCO grew out of the corresponding parts of the League Secretariat, while the Mandates System of the League was taken over by the United Nations Trusteeship System. The League Treaty Series was maintained without interruption by the United Nations, and many other activities such as the control of narcotic drugs and work for refugees passed from the old organization to the new one.

The basis of both the League of Nations and the United Nations is the pledge by sovereign states to cooperate, a pledge which involves some measure of sacrifice of sovereignty in the common interest. Both organizations were designed as an intermediate base between the international relations of traditional diplomacy, which had become obsolescent with the disasters of the First World War, and were proved inadequate, and even dangerous, with the Second World War, and the theoretical, ultimate aim of a world legislature, if not a world government. Both organizations therefore show the weaknesses of a transitional state—great aims with small means, great responsibilities with little authority, great expectations clouded by deep suspicions, and hopes for the future constantly blurred by fears and prejudices from the past.

National sovereignty is, understandably, a jealously guarded possession. The harmonizing of national sovereignty with the wider interest, in a way that is acceptable to the governments and peoples concerned, is the main task, and necessity, of international organization. The League's experience made this necessity clear, and we can already see a considerable advance since 1919. Certain European organizations in particular, such as the Coal and Steel Community and the Common Market, have gone far in the direction of pooling resources, coordinating policy and limiting national sovereignty in certain economic fields.

The Charter shows some formal advances over the Covenant in the matter of sovereignty. For example, it forbids the use of force by a state in a manner inconsistent with the purposes of the Organization and obligates the members to supply armed forces and other assistance to the Security Council and to apply measures called for by the Council.

In the United Nations there have also been practical indications of a changing attitude towards the sanctity of national sovereignty. The acceptance of a United Nations peace-keeping force on the territory of a sovereign state is one such instance, and the provision of contingents of national armies to serve under United Nations command is another. These are small beginnings, but impotant ones. There is also, I hope, an increasing recognition of the impartiality and objectivity of the United Nations Secretariat. Despite these changes, the United Nations still has only to a very limited extent a separate existence, and possibilities of action, independent of the will of member governments and the policies of member states. In a given situation it can advance no further than the parties concerned permit. As my distinguished predecessor pointed out, its capacity to act is, in fact, still to a large extent restricted by fundamental national reactions.

There were major differences in the origins and environment of the League and the United Nations. The League was directly linked with the outcome of the First World War and was thus, from the first, dominated by the European situation. The Covenant of the League was an integral part of the Treaty of Versailles. The League was therefore an aspect of the postwar settlement, with all the advantages and disadvantages of such a position. The United Nations Charter on the other hand was drafted before the end of the Second World War and was expressly *not* a part of the postwar settlement. In a sense the League was thus tied from the first to the *status quo* with strong overtones from the past. The United Nations Charter, on the other hand, starting with a statement of purposes and principles for the guidance of the Organization and its members, looks firmly to the future. It is this difference perhaps more than any other that has given the United Nations its vitality.

The Covenant was a remarkable document for its time. Its articles on the reduction in armaments, on aggression, on the judicial settlement of disputes and resort to the Permanent Court of International Justice, on sanctions and on the use of armed force to protect the covenants of the League, were great political innovations in the world of 1919 and have been taken up and developed in the corresponding articles of the United Nations Charter. Unfortunately, in the critical 1930's the leadership, the confidence and the courage to apply them effectively were lacking, and with disastrous results. The soundness of the principles underlying them was reinforced rather than invalidated by this failure.

In other respects the League's Covenant lacked the dynamism of the Charter. Thus the Covenant lacked a clear statement of such an important objective as development towards self-government or independence, and emphasis on the necessity of economic and social development and human rights as an essential complement to political and juridical, and even military, arrangements to establish a firm basis for peace. The United Nations Charter has provided, in practice, a more flexible instrument than the League Covenant, over a wider field. The abandonment of the over-all rule of unanimity which prevailed in the League Council and Assembly is one symptom of this flexibility. The Security Council has a far wider discretion than the League Council had in determining what constitutes an act of aggression; while the system of specialized agencies makes possible much wider and more functional operation in the economic and social field.

The world of the League was in some ways a far less articulate world than we have today. A large proportion of the world's population was then still in colonial status and played little or no part in the world's affairs. This fact gave a basic lack of representative balance to the League's position as a world organization, which was aggravated by other factors relating to membership. Despite the primary role of President Wilson in its creation, the United States, by one of history's major ironies, was never a member of the League. The USSR only became a member in 1934, at which time both Germany and Japan had given notice of their withdrawal, to be followed two years later by Italy. Thus the major effort to maintain peace and security in a critical time through the League devolved upon France and Great Britain and had an essentially European basis, which deprived it of much of the moral authority of a truly global organization.

In this regard, the history of the United Nations presents a striking contrast in its steady progress toward universality. Existing in a time of rapid historic change, its membership has more than doubled since its inception, and the majority of its 113 members now come from Africa and Asia. It is thus more broadly based and less dominated by the greater powers, although the great powers, of course, play an immensely important role in its activities.

It derives added strength and balance from the activities and efforts of the smaller nations, which protect it to some extent from the buffetings of great power rivalries. Unlike the League, from which 14 countries withdrew during its active history, leaving it with a membership of 53 in 1939, no country has ever withdrawn from the United Nations, however adverse its position in the United Nations might appear to be at any given time.

In its predominantly European setting the successive breaches of the Covenant in the 1930's by Mussolini's Italy, and later, Hitler's Germany, paralyzed the League and rendered it ineffective, while the rise of economic nationalism after the depression of 1929 overwhelmed the promise of its earlier efforts in the economic field. Undoubtedly the mood of the 1930's turned against the system of the League Covenant. It was a bewildering mood, and they were confused and dismal times, when it seemed as if mankind had obsessively condemned itself to learn all over again the clear lessons of the First World War. The League Covenant became the victim of ultra-nationalist propaganda from all sides. This propaganda, actively pursued by many people in positions of power and responsibility, frustrated the League's efforts, grudged its successes and rejoiced in its failures. Confidence in its promise was undermined, and the system went down to a tragic and inglorious defeat. Only after five years of world war did the victorious nations rally themselves to repeat, with a conviction born of horror, the noble experiment.

In practice it could be said that the League tended to be legalistic in the face of crisis, while the United Nations has been pragmatic. Since the Covenant condemned "resort to war", the Japanese action in Manchuria in the early 1930's was justified as a "police action". The world has learned, in the cruelest way, the danger of such euphemisms. The Charter, of course, expressly forbids the threat as well as the use of force. The successful peace-keeping operations of the United Nations have been essentially improvised responses to particularly urgent problems. None of these operations was clearly foreshadowed in the Charter. The world has become a much smaller and more closely interrelated place in the last 30 years, and trouble can now spread and escalate much faster and with infinitely greater devastation. The relatively greater speed and informality in action of the United Nations in meeting danger, as compared to the League, reflects this fact as much as it does the heightened determination of nations to avoid a third and even more terrible war.

There were also inherent reasons for this change of attitude and pace in the changing environment in which the United Nations has worked for its first 19 years. Due partly to the lack of unanimity among the great powers and partly to the radical change in the nature of war resulting from the development of nuclear and thermonuclear weapons, there has been a gradual change in general attitudes on questions of international security in the United Nations.

There has tended to be a tacit transition from the concept of collective security, as set out in Chapter VII of the United Nations Charter, to a more realistic idea of peace-keeping in a changing world. There has also been a change in emphasis, for the time being at least, from the use of the military forces of the great powers, as contemplated in the Charter, to the use in practice of the military resources of the smaller powers, which has the advantage of not entangling United Nations action in the conflicts of the Cold War.

Already the concept of absolute sovereignty of a state is unreal, for no country can now exist in isolation. The Charter of the United Nations has taken away the sovereign right to go to war, or even to threaten the use of force in any international dispute. The International Court provides a tribunal for the judicial settlement of legal questions between nations. Many states have given the International Court a wide compulsory jurisdiction.

In the political field, even when there has been open conflict between states, and armed force has been used or threatened, there has been an increasing tendency for the principles of the Charter of the United Nations, rather than military power, to prevail, and on a number of occasions since 1945, the Charter has been a factor in actually preventing or in halting war. The principles of the Charter are clearly acceptable to most of mankind. The acceptance of their practical application, however, involving as it does concepts of national sovereignty long held sacred, is a longer and more difficult task—a task in which the League of Nations failed. If the United Nations has, so far, had more success and has made practical progress in applying the principles of the Charter, it is largely because public thinking on international issues has made great advances and because the dangers to be avoided are greater than ever.

We are now moving away quickly from the world of compartmentalized self-sufficiency into a world where human solidarity daily becomes more essential. Already in humanitarian questions this solidarity is real, as we can see from international responses to natural and other disasters. It is becoming more real in the economic field, and it is clearly a necessity, though not yet a practical reality, in the political field. Here the governments of the world, associated in the United Nations, must realize the ideals which were already accepted in 1919 in the Covenant of the League and were reaffirmed in 1945 in the Charter of the United Nations.

We can thus see how far the world has actually come since 1919 in making the ideas and ideals of the Covenant of the League of Nations into acceptable reality. If we are to make the next step toward world authority and then onward to a world government, it will be by the growth in authority and prestige of the institutions and agencies of the United Nations, and by the development of the provisions of the Charter and the Statute of the International Court. If we can make those documents accepted as binding law, as every government in the United Nations is pledged to accept, then we are on the right path to world authority.

43. *TWO DIFFERING CONCEPTS OF UNITED NATIONS ASSAYED*/ DAG HAMMARSKJÖLD*

I

Debates and events during the year since the publication of the last report to the General Assembly have brought to the fore different concepts of the United Nations, the character of the Organization, its authority and its structure.

On the one side, it has in various ways become clear that certain members conceive of the Organization as a static conference machinery for resolving conflicts of interest and ideologies with a view to peaceful coexistence, within the Charter, to be served by a Secretariat which is to be regarded not as fully internationalized but as representing within its ranks those very interests and ideologies.

Other members have made it clear that they conceive of the Organization primarily as a dynamic instrument of governments

* Dag Hammarskjöld, "Two Differing Concepts of United Nations Assayed," *United Nations Review*, Vol. 8, No. 9 (September 1961), pp. 12–17.

through which they, jointly and for the same purpose, should seek such reconciliation but through which they should also try to develop forms of executive action, undertaken on behalf of all members, and aiming at forestalling conflicts and resolving them, once they have arisen, by appropriate diplomatic or political means, in a spirit of objectivity and in implementation of the principles and purposes of the Charter.

Naturally, the latter concept takes as its starting point the conference concept, but it regards it only as a starting point, envisaging the possibility of continued growth to increasingly effective forms of active international cooperation, adapted to experience, and served by a Secretariat of which it is required that, whatever the background and the views of its individual members, their actions be guided solely by the principles of the Charter, the decisions of the main organs and the interests of the Organization itself.

The first concept can refer to history and to the traditions of national policies of the past. The second can point to the needs of the present and of the future in a world of ever-closer international interdependence where nations have at their disposal armaments of hitherto unknown destructive strength. The first one is firmly anchored in the time-honored philosophy of sovereign national states in armed competition of which the most that may be expected in the international field is that they achieve a peaceful coexistence. The second one envisages possibilities of intergovernmental action overriding such a philosophy, and opens the road toward more developed and increasingly effective forms of constructive international cooperation.

It is clearly for the governments, members of the Organization, and for these governments only, to make their choice and decide on the direction in which they wish the Organization to develop. However, it may be appropriate to study these two concepts in terms of the purposes of the Organization as laid down in the Charter and, in this context, also to consider the character and the significance of the decisions of the Organization as well as its structure.

II

The purposes and principles of the Charter are set out in its preamble and further developed in a series of articles, including some which may seem to be primarily of a procedural or administrative nature. Together, these parts of the Charter lay down some basic rules of international ethics by which all member states have committed themselves to be guided. To a large extent, the rules reflect standards accepted as binding for life within states. Thus, they appear, in the main, as a projection into the international arena and the international community of purposes and principles already accepted as being of national validity. In this sense, the Charter takes a first step in the direction of an organized international community, and this independently of the organs set up for international cooperation. Due to different traditions, the state of social development and the character of national institutions, wide variations naturally exist as to the application in national life of the principles reflected in the Charter, but it is not too difficult to recognize the common elements behind those differences. It is therefore not surprising that such principles of national application could be transposed into an agreed basis also for international behavior and cooperation.

In the preamble to the Charter, member nations have reaffirmed their faith "in the equal rights of men and women and of nations large and small," a principle which also has found many other expressions in the Charter.

Thus, it restates the basic democratic principle of equal political rights, independently of the position of the individual or of the member country in respect of its strength, as determined by territory, population or wealth. The words just quoted must, however, be considered as going further and imply an endorsement as well of a right to equal economic opportunities.

It is in the light of the first principle that the Charter has established a system of equal votes, expressing "the sovereign equality of all its members," and has committed the Organization to the furtherance of self-determination, self-government and independence. On the same basis, the Charter requires universal respect for and observance of human rights and fundamental freedoms for all "without distinction as to race, sex, language or religions."

It is in the light of the latter principle—or, perhaps, the latter aspect of the same basic principle—that the Charter, in Article 55, has committed the members to the promotion of higher standards of living, full employment and conditions of economic and social progress and development as well as to solutions of international economic and related problems. The pledge of all members to take joint and separate action, in cooperation with the Organization, for the achievement of these purposes has been the basis for the far-reaching economic and technical assistance channelled through or administered by the Organization, and may rightly be considered as the basic obligation reflected also in such economic and technical assistance as member governments have been giving, on a bilateral basis, outside the framework of the Organization.

It would seem that those who regard the Organization as a conference machinery, "neutral" in relation to the direction of policies on a national or international basis and serving solely as an instrument for the solution of conflicts by reconciliation, do not pay adequate attention to those essential principles of the Charter to which reference has just been made. The terms of the Charter are explicit as regards the equal political rights of nations as well as of individuals and, although this second principle may be considered only as implicit in the terms of the Charter, they are clear also as regards the demand for equal economic opportunities for all individuals and nations. So as to avoid any misunderstanding, the Charter directly states that the basic democratic principles are applicable to nations "large and small" and to individuals without distinction "as to race, sex, language and religion," qualifications that obviously could be extended to cover also other criteria such as, for example, those of an ideological character which have been used or may be used as a basis for political or economic discrimination.

In the practical work of the Organization these basic principles have been of special significance in relation to countries under colonial rule or in other ways under foreign domination. The General Assembly has translated the principles into action intended to establish through self-determination a free and independent life as sovereign states for peoples who have expressed in democratic forms their wish for such a status. Decisive action has in many cases been taken by member governments, and then the United Nations has had only to lend its support to their efforts. In other cases, the main responsibility has fallen on the Organization itself. The resolution on colonialism, adopted by the General Assembly at its fifteenth session, may be regarded as a comprehensive restatement in elaborated form of the principle laid down in the Charter. Results of developments so far have been reflected in the birth of a great number of new national states and a revolutionary widening of the membership of the Organization.

The demand for equal economic opportunities has, likewise, been—and remains—of special significance in relation to those very countries which have more recently entered the international arena as new states. This is natural in view of the fact that, mostly, they have been in an unfavorable economic position, which is reflected in a much lower per capita income, rate of capital supply and degree of technical development, while their political independence and sovereignty require a fair measure of economic stability and economic possibilities in order to gain substance and full viability.

In working for the translation into practical realities in international life of the democratic principles which are basic to the Charter, the Organization has thus assumed a most active role and it has done so with success, demonstrating both the need and the possibilities for such action.

Further, in the preamble to the Charter it is stated to be a principle and purpose of the Organization "to establish conditions under which justice and respect for the obligations arising from treaties and other sources of international law can be maintained." In these words—to which, naturally, counterparts may be found in other parts of the Charter—it gives expression to another basic democratic principle, that of the rule of law. In order to promote this principle, the Charter established the International Court of Justice, but the principle permeates the approach of the Charter to international problems far beyond the sphere of competence of the Court. As in national life, the principle of justice—which obviously implies also the principle of objectivity and equity in the consideration of all matters before the General Assembly or the Security Council—must be considered as applicable without distinction or discrimination, with one measure and one standard valid for the strong as well as for the weak. Thus, the demand of the Charter for a rule of law aims at the substitution of right for might and makes of the Organization the natural protector of rights which countries, without it, might find it more difficult to assert and to get respected.

The principle of justice can be regarded as flowing naturally from the principles of equal political rights and equal economic opportunities, but it has an independent life and carries, of itself, the world community as far in the direction of an organized international system as the two first-mentioned principles. It has deep roots in the history of the efforts of man to eliminate from international life the anarchy which he had already much earlier overcome on the national level, deeper indeed than the political and economic principles which, as is well known, were much later to get full acceptance also in national life. Long before the United Nations and long before even the League of Nations, governments were working toward a rule of justice in international life through which they hoped to establish an international community based on law, without parliamentary or executive organs, but with a judicial procedure through which law and justice could be made to apply.

The Charter states and develops the three principles mentioned here as a means to an end: "to save succeeding generations from the scourge of war." This adds emphasis to the concept, clearly implied in the Charter, of an international community for which the Organization is an instrument and an expression and in which anarchic tendencies in international life are to be curbed by the introduction of a system of equal political rights, equal economic opportunities and the rule of law. However, the Charter goes one step further, drawing a logical conclusion both from the ultimate aim of the Organization and from the three principles. Thus, it outlaws the use of armed force "save in the common interest." Obviously, the Charter cannot, on the one side, establish a rule of law and the principle of equal rights for "nations large and small" and, on the other hand, permit the use of armed force for national ends, contrary to those principles and, therefore, not "in the common interest." Were nations, under the Charter, to be allowed, by the use of their military strength, to achieve ends contrary to the principle of the equality of members and the principle of justice, it would obviously deprive those very principles of all substance and significance. One practical expression of this approach, which may be mentioned here, is that the organs of the United Nations have consistently maintained that the use of force, contrary to the Charter as interpreted by those organs, cannot be permitted to yield results which can be accepted as valid by the Organization and as establishing new rights.

In the Charter, the right to the use of force is somewhat more extensive than may seem to be the case from a superficial reading of the phrase "save in the common interest." Thus, apart from military action undertaken pursuant to a decision of the Security Council for repression of aggression—that is, for upholding the basic Charter principles—the Charter opens the door to the use of armed force by a nation in exercise of its inherent right to resist armed attack. This is a point on which, both in theory and in practice, the development of international law is still at a very early stage. As is well known, no agreement has been reached on a definition of aggression, beyond that found in Article 2, paragraph 4, of the Charter, and the Organization has several times had to face situations in which, therefore, the rights and wrongs in a specific case of conflict have not been clarified. It would be a vitally important step forward if wider agreement could be reached regarding the criteria to be applied in order to distinguish between legitimate and illegitimate use of force. History is only too rich in examples of armed aggression claimed as action in self-defence. How could it be otherwise, when most cases of armed conflict are so deeply rooted in a history of clashes of interests and rights, even if, up to the fatal moment of the first shot, those clashes have not involved recourse to the use of armed force?

In recognition of this situation and in the light of historical experience, the Charter makes yet another projection into international life of solutions to conflicts tested in national life, and establishes the final principle that the Organization shall "bring about by peaceful means and in conformity with the principles of justice and international law, adjustment or settlement of international disputes or situations which might lead to a breach of the peace." This principle, as quoted here from Article 1 of the Charter, is further developed specifically in Article 33, which requires parties to any dispute, the consequence of which is likely to endanger the maintenance of international peace and security, to "seek a solution by negotiation, inquiry, mediation, conciliation, arbitration, judicial settlement, resort to regional agencies or arrangements, or other peaceful means of their own choice." It is in this sphere that the Security Council has had, and is likely to continue to have, its main significance, both directly as a forum before which any dispute threatening peace and security can be brought up for debate and as an organ which directly, or through appropriate agents, may assist the parties in finding a way out and, by preventive diplomacy, may forestall the outbreak of an armed conflict. It seems appropriate here to draw attention especially to the right of the Security Council under Article 40 to "call upon the parties concerned to comply with such provisional measures as it deems necessary or desirable" for the prevention of any aggravation of a situation threatening peace and security, and to the obligation of members to comply with a decision on such measures.

It is in the light of the approach to international coexistence in our world today, which is thus to be found in the Charter, that judgment has to be passed on the validity of the different conceptions of the Organization which in recent times have become increasingly apparent. As already pointed out, the basic principles regarding the political equality of nations and their right to equal economic opportunities are difficult to reconcile with the view that the Organization is to be regarded only as a conference machinery for the solution, by debate and joint decisions, of conflicts of interest or ideology. It seems even more difficult to reconcile these principles with a view according to which equality among members should be reflected in the establishment of a balance between power blocs or other groupings of nations. The same difficulty is apparent as regards the principle of justice and the principle of prohibiting the use of armed force. It is easier to apply the conference concept to the principle of prevention of conflict through negotiation, but also on this point the difficulties become considerable if it is recognized that such solutions as may be sought by the Organization should be solutions based on the rules of equality and justice.

III

The General Assembly, the Security Council and other collective organs of the United Nations have features in common with a standing international diplomatic conference, but their procedures go beyond the forms of such a conference and show aspects of a parliamentary or quasi-parliamentary character.

While decisions of a conference, in order to commit its participants, must be based on their subsequent acceptance of the decisions, the organs of the United Nations act on the basis of voting, with the decisions being adopted if supported by a majority. However, the decisions of the Assembly have, as regards member states, only the character of recommendations (except for financial assessments and certain other types of organizational action) so that obligations like those arising out of an agreement, coming into force after a conference, do not normally flow from them. But although the decisions, legally, are only recommendations, they introduce an important element by expressing a majority consensus on the issue under consideration.

Naturally, such a formula leaves scope for a gradual development in practice of the weight of the decisions. To the extent that more respect, in fact, is shown to General Assembly recommendations by the member states, they may come more and more close to being recognized as decisions having a binding effect on those concerned, particularly when they involve the application of the binding principles of the Charter and of international law.

Both those who regard a gradual increase in the weight of decisions of the General Assembly as necessary, if progress is to be registered in the direction of organized peaceful coexistence within the Charter, and those who oppose such a development, have to recognize that, with certain variations in individual cases, the practice still is very close to the restrictive Charter formula. Experience shows that even countries which have voted for a certain decision may, later on, basing themselves on its character of merely being a recommendation, refuse to follow it or fail to support its implementation, financially or in other respects.

What has been said applies generally to the collective organs of the Organization, but, as is well known, the Charter has gone one step further beyond the conference concept, in the direction of the parliamentary concept, in the case of the Security Council. In Article 25 member states of the United Nations have agreed to "accept and carry out the decisions of the Security Council in accordance with the present Charter," thus, by agreement, making the decisions of the Council mandatory, except, of course, when such decisions take the form of "recommendations" within the terms of Chapter VI or certain other Articles of the Charter. They have further, in Article 49, undertaken to "join in affording mutual assistance in carrying out the measures decided upon by the Security Council."

This agreed mandatory nature of certain Security Council decisions might have led to a demand for unanimity in the Council, a unanimity which was the rule for the Council of the League of Nations. Even so, however, the arrangement would have gone beyond the conference principle with its requirement that no decision reached in an international organ should be binding on an individual member short of his agreement. With the present arrangements, requiring a majority of seven and the concurring votes of the permanent members, a bridge between the traditional conference approach and a parliamentary approach is provided by the commitment in Article 25 to agree to the carrying out of the decisions in the Council which should be considered as giving the Council its authority by general delegation as indeed stated in Article 24, paragraph 1.

What clearly remains within the Council of the traditional conference and agreement pattern is the condition that its decisions of a nonprocedural character must be supported by the unanimous vote of the five permanent members, thus avoiding for those members the risk of being bound by a decision of the Council which has not met with their agreement. It may be observed that this special position for the permanent members, apart from other reasons, has the justification that, without such a rule, the other members of the organization, in complying with a Security Council decision, might find themselves unwillingly drawn into a big power conflict.

In spite of the delegated authority which the Council may be considered as exercising, and the condition that decisions must be agreed to by the permanent members, the experience of the Organization, as regards the implementation of Council decisions, is uneven and does not indicate full acceptance in practice of Article 25. In this case also, examples can be given of a tendency to regard decisions, even when taken under Chapter VII, as recommendations binding only to the extent that the party concerned has freely committed itself to carry them out; there is here a clear dichotomy between the aims of the Charter and the general political practice at its present stage of development. Such cases refer not only to members outside the Council, or, perhaps, members inside the Council, who have not supported a specific decision, but also to members within the Council who have cast their votes in favor of a decision but who later on are found to reserve for themselves at least a right to interpret the decision in ways which seem to be at variance with the intentions of the Council. The ambiguity of this situation emerges with special force in cases where such attitudes have been taken by permanent members of the Council, who are considered to shoulder the responsibility for the maintenance of peace and security which is reflected in the special position they hold within the Council. Obviously, the problem whether the intended legal weight is given to decisions of the Security Council arises in practice not only in cases of noncompliance but also in cases of a refusal to shoulder the financial consequences of a decision of the Council.

These observations—which have been limited to a reminder of the Charter rules and a factual reminder also of the experiences in practice—point to a situation which in any evaluation of the United Nations must be given the most serious consideration by members. For the judgment on the various concepts of the United Nations which are put forward, it is one thing to note what the Charter stipulates; it is an entirely different but ultimately more important question as to what the situation is in practice and what, in fact, is the weight given to decisions of the Organization when they go beyond the conference pattern of agreement.

For those who maintain the conference concept of the Organization, it is natural to side-step the mandatory nature of decisions by the Security Council. For those who take a different view, it is equally natural and essential to work for a full and general acceptance of the Charter rules. Were those to be right who hold that the Charter, on the points discussed here and, maybe, also as regards the five basic principles discussed in the first part of this introduction, is ahead of our time and the political possibilities which it offers, such a view still would not seem to justify the conclusion that the clear approach of the Charter should be abandoned. Rather, it would indicate that member nations jointly should increase their efforts to make political realities gradually come closer to the pattern established by the Charter.

In the light of such considerations, the significance of the outcome of every single conflict on which the Organization has to take a stand and the weight given to its decisions in such a conflict stand out very clearly. A failure to gain respect for decisions or actions of the Organization within the terms of the Charter is often called a failure for the Organization. It would seem more correct to regard it as a failure of the world community, through its member nations and in particular those most directly concerned, to cooperate in order, step by step, to make the Charter a living reality in practical political action as it is already in law.

Were such cooperation, for which the responsibility naturally rests with each single member as well as with all members collectively, not to come about, and were the respect for the obligations flowing from Article 25 of the Charter to be allowed to diminish, this would spell the end of the possibilities of the Organization to grow into what the Charter indicates as the clear intention of the founders, as also of all hopes to see the Organization grow into an increasingly effective instrument, with increasing respect for recommendations of the General Assembly as well.

What this would mean for the value of the Organization as protector of the aims, principles and rights it was set up to further and safeguard is obvious. The effort through the Organization to find a way by which the world community might, step by step, grow into organized international cooperation within the Charter must either progress or recede. Those whose reactions to the work of the Organization hamper its development or reduce its possibil-

ities of effective action may have to shoulder the responsibility for a
return to a state of affairs which governments had already found too
dangerous after the First World War.

IV

The growth of the United Nations out of the historic conference
pattern—which, as observed earlier in this introduction, at all events
naturally remains the starting point in all efforts of the Organization—is clearly reflected in what, in the light of experience, may
seem to be a lack of balance in the Charter. While great attention is
given to the principles and purposes, and considerable space is
devoted to an elaboration of what may be called the parliamentary
aspects of the Organization, little is said about executive arrangements. This does not mean that the Charter in any way closes the
door to such arrangements or to executive action, but only that, at
the stage of international thinking crystallized in the Charter, the
conference approach still was predominant, and that the needs for
executive action, if the new Organization was to live up to expectations and to its obligations under the Charter, had not yet attracted
the attention they were to receive in response to later developments.

The key clause on the executive side may be considered to be
Article 24, in which it is said that "in order to assure prompt and
effective action by the United Nations, its members confer on the
Security Council primary responsibility for the maintenance of
international peace and security."

On that basis the Security Council is given the right, under
Article 29, to establish such subsidiary organs as it deems necessary
for the performance of its functions, the right under Article 40 to
decide on so-called provisional measures, the right to use, for the
purposes of the Charter, under certain conditions, armed forces
made available to the Council, the right under Article 48 to request
from governments action on the Council's behalf, as well as the
right to request of the Secretary-General to "perform . . . such
functions as are entrusted to him" by the Council.

The various clauses here briefly enumerated open a wide range
of possibilities for executive action undertaken by, and under the
aegis of, the Security Council. However, no specific machinery is
set up for such action by the Council, apart from the Military Staff
Committee, with planning responsibilities in the field of the possible
use of armed force by the Security Council under Chapter VII of

the Charter. In fact, therefore, the executive functions and their form have been left largely to practice, and it is in the field of the practices of the Organization that cases may be found in the light of which it is now possible to evaluate the ways in which the Organization may develop its possibilities for diplomatic, political or military intervention of an executive nature in the field.

The forms used for executive action by the Security Council—or when the Council has not been able to reach decisions, in some cases, by the General Assembly—are varied and are to be explained by an effort to adjust the measures to the needs of each single situation. However, some main types are recurrent. Subcommittees have been set up for fact-finding or negotiation on the spot. Missions have been placed in areas of conflict for the purpose of observation and local negotiation. Observer groups of a temporary nature have been sent out. And, finally, police forces under the aegis of the United Nations have been organized for the assistance of the governments concerned with a view to upholding the principles of the Charter. As these, or many of these, arrangements require centralized administrative measures, which cannot be performed by the Council or the General Assembly, members have to a large extent used the possibility to request the Secretary-General to perform special functions by instructing him to take the necessary executive steps for implementation of the action decided upon. This has been done under Article 98, as quoted above, and has represented a development in practice of the duties of the Secretary-General under Article 97.

The character of the mandates has, in many cases, been such that in carrying out his functions the Secretary-General has found himself forced also to interpret the decisions in the light of the Charter, United Nations precedents and the aims and intentions expressed by the members. When that has been the case, the Secretary-General has been under the obligation to seek guidance, to all possible extent, from the main organs; but when such guidance has not been forthcoming, developments have sometimes led to situations in which he has had to shoulder responsibility for certain limited political functions, which may be considered to be in line with the spirit of Article 99 but which legally have been based on decisions of the main organs themselves, under Article 98, and thus the exclusive responsibility of member states acting through these organs. Naturally, in carrying out such functions the Secretariat has remained fully subject to the decisions of the political bodies.

This whole development has lately become a matter of controversy, natural and, indeed, unavoidable in the light of differences of approach to the role of the Organization to which attention has been drawn earlier in this introduction. While the development is welcomed by member nations which feel a need of growth as regards the possibilities of the Organization to engage in executive action in protection of the Charter principles, it is rejected by those who maintain the conference concept of the Organization. The different opinions expressed on the development are only superficially related to this or that specific action and the way in which it is considered to have been carried through. They are also only superficially related to the choice of means used for translating decisions into action. The discussion regarding the development of executive functions is basically one confronting the same fundamentally different concepts of the Organization and its place in international politics, which could be seen also in the different attitudes toward the legal weight of decisions of the Organization.

It is in this context that the principle embodied in Article 100 of the Charter is of decisive significance. This principle, which has a long history, establishes the international and independent character of the Secretariat. Thus, it is said that the Secretary-General and the staff of the Secretariat "shall not seek or receive instructions from any Government or from any other authority external to the Organization," and that they "shall refrain from any action which might reflect on their position as international officials responsible only to the Organization." In the same Article, the members of the United Nations undertake to respect "the exclusively international character of the responsibilities of the Secretary-General and the staff and not to seek to influence them in the discharge of their responsibilities."

The significance of the principle stated in Article 100 is a dual one. It envisages a Secretariat so organized and developed as to be able to serve as a neutral instrument for the Organization, were its main organs to wish to use the Secretariat in the way which has been mentioned above and for which Article 98 has opened possibilities. But in doing so, the principle also indicates an intention to use the Secretariat for such functions as would require that it have an exclusively international character.

In the traditional conference pattern, participants in a meeting are mostly serviced by a secretariat drawn from the same countries as the participants themselves, and constituting a mixed group regarding which there is no need to demand or maintain an exclusively international character. It is therefore natural that those who favor the conference approach to the United Nations tend to give to Article 100 another interpretation than the one which the text calls for, especially in the light of its historical background and its background also in other clauses of the Charter.

There is no reason to go more deeply into this special problem here. Suffice it to say that, while the Organization, if regarded as a standing diplomatic conference, might well be serviced by a fully international Secretariat but does not need it, the other approach to the Organization and its role cannot be satisfied with anything less than a secretariat of an exclusively international character, and thus cannot be reconciled with a secretariat composed on party lines and on the assumption that the interests represented in the main organs in this manner should be represented and advocated also within the Secretariat. Thus, again, the choice between conflicting views on the United Nations Secretariat is basically a choice between conflicting views on the Organization, its functions and its future.

In order to avoid possible misunderstandings, it should be pointed out here that there is no contradiction at all between a demand for a truly international Secretariat and a demand, found in the Charter itself, for as wide a "geographical" distribution of posts within the Secretariat as possible. It is, indeed, necessary precisely in order to maintain the exclusively international character of the Secretariat that it be so composed as to achieve a balanced distribution of posts on all levels among all regions. This, however, is clearly something entirely different from a balanced representation of trends or ideologies. In fact, if a realistic representation of such trends is considered desirable, it can and should be achieved without any assumption of political representation within the ranks of the Secretariat, by a satisfactory distribution of posts based on geographical criteria.

The exclusively international character of the Secretariat is not tied to its composition but to the spirit in which it works and to its insulation from outside influences, as stated in Article 100. While it may be said that no man is neutral in the sense that he is without opinions or ideals, it is just as true that, in spite of this, a neutral Secretariat is possible. Anyone of integrity, not subjected to undue pressures, can, regardless of his own views, readily act in an "exclusively international" spirit and can be guided in his actions on behalf of the Organization solely by its interests and principles and by the instructions of its organs. . . .

44. *THE DISUNITED NATIONS**/
CHARLES DE GAULLE

The United Nations Organization and its institutions were created in 1945 on the basis of a Charter, and with purposes which France at that time approved. I was, myself, at that time at the head of my country and in this capacity I was one of the founders of the United Nations at the request of President Roosevelt and then of President Truman, who were its promoters.

There was an executive council, the Security Council, which was a sort of Government composed of the five big powers, that is to say, the United States, the Soviet Union, Great Britain, China and France. And then there was a kind of non-legislative deliberative parliament, the General Assembly. The General Assembly, at that time, was supposed to debate only on subjects which were submitted to it by the Security Council. I will add that the General Assembly then included only about forty States, which had been in existence for a long time, which were endowed with cohesion and unity, and which were used to international relations and to the traditions, obligations and responsibilities which these relations entail.

In the Security Council each of the members—each of the big powers—had the veto power. And then finally in the General Assembly, in accordance with what France had wanted and had obtained in San Francisco, it was necessary—and it still is—to have a two thirds majority in order to pass a resolution.

It seems that all these procedures would enable the States to establish contact with each other, to examine world questions jointly and to promote peace while restricting demagogic activities.

As for the Charter, it was designed to prevent the Organization from interfering in the affairs of each State and it could intervene only on the explicit request of a government.

Finally, among the intentions which had inspired its creation there was the desire, perhaps the illusion of the Western nations—in any case of the Americans—to bring the Soviets to cooperate with the West. We know what has happened.

* Ambassade de France, Service de Presse et d'Information, *President De Gaulle Holds Fourth Press Conference* (New York, 1961), pp. 7–8. Reprinted by permission.

Today it must be said that the United Nations really do not in any way resemble what they were or ought to have been at the start. First of all, the Security Council no longer comprises—is far from comprising—only the big powers, but also several powers elected in turn, and then there is an undetermined number of delegations attending all debates of the Security Council, depending on the subjects under discussion. As for the General Assembly, at the present time it has assumed all powers. It can deliberate on everything, without and even against the advice of the Security Council, which is thus dispossessed of its essential prerogative. In addition, this General Assembly now includes the representatives of more than one hundred States—soon they will number one hundred twenty—most of which, at least many of which, are improvised States and believe it their duty to stress grievances or demands with regard to the older nations, rather than elements of reason and progress.

As for the Charter, it now inconveniences every one and there is no one who can enforce its application. As regards the hoped-for cooperation between East and West within the United Nations, we can see its results.

So that now the meetings of the United Nations are no more than riotous and scandalous sessions where there is no way to organize an objective debate and which are filled with invectives and insults proffered especially by the Communists and by those who are allied with them against the Western nations.

And then, as the United Nations becomes a scene of disturbance, confusion and division, it acquires the ambition to intervene in all kinds of matters. This is especially true of its officers. It is anxious to assert itself—even by force of arms—as it did in the Congo.

The result is that it carries to the local scene its global incoherence, the personal conceptions of its various agents and the individual partiality of each of the States which send their contingents with their own orders—send them, then withdraw them.

Under these conditions, France does not see how she can adopt any other attitude toward the United, or Disunited, Nations than that of the greatest reserve. In any case, she does not wish to contribute her men or her money to any present or eventual undertaking of this organization—or disorganization. Of course we hope that the day will come when common sense will again prevail and when the reasonable nations, noting the results of experience, will wish to resume this great world undertaking on a new basis.

In my opinion, this will be achieved if Europe succeeds in organizing itself and consequently in asserting its power, its reason and its experience in the world. Then Europe will be able to take the necessary steps.

14

FUNCTIONALISM AND REGIONALISM

The spiritual father of the functional approach to international organization is David Mitrany, of Princeton University's Institute for Advanced Study. The first selection—an article which appeared in the British journal *International Affairs* in 1948 —is a stimulating presentation of his views. Mitrany's best known book is *A Working Peace System*.

The second selection is by an outstanding practitioner of functionalism: Paul G. Hoffman. The author heads the United Nations Development Programme, a program of economic and technical assistance to the developing countries. He delivered this address to the Columbia University Conference on International Economic Development on February 20, 1970.

Regionalism has developed to the greatest extent in Western Europe, particularly after the Second World War. But the ideal of closer cooperation and integration of the European states has existed for many centuries. One of the adherents of this ideal was Napoleon Bonaparte (1769–1821), according to the statements which he made while he was imprisoned on Saint Helena. The third selection consists of his highly interesting reflections on this subject.

The most exciting and far-reaching experiment in regional-functional organization is the European Economic Community. The fourth selection is a speech by Walter Hallstein to a joint meeting of Harvard University and the Massachusetts Institute of Technology on May 22, 1961. Hallstein was the dynamic first President of the E.E.C.'s Commission, and in many respects regarded himself as the first "prime minister of Europe."

45. *THE FUNCTIONAL APPROACH TO WORLD ORGANIZATION**/DAVID MITRANY*

It seems to be the fate of all periods of transition that reformers are more ready to fight over a theory than to pull together on a problem. At this stage I can only ask to be given credit for the claim that I do not represent a theory. I represent an anxiety. At home, when we want change or reform, we state our objectives in such terms that all may see how we may attain them. When it comes to the international world, where we are faced with old and stubborn habits of mind and feeling and political dogmas, where the change we have in mind must close one of the ponderous tomes of history and open up a new one, it seems that nothing will do but the perfect goal and winged results.

If we compare the general mood of 1919, when everybody was keen to get back to what had gone before, with the mood of 1948 one generation later, when the need for an active international society is almost universally taken for granted—we are justified in regarding the change as progress indeed; a change in outlook without which all schemes for international peace would, as in past centuries, remain but noble dreams. Yet, even with that change,

* David Mitrany, "The Functional Approach to World Organization," reprinted by permission of the Society for a World Service Federation from *A Working Peace System*, published by Quadrangle Books, Inc.

present schemes may likewise remain noble dreams if they are beyond the reach of the ways and means of human government. "Government is a practical thing," Burke wrote to the Sheriffs of Bristol, and we should beware of elaborating political forms "for the gratification of visionaries." It is the task of experts, whether individuals or groups, to pass now beyond fine appeals and ideal formulae. Expert vagueness will merely result in popular vacuousness. If that popular receptiveness to the idea of international organization is to ripen into an informed public opinion, it must now be fed with a diet of hard facts and practicable measures, so that it may know how to press and support Governments in the pursuit of an active international policy. How otherwise can it be explained why, with such broad goodwill and sense of urgency, so little has been fulfilled?

The general outlook, therefore, is promising. When we come to examine present trends more concretely, two stand out above all—the trend for national self-government, and the trend for radical social change. The two are at work in different strengths in different parts of the world, but they merge into each other. Even in Europe, where state-making seems near to completion, the transformation of society is taking place on a national basis; while in the Middle East, in South-East Asia and elsewhere, the new States express social revolution as much as political revolution. Speaking internationally, therefore, there is in this social nationalism or national socialism an actual danger of regression. The modern political trend has led increasingly to the splitting up of the world into independent States; the idea of national self-government was taken as the guide of the peace settlement of 1919 and is still strongly at work in the Middle East, in South-East Asia, and is stirring in Africa too. At the same time the modern division of labour had tended to weld peoples and countries together, and it is that unity which is in danger of being loosened by the new conception of the State. It is not my part to discuss whether the trend is desirable or inevitable, but merely to establish that these are the conditions from which our international house-building must start. We are favoured by the need and habit of material co-operation, we are hampered by the general clinging to political segregation. How to reconcile these two trends, both of them natural and both of them active, is the main problem of political architecture at present.

In the light of that problem ideas and schemes for international organization can be brought, speaking broadly, under one of three categories: (i) a general and fairly loose association, like the League of Nations and the United Nations, (ii) a federal system and (iii) functional arrangements.

The League of Nations and now the United Nations, as their names imply, rest upon national separateness. They are loose associations for occasional specific joint action, in regard to each of which each member remains on the whole free to participate or not. They are clubs which make joint action easier, if wanted, and in the United Nations facilities for economic and social action are much improved; but they cannot prescribe such action, much less take it on their own authority.

Our short but tense experience since the creation of the United Nations has shown that such a loose arrangement is inadequate in scope and uncertain in working. Hence, no doubt, the widespread interest in the federal idea, in a variety of forms. Federalism is one of the great inventions of political theory and life. It came to us from the New World and has been adopted in a number of places especially in newer political groupings. It has served admirably where a number of adjacent and related provinces or countries, while retaining separate identity, wanted to join together for some general purpose. Federation has been the political equivalent of a company with limited liability. Habitually, federal experiments rest upon a number of similar elements: a degree of close kinship or relationship, a will to unity, but with it a clear intent to manage most affairs severally. How does all this apply to the international scene?

We are presented with a choice of proposals for international federation, advocating variously and vaguely European federation or Western federation or democratic federation or, more ambitiously, world federation. The fact that there are so many differing proposals show that they do not rest on any inherent element of kinship or close relationship. Any of them may be desirable, but we have no proof that any is desired. The will to unite is not self-evident. Indeed most of these ideas, like that for European federation, are pressed from outside upon countries which themselves have shown no sign of taking the initiative, as a corrective to their former individualistic ways—a novel idea of political marriage by sentence of the court. Or alternatively they are urged to federate so as to be able to stand up to other political groupings. The advice may be sound, but it is an argument for a new nationalism not for a new internationalism. Hitherto federation has indeed merely created a new separate political unit which in the process, as in Germany, did bring peace within the group. There is no evidence that it would necessarily contribute to peace between it and other groups. The prospect of two powerful federations, for instance, facing each other in Europe is not enchanting. It would not check one of the present general trends, that of political division: it would change the dimensions of nationalism, but not its nature.

Let us take the most hopeful view as to the will of the countries to unite, and leave aside for the moment this negative view of peace. The main question is—would some kind of international federation under present conditions strengthen the trend for material integration, so as to make of it a general and positive foundation for peace? A federation comes into being for certain specific ends, and for those *only*. A federation unites, but it also restricts. It rests on a rigid division of powers and functions between territorial authorities which have equal status; and that division is usually and necessarily laid down in a written constitution provided with an armoury of safeguards against its being lightly tampered with. In the volume of essays on Federal Planning[1] Professor Wheare granted that federal government is by its nature conservative and legalistic. Every attempt to give the central government some new function and power has to knock at the massive and rusty gates of the constitution. The efforts of the Canadian Government to change the fiscal arrangements of the federation have been blocked so far, in spite of long discussion and patent need. In Australia repeated efforts for economic and social action have been similarly defeated; and the recent decision to nationalize the banking system has shaken the political structure and temper of the country. Even in such a dynamic country as the United States, the sin of unconstitutionality has plagued efforts at social reform—such as the prohibition of child labour in factories—and killed or maimed most of the original New Deal measures. The now universally admired and imitated T.V.A. scheme had to sustain, on grounds of unconstitutionality, fifty-one suits before the Supreme Court before it was allowed to settle down to its great work.

It is curious how those who urge the use of the federal idea internationally have neglected this central characteristic of it. Jefferson, who politically was wise beyond a man's measure, fore-

[1] P. Ransome, Ed., *Studies in Federal Planning* (London, Macmillan, 1943).

saw this and would have liked the constitution to include a provision for its periodical revision every ten years. It so happens that such a provision and for such a term was part of the Austro-Hungarian federal arrangement, the so-called *Anschluss*, with the result that every term became a crisis with a threat of dissolution—which led the irrepressible Vienna wits to speak of it as "Monarchie auf Kündigung." Yet such a refractory attitude is not unreasonable. New functions and new powers allowed to the supposedly co-equal central authority, however beneficent the social purpose, have a cumulative effect politically, and a sufficient number of them would before long permanently change the balance upon which the federation was established. It took almost twenty years of difficult negotiation, as Professor Brady points out,[1] to find a basis for the federation of Australia, and the reluctance to see it changed is therefore understandable. An international federation, to come into being at all, would have to start upon a very narrow basis and very rigid arrangements as to form and functions; and the reluctance to allow these to be disturbed would be correspondingly deeper.

In an international federation every adaptation, every amendment, would have to pass the gauntlet of jealous discussions between countries which have newly come together and differ in their political background. Even in agreed common matters the pace is that of the slowest member of the federation; issues which divide deeply have to be skirted. But in our time conditions and needs and problems are apt to change rapidly. The constitution would have to be continuously adapted, or the difficulty of doing this would hobble the life and government of the federation. Can such an instrument be made to fit the revolutionary mood which, whatever we may think of it, is surging in most parts of the world? Some may have been puzzled that the most revolutionary of all governments, which ideologically believes in world unity and in the proscription of the State, at the United Nations, and on every possible occasion, insists on a strict observance of national sovereignty. The explanation may be found in a recent article on sovereignty by Professor Levin,[2] a leading Soviet jurist, who uses this very argument—that any and every people must be free to transform its social organization with full power of its own to do so, and without external

[1] Alexander Brady, "Dominion Nationalism and the Commonwealth" (*Canadian Journal of Economics and Political Science*, February, 1944, p. 9).

[2] J. D. Levin, "The Problem of Sovereignty in the U.N. Statute" (*Sovetskoe Gosudarstvo i Pravo*, No. 1, 1947, p. 16).

interference or complications. Professor Levin is obviously right in assuming that this would not be possible under some rigid and comprehensive form of political association. If a federal House cannot be half free and half slave, neither can it be half capitalist and half communist. Every attempt at deep change in one part would put in jeopardy the persistence of the whole; for the alternative would appear to the legalists as disruption, and to the reformers as stagnation.

A federal system has many bright virtues. But in form and working it is a combination of rigidities—rigid in its framework, whether geographical or ideological; rigid in its consititution, which has to be formal and unchallenged; rigid in its general life, because of the limits and obstacles it places to fresh common action. If under present conditions of political nationalism an international federation is difficult to achieve, under present conditions of social revolution it would be difficult to maintain. It would have little prospect, except on the lowest common denominator as regards membership—such as the Benelux or the Scandinavian groups—or lowest common denominator as regards federal activity. But if a dynamic federal grouping is not possible, a laggard federal grouping would be meaningless now.

When the present federations came into being, their chief central functions were common defence and foreign policy. These are indeed the functions, with a common budget for their purpose, that Mr. Lionel Curtis considers sufficient to start the federal arrangement which he has advocated so eloquently and devotedly. But does this not again neglect the historical perspective? Not only do the number of functions which need to be carried out jointly change; their character is apt to change even more rapidly. A hundred or even fifty years ago defence and foreign policy were limited affairs in relation to the total life of the community. Now they embrace between them control of material resources and of the organization of industry, control of manpower and of training, and even control of communications as of education and opinion—with corresponding sweeping control of trade and of fiscal and financial policy.

Federation, to sum up, was invented and adopted when, in general, the functions of government were limited, and those of central government were deliberately intended to be restricted; now we live somewhat feverishly and precariously in an era of centralized planning. It was born in times of enthusiasm for constitutions;

now we are in a pragmatic mood that scorns formal rules and restrictions. Federalism was meant to put into the hands of central authority the least possible functions of common life; now it could only mean leaving in the hands of the individual authority the least possible functions of local life. If federation were to do all the things for political security and for social security that present trends demand—inevitably through the instrument of central authority—it could only end in the paradox that the federal idea would be proclaimed only to be organized out of existence.

The foregoing examination of the difficulties of the federal idea is not made from any inclination to be critical. It is rather from a complete conviction that in this awkward field we cannot make progress by propounding schemes which have a pleasant symmetry without regard to the rough and shifty terrain on which they have to be grounded; and in looking at the federal idea against present conditions and needs I have really been trying to bring out the sociological framework within which any effort towards international government would have to work. That framework, shaped as it is essentially by the will for national distinctness and the need for social integration, shows that our end will be difficult to achieve simply by changing the dimensions of traditional political instruments. That being so, we are bound to look for a new political device, and the device which seems to fit that framework is the functional idea—not as a new invention, but as a new application.

It so happens that the functional approach has been used a great deal in established federations, very successfully by the New Deal, with the T.V.A. scheme as its outstanding example. It may be as well to deal here with two circumstantial points. If, it may be said, existing federations have been able to do all that, does not this break the argument that the federal idea cannot be helpful internationally? Existing federations can sometimes push aside or get round formal federal partitions because they *are* old-established federations. Generations of common life and experience have welded them into a community, with a common outlook and common problems expressed in the programmes of national parties; and common central government has come to be taken for granted, with state or provincial governments, with perhaps the exception of Quebec—a significant exception—more on the level of local administrative bodies. In most cases the problem, therefore, was not so much to create a common policy as to consolidate a group of similar or identical policies. And yet even in such old-established federations, in times of crisis, these collective doings were expanded not by changing federal arrangements but rather by circumventing them. In no case was there any deliberate change in the formal gradation of power; the federal governments took upon themselves many new tasks with tacit national consent, and thus acquired new power by functional accretion, not by constitutional revision. In the United States the one attempt at constitutional change, to increase the membership of the Supreme Court, was also the only issue on which President Roosevelt was utterly defeated, though its effect would have been mild compared with the tremendous impact of the New Deal.

The United States took this line boldly also in starting new connections with neighbouring States—not only in the close war-time arrangements with Canada, which were a matter of expediency, but in permanent measures. The Alcan Highway has created a strip of international administration running from the United States through Canada to Alaska; the arrangement with Mexico for the development of the Rio Grande has turned a dividing river into a joint enterprise; and pan-American developments are likely to follow the same line. These experiments have a particular lesson for the wider international problem. It is not only that they can be made, but that the United States has found it easier to complete the Alcan arrangement with Canada and the Rio Grande arrangement with Mexico than to get its own T.V.A. scheme going. The first two were made with sovereign countries which retained their sovereignty except in so far as it was pooled for a specific joint functional undertaking. The other experiment affected federal units which were reluctant to part with any of their share of power, and tried hard to maintain the balance laid down in the American constitution. In a more extreme way the point is illustrated by the insistence of the Australian Government, against American reluctance, that some form of international undertaking to work for "full employment" be included in the San Francisco Charter, with the purpose of getting in this way the right to take internal action which would otherwise be beyond its constitutional power—a striking and novel way of asking for international obligations to get over federal obstructions. The incident also illustrates how the content of "foreign policy" is changing. In the United States and in other federations, in other words, necessary joint action was possible in the face of constitutional obstacles because it could rely on an old and live sense of national unity. A new international federation would have no such unity, and the constitutional barriers would thus obstruct all the more starkly at every corner. And even those old federations have found it at times easier to make functional arrangements with foreign States than within themselves.

The truth is that by its very nature the constitutional approach emphasizes the individual index of power; the functional approach emphasizes the common index of need. There are many such needs which cut across national boundaries, and an effective beginning could be made by providing joint government for them. On such lines, the emergence of so many new national States, which politically adds to our difficulties, might even be put into the service of international unification. If they are to achieve a promising social foundation for their political independence they need many things in the way of material and technical help and service which are beyond their means and experience; and, as in the case of the Marshall Plan, such needs should be used deliberately and insistently to set up lines for joint international action.

The universal popular claim for social security could likewise be turned into a channel for international unity. For it is important to note that the new nationalism is everywhere a peculiarly social nationalism; like the nineteenth century nationalism, each wants to have its own national house but, unlike the earlier nationalism, it is especially intent upon a new social life within that house. There may be much to be said for one solid international block of flats, but as long as people choose to live in detached national houses we could go a long way by supplying joint social and other services. Only in some such way is there any prospect, for instance, of mending the breach in the political unity of India, and of leading gradually to a unity of natural common interests; whereas any suggestion for political reunion would only serve to make even such practical proposals suspect. Again, this seems the only possible hope of mending the division between Arabs and Jews in Palestine; and, indeed, of building some true unity among the Arab countries themselves, along the path so admirably mapped out by the Middle East Supply Centre during the war. In the Danubian region, in spite of much ideological fraternizing, Mr. Dimitrov's mere reference to a federal link-up at once brought a rebuke from Moscow, and little response from his neighbours; but those same countries are apparently working on a scheme for a Danube Valley Authority. Nor is there any other way of dealing with the vital problem of the Ruhr. If the region is to remain German, if French fears for security are to be assuaged, if the claims of neighbouring allied countries for a share of its products are to be met, and at the same time, German workers are to be given the prospect of a decent life, only a Ruhr Valley Authority under non-political international functional management would have any prospect of meeting these varied and mixed claims. Two points might be made on this which will bring out the contrast beetween the political and the functional approach: first, that an R.V.A. could be started at any time without waiting for a Western Union, while a Western Union would still have to work through an R.V.A.; and, secondly, that Soviet Russia could at any time be brought into the partnership of an autonomous R.V.A., but not in a Western Union. The enclosing of an R.V.A. within a full Western system would inevitably dig a moat against wider co-operation.

It would be instructive to examine the structure and working of the wartime functional arrangements, or the work of the international Labour Organization in giving a common direction to policies of social improvement without encroaching on State sovereignty. The French, Belgian and British Governments are now working out lines of co-operation for their African territories, ranging from sanitation, irrigation and soil conservation, to the common use of communications and other services, with a view to co-ordinating economic, educational and administrative policies.

It is not only to the field of government and economics that the functional approach brings relief. In the noteworthy sermon which the Archbishop of Canterbury preached before the University of Cambridge in November 1946,[1] he boldly admitted that all schemes of reunion between the English churches had failed because, as he insisted, they had tried a constitutional reunion, and he called for a different approach simply by the exchange of ministers and pulpits. "It is because I fear a stalemate," said Dr. Fisher, "that I venture to throw out this suggestion—Can we grow to full communion with each other before we write a constitution?" The evolution of the Flemish problem in Belgium is also instructive. The political separatist movement during the First World War created a bitter reaction in the country and almost led to civil strife. Since then, by gradual quiet changes, the Flemings have obtained complete autonomy in education—the University of Ghent is now completely Flemish and that of Liége completely French—and almost as wide autonomy in the administration of the Flemish area; in addition,

[1] Speech by Dr. Geoffrey Fisher, November 3, 1946 before the University of Cambridge. Reported in *The Times*, November 4, 1946.

there has been growing cultural association with Holland. The instructive point is that no constitutional provision has so far legalized this evolution, while talk of separation has died out among the Flemings.

Earlier in this paper I instanced the many varieties of the federal idea competing for public support as one proof of its weakness. There are as many, if not more schemes for functional experiment. Does that not show a similar fragility of conception? Perhaps nothing brings out more clearly how different is the core of the political from the functional approach. In the first the several schemes are mutually exclusive—a State cannot be in both a European or an Empire federation, or in both a European and a democratic federation. Functional schemes are at best complementary, each helping the others, and at worst independent of each other. Any one can be started at any time whether the others are accepted or not, and any one may live and prosper even if others fail or are abandoned. In such changing times they have the invaluable virtue of autonomous existence, and likewise of autonomous development. A scheme started by a few countries for transport, or for oil, and so on, could later be broadened to include belated members, or reduced to let reluctant ones drop out. Moreover they can vary in their membership, countries could take part in some schemes and perhaps not in others, whereas in any political arrangement such divided choice would obviously not be tolerable. Functional "neutrality" is possible, where political "neutrality" is not. In addition, functional arrangements have the virtue of technical self-determination, one of the main reasons which makes them more readily acceptable. The nature of each function tells of itself the scope and powers needed for its effective performance. All these elements are capable of concrete measurement, and unlike rigid political arrangements, they are therefore capable of concrete adjustment, in keeping with changes in the conditions of the function. The requirements of a federal authority for the conduct, for instance, of the common foreign policy must always be a matter of political bargaining. The requirements of a functional authority in charge of oil or aviation or of a Danube Valley Authority, at any given time for the clear-cut task entrusted to it, would be a matter of factual audit.

These characteristcis of the functional approach therefore help to mitigate the obstinate problem of equal sovereignty. In this approach it is not a matter of surrendering sovereignty, but merely of pooling so much of it as may be needed for the joint performance of the particular task. In such practical arrangements Governments have not, as in political systems, to safeguard their right to equal voting, but can allow a special position to the countries which have a special responsibility in the task concerned, so long as the service is performed for the benefit of all. All this is completely in keeping with the whole trend of modern government. Twentieth century government means less a division of powers than an integration of functions; administration and administrative law are its characteristic tools, and such functional arrangements would simply mean giving international range to administrative organs and administrative jurisdiction, in accordance with the nature of each task. They would also be in harmony with the social philosophy of our time. As Sir John Boyd Orr has said of his particular responsibility, "here in this world food plan we have the means whereby the nations could begin to co-operate on something which would do none of them harm and do all of them good."[1] If Governments have the welfare of their own peoples at heart they could let such organizations get to work; and if the organizations are successful and their number grows, world government will gradually evolve through their performance. From the point of view of normal daily life, to quote the late Professor Hobhouse, "the life of a community may be regarded as the sum of the functions performed by its members." And conversely, one might add, the performance of a number of common functions is the way to create a normal community. If one were to visualize a map of the world showing economic and social activities, it would appear as an intricate web of interests and relations crossing and recrossing political divisions—not a fighting map of States and frontiers, but a map pulsating with the realities of everyday life. They are the natural basis for international organizations: and the task is to bring that map, which is a functioning reality, under joint international government, at least in its essential lines. The political lines will then in time be overlaid and blurred by this web of joint relations and administrations.

Close association of States can be either comprehensive or selective. Clearly the first is the ideal—all countries working together for their common good. But if it cannot be comprehensive, if it has to be selective, it is better that it be selective on lines of special activities rather than of sectional groups. Any one country may join a particular activity, but a set group cannot help being exclusive;

[1] Speech in the House of Commons, April 4, 1946, reported in *The Times,* April 5, 1946.

and, in the words of Dr. Johnson, "such is the disposition of man that whatever makes a distinction creates rivalry." Seen in this light the functional approach implies not merely a change of political device but a change of political outlook. It should help to shift the emphasis from political issues which divide, to those social issues in which the interest of the peoples is plainly akin and collective; to shift the emphasis from power to problem and purpose.

In all societies there are both harmonies and disharmonies. It is largely within our choice which we pick out and further. Since the end of the war we have had brutal illustration of this truth at peace conferences, at meetings of the United Nations at which the new international life was supposed to be born. We must begin anew, therefore, with a clear sense that the nations can be bound together into a world community only if we link them up by what unites, not by what divides. In the second place, ways and means to that end must be fitted to that purpose. They have to be adequate, but they also must be relevant; and if they are to be relevant they must start from the conditions which are around us. They must avoid reaction, but also avoid Utopia. We can ask our fellow men to look beyond the national State; we cannot expect them to feel themselves at once members of a world State. During his first months as President, Jefferson wrote to a friend that he realized how short he would fall of achieving all that reason and experience justified, but "when we reflect how difficult it is to move or inflect the great machine of society, how impossible to advance the notions of a whole people suddenly to ideal right, we see the wisdom of Solon's remark, that no more good must be attempted than the nation can bear."

That is wise judgment. But in our case, and in our time, what the nations can bear shows a distinction. Taken by and large, they seem unable to bear much interference with their political independence, but they can bear quite a lot when it comes to economic and social action. That distinction gives a first guiding line for any international arrangement. The next question is, how such economic and social action might be organized to lead us to international community and international government. In our own countries we are getting accustomed to putting nearly all such action into the hands of central government. Are we ready to follow the same course in the international sphere? If so, a federation, with its restrictive political machinery, is in any case hardly the proper instrument. A federation leaving those social and economic activities in the hands of its national members would in this respect be little more than a replica of the United Nations, under a different guise and name. If, on the other hand, those activities are entrusted to a centralized international authority with corresponding powers and means, it will have to be hardly less than a full-fledged international government. These tasks must of necessity be performed jointly and controlled centrally; therefore, the true choice is not between the present competitive nationalisms and a lame international federation, but between a full-fledged and comprehensive world government and equally full-fledged but specific and separate functional agencies.

46. SUCCESS, FAILURE . . . AND THE FUTURE*/ PAUL G. HOFFMAN

The timing of this Conference [on international economic development] could hardly be more propitious, since there is an unprecedented wealth of material for it to examine. During the last several months, the entire field of development has been probed with a care and intensity rarely given to any subject in the history of mankind. For example, our United Nations Development Programme alone has been put under scrutiny by a Committee of Seven, a Committee of Fourteen, and a Committee of Fifty-Four. We've also been included, to a greater or lesser degree, in the investigations of the Pearson Commission, the Tinbergen Commission and, of course, the distinguished group headed by Sir Robert Jackson which has recently issued its report on the development assistance capacity of the United Nations family as a whole. Since last summer, I would guess that I have personally read no less than 3,000 pages of reports and of comments on reports. . . .

From my own standpoint, looking back at the record of development progress achieved in the 1960s, I see a mixture of failures and successes in which, I believe, the gains outweigh the set-backs. A complete accounting would, of course, take hours if not days to

* Address by Paul G. Hoffman, Administrator of the United Nations Development Programme, to Columbia University Conference on International Economic Development, 20 February, 1970.

render. But let me try to cast up very briefly a partial balance sheet, as I evaluate it, starting with some items on the debit side.

One of the failures of the first Development Decade must, I think, be laid on the doorstep of the professionals in the field. What I have in mind is the fact that administrators of development assistance programs often failed to look at their work in the proper perspective. On the one hand they stressed, and rightfully so, that the primary responsibility for speeding development progress rested with the low-income countries themselves. And they acknowledged that these countries were, in fact, bearing from 80 to 85% of all the costs involved. Yet, too often they seemed to feel that external aid—even though it represented only a relatively small part of total development expenditures—should rightly be used as a tool by which the donor countries could manipulate the economic and social policy decisions of recipient governments. In effect, what the administrators of aid programs were saying was: "Father knows best." I think this is wrong on two counts. First of all, it assumes that we in the industrialized countries have all the answers to other peoples' problems. Actually, as you are aware, we are having some difficulties in successfully solving our own. Secondly, it negates the concept of helping developing countries to help themselves, and prolongs their period of dependence rather than hastening the day when they can stand on their own feet unsupported.

Our counterparts in the low-income nations did, of course, make their own share of mistakes—as was only natural in a field where so much had to be done in so little time under such great pressures and with so many unknowns involved. Fortunately, I think that this whole picture is changing. We administrators of aid are acquiring a good deal of humility. Our opposite numbers in the low-income countries are amassing a wealth of knowledge and experience. As this first Development Decade comes to an end our relationships are increasingly close, and we are talking to each other in a language that both sides pretty clearly understand.

A second failure of the 1960s was the failure to adopt certain policies which would make it progressively easier for the low-income countries to *earn* the foreign exchange they need as the high-octane fuel for progress. A great deal has been said in recent years—and some of it in rather harsh words—about what the industrialized countries did or failed to do to help the low-income nations improve their trading position. Whatever the merits of either side's case in this controversy may be, there is little doubt that many of the trade practices followed by donor countries made it difficult for the developing nations to achieve a favourable balance of payments— so that what was given by the right hand of aid was often taken back by the left hand of trade. However, another potentially important approach to this problem was almost completely overlooked during the 1960s. It has now been brought to the forefront by my good friend, Sir Arthur Lewis. He suggests that the less developed countries shift the focus of their efforts away from trying to increase sizably their sales to the industrialized nations under what, for the foreseeable future, must remain highly unfavourable competitive conditions. He urges, instead, the establishment of a new network of trading relationships among the less developed countries themselves, and the creation of a new set of institutions for financing such trade. With these recommendations, I very strongly agree.

But the most dangerous failure of the 60s, in my judgment, was the failure of the industrialized countries fully to meet their responsibilities, and to fully take advantage of their opportunities, in the provision of development aid. Put quite bluntly, they did not furnish enough money to get the job done as it should and could have been done. And although the total transfer of resources from the richer to the poorer countries increased somewhat toward the end of the first Development Decade, the proportion of this total represented by *official* aid declined. This is why I regard as particularly important and timely the recommendation of the Pearson Commission that, by no later than 1975, seven-tenths of all resource transfers from the wealthier to the poorer nations should be in the form of *official* development assistence. This is not intended in any way to down-grade the importance of *private* development investments. In fact, I would like to see such investments sharply increased. But official aid must, for many years ahead, remain the backbone of the effort, because there are critical development fields —among them the building of schools, roads, health facilities, rural and urban public services, and other vital elements of infrastructure —into which private capital will rarely if ever go for lack of a profit incentive.

The fact that the wealthier nations did not raise their official development assistance to adequate levels sprang from what might be called two "sub-failures". The first of these was a failure by governments to present to their publics an *accurate* picture of what development assistance really costs the tax-payer. Until quite recently, for example, no distinction was made between official aid for which the tax-payer must bear some of the cost and private development flows which cost him nothing. This point at least is now being clarified. However, the true costs of official aid itself are still very widely misunderstood, mainly because a *gross* rather than a *net* figure is still very widely used. But in order to arrive at a valid estimate of the burden that official aid imposes on the tax-payer, one must deduct from the gross that component represented by sound bankable loans, by the repayment of interest on such loans, and by an appropriate part of assistance granted in the form of soft loans. The results of this process are quite educational. For example, the *total* transfer of resources from the richer to the poorer countries in 1969 has probably amounted to something in the neighborhood of \$12 or \$13 billion. But deducting from that figure all private investments and those portions of the gross official flows I have just mentioned would give us a net of only around \$4 billion. And it is that \$4 billion only for which the tax-payers had to dig into their pockets, during a year in which they laid out over \$150 billion for military purposes.

The second sub-failure which contributed in a major way to inadequate levels of aid during the 1960s was a failure to get general acceptance of the idea that development assistance is not charity but a sound long-term investment in global economic growth. And I furthermore believe that we will never see development assistance flows reaching a sufficient level until there is widespread understanding—in both the richer and poorer countries—of the need which both fully share for an expanding world economy. Put another way, there is no country so rich that is cannot profit from a higher level of world trade, and no country so poor that it cannot help itself and its neighbors by contributing to the attainment of this higher level.

I have repeatedly used the phrase "adequate levels of assistance", and I suppose I should clarify what I have in mind by this term. In a general sense, I would say that adequate levels of assistance are those which are high enough to allow the developing countries to speed their economic and social progress at the fastest pace of which they are capable. And if I had to place a dollar figure on this amount, my best guess would be that it should reach around \$20 billion a year gross which might net down to around a \$7 or \$8 billion cost to the tax-payers of the donor nations.

Now, despite all the failures I have mentioned, the first Development Decade must, I believe, be considered a great success. To begin with, not only did the developing nations as a group reach—by the end of that decade—the target of an average 5% yearly increase in GNP. There were also a good many countries which exceeded that pace, and a few which registered growth rates either in total GNP or in key individual economic sectors above those ever achieved by any of the industrialized nations. And in many, though not all, of the low-income countries there were improvements in the quality of human life as well as in statistical indices.

Secondly, a very large number of highly successful development projects were implemented throughout the world. Over the last ten years, many millions of acres of land have been brought under far more fruitful cultivation than ever before. Rivers have been harnessed to produce many millions of kilowatt hours of added hydro-electric power. Many millions of tons of economically valuable raw materials have been located and put to work. Above all, many millions of men and women have been educated and trained to make more of their own potentials and contribute more to the progress of their countries. If I may add a purely personal note, I must tell you that I get a great deal of satisfaction from one piece of work in this general area which was largely financed by the UNDP. This is the intercontinental project designed to help increase agricultural production by reducing the enormous damage to growing crops which has been caused for centuries by the ravenous desert locust. A friend of mine, perhaps too kind a friend, once told me that the billions of dollars saved by the activities of this one project more than justified the entire UNDP programme.

A third very major success has been the phenomenal growth during the last ten years of development-related technologies. As specialists in this field, you are all well aware of the tremendous potential of the so-called "green revolution" which has already produced new strains of rice, wheat, and legumes that have more than doubled output per acre in many areas of the world. For my own part, I find even more exciting what I have learned about present and prospective advances in increasing the protein content of cereal and vegetable foodstuffs—advances that could save hundreds of millions of children from crippling mental and physical damage.

This nutritional enrichment of agricultural produce brings to mind a remark by George Harrar, President of the Rockefeller Foundation, to the effect that for centuries the plants have been giving us what *they wanted*, and that now the time is coming when they can be made to give us what *we need*. Much of it has been achieved through using nuclear radiation to induce genetic changes in widely grown food crops such as corn. But the peaceful atom is also at work in many related fields. For example, radioactive isotopes and other nuclear-based technologies are now being used to insure that the right amount of fertilizer is applied in the right place at the right time—to greatly improve groundwater management practices—to prevent and cure animal diseases—and to preserve food from spoilage.

There is one further technological breakthrough in agriculture which I should like to mention because it exemplifies something of what has been achieved through *international cooperation for development*—itself a field of quiet but revolutionary progress during the 1960s. Scottish scientists attending a conference in New Zealand learned of a newly-discovered Japanese method for testing the quality of seeds which seemed very promising but was too complex and costly for widespread use. In one year of applied research they so simplified this process that now almost any farmer anywhere can, within twenty-four hours and for a few pennies, determine whether his seeds will produce good, fair or poor crops.

Revolutionary results can also soon be expected from advances in aerospace science. Considerable publicity has been given to the promise offered by geodetic and earth resources satellites—for finding and classifying mineral deposits, potentially arable soils, and schools of food-fish; as well as for detecting areas of plant and timber disease in time to take effective counter-measures. It will not be long before this promise is realized, or before "television switchboards" are in orbit to relay to the developing countries basic educational programs, as well as instruction in modern farming, health-care, and family planning methods. And I was recently told by the head of a company specializing in high-altitude aerial photography that his firm has already proven-out a new reconnaissance technique which can locate likely deposits of industrial metals, petroleum and many other valuable resources beneath the land and under the seas at much lower cost and in half the time that is presently required.

To sum it all up, the past ten years have seen the greatest progress by far toward fuller utilization of the world's natural and human resources of any similar period in history. If I may interject one further personal note, it is particularly gratifying that the UNDP —in the field of human resources development—was able, during the decade, to help finance and administer no less than 387 projects for education and training with a total cost of over $1.1 billion, of which recipient governments provided nearly 75%. Through the work of these projects, almost 600,000 men and women of the developing countries acquired or upgraded skills critically needed for speeding the progress of their nations.

Now, what makes such gains in resource utilization by the low-income countries so significant, is the fact that it has laid the necessary groundwork for a real surge forward on all sectors of the development front during the 1970s. And while we are on the subject of the future, I'd like to dream just a little about an ideal world that has never existed and can never be completely attained. It would be a world in which, as the result of continually improving technology and its continually wiser use, all the world's natural resource potentials would be fully exploited for the benefit of mankind. More importantly, it would be a world in which every child born would be a *wanted* child—a child who could be adequately cared for, fed, schooled, housed, clothed and given the opportunity to make as much of himself as his inborn talents would allow.

This is, of course, a very different world from the one we have today. For example—and I frequently cite these figures because I know of nothing that more clearly defines the reason that poor countries *are* poor—I would guess that the developing nations as a whole can now productively use only a little bit over 20% of their natural resource potentials. And I would say flat out that the productive employment of man, woman and youth power potentials comes to no more than 10%. Clearly, any country which can only employ one-fifth of its material wealth and only one-tenth of its peoples' energies is about in the same position as a man whose feet are hobbled trying to climb a ladder whose rungs are greased.

What then should be our priorities for the 1970s? What goals should we aim to achieve during the second Development Decade?

First of all, I think we should try to bring the level of natural resource utilization throughout the developing world up from 20% to perhaps 30%. Even more urgently, we should seek to raise manpower utilization from 10% to 20%. It is my personal belief that if the low-income countries continue their own very major efforts—and if external assistance is made available on the scale I earlier suggested—then these are not unrealistic goals.

Secondly, we must give urgent attention to checking the soaring spiral of population growth which has particularly ominous implications for the world's low-income countries. Just a few facts and figures are needed to dramatize the magnitude of the crisis that is brewing.

Despite widespread and generally effective efforts at basic education—efforts which have measurably reduced the *percentage* of adults who cannot read and write—the *total number* of illiterates in the world next year will probably reach a new record high of some 810 million, the overwhelming majority being found in the developing countries. In fact, because of population growth, even if illiteracy could be reduced at twice the present rate, that figure would still be considerably in excess of 700 million. Moreover, during the next ten years, the developing countries, with more than 75 million of their adult citizens now unemployed, will experience a net increase in their available labor force of an additional 226 million.

It is true that the much-publicized danger of widespread famine can probably go on being averted for a long while even if present birth rates are maintained. And the problems of meeting other strictly *material* needs could perhaps also be solved, although at very high cost. But what cannot be done, by any stretch of the imagination, is to furnish a global population which is growing at its present rate with the minimal services and amenities needed for a decent way of life. Furthermore, the present pace of population increase threatens to make the problems of living together as a reasonably harmonious human community just about totally unmanageable. Imagine, if you will, every square mile on earth having a population density equal to that of Manhattan island today—which is what we face within one hundred years unless things change rather radically—and you can see the catastrophe that could easily befall us from planetary overcrowding.

Finally, very high priority must be given over the next 10 years to the protection of the natural environment—of the water we drink, the air we breathe, and the land that provides us with a living. For increasing pollution has by now become a baneful partner to the blessings of increased productivity.

In the case of the low-income countries, there is probably still time to provide the proverbial ounce of prevention instead of the many, many pounds of cure required in the industrialized nations. Yet I can tell you from personal experience that, even in the developing nations, it would be extremely dangerous to waste any time at all in coping with pollution problems. For I very vividly remember the pleas for conservation that were issued by Theodore Roosevelt and Gifford Pinchot over 50 years ago in the United States. Those pleas went almost completely unheeded—so that today it will cost many billions of dollars to clean up the Hudson River basin alone, not to mention the damage that pollution has already caused to the health of our people and the decency of our surroundings.

In closing I would like to offer one bit of purely personal thinking about the attitudes and understandings with which we need to approach the challenges of the second Development Decade. Specifically, we must, I feel, begin to accept the term *"global"* development as being a literal not a figurative description of the goal we seek to attain. For the entire world, and not just some of its parts, is threatened by escalating population growth; by the fouling of rivers, oceans, soils and air; by a growing alienation of the rich and privileged from the poor and deprived. The whole world, too, is troubled by an excessive and unnatural discord between the generations, and by needless hostility among people who happen to have varying amounts of pigmentation in their skins. I do not see how problems such as these can ever be solved except in a global context. And I am convinced that the whole world stands to profit in a way it never could have profited before from pooling its creative energies and its productive efforts.

Thus I devoutly hope that the peoples of the wealthier countries will come to realize that what they have heretofore called "foreign aid" is, in fact, the best and most rewarding form of "self-help." I hope, no less, that the peoples of the developing countries will put aside the idea they belong to a "third world" whose needs and aspirations are somehow totally different from, or in opposition to, the basic needs and aspirations of all the rest.

Accepting such points of view will not be easy, for they run counter to some deeply implanted and emotionally powerful beliefs. Yet accepted they must be and rather quickly at that. For the overridingly important fact of present day life is the fact that this has become one world in every aspect of any importance to the survival and well-being of mankind. And one cannot ignore facts of this magnitude for any length of time with impunity.

47. *THE UNIFICATION OF EUROPE** /
NAPOLEON BONAPARTE

One of my greatest ideas was to bring together and integrate the peoples united by geography, but divided and split apart by revolutions and politics. In Europe we thus find, even though in a condition of disunity, more than thirty million Frenchmen, fifteen million Spaniards, fifteen million Italians, and thirty million Germans. I would have liked to make each of these peoples into a single entity and a true nation. With such a retinue I would have appeared proudly before posterity, and I would have earned the blessing of ages. I would have felt worthy of this glory!

After this simplification of the situation, I would have had a better opportunity to devote myself to the beautiful ideal of civilization. In that state of things, there would have been more chances to introduce everywhere the unity of laws, principles, opinions, sentiments, viewpoints, and interests. Then perhaps under the favorable condition of universal enlightenment, it would have become permissible to dream of the adoption of the system of the American Congress or of the Amphictyonic League in Greece by the great European family of nations. What a great prospect of power, grandeur, happiness, and prosperity! What a grand and magnificent spectacle!

The unification of the thirty or forty million Frenchmen was already attained and perfected; that of the fifteen million Spaniards was on the verge of being achieved, too. The unification of the fifteen million Italians was already well under way: it only needed to grow further, and each day their unity of principles and legislation, of thought and feeling—that certain and infallible cement of human aggregations—matured. . . . The unification of the Germans had to proceed at a slower pace; consequently I did not do more than reduce the monstrous complexity of their country. Not that they were not ready for centralized rule: on the contrary, they were more than ready for it—they could have resisted us blindly before

* Comte de Las Cases, *Mémorial de Sainte-Hélène: Journal de la Vie Privée et des Conversations de l'Empereur Napoléon, à Sainte Hélène* (London: Colburn and Bossange, 1823), remarks on November 11, 1816. Translated by Eva Tamm Lijphart and Arend Lijphart.

grasping our intentions. How is it possible that no German prince has understood the disposition of his nation, or that no one has known how to take advantage of it? Certainly, if heaven had decreed that I be born a German prince, I would have governed thirty million united Germans, and I would have guided them unfailingly through the numerous crises of our time. And if my estimate of them is correct, I also believe that, once they would have elected me and proclaimed me as their leader, they would never have forsaken me, and I would not be here [on Saint Helena] now. . . .

Be that as it may, this unity will come about sooner or later by the force of circumstances. The impulse has been given, and I do not think that after my fall and the disappearance of my system, any other grand equilibrium will be possible in Europe except the aggregation and the confederation of the great nations. The first sovereign who, in the first major crisis, will espouse in good faith the cause of the peoples, will find himself at the head of all of Europe, and will be free to do whatever he wishes.

48. ECONOMIC INTEGRATION AND POLITICAL UNITY IN EUROPE*/ WALTER HALLSTEIN

What I should like to discuss tonight is the political response that we in the West are making to the challenges that face us today. That which concerns me most directly is the creation of what is known as the European Economic Community—of whose Commission I have the honour to be President. In name, as you know, it is 'economic': but what I want to stress tonight is that it is also political. Note that I say 'it *is* political'—not just that it tends towards a political goal. That goal has been described by none less than Winston Churchill as 'a United States of Europe'. My aim tonight is to show that the future has already begun.

As you know, it was in 1950 that Germany, France, Italy, and the Benelux countries set up the European Coal and Steel Community. It was in 1957 that they set up Euratom—the Atomic Energy Community—and the so-called Common Market—the European

* Walter Hallstein, *Economic Integration and Political Unity in Europe* (London: Information Service of the European Communities, 1961).

Economic Community. These are economic organizations—but they are also highly political.

The Obligations of Membership

The question may arise: Why does the European Economic Community have only six members? Well, it is not because we are some kind of an exclusive club. Our number was not decided by those who joined, but rather by those who did not join. Our founding Treaty holds out two possibilities for European states—full membership, or association. Full membership means full acceptance of the Treaty and the institutions it establishes. It means acceptance of the political significance and dynamism of these institutions. A full member must agree to build common policy in a wide range of endeavour. Association, on the other hand, is only partial membership. An associate takes on only a part of the obligations of our Treaty and enjoys only a portion of the rights of full members.

The basic economic idea underlying the Common Market is that the resources of modern technology can only be used to the full if the economic area within which they are developed is large enough. In the economic sphere, the modern world is a world of continents, of markets and economies on the grand scale. Divided economies and divided markets mean small-scale efforts, which in turn mean waste and relative poverty. In the United States, with its huge common market of some 180 million people, some seventy million men and women—the working population—in 1960 produced the equivalent of more than 503 billion dollars. In the same year in the Community countries, with a combined population of nearly 170 million, a working population even larger than that of the United States produced the equivalent of only some 180 billion dollars—little more than one-third of what a smaller working population in America produced in the same time. You may say, quite rightly: 'But American industry is more capital-intensive.' But why is this so? Because it can afford to produce for the vast American home market, and can thus afford the massive investments that a large market both requires and makes possible. Only by establishing in Europe a home market of this scale can we hope to play our full part in producing and exploiting the world's wealth.

NOT JUST FREE TRADE

The idea of a single large home market, therefore, lies at the heart of the movement for economic integration. But this in itself involves political issues. It is not just a movement for free trade between separate economies. It is a movement to fuse markets—and economies—into one, and to establish within that 'common market' the conditions and characteristics of any single national market. This means sweeping away the classical barriers to trade, tariffs and quotas. It means removing less obvious barriers—various types of discrimination; legislative barriers; glaring tax differences, and so on. It means ensuring that private barriers do not divide the market— for example, market-sharing agreements and the activities of trusts. It means maintaining the external conditions of a single home market, by making uniform for the whole area the conditions in which imports may enter it. This entails merging the separate national customs tariffs *vis-à-vis* the rest of the world into one single, common tariff, and applying a single common policy for external trade. All these are matters of political importance.

A SINGLE ECONOMIC POLICY

And a common market goes even further than this. Within a home market, not only goods, but persons, services, and capital, can circulate freely. The same must apply to a common market composed of numerous states. A home market means a home market for agriculture: therefore it cannot be left out of a common market—or not, at least, without running into the risk of favouring one partner unfairly against another, and thus leaving the whole edifice not only incomplete but lop-sided. Nor, in the delicate matter of agriculture, where so many stubborn traditions and such deep political passions are involved, can things be left to look after themselves. A common market in agriculture inescapably involves a common agricultural policy to replace the often conflicting policies of the national states. Much the same is true of transport—another field where full and free competition is not yet a practicable goal. Finally, and most difficult of all, if we seek to establish a single home market and a single economy, we must progressively fuse into one our separate national policies and move towards one economic policy for the Community as a whole.

This, in a nutshell, is the philosophy behind the Common Market Treaty. But let me state it more concisely still. The statement is not mine. It comes from one of the last documents produced by the League of Nations, and issued by the United Nations in 1947. Here it is: 'For a customs union to exist it is necessary to allow free movement of goods within the union. For a customs union to be a reality, it is necessary to allow free movement of persons. For a customs union to be stable it is necessary to maintain free exchangeability of currency and stable exchange rates within the union. This implies, *inter alia*, free movement of capital within the union. When there is free movement of goods, persons, and capital in an area, diverse economic policies concerned with maintaining economic activity cannot be pursued'.[1]

Federal Institutions

Economically, therefore, those states that commit themselves to the Common Market commit themselves to a far-reaching process of integration into a single unit. Is this not a far-reaching political commitment? Let me continue the quotation that I cited just now. It goes on: 'To assure uniformity of policy some political mechanism is required'. Ladies and gentlemen, I do not need to remind you that our European Community has established an institutional mechanism whose salient features are federal. They are founded upon the principal of democratic control, embodied in the European Parliament, which is really the active beginnings of a Parliament: it has the one great power of overthrowing the executive organ of the Community, *i.e.* the Commission, and a number of much lesser powers, such as that of constantly putting questions, being legally entitled to an answer, and the right to be consulted on most occasions when the Community proposes to legislate. It is my belief that these powers must be augmented in the future, particularly when the Parliament—which at present is chosen by and from the national Parliaments—becomes the direct expression of democratic opinion by being directly elected by universal suffrage.

The Community institutions, then, are subject to democratic control. They are also subject to the rule of law. This finds its

[1] 'Customs Union—a League of Nations contribution to the study of customs union problems', Lake Success, New York, 1947, p. 74.

expression in the Community's Court of Justice—the nearest parallel, perhaps, to your own Supreme Court.

The representatives of the Member Governments sit in the Community's Council of Ministers. This, too, is a federal organ—since unlike those of international organizations, its decisions are taken, as a rule, by majority vote, thus making it often impossible for one Member State to impose its veto. This is a built-in guarantee of progress: it is vital to the success of the whole enterprise.

TASKS OF THE EXECUTIVES

I have left until last the so-called 'Executives' of the Community. These are fully independent of the Member States in that their Members—some of them ex-Ministers even—are no longer national representatives: they are expressly forbidden to take instructions, and are responsible exclusively to the European Parliament. Their discussions are not public, and once a decision has been reached, the Executive concerned has collective responsibility for it: decisions are reached, of course, by simple majority. I said just now 'so-called' Executives, because although the analogy with the executive branch of a classical constitution is a close one, it is not complete. The most important rôle of the Executives—apart from certain domains where they take and apply decisions directly affecting the Community as a whole—is threefold. The Commission is first a motor, to stimulate and initiate Community action. It has the sole right to propose action in a large number of fields, and its proposals can only be modified by a unanimous vote of the national representatives in the Council. Secondly, the Commission is a watchdog, one of the guardians of the Treaty, keeping Governments and others up to the mark. It must take offenders before the Court of Justice: in at least two cases, it has already done so. Thirdly, it plays the part of an honest broker, helping to bring about agreement among the Member States, and to ensure thereby that action is taken. Indeed, the basic secret of the Community's smooth working is the constant collaboration—and division of labour—between the national representatives in the Council and the independent Commission. I need not stress the crucial importance of all these rôles.

Nor, I think, do I need to point out that all this panoply of institutions is itself highly political. It is certainly, in the words of the League of Nations report I quoted earlier, 'some political mechanism'. Not only this, but the subject-matter of its actions is itself political. Let me make one final quotation from the League of

Nations text: 'The greater the interference of the state in economic life, the greater must be the political integration'. For what we are doing, ladies and gentlemen, is not just integrating the action of employers, workers, merchants, or consumers. What is being integrated is the part played by the national states in creating the conditions within which economic activity takes place. I need not remind you how greatly the rôle of the state in this field has increased since, say, half a century ago, even in the freest and most liberal economies. Indeed, in some respects I think it may be true to say that the effect of economic integration is to make those economies more free, and certainly more liberal, than under a purely national economic régime. When one thinks of agriculture, for instance, it becomes clear that integration means a degree of liberation from innumerable national protective measures. It is also clear that this task is long, difficult, and delicate—precisely because its subject-matter is so highly political—and, indeed, politically explosive. Let me repeat: highly political. If we have learned anything in the years of experience which we have had since the European Coal and Steel Community first opened the common market for coal in 1953, it is this: that these apparently humdrum economic tasks are in reality very much more. And that 'very much more', which is political, is of the very greatest importance, not only to the Community, but also—and most particularly—to our friends in the rest of the world.

'We are not in business . . . we are in politics'

This is especially so, I think, in the case of the United States. It is important because it guarantees that we are serious—that we are in earnest. We are not in business to promote tariff preferences, to establish a discriminatory club, to form a larger market to make us richer, or a trading bloc to further our commercial interests. We are not in business at all: we are in politics. Our aim is to help ourselves, and so help others: to rid Europe of the crippling anomalies of the past, and enable her to pull her full weight in building tomorrow's world.

This task is urgent; and it is a task that does not concern us alone, or our economies alone. It is a political task, and a political task for us all.

THE CHALLENGE

Do I need to remind you, indeed, of how fast our world is changing? It is this single fact, I think, that distinguishes our age from the nineteenth century.

Only a few years ago, children's books were full of the wonders of the new twentieth century: automobiles, aircraft, telephones, radio. We all knew, we all said, that these inventions were going to transform our world, reducing distances, bringing peoples closer together. All this has happened. So rapidly have new wonders replaced the old that now, in the age of television, atomic energy, and space travel, we look back with affectionate nostalgia to the age of the early automobile, the biplane with fixed undercarriage, the Bell telephone, and the old crystal radio. Yet when we look at our political life, at our international relations, how far have we really accepted the political consequences of even those far-off inventions? And how much less have we applied to our whole way of thinking the consequences of more recent advance! We are running a race with destiny; we cannot afford to run it in period costume.

As I have suggested, there are signs of progress. After the first World War, a great President of the United States, Woodrow Wilson, outlined the famous 'Fourteen Points'. As a step forward at the time, this programme was remarkable. It sought to outlaw what were then seen as the causes of war: secret treaties, naval jealousies, the arms race, colonial rivalries. But seen from a distance of over forty years, the Fourteen Points look most remarkable as a symptom of their own age and a consecration of nationalism. In the words of a recent historian, their aim was to achieve justice 'by making states more perfect nation-states'.[2]

After World War II, attitudes had changed. The old League of Nations was replaced by the United Nations—and the change of name was significant. A new network of international organizations came into being, expressing the general recognition that even 'perfect' nation-states must acknowledge some degree of organized interdependence. But even this was only a belated attempt to face the political consequences of changes that had already occurred in the early years of this century. It was the first conscious effort to

[2] David Thomson: 'Europe Since Napoleon', London, 1957, p. 534.

draw the logical conclusions from technical inventions now long past.

THE RESPONSE: INTEGRATION

It was not until 1950, in fact, that the process went one stage further, and the concept of the nation-state itself began to be modified in practice. Hitherto, the attempt to create a new order in the world had been limited to intensifying international co-operation between separate states. Now, for the first time, it began to take the form of integrating those states together, to reflect in their political life and political organization, the radical changes brought about in the first instance by technological advance. This, in fact, was the beginning of the European Community: it is yet another reason for stressing its political nature. For, if co-operation was the political response to the invention of automobiles, aircraft, telephones, and radio, then economic integration is the political response to those even more spectacular innovations of the jet age, of the atomic age, of which the latest instance is space travel by human beings.

Mention of this fact, I think, recalls that what we face, in this changing world, is more than a purely technological challenge. That challenge is political, too. Indeed, one may well ask whether the efforts which the countries of the European Community are making would have taken shape had there not been a direct political stimulus—I may even say a direct political threat. Certainly, the process of uniting Western Europe has been greatly accelerated by the fact that Europe as a whole is divided by the Iron Curtain. Paul-Henri Spaak, in his brilliant little book on NATO, takes as his starting point the thirteenth of March, 1948, when the Czech Foreign Minister, Jan Masaryk, committed suicide—or was murdered: but he rightly points out that this was only the culminating point in a whole series of events. Since the War, indeed, Europe has been menaced by political forces whose aim it is to destroy the Western way of life. Those forces are very close to us. They are very strong. They are constantly growing stronger. Driven by a pseudo-religious sense of mission, organized with great efficiency, and backed by ever-growing resources, they challenge us in all spheres—military, political, and economic. Locked in the military balance of power, we may yet find ourselves attacked in our political and economic life: all over the world, indeed, the struggle is on. Call it, if you will, 'competitive co-existence'; what is clear is that this kind of competition is no mere friendly rivalry, but a political and economic challenge that must be met by economic and political means. Faced on the one hand by Communist empire-building and on the other by Communist economic planning, we have to prove that our free system not only is better, but works better.

Never Purely Economic

In this context, can we regard the integration of Europe as a purely economic phenomenon? Is it, indeed, has it ever been, a purely economic affair?

As a matter of recent experience, the answer is 'no'. There was the plan—unhappily it came to nothing—for a European army, the European Defence Community. What more strikingly political proposal could be imagined? With it went the proposal for a European Political Community. Both failed—not so much because of a general lack of the will to achieve them, as because of particular political circumstances, among others a virulent and largely Communist inspired propaganda campaign against them.

But this failure was not the signal for retreat. Less than a year later came the Messina Conference and the proposals for the Common Market and Euratom. And their goal is not only, as I have said, the economic integration of Europe, with all the political overtones that this implies. It is also to carry one stage further an essentially political movement. It is no accident, for example, that the Euratom Treaty should contain the germ of a 'European University'. It is no paradox that the Community countries should now be feeling their way towards a unity of political action, partly under the stimulus of the suggestions made last year by President de Gaulle.

FROM CO-OPERATION TO INTEGRATION

All this, moreover, falls in line with the natural evolution of Europe itself. In that sense, in seeking political unity, we have history on our side. Even a generation ago, we used to speak of 'the concert of the Powers'. Traditionally, the structure of Europe consisted of a multiplicity of separate states with their own separate structures, which although they did not always act in total isolation from each other, came together only in temporary and *ad hoc* groupings. Basically, the system rested upon the balance of power between

France and Germany, with—often—Great Britain in the rôle of moderator between them. It was a contrapuntal concert of Europe with conductors—sometimes—from outside the European continent.

That concert is silenced. It reached its finale in 1939—a bitter and tragic finale that continued for six years. Then, if not before, it became obvious that the nineteenth century system so masterfully employed by Bismarck could no longer endure in the twentieth century. It gave place to the system of Schuman, of Adenauer, of Sforza, of De Gasperi, of Spaak, and a whole new generation of statesmen. In place of the balance of power, they created the fusion of interests. In place of the *ad hoc* groupings of separate states, they proposed the pooling of problems and resources. In place of co-operation, they worked for integration. In place of the concert of the Powers, they set as their goal an ever closer union, shaped by common institutions, and built upon deeds, not words.

NEED FOR A POLITICAL CHOICE

These things did not happen automatically: in politics, nothing does. They demanded a clear choice, and a political choice. Need I add that this fundamental political decision has already borne unmistakably political fruit? In 1946, just a year after the War, Winston Churchill called for a reconciliation of France and Germany 'within a kind of United States of Europe'. Ladies and gentlemen, those words were prophetic. There has been a transformation of Germany's relations with France. Fifty years ago, my teacher in Mainz on the Rhine used to tell us that France was Germany's 'natural enemy', ordained by providence as such for all time. A few miles away, no doubt, little French boys were being taught the same pernicious nonsense—from the opposite point of view. Today, it would be laughable—if its past consequences had not been so tragic.

Those consequences themselves are a further political factor in the story. You in the United States are commemorating this year the hundredth anniversary of the Civil War. The War of 1939 to 1945, was, I sincerely hope, the last civil war in Western Europe. From your Civil War you emerged as a nation: from ours we emerged as a nascent Community. Nor is it by chance that the geographical area of the Six founder States of the European Community is almost identical with that which was brought to the brink of destruction, both materially, and psychologically, by the Nazi-Fascist monster and by the second World War. The former debased the concept of national sovereignty: the latter emptied it of substance. Frontiers seem less real when they can be flattened by tanks or ignored by intercontinental missiles.

IMMENSE POLITICAL CHANGES

But these brutal political facts—facts that we have had to face most clearly in Europe itself—are themselves only part of the immense political changes which have been transforming the whole world during this century. I said just now that in the economic sphere the world map is no longer made up of countries: it is made up of continents. This is true also in the political sphere. We are familiar with the idea of two great world powers—the United States and the Soviet Union. We are becoming familiar with the emergence of Communist China, with the rapid changes on the continent of Africa, with new prospects and new dangers in Latin America. Here, too, is a political challenge, but of a different kind. It is a challenge of scale, a challenge of size. In a world of giants, we cannot afford to be midgets. Here, then, is a further political motive for seeking real unity—political unity—in Europe.

Towards an Atlantic Community

This does not mean, of course, that we are seeking to create some kind of 'third force' in Europe, some kind of divisive factor within the Atlantic Alliance. Indeed, the same political challenge that is leading us to unite in Europe makes it all the more necessary for us to cement our European Community within the larger and perforce looser community that is the Atlantic Community. If we are seeking to create what has been called 'a second America in the West', it is because we wish to become a strong and valid partner for the 'first' America—to be one of the pillars upon which the Alliance itself is built. Not only do we believe in 'interdependence': we owe to it whatever progress we have achieved since the War. We shall never forget the foresight, the imagination, and the sheer generosity with which the United States helped to restore Europe after World War II. Today, that phase is over. Europe is on her feet again, and charity can be replaced by co-operation. And we need to co-operate —to defend ourselves, to help others, to fight poverty, to make a real attack on all those problems which not even the European Community as a whole, not even the United States as a whole, can tackle effectively alone. Can a so-called 'third force' maintain the NATO shield by itself? Can it meet by itself the needs of the developing countries? Can it alone solve the problems of booms and slumps, of currency reserves, of agricultural surpluses? Of course not. Ladies and gentlemen, we must rally the forces of the Atlantic Community to tackle these problems together, and to create a new economic order in the free world. What better way to begin than by uniting the European partners in this great venture? Already, indeed, the creation of the European Community is beginning to exert a cohesive effect. Without it, would Great Britain now be rethinking her whole relationship to continental Europe? Without it, should we have seen those other steps forward that have culminated in the formation of the O.E.C.D.? The stone once cast into the pool, the rings broaden out into ever widening circles.

I do not wish to claim too much for the European Community. But I do believe, and tonight I hope to have shown you *why* I believe—that the movement for European integration, far from being a mere movement for technocrats, for economists, is one that is essentially political, and therefore one that concerns all of us. It is a movement that is still in progress. Not all the problems are solved as yet—nor are all the dangers overcome, but we are determined, and we are hopeful.

Moreover, if there is one conclusion that emerges inescapably from what I have been saying here tonight it is that the political integration of Europe can only make its full contribution to the strength and safety of us all if it goes hand in hand with ever closer links across the Atlantic. It now takes less time to cross the Atlantic than it once took to cross the Mediterranean; and as the ocean that both divides and joins us, the Atlantic is indeed the Mediterranean of our own day.

A New and Creative Approach

I do not need to remind you of the many problems that we share, the many tasks that we must face together. Let me mention only three of them. There is the problem of our international monetary system, and the repercussions that even minor changes may have on the safety of all our currencies, the fruits of our thrift and industry, and even the stability of our political life. There is the problem of agricultural production in the age of modern technology—the problem of surpluses, and the problem of adaptation on the land. And finally, there is the pressing need to work together to help the world's developing countries—what Dean Rusk has rightly called 'a matter of life and death for freedom'. These are some of the problems that the new Organization for Economic Co-operation and Development will be tackling in the years to come—with the full participation of both the European Community and the United States, as well as of our other friends and partners in the free world. How important that partnership is I do not need to stress.

We for our part believe that the even closer partnership we are establishing in the European Community is one of the very few new political inventions that we in the West have made since World War II. We are determined to use it, in collaboration with the United States and with the West as a whole, to make a new and creative approach to the many other political and economic problems that face us all throughout the globe. With the help of our friends, with your help, we shall succeed.

15

INTERNATIONAL LAW

International law is one of the oldest attempts to bring a measure of order and peace to our troubled world. Hugo Grotius (1583–1645) is generally considered to be the "Father of International Law." The first selection is from the Prolegomena to his *On the Law of War and Peace*. In the Prolegomena, Grotius pays special attention to the nature and binding character of international law.

In the second selection, John Stuart Mill (1806–73) compares and contrasts international and domestic (municipal) law. One of his criticisms, which is also frequently voiced today, is that international law tends to favor the status quo and is inherently conservative. For instance, he condemns the legal principle of non-intervention, although on political grounds he is not always in favor of intervention—even for worthy causes.

The third and fourth selections contain analyses of the nature and function of international law by Philip C. Jessup and Richard M. Nixon. Jessup was a judge on the International Court of Justice in The Hague from 1961 to 1970. He made these remarks at the "Pacem in Terris Conference" held in New York in February 1965. President Nixon's comments on international law were contained in an address to the Academy of Political Science in New York on April 13, 1959, when he was Vice President of the United States.

49. *PROLEGOMENA TO THE LAW OF WAR AND PEACE*/HUGO GROTIUS*

The municipal law of Rome and of other states has been treated by many, who have undertaken to elucidate it by means of commentaries or to reduce it to a convenient digest. That body of law, however, which is concerned with the mutual relations among states or rulers of states, whether derived from nature, or established by divine ordinances, or having its origin in custom and tacit agreement, few have touched upon. Up to the present time no one has treated it in a comprehensive and systematic manner; yet the welfare of mankind demands that this task be accomplished. . . .

Such a work is all the more necessary because in our day, as in former times, there is no lack of men who view this branch of law with contempt as having no reality outside of an empty name. On the lips of men quite generally is the saying of Euphemus, which Thucydides quotes, that in the case of a king or imperial city nothing is unjust which is expedient. Of like implication is the statement that for those whom fortune favors might makes right, and that the administration of a state cannot be carried on without injustice.

Furthermore, the controversies which arise between peoples or kings generally have Mars as their arbiter. That war is irreconcilable with all law is a view held not alone by the ignorant populace;

* Hugo Grotius, *De Jure Belli ac Pacis Libri Tres*, trans. Francis W. Kelsey (Oxford: The Clarendon Press, 1925), Vol. 2, pp. 9–18.

expressions are often let slip by well-informed and thoughtful men which lend countenance to such a view. Nothing is more common than the assertion of antagonism between law and arms. . . .

Since our discussion concerning law will have been undertaken in vain if there is no law, in order to open the way for a favorable reception of our work and at the same time to fortify it against attacks, this very serious error must be briefly refuted. In order that we may not be obliged to deal with a crowd of opponents, let us assign to them a pleader. And whom should we choose in preference to Carneades? For he had attained to so perfect a mastery of the peculiar tenet of his Academy that he was able to devote the power of his eloquence to the service of falsehood not less readily than to that of truth.

Carneades, then, having undertaken to hold a brief against justice, in particular against that phase of justice with which we are concerned, was able to muster no argument stronger than this, that, for reasons of expediency, men imposed upon themselves laws, which vary according to customs, and among the same peoples often undergo changes as times change; moreover, that there is no law of nature, because all creatures, men as well as animals, are impelled by nature toward ends advantageous to themselves; that, consequently, there is no justice, or, if such there be, it is supreme folly, since one does violence to his own interests if he consults the advantage of others.

What the philosopher here says, and the poet reaffirms in verse,

And just from unjust Nature cannot know,

must not for one moment be admitted. Man is, to be sure, an animal, but an animal of a superior kind, much farther removed from all other animals than the different kinds of animals are from one another; evidence on this point may be found in the many traits peculiar to the human species. But among the traits characteristic of man is an impelling desire for society, that is, for the social life—not of any and every sort, but peaceful, and organized according to the measure of his intelligence, with those who are of his own kind; this social trend the Stoics called "sociableness." Stated as a universal truth, therefore, the assertion that every animal is impelled by nature to seek only its own good cannot be conceded.

Some of the other animals, in fact, do in a way restrain the appetency for that which is good for themselves alone, to the advantage now of their offspring, now of other animals of the same species. This aspect of their behavior has its origin, we believe, in some extrinsic intelligent principle, because with regard to other actions, which involve no more difficulty than those referred to, a like degree of intelligence is not manifest in them. The same thing must be said of children. In children, even before their training has begun, some disposition to do good to others appears, as Plutarch sagely observed; thus sympathy for others comes out spontaneously at that age. The mature man in fact has knowledge which prompts him to similar actions under similar conditions, together with an impelling desire for society, for the gratification of which he alone among animals possesses a special instrument, speech. He has also been endowed with the faculty of knowing and acting in accordance with general principles. Whatever accords with that faculty is not common to all animals, but peculiar to the nature of man.

This maintenance of the social order, which we have roughly sketched, and which is consonant with human intelligence, is the source of law properly so called. To this sphere of law belong the abstaining from that which is another's, the restoration to another of anything of his which we may have, together with any gain which we may have received from it; the obligation to fulfill promises, the making good of a loss incurred through our fault, and the inflicting of penalties upon men according to their deserts.

From this signification of the word "law" there has flowed another and more extended meaning. Since over other animals man has the advantage of possessing not only a strong bent toward social life, of which we have spoken, but also a power of discrimination which enables him to decide what things are agreeable or harmful (as to both things present and things to come), and what can lead to either alternative, in such things it is meet for the nature of man, within the limitations of human intelligence, to follow the direction of a well-tempered judgment, being neither led astray by fear or the allurement of immediate pleasure, nor carried away by rash impulse. Whatever is clearly at variance with such judgment is understood to be contrary also to the law of nature, that is, to the nature of man.

To this exercise of judgment belongs moreover the rational allotment to each man, or to each social group, of those things which are properly theirs, in such a way as to give the preference now to him who is more wise over the less wise, now to a kinsman rather than to a stranger, now to a poor man rather than to a man of means, as the conduct of each or the nature of the thing suggests. Long ago the view came to be held by many that this discriminating allotment is a part of law, properly and strictly so called; nevertheless law, properly defined, has a far different nature, because its essence lies in leaving to another that which belongs to him, or in fulfilling our obligations to him.

What we have been saying would have a degree of validity even if we should concede that which cannot be conceded without the utmost wickedness, that there is no God, or that the affairs of men are of no concern to him. The very opposite of this view has been implanted in us partly by reason, partly by unbroken tradition, and confirmed by many proofs as well as by miracles attested by all ages. Hence it follows that we must without exception render obedience to God as our Creator, to whom we owe all that we are and have, especially since in manifold ways he has shown himself supremely good and supremely powerful, so that to those who obey him he is able to give supremely great rewards, even rewards that are eternal, since he himself is eternal. We ought, moreover, to believe that he has willed to give rewards, and all the more should we cherish such a belief if he has so promised in plain words; that he has done this, we Christians believe, convinced by the indubitable assurance of testimonies.

Herein, then, is another source of law besides the source in nature, that is, the free will of God, to which beyond all cavil our reason tells us we must render obedience. But the law of nature of which we have spoken, comprising alike that which relates to the social life of man and that which is so called in a larger sense, proceeding as it does from the essential traits implanted in man, can nevertheless rightly be attributed to God because of his having willed that such traits exist in us. In this sense, too, Chrysippus and the Stoics used to say that the origin of law should be sought in no other source than Jupiter himself; and from the name Jupiter the Latin word for law (*ius*) was probably derived. . . .

Again, since it is a rule of the law of nature to abide by pacts (for it was necessary that among men there be some method of obligating themselves one to another, and no other natural method can be imagined), out of this source the bodies of municipal law have arisen. For those who had associated themselves with some group, or had subjected themselves to a man or to men, had either expressly promised, or from the nature of the transaction must be understood impliedly to have promised, that they would conform to that which should have been determined, in the one case by the majority, in the other by those upon whom authority had been conferred.

What is said, therefore, in accordance with the view not only of Carneades but also of others, that

> Expediency is, as it were, the mother
> Of what is just and fair,

is not true, if we wish to speak accurately. For the very nature of man, which even if we had no lack of anything would lead us into the mutual relations of society, is the mother of the law of nature. But the mother of municipal law is that obligation which arises from mutual consent; and since this obligation derives its force from the law of nature, nature may be considered, so to say, the great-grand-mother of municipal law.

The law of nature nevertheless has the reinforcement of expediency; for the author of nature willed that as individuals we should be weak, and should lack many things needed in order to live properly, to the end that we might be the more constrained to cultivate the social life. But expediency afforded an opportunity also for municipal law, since that kind of association of which we have spoken, and subjection to authority, have their roots in expediency. From this it follows that those who prescribe laws for others in so doing are accustomed to have or ought to have some advantage in view.

But just as the laws of each state have in view the advantage of that state, so by mutual consent it has become possible that certain laws should originate as between all states, or a great many states; and it is apparent that the laws thus originating had in view the advantage, not of particular states, but of the great society of states. And this is what is called the law of nations, whenever we distinguish that term from the law of nature.

This division of law Carneades passed over altogether. For he divided all law into the law of nature and the law of particular countries. Nevertheless if undertaking to treat of the body of law which is maintained between states—for he added a statement in regard to war and things acquired by means of war—he would surely have been obliged to make mention of this law.

Wrongly, moreover, does Carneades ridicule justice as folly. For since, by his own admission, the national who in his own country obeys its laws is not foolish, even though, out of regard for that law he may be obliged to forego certain things advantageous for himself, so that nation is not foolish which does not press its own advantage to the point of disregarding the laws common to nations. The reason in either case is the same. For just as the national who violates the law of his country in order to obtain an immediate advantage breaks down that by which the advantage of himself and his posterity are for all future time assured, so the state which transgresses the laws of nature and of nations cuts away also the bulwarks which safeguard its own future peace. Even if no advantage were to be contemplated from the keeping of the law, it would be a mark of wisdom, not of folly, to allow ourselves to be drawn toward that to which we feel that our nature leads.

Wherefore, in general, it is by no means true that

> You must confess that laws were framed
> From fear of the unjust,

a thought which in Plato someone explains thus, that laws were invented from fear of receiving injury, and that men are constrained by a kind of force to cultivate justice. For that relates only to the institutions and laws which have been devised to facilitate the enforcement of right, as when many persons in themselves weak, in order that they might not be overwhelmed by the more powerful, leagued themselves together to establish tribunals and by combined force to maintain these, that as a united whole they might prevail against those with whom as individuals they could not cope.

And in this sense we may readily admit also the truth of the saying that right is that which is acceptable to the stronger, so that we may understand that law fails of its outward effect unless it has a sanction behind it. In this way Solon accomplished very great results, as he himself used to declare,

> By joining force and law together,
> Under a like bond.

Nevertheless law, even though without a sanction, is not entirely void of effect. For justice brings peace of conscience, while injustice causes torment and anguish, such as Plato describes, in the breasts of tyrants. Justice is approved, and injustice condemned, by the common agreement of good men. But, most important of all, in God injustice finds an enemy, justice a protector. He reserves his judgments for the life after this, yet in such a way that he often causes their effects to become manifest even in this life, as history teaches by numerous examples.

Many hold, in fact, that the standard of justice which they insist upon in the case of individuals within the state is inapplicable to a nation or the ruler of a nation. The reason for the error lies in this, first of all, that in respect to law they have in view nothing except the advantage which accrues from it, such advantage being apparent in the case of citizens who, taken singly, are powerless to protect themselves. But great states, since they seem to contain in themselves all things required for the adequate protection of life, seem not to have need of that virtue which looks toward the outside, and is called justice.

But, not to repeat what I have said, that law is not founded on expediency alone, there is no state so powerful that it may not at some time need the help of others outside itself, either for purposes of trade, or even to ward off the forces of many foreign nations united against it. In consequence we see that even the most powerful peoples and sovereigns seek alliances, which are quite devoid of significance according to the point of view of those who confine law within the boundaries of states. Most true is the saying that all things are uncertain the moment men depart from law.

If no association of men can be maintained without law, as Aristotle showed by his remarkable illustration drawn from brigands, surely also that association which binds together the human race, or binds many nations together, has need of law; this was perceived by him who said that shameful deeds ought not to be committed even for the sake of one's country. Aristotle takes sharply to task those who, while unwilling to allow anyone to exercise authority over themselves except in accordance with law, yet are quite indifferent as to whether foreigners are treated according to law or not. . . .

50. *THE CUSTOM OF NATIONS** / *JOHN STUART MILL*

. . . what is the law of nations? Something, which to call a law at all, is a misapplication of terms. The law of nations is simply the custom of nations. It is a set of international usages, which have

* John Stuart Mill, *Dissertations and Discussions: Political, Philosophical and Historical* (London: Parker and Son, 1859, 1867), Vol. II, pp. 378–81, Vol. III, pp. 173–77.

grown up like other usages, partly from a sense of justice, partly from common interest or convenience, partly from mere opinion and prejudice. Now, are international usages the only kind of customs which, in an age of progress, are to be subject to no improvement? Are they alone to continue fixed, while all around them is changeable? The circumstances of Europe have so altered during the last century, that the constitutions, the laws, the arrangements of property, the distinctions of ranks, the modes of education, the opinions, the manners,—everything which affects the European nations separately and within themselves, has changed so much, and is likely to change so much more, that in no great lapse of time they will be scarcely recognizable; and is it in their collective concerns, their modes of dealing with one another, that their circumstances, their exigencies, their duties and interests, are absolutely unchanged? What is called the law of nations is as open to alteration, as properly and even necessarily subject to it when circumstances change or opinions alter, as any other thing of human institution.

And, mark, in the case of a real law, of anything properly called a law, it is possible to maintain (however erroneous may be the opinion) that there is never any necessity for disobeying it; that it should be conformed to while it exists, the alternative being open of endeavouring to get it altered. But in regard to that falsely-called law, the law of nations, there is no such alternative; there is no ordinance or statute to repeal; there is only a custom, and the sole way of altering that, is to act in opposition to it. A legislature can repeal laws, but there is no Congress of nations to set aside international customs, and no common force by which to make the decisions of such a Congress binding. The improvement of international morality can only take place by a series of violations of exsiting rules; by a course of conduct grounded on new principles, and tending to erect these into customs in their turn.

Accordingly, new principles and practices are, and have been, continually introduced into the conduct of nations towards one another. To omit other instances, one entirely new principle was for the first time established in Europe, amidst general approbation, within the last thirty years. It is, that whenever two countries, or two parts of the same country, are engaged in war, and the war either continues long undecided, or threatens to be decided in a way involving consequences repugnant to humanity or to the general interest, other countries have a right to step in; to settle among themselves what they consider reasonable terms of accommodation, and if these are not accepted, to interfere by force, and compel the recusant party to submit to the mandate. This new doctrine has been acted on by a combination of the great powers of Europe, in three celebrated instances: the interference between Greece and Turkey at Navarino; between Holland and Belgium at Antwerp; and between Turkey and Egypt at St. Jean d'Acre. It is too late in the day, after these precedents, to tell us that nations may not forcibly interfere with one another for the sole purpose of stopping mischief and benefiting humanity.

Can any exigency of this sort be stronger—is any motive to such interference of a more binding character—than that of preventing the liberty of a nation, which cares sufficiently for liberty to have risen in arms for its assertion, from being crushed and trampled out by tyrannical oppressors, and these not even of its own name and blood, but foreign conquerors? The customs, or falsely called laws of nations, laid down in the books, were made for an age like that of Louis XIV to prevent powerful and ambitious despots from swallowing up the smaller states. For this purpose they were well adapted. But the great interests of civilized nations in the present age, are not those of territorial attack and defence, but of liberty, just government, and sympathy of opinion. For this state of things what is called the law of nations was not made; and in no state of things at all analogous to this, has that so-called law ever been, in the smallest degree, attended to. There was once in Europe a time when, as much as at present, the most important interests of nations, both in their domestic and in their foreign concerns, were interests of opinion: it was the era of the Reformation. Did any one then pay the least regard to the pretended principle of non-interference? Was not sympathy of religion held to be a perfectly sufficient warrant for assisting anybody? Did not Protestants aid Protestants, wherever they were in danger from their own governments? Did not Catholics support all other Catholics in suppressing heresy? What religious sympathies were then, political ones are now; and every liberal government or people has a right to assist struggling liberalism, by mediation, by money, or by arms, wherever it can prudently do so; as every despotic government, when its aid is needed or asked for, never scruples to aid despotic governments. . . .

A Few Words on Non-Intervention

With respect to the question, whether one country is justified in helping the people of another in a struggle against their government for free institutions, the answer will be different, according as the yoke which the people are attempting to throw off is that of a purely native government, or of foreigners; considering as one of foreigners, every government which maintains itself by foreign support. When the contest is only with native rulers, and with such native strength as those rulers can enlist in their defence, the answer I should give to the question of the legitimacy of intervention is, as a general rule, No. The reason is, that there can seldom be anything approaching to assurance that intervention, even if successful, would be for the good of the people themselves. The only test possessing any real value, of a people's having become fit for popular institutions, is that they, or a sufficient portion of them to prevail in the contest, are willing to brave labour and danger for their liberation. I know all that may be said. I know it may be urged that the virtues of freemen cannot be learnt in the school of slavery, and that if a people are not fit for freedom, to have any chance of becoming so they must first be free. And this would be conclusive, if the intervention recommended would really give them freedom. But the evil is, that if they have not sufficient love of liberty to be able to wrest it from merely domestic oppressors, the liberty which is bestowed on them by other hands than their own, will have nothing real, nothing permanent. No people ever was and remained free, but because it was determined to be so; because neither its rulers nor any other party in the nation could compel it to be otherwise. If a people—especially one whose freedom has not yet become prescriptive—does not value it sufficiently to fight for it, and maintain it against any force which can be mustered *within* the country, even by those who have the command of the public revenue, it is only a question in how few years or months that people will be enslaved. Either the government which it has given to itself, or some military leader or knot of conspirators who contrive to subvert the government, will speedily put an end to all popular institutions: unless indeed it suits their convenience better to leave them standing, and be content with reducing them to mere forms; for, unless the spirit of liberty is strong in a people, those who have the executive in their hands easily work any institutions to the purposes of despotism. There is no sure guarantee against this deplorable issue, even in a country which has achieved its own freedom; as may be seen in the present day by striking examples both in the Old and New Worlds: but when freedom has been achieved *for* them, they have little prospect indeed of escaping this fate. When a people has had the misfortune to be ruled by a government under which the feelings and the virtues needful for maintaining freedom could not develop themselves, it is during an arduous struggle to become free by their own efforts that these feelings and virtues have the best chance of springing up. Men become attached to that which they have long fought for and made sacrifices for; they learn to appreciate that on which their thoughts have been much engaged; and a contest in which many have been called on to devote themselves for their country, is a school in which they learn to value their country's interest above their own.

It can seldom, therefore—I will not go so far as to say never—be either judicious or right, in a country which has a free government, to assist, otherwise than by the moral support of its opinion, the endeavours of another to extort the same blessing from its native rulers. We must except, of course, any case in which such assistance is a measure of legitimate self-defence. If (a contingency by no means unlikely to occur) this country, on account of its freedom, which is a standing reproach to despotism everywhere, and an encouragement to throw it off, should find itself menaced with attack by a coalition of Continental despots, it ought to consider the popular party in every nation of the Continent as its natural ally: the Liberals should be to it, what the Protestants of Europe were to the Government of Queen Elizabeth. So, again, when a nation, in her own defence, has gone to war with a despot, and has had the rare good fortune not only to succeed in her resistance, but to hold the conditions of peace in her own hands, she is entitled to say that she will make no treaty, unless with some other ruler than the one whose existence as such may be a perpetual menace to her safety and freedom. These exceptions do but set in a clearer light the reasons of the rule; because they do not depend on any failure of those reasons, but on considerations paramount to them, and coming under a different principle.

But the case of a people struggling against a foreign yoke, or against a native tyranny upheld by foreign arms, illustrates the reasons for non-intervention in an opposite way; for in this case the reasons themselves do not exist. A people the most attached to freedom, the most capable of defending and of making a good use of free institutions, may be unable to contend successfully for them against the military strength of another nation much more powerful. To assist a people thus kept down, is not to disturb the balance of forces on which the permanent maintenance of freedom in a

country depends, but to redress that balance when it is already unfairly and violently disturbed. The doctrine of non-intervention, to
be a legitimate principle of morality, must be accepted by all governments. The despots must consent to be bound by it as well as the
free States. Unless they do, the profession of it by free countries
comes but to this miserable issue, that the wrong side may help the
wrong, but the right must not help the right. Intervention to enforce
non-intervention is always rightful, always moral, if not always
prudent. Though it be a mistake to *give* freedom to a people who do
not value the boon, it cannot but be right to insist that if they do
value it, they shall not be hindered from the pursuit of it by foreign
coercion. . . .

51. *ON THE WORLD COMMUNITY**/

PHILIP C. JESSUP

The encyclical [*Pacem in Terris*] that is the basis for all of our
considerations at this Convocation does not cover the problem of
law or the rule of law in detail. It would not be expected that it
should. It does contain references to law and justice, and law cannot
exist without justice. It also contains references to the need for
international organization and specifically the United Nations, and
law cannot exist apart from organization.

The rule of law has both simple and complex aspects. It is
simple in the sense that every human society has regulated its inter-
relationships, whether of individuals or of groups, by some rule of
law. That law which is established exists though it be violated.
Unhappily, law and violation of law are facts confirmed to us all in
our daily experience of life and in our daily reading of the headlines
of the newspapers, whether they apply to situations inside states or
to relations among the states of the world.

But law is not only a group of prohibitions or provisions for
penalties, as in what we call "criminal law." More importantly,

* Philip C. Jessup, Statement at the International Convocation on the Requirements of Peace held in New York City in February 1965, in *On the
World Community* (Santa Barbara: Center for the Study of Democratic Institutions, 1965), pp. 11–12. Reprinted by permission.

perhaps, law is the method by which society has always created devices to enable people to work together for the accomplishment of their proper ends and for the common good. That is why, in our domestic system, basic institutions like those of marriage and the family are creations of law. The institution of property is a creation of law. Practically all of our economic and business life proceeds on the basis of a great legal creation—the corporation. The same thing has been true in the international field, although we grant that the development of international law has not been perfected to the extent to which law has been perfected inside national societies.

Take the Charter of the United Nations, which is itself a treaty, a contract, a legal document. It says that the members of the United Nations are "states." We take it for granted that we know what states are, just as we take it for granted that we know what "corporations" are in the business life of the community. But the "state" in the international sense is a legal creation; it is a notion that has evolved over the centuries.

The United Nations itself, as an international organization, is a legal device, in the same way as the corporation in national law is a legal device for accomplishing certain definite ends. Within the general family of organizations of the United Nations there is a nexus of international organizations by which the affairs of the world are carried on. Through these it is possible to post a letter in New York and have it delivered in Germany or in Hong Kong or in Buenos Aires; the world community is enabled to quarantine diseases or to check plague as it never could in the past; there is an exchange of weather information so vital now to air transport and to sea transport. All of these are developed by treaties, and treaties are law, and they so remain even when they are broken.

We are told, and it is true, that coexistence is not merely an aspiration but a fact. The Soviet Union and the United States coexist, but they do not coexist in a vacuum. States do not sit off, one here, and one there, and merely glare at each other. They have inter-relationships, and those inter-relationships must be—and are— determined by various legal rules. That is why, for instance, in the ordinary mechanics of international society, there is an exchange of ambassadors and consular officers who perform numerous functions that enable the relationships of states to proceed in an orderly way. That is why, for another example, there are agreements as to which planes of which countries may fly which routes, and agreements about the allocation of radio wave lengths so as to distribute these necessary services among the various states of the world without undue conflict.

There are those who talk of the need for gradual evolution of human institutions. There are others who are impatient and say, no, we must have a panacea, we must have world law tomorrow and that will assure the peace. But let us consider the Secretary-General of the United Nations as the super-apothecary of the world, to whom everyone comes with a prescription for peace. It seems to me that our super-apothecary must reply: the prescription for peace is compounded of elements drawn from all over the face of the globe. There is an herb that grows on some unclimbed summit of some great mountain; there is another that may be found in the swamps of impenetrable jungles in tropical areas; there is a third that blooms in the desert, perhaps when it rains once in ten years or even once in a millennium; and all of these, and others, must be gathered and brewed before we can succeed in finding the prescription for the panacea that the impatient ask for now.

If we think of the leader of the world organization as a physician who is asked to eliminate from the world the virus of hate, the virus of envy, the virus of jealousy, the viruses that poison international relations, he is bound to reply that there is no super-drug that will conquer these viruses. All that our medications can do is to counter the possible development of other ills which follow in the train of the virus and to which the system, weakened by the virus, may be subjected unless proper care is taken. And so it is with the rule of law. It is not a panacea, nor is it something already achieved.

One of the great difficulties standing in the way of the full development of law in the international community is the concept known as sovereignty. Sovereignty is a quicksand. If one tries to build upon it, the entire legal structure sinks and perishes. Sovereignty in the sense of the unregulated will of states to do as they please is absolutely incompatible with the international rule of law. People do not always realize that every time a state enters into a treaty—as, for example, a treaty limiting nuclear tests—it is not only *exercising* its sovereignty but *limiting* its sovereignty by prohibiting itself from doing certain things in the future.

I feel bound to say that the jurists and international lawyers of the Soviet Union do not share this point of view about sovereignty. To them the preservation of sovereignty is the keynote and the necessary foundation of the operation of the United Nations. Perhaps this is why, in the application of international law to the solution of international disputes, there are so few governments of the world prepared to submit their controversies to the existing international tribunal, the International Court of Justice.

It is necessary to add, however, that this unwillingness to submit disputes is not always related merely to an over-emphasis on state sovereignty but is sometimes inspired by the same considerations that lead attorneys in the domestic field to urge their clients to settle cases out of court by negotiation instead of submitting them to the hazard of litigation. Foreign offices of governments function with the aid of legal advisers. Since they are generally cautious lawyers, they say: Don't submit it to the Court, you might lose; whereas if you just sit back, perhaps nothing will happen. This is hardly the way to promote the international rule of law. On the other hand, it was Elihu Root who used to describe developments in international peace by way of the old English expression, "Leg over leg, the dog went to Dover." If Dover represents the ultimate goal of peace, we shall attain it only by that cautious, slow, and sometimes discouraging route.

In the meantime, there is law; there are institutions for the application of law; and it is possible today for governments, like individuals, to take the advice of Shakespeare and do as adversaries do in law, "Strive mightily but eat and drink as friends."

52. *WORLD PEACE THROUGH WORLD LAW* */ RICHARD M. NIXON*

The Rule of Law

An invitation to address this distinguished audience is one of the most flattering and challenging a man in my position could receive.

Flattering because the very name of this organization at least implies that the profession which I am proud to represent can properly be described as a science rather than by some of the far less complimentary terms usually reserved for politics and politicians.

And challenging because I realize that an Academy of Political

* Address by Richard M. Nixon, Vice President of the United States, before The Academy of Political Science, April 13, 1959.

Science expects a speech of academic character. I hasten to add, however, if it is proper to quote a Princeton man at a Columbia gathering, that in using the term "academic" I share Woodrow Wilson's disapproval of the usual connotation attached to that word. Speaking on December 28, 1918, in London's Guildhall he said: "When this war began a league of nations was thought of as one of those things that it was right to characterize by a name which, as a university man, I have always resented. I was said to be academic, as if that in itself were a condemnation, something that men could think about but never get."

In my view, the primary function of the practicing politician and of the political scientist is to find ways and means for people to get those things they think about; to make the impractical practical; to put idealism into action.

Question of Survival

It is in that spirit, that I ask you to analyze with me tonight the most difficult problem confronting our society today. It is, as I am sure we will all agree, the simple but over-riding question of the survival of our civilization. Because while none of us would downgrade the importance of such challenging problems as the control of inflation, economic growth, civil rights, urban redevelopment—we all know that the most perfect solutions of any of our domestic problems will make no difference at all if we are not around to enjoy them.

Perhaps at no time in the course of history have so many people been so sorely troubled by the times and dismayed by the prospects of the future. The almost unbelievably destructive power of modern weapons should be enough to raise grave doubts as to mankind's ability to survive even were we living in a world in which traditional patterns of international conduct were being followed by the major nations. But the threat to our survival is frighteningly multiplied when we take into account the fact that these weapons are in the hands of the unpredictable leaders of the Communist world as well as those of the free world.

. . . Even though our dedication to strength will reduce sharply the chances of war by deliberate overt act, as long as the rule of force retains its paramount position as the final arbiter of international disputes, there will ever remain the possibility of war by miscalculation. If this sword of annihilation is ever to be removed from its precarious balance over the head of all mankind, some more positive courses of action than massive military deterrence must somehow be found.

It is an understandable temptation for public men to suggest that some "bold new program" will resolve the human dilemma—that more missiles, more aid, more trade, more exchange, or more meetings at the Summit will magically solve the world's difficulties.

No Panacea

The proposals that I will suggest tonight are not offered as a panacea for the world's ills. In fact, the practice of suggesting that any one program, whatever its merit, can automatically solve the world's problems is not only unrealistic but, considering the kind of opponent who faces us across the world today, actually can do more harm than good in that it tends to minimize the scope and gravity of the problems with which we are confronted, by suggesting that there may be one easy answer.

But while there is no simple solution for the problems we face, we must constantly search for new practical alternatives to the use of force as a means of settling disputes between nations.

Alternative to Force

Men face essentially similar problems of disagreement and resort to force in their personal and community lives as nations now do in the divided world. And, historically, man has found only one effective way to cope with this aspect of human nature—the rule of law.

More and more the leaders of the West have come to the conclusion that the rule of law must somehow be established to provide a way of settling disputes among nations as it does among individuals. But the trouble has been that as yet we have been unable to find practical methods of implementing this idea. Is this one of these things that men can think about but cannot get? . . .

United States Must Take Initiative

I am now convinced, and in this I reflect the steadfast purpose of the President, and the wholehearted support of the Secretary of

State and the Attorney General, that the time has now come to take the initiative in the direction of establishment of the rule of law in the world to replace the rule of force.

Under the Charter of the United Nations and the Statute of the International Court of Justice, institutions for the peaceful composing of differences among nations and for law-giving exist in the international community. Our primary problem today is not the creation of new international institutions, but the fuller and more fruitful use of the institutions we already possess.

The International Court of Justice is a case in point. Its relative lack of judicial business—in its 12-year history an average of only two cases a year have come before the tribunal of fifteen outstanding international jurists—underlines the untried potentialities of this Court. While it would be foolish to suppose that litigation before the Court is the answer to all the world's problems, this method of settling disputes could profitably be employed in a wider range of cases than is presently done.

Reservation Should Be Modified

As the President indicated in his State of the Union message, it is time for the United States to reexamine its own position with regard to the Court. Clearly all disputes regarding domestic matters must remain permanently within the jurisdiction of our own courts. Only matters which are essentially international in character should be referred to the International Court. But the United States reserved the right to determine unilaterally whether the subject matter of a particular dispute is within the domestic jurisdiction of the United States and is therefore excluded from the jurisdiction of the Court. As a result of this position on our part, other nations have adopted similar reservations. This is one of the major reasons for the lack of judicial business before the Court.

To remedy this situation the Administration will shortly submit to the Congress recommendations for modifying this reservation. It is our hope that by our taking the initiative in this way, other countries may be persuaded to accept and agree to a wider jurisdiction of the International Court. . . .

Negotiation Is Not Enough

Turning to the political area, we have now come far enough along in the great historic conflict between the free nations and the Communist bloc to know that negotiation and discussion alone will not necessarily resolve the fundamental issues between us. This has proved to be the case whether the negotiations took place through the very helpful processes of the United Nations, or at the conference table of foreign ministers, or even at what we now call the Summit.

What emerges, eventually, from these meetings at the conference table are agreements. We have made a great many agreements with the Soviet leaders from the time of Yalta and Potsdam. A major missing element in our agreements with the Soviet leaders has been any provision as to how disputes about the meaning of the agreements in connection with their implementation could be decided.

Looking back at the first Summit Conference at Geneva, for example, we find that it produced an agreement, signed by the Soviet leaders, which elevated the hopes of the entire world.

It should be noted, however, that the President and the Secretary of State repeatedly warned both before and after the holding of the conference that success could be measured only in deeds. One of the announced purposes of the conference was to test the Soviet sincerity by the standard of performance.

The Summit Conference has since been characterized by some as a failure, but in terms of agreements, as such, it was a success.

Let me quote briefly from that agreement: "The heads of government, recognizing their common responsibility for the settlement of the German question and the reunification of Germany, have agreed that the settlement of the German question and the reunification of Germany by means of free elections shall be carried out in conformity with the national interests of the German people and the interests of European Security."

Problem of Interpretation

In other words, those who participated in the Conference, including

Mr. Khrushchev, agreed at Geneva on a sound method for dealing with the German problem—the very same problem from which he has now fathered the new crisis at Berlin. But while the agreement seemed clear, as events subsequently developed, Mr. Khrushchev's understanding of its meaning was ostensibly different from ours.

The crucial question remained—how was the agreement to be effective when the parties disagreed as to what it meant? This is typical of a problem that can arise wherever any agreement is entered into between nations.

In looking to the future what practical steps can we take to meet this problem? I will not even suggest to you that there is any simple answer to this question. For obviously there can be none. But I do believe there is a significant step we can take toward finding an answer.

Specific Proposals

We should take the initiative in urging that in future agreements provisions be included to the effect: (1) that disputes which may arise as to the interpretation of the agreement should be submitted to the International Court of Justice at The Hague; and (2) that the nations signing the agreement should be bound by the decision of the Court in such cases.

Such provisions will, of course, still leave us with many formidable questions involving our relationships with the Communist nations in those cases where they ignore an agreement completely apart from its interpretation. But I believe this would be a major step forward in developing a rule of law for the settlement of political disputes between nations and in the direction all free men hope to pursue. If there is no provision for settling disputes as to what an international agreement means and one nation is acting in bad faith, the agreement has relatively little significance. In the absence of such a provision an agreement can be flagrantly nullified by a nation acting in bad faith whenever it determines it is convenient to do so.

While this proposal has not yet been adopted as the official United States position, I have discussed it at length with Attorney General Rogers and with officials of the State Department and on the basis of these discussions I am convinced that it has merit and should be given serious consideration in the future.

Not a Western Instrumentality

The International Court of Justice is not a Western instrumentality. It is a duly constituted body under the United Nations Charter and has been recognized and established by the Soviet Union along with the other signatories to the Charter.

There is no valid reason why the Soviets should not be willing to join with the nations of the Free World in taking this step in the direction of submitting differences with regard to interpretation of agreements between nations to a duly established international court and thereby further the day when the rule of law will become a reality in the relations between nations.

And, on our part, as Secretary Dulles said in his speech before the New York State Bar Association on January 31: "Those nations which do have common standards should, by their conduct and example, advance the rule of law by submitting their disputes to the International Court of Justice, or to some other international tribunal upon which they agree."

Importance of Example

We should be prepared to show the world by our example that the rule of law, even in the most trying circumstances, is the one system which all free men of good will must support.

In this connection it should be noted that at the present time in our own country our system of law and justice has come under special scrutiny, as it often has before in periods when we have been engaged in working out basic social relationships through due process of law. It is certainly proper for any of us to disagree with an opinion of a court or courts. But all Americans owe it to the most fundamental propositions of our way of life to take the greatest care in making certain that our criticisms of court decisions do not become attacks on the institution of the court itself.

Mr. Khrushchev has proclaimed time and again that he and his associates in the Kremlin, to say nothing of the Soviet peoples, desire only a fair competition to test which system, Communism or free capitalism, can better meet the legitimate aspirations of mankind for a rising standard of living.

Perhaps it is significant that the leaders of the Free World do not feel obliged to so proclaim so often. The world knows that this is the only kind of competition which the free nations desire. It is axiomatic that free people do not go to war except in defense of freedom. So obviously we welcome this kind of talk from Mr. Khrushchev. We welcome a peaceful competition with the Communists to determine who can do the most for mankind.

Need for an Umpire

Mr. Khrushchev also knows, as we do, that a competition is not likely to remain peaceful unless both sides understand the rules and are willing to have them fairly enforced by an impartial umpire. He has pointedly reminded the world that Soviet troops are not in Germany to play skittles. The free peoples passionately wish that Mr. Khrushchev's troops, as well as their own, could find it possible to play more skittles and less atomic war games. But we remind him that his troops could not even play skittles without rules of the game.

If the Soviets mean this talk of peaceful competition, then they have nothing to fear from the impartial rules impartially judged which will make such peaceful competition possible.

The Soviet leaders claim to be acutely aware of the lessons of history. They are constantly quoting the past to prove their contention that Communism is the wave of the future. May I call to their attention one striking conclusion that is found in every page of recorded history. It is this: the advance of civilization, the growth of culture, and the perfection of all the finest qualities of mankind have all been accompanied by respect for law and justice and by the constant growth of the use of law in place of force.

The barbarian, the outlaw, the bandit are symbols of a civilization that is either primitive or decadent. As men grow in wisdom, they recognize that might does not make right; that true liberty is freedom under law; and that the arrogance of power is a pitiful substitute for justice and equity.

World Peace Through World Law

Hence once again we say to those in the Kremlin who boast of the superiority of their system: "Let us compete in peace, and let our course of action be such that the choice we offer uncommitted peoples is not a choice between progress and reaction, between high civilization and a return to barbarism, between rule of law and the rule of force."

In a context of justice, of concern for the millions of men and women who yearn for peace, of a constant striving to bring the wealth abounding in this earth to those who today languish in hunger and want—in such a context, competition between the Communist world and the Free World would indeed be meaningful. Then we could say without hesitation: Let the stronger system win, knowing that both systems would be moving in a direction of a world of peace, with increasing material prosperity serving as a foundation for a flowering of the human spirit.

We could then put aside the hatred and distrust of the past and work for a better world. Our goal will be peace. Our instrument for achieving peace will be law and justice. Our hope will be that, under these conditions, the vast energies now devoted to weapons of war will instead be used to clothe, house, and feed the entire world. This is the only goal worthy of our aspirations. Competing in this way, nobody will lose, and mankind will gain.

16

DISARMAMENT AND ARMS CONTROL

This chapter deals with disarmament in the broadest sense, including the reduction and control of armaments. One of the earliest disarmament proposals is Jeremy Bentham's plan for mutual reduction of troops. Bentham (1748–1832) included this idea as a vital element of his "plan for an universal and perpetual peace." Other features of this plan were the complete withdrawal from the colonies, the establishment of an international court of justice, and the abolition of secret diplomacy.

In his famous encyclical *Pacem in Terris,* Pope John XXIII made a stirring plea for disarmament. This part of the encyclical is reprinted as the second selection in this chapter.

Approximately two months before the Nuclear Test Ban Treaty was signed in 1963 —a significant breakthrough in postwar disarmament negotiations—President John F. Kennedy discussed the rationale behind his efforts for peace including steps toward disarmament. He delivered his widely hailed speech "Toward a Strategy of Peace" at commencement exercises of The American University in Washington, D.C., on June 10, 1963.

The final selection is Jerome D. Frank's discussion of the disarmament question from a psychological point of view. Frank is Professor of Psychiatry at the Johns Hopkins University School of Medicine.

53. *TREATIES LIMITING THE NUMBER OF TROOPS*/ JEREMY BENTHAM*

Proposition XII.—That for the maintenance of such a pacification [the general and permanent pacification for all Europe], general and perpetual treaties might be formed, limiting the number of troops to be maintained.[1]

If the simple relation of a single nation with a single other nation be considered, perhaps the matter would not be very difficult. The misfortune is, that almost everywhere compound relations are found. On the subject of troops,—France says to England, Yes I would voluntarily make with you a treaty of disarming, if there were only you; but it is necessary for me to have troops to defend me from the Austrians. Austria might say the same to France; but it is necessary to guard against Prussia, Russia, and the Porte. And the like allegation might be made by Prussia with regard to Russia.

Whilst as to naval forces, if it concerned Europe only, the difficulty might perhaps not be very considerable. To consider France, Spain and Holland, as making together a counterpoise to the power of Britain,—perhaps on account of the disadvantages which accompany the concert between three separate nations, to say nothing of the tardiness and publicity of procedures under the Dutch Constitu-

---

* Jeremy Bentham, "A Plan for an Universal and Perpetual Peace," *Works* (Edinburgh: William Tait, 1843), Vol. II, pp. 550–52.

[1] Precedents.—(a) Convention of disarmament between France and Britain 1787,—this is a precedent of the measure or stipulation itself; (b) Armed neutrality code,—this is a precedent of the mode of bringing about the measure, and may serve to disprove the impossibility of a general convention among nations; (c) Treaty forbidding the fortifying of Dunkirk.

tion,—perhaps England might allow to all together a united force equal to half or more than its own.

An agreement of this kind would not be dishonourable. If the covenant were on one side only, it might be so. If it regard both parties together, the reciprocity takes away the acerbity. By the treaty which put an end to the first Punic war, the number of vessels that the Carthaginians might maintain was limited. This condition was it not humiliating? It might be: but if it were, it must have been because there was nothing correspondent to it on the side of the Romans. A treaty which placed all the security on one side, what cause could it have had for its source? It could only have had one— that is the avowed superiority of the party thus incontestably secured,—such a condition could only have been a law dictated by the conqueror to the party conquered. The law of the strongest. None but a conqueror could have dictated it; none but the conquered would have accepted it.

On the contrary, whatsoever nation should get the start of the other in making the proposal to reduce and fix the amount of its armed force, would crown itself with everlasting honour. The risk would be nothing—the gain certain. This gain would be, the giving an incontrovertible demonstration of its own disposition to peace, and of the opposite disposition in the other nation in case of its rejecting the proposal.

The utmost fairness should be employed. The nation addressed should be invited to consider and point out whatever further securities it deemed necessary, and whatever further concessions it deemed just.

The proposal should be made in the most public manner:—it should be an address from nation to nation. This, at the same time that it conciliated the confidence of the nation addressed, would make it impracticable for the government of that nation to neglect it, or stave it off by shifts and evasions. It would sound the heart of the nation addressed. It would discover its intentions, and proclaim them to the world.

The cause of humanity has still another resource. Should Britain prove deaf and impracticable, let France, without conditions, emancipate her colonies, and break up her marine. The advantage even upon this plan would be immense, the danger none. The colonies I have already shown are a source of expense, not of revenue,—of burthen to the people, not of relief. This appears to be the case, even upon the footing of those expenses which appear upon the face of them to belong to the colonies, and are the only ones that have hitherto been set down to their account. But in fact the whole expense of the marine belongs also to that account, and no other. What other destination has it? What other can it have? None. Take away the colonies, what use would there be for a single vessel, more than the few necessary in the Mediterranean to curb the pirates.

In case of a war, where at present (1789) would England make its first and only attack upon France? In the colonies. What would she propose to herself from success in such an attack? What but the depriving France of her colonies. Were these colonies—these bones of contention—no longer hers, what then could England do? what could she wish to do?

There would remain the territory of France; with what view could Britain make any attack upon it in any way? Not with views of permanent conquest;—such madness does not belong to our age. Parliament itself, one may venture to affirm, without paying it any very extraordinary compliment, would not wish it. It would not wish it, even could it be accomplished without effort on our part, without resistance on the other. It would not, even though France herself were to solicit it. No parliament would grant a penny for such a purpose. If it did, it would not be a parliament a month. No king would lend his name to such a project. He would be dethroned as surely and as deservedly as James the Second. To say, I will be king of France, would be to say, in other words, I will be absolute in England.

Well, then, no one would dream of conquest. What other purpose could an invasion have? The plunder and destruction of the country. Such baseness is totally repugnant, not only to the spirit of the nation, but to the spirit of the times. Malevolence could be the only motive—rapacity could never counsel it; long before an army could arrive anywhere, everything capable of being plundered would be carried off. Whatever is portable, could be much sooner carried off by the owners, than by any plundering army. No expedition of plunder could ever pay itself.[2]

[2] This brings to recollection the achievements of the war from 1755 to 1763. The struggle betwixt prejudice and humanity produced in conduct a result truly ridiculous. Prejudice prescribed an attack upon the enemy in his own territory,—humanity forbade the doing him any harm. Not only nothing was gained by these expeditions, but the mischief done to the country invaded was not nearly equal to the expense of the invasion. When a Japanese rips open his own belly, it is in the assurance that his enemy will follow his example. But in this instance, the Englishman ripped open his own belly that the Frenchman might get a scratch. Why was this absurdity acted? Because we were at war,—and when nations are at war something must be done, or at least appear to be done; and there was nothing else to be done. France was already stripped of all its distant dependencies.

Such is the extreme folly, the madness of war: on no supposition can it be otherwise than mischievous, especially between nations circumstanced as France and England. Though the choice of the events were absolutely at your command, you could not make it of use to you. If unsuccessful, you may be disgraced and ruined: if successful, even to the height of your wishes, you are still but so much the worse. You would still be so much the worse, though it were to cost you nothing. For not even any colony of your own planting, still less a conquest of your own making, will so much as pay its own expenses.

The greatest acquisitions that could be conceived would not be to be wished for,—could they even be attained with the greatest certainty, and without the least expense. In war, we are as likely not to gain as to gain—as likely to lose as to do either: we can neither attempt the one, nor defend ourselves against the other, without a certain and most enormous expense.

Mark well the contrast. All trade is in its essence advantageous— even to that party to whom it is least so. All war is in its essence ruinous; and yet the great employments of government are to treasure up occasions of war, and to put fetters upon trade.

Ask an Englishman what is the great obstacle to a secure and solid peace, he has his answer ready:—It is the ambition, perhaps he will add, the treachery of France. I wish the chief obstacle to a plan for this purpose were the dispositions and sentiments of France!— were that all, the plan need not long wait for adoption.

Of this visionary project, the most visionary part is without question that for the emancipation of distant dependencies. What will an Englishman say, when he sees two French ministers[3] of the highest reputation, both at the head of their respective departments, both joining in the opinion, that the accomplishment of this event, nay the speedy accomplishment of it, is inevitable, and one of them scrupling not to pronounce it as eminently desirable.

It would only be the bringing things back on these points to the footing they were on before the discovery of America. Europe had then no colonies—no distant garrisons—no standing armies. It would have had no wars but for the feudal system—religious antipathy—the rage of conquest—and the uncertainties of succession. Of these four causes, the first is happily extinct everywhere—the second and third almost everywhere, and at any rate in France and England

---

[3] Turgot and Vergennes.

—the last might, if not already extinguished, be so with great ease.

The moral feelings of men in matters of national morality are still so far short of perfection, that in the scale of estimation, justice has not yet gained the ascendency over force. Yet this prejudice may, in a certain point of view, by accident, be rather favourable to this proposal than otherwise. Truth, and the object of this essay, bid me to say to my countrymen, it is for you to begin the reformation —it is you that have been the greatest sinners. But the same considerations also lead me to say to them, you are the strongest among nations: though justice be not on your side, force is; and it is your force that has been the main cause of your injustice. If the measure of moral approbation had been brought to perfection, such positions would have been far from popular, prudence would have dictated the keeping them out of sight, and the softening them down as much as possible.

Humiliation would have been the effect produced by them on those to whom they appeared true—indignation on those to whom they appeared false. But, as I have observed, men have not yet learned to tune their feelings in unison with the voice of morality in these points. They feel more pride in being accounted strong, than resentment at being called unjust: or rather, the imputation of injustice appears flattering rather than otherwise, when coupled with the consideration of its cause. I feel it in my own experience; but if *I*, listed as I am as the professed and hitherto the only advocate in my own country in the cause of justice, set a less value on justice than is its due, what can I expect from the general run of men?

54. *DISARMAMENT** / *POPE JOHN XXIII*

. . . it is with deep sorrow that we note the enormous stocks of armaments that have been and still are being made in more economically developed countries, with a vast outlay of intellectual and economic resources. And so it happens that, while the people of these countries are loaded with heavy burdens, other countries as a

* Pope John XXIII, *Pacem in Terris*, text as published in *The New York Times* (June 11, 1963), p. 18. © 1963 by The New York Times Company. Reprinted by permission.

result are deprived of the collaboration they need in order to make economic and social progress.

The production of arms is allegedly justified on the grounds that in present-day conditions peace cannot be preserved without an equal balance of armaments. And so, if one country increases its armaments, others feel the need to do the same; and if one country is equipped with nuclear weapons, other countries must produce their own, equally destructive.

Consequently, people live in constant fear lest the storm that every moment threatens should break upon them with dreadful violence. And with good reason, for the arms of war are ready at hand. Even though it is difficult to believe that anyone would deliberately take the responsibility for the appalling destruction and sorrow that war would bring in its train, it cannot be denied that the conflagration may be set off by some uncontrollable and unexpected chance. And one must bear in mind that, even though the monstrous power of modern weapons acts as a deterrent, it is to be feared that the mere continuance of nuclear tests, undertaken with war in mind, will have fatal consequences for life on the earth.

Justice, then, right reason and humanity urgently demand that the arms race should cease. That the stockpiles which exist in various countries should be reduced equally and simultaneously by the parties concerned. That nuclear weapons should be banned. And that a general agreement should eventually be reached about progressive disarmament and an effective method of control. In the words of Pius XII, our predecessor of happy memory: "The calamity of a world war, with the economic and social ruin and the moral excesses and dissolution that accompany it, must not be permitted to envelop the human race for a third time."

All must realize that there is no hope of putting an end to the building up of armaments, nor of reducing the present stocks, nor, still less, of abolishing them altogether, unless the process is complete and thorough and unless it proceeds from inner convictions: unless, that is, everyone sincerely cooperates to banish the fear and anxious expectation of war with which men are oppressed. If this is to come about, the fundamental principle on which our present peace depends must be replaced by another, which declares that the true and solid peace of nations consists not in equality of arms, but in mutual trust alone. We believe that this can be brought to pass, and we consider that it is something which reason requires, that it is eminently desirable in itself and that it will prove to be the source of many benefits.

In the first place, it is an objective demanded by reason. There can be, or at least there should be, no doubt that relations between states, as between individuals, should be regulated not by the force of arms, but by the light of reason, by the rule, that is, of truth, of justice and of active and sincere cooperation.

Secondly, we say that it is an objective earnestly to be desired in itself. Is there anyone who does not ardently yearn to see war banished, to see peace preserved and daily more firmly established?

And finally, it is an objective which will be a fruitful source of many benefits, for its advantages will be felt everywhere, by individuals, by families, by nations, by the whole human family. The warning of Pius XII still rings in our ears: "Nothing is lost by peace. Everything may be lost by war."

Since this is so, we, the vicar on earth of Jesus Christ, Saviour of the world and author of peace, and as interpreter of the very profound longing of the entire human family, following the impulse of our heart, seized by anxiety for the good of all we feel it our duty to beseech men, especially those who have the responsibility of public affairs, to spare no labor in order to insure that the world events follow a reasonable and human course.

In the highest and most authoritative assemblies, let men give serious thought to the problem of a peaceful adjustment of relations between political communities on a world level: an adjustment founded on mutual trust, on sincerity in negotiations, on faithful fulfillment of obligations assumed. Let them study the problem until they find that point of agreement from which it will be possible to commence to go forward towards accords that will be sincere, lasting and fruitful.

We, for our part, will not cease to pray God to bless these labors so that they may lead to fruitful results.

55. *TOWARD A STRATEGY OF PEACE* /

JOHN F. KENNEDY

"There are few earthly things more beautiful than a University," wrote John Masefield, in his tribute to the English universities—and

* John F. Kennedy, "Toward a Strategy of Peace," *The Department of State Bulletin,* Vol. 49, No. 1253 (July 1, 1963), pp. 2-6.

his words are equally true here. He did not refer to spires and towers, to campus greens and ivied walls. He admired the splendid beauty of the university, he said, because it was "a place where those who hate ignorance may strive to know, where those who perceive truth may strive to make others see."

I have, therefore, chosen this time and this place to discuss a topic on which ignorance too often abounds and the truth is too rarely perceived—yet it is the most important topic on earth: world peace.

What kind of peace do I mean? What kind of peace do we seek? Not a *Pax Americana* enforced on the world by American weapons of war. Not the peace of the grave or the security of the slave. I am talking about genuine peace, the kind of peace that makes life on earth worth living, the kind that enables men and nations to grow and to hope and to build a better life for their children—not merely peace for Americans but peace for all men and women, not merely peace in our time but peace for all time.

I speak of peace because of the new face of war. Total war makes no sense in an age when great powers can maintain large and relatively invulnerable nuclear forces and refuse to surrender without resort to those forces. It makes no sense in an age when a single nuclear weapon contains almost 10 times the explosive force delivered by all of the Allied air forces in the Second World War. It makes no sense in an age when the deadly poisons produced by a nuclear exchange would be carried by the wind and water and soil and seed to the far corners of the globe and to generations yet unborn.

Today the expenditure of billions of dollars every year on weapons acquired for the purpose of making sure we never need to use them is essential to keeping the peace. But surely the acquisition of such idle stockpiles—which can only destroy and never create— is not the only, much less the most efficient, means of assuring peace.

I speak of peace, therefore, as the necessary rational end of rational men. I realize that the pursuit of peace is not as dramatic as the pursuit of war, and frequently the words of the pursuer fall on deaf ears. But we have no more urgent task.

Some say that it is useless to speak of world peace or world law or world disarmament—and that it will be useless until the leaders of the Soviet Union adopt a more enlightened attitude. I hope they do. I believe we can help them do it. But I also believe that we must reexamine our own attitude, as individuals and as a nation, for our attitude is as essential as theirs. And every graduate of this school, every thoughtful citizen who despairs of war and wishes to bring peace, should begin by looking inward—by examining his own attitude toward the possibilities of peace, toward the Soviet Union, toward the course of the cold war, and toward freedom and peace here at home.

The Possibilities of Peace

First: Let us examine our attitude toward peace itself. Too many of us think it is impossible. Too many think it unreal. But that is a dangerous, defeatist belief. It leads to the conclusion that war is inevitable, that mankind is doomed, that we are gripped by forces we cannot control.

We need not accept that view. Our problems are manmade; therefore they can be solved by man. And man can be as big as he wants. No problem of human destiny is beyond human beings. Man's reason and spirit have often solved the seemingly unsolvable, and we believe they can do it again.

I am not referring to the absolute, infinite concept of universal peace and good will of which some fantasies and fanatics dream. I do not deny the values of hopes and dreams, but we merely invite discouragement and incredulity by making that our only and immediate goal.

Let us focus instead on a more practical, more attainable peace, based not on a sudden revolution in human nature but on a gradual evolution in human institutions—on a series of concrete actions and effective agreements which are in the interest of all concerned. There is no single, simple key to this peace, no grand or magic formula to be adopted by one or two powers. Genuine peace must be the product of many nations, the sum of many acts. It must be dynamic, not static, changing to meet the challenge of each new generation. For peace is a process, a way of solving problems.

With such a peace there will still be quarrels and conflicting interests, as there are within families and nations. World peace, like community peace, does not require that each man love his neighbor; it requires only that they live together in mutual tolerance, submitting their disputes to a just and peaceful settlement. And history teaches us that enmities between nations, as between individuals, do not last forever. However fixed our likes and dislikes may seem, the tide of time and events will often bring surprising changes in the relations between nations and neighbors.

So let us persevere. Peace need not be impracticable, and war need not be inevitable. By defining our goal more clearly, by making it seem more manageable and less remote, we can help all peoples to see it, to draw hope from it, and to move irresistibly toward it.

Common Interests of U.S. and Soviet Union

Second: Let us reexamine our attitude toward the Soviet Union. It is discouraging to think that their leaders may actually believe what their propagandists write. It is discouraging to read a recent authoritative Soviet text on military strategy and find, on page after page, wholly baseless and incredible claims—such as the allegation that "American imperialist circles are preparing to unleash different types of wars . . . that there is a very real threat of a preventive war being unleashed by American imperialists against the Soviet Union . . . [and that] the political aims of the American imperialists are to enslave economically and politically the European and other capitalist countries . . . [and] to achieve world domination . . . by means of aggressive wars."

Truly, as it was written long ago: "The wicked flee when no man pursueth." Yet it is sad to read these Soviet statements—to realize the extent of the gulf between us. But it is also a warning—a warning to the American people not to fall into the same trap as the Soviets, not to see only a distorted and desperate view of the other side, not to see conflict as inevitable, accommodation as impossible, and communication as nothing more than an exchange of threats.

No government or social system is so evil that its people must be considered as lacking in virtue. As Americans we find communism profoundly repugnant as a negation of personal freedom and dignity. But we can still hail the Russian people for their many achievements—in science and space, in economic and industrial growth, in culture and in acts of courage.

Among the many traits the peoples of our two countries have in common, none is stronger than our mutual abhorrence of war. Almost unique among the major world powers, we have never been at war with each other. And no nation in the history of battle ever suffered more than the Soviet Union suffered in the course of the

Second World War. At least 20 million lost their lives. Countless millions of homes and farms were burned or sacked. A third of the nation's territory, including nearly two-thirds of its industrial base, was turned into a wasteland—a loss equivalent to the devastation of this country east of Chicago.

Today, should total war ever break out again—no matter how—our two countries would become the primary targets. It is an ironical but accurate fact that the two strongest powers are the two in the most danger of devastation. All we have built, all we have worked for, would be destroyed in the first 24 hours. And even in the cold war, which brings burdens and dangers to so many countries—including this nation's closest allies—our two countries bear the heaviest burdens. For we are both devoting massive sums of money to weapons that could be better devoted to combating ignorance, poverty, and disease. We are both caught up in a vicious and dangerous cycle in which suspicion on one side breeds suspicion on the other and new weapons beget counterweapons.

In short, both the United States and its allies, and the Soviet Union and its allies, have a mutually deep interest in a just and genuine peace and in halting the arms race. Agreements to this end are in the interests of the Soviet Union as well as ours, and even the most hostile nations can be relied upon to accept and keep those treaty obligations, and only those treaty obligations, which are in their own interest.

So let us not be blind to our differences, but let us also direct attention to our common interests and to the means by which those differences can be resolved. And if we cannot end now our differences, at least we can help make the world safe for diversity. For in the final analysis our most basic common link is that we all inhabit this planet. We all breathe the same air. We all cherish our children's future. And we are all mortal.

The Pursuit of Peace

Third: Let us reexamine our attitude toward the cold war, remembering that we are not engaged in a debate, seeking to pile up debating points. We are not here distributing blame or pointing the finger of judgment. We must deal with the world as it is and not as it might have been had the history of the last 18 years been different.

We must, therefore, persevere in the search for peace in the hope that constructive changes within the Communist bloc might bring within reach solutions which now seem beyond us. We must conduct our affairs in such a way that it becomes in the Communists' interest to agree on a genuine peace. Above all, while defending our own vital interests, nuclear powers must avert those confrontations which bring an adversary to a choice of either a humiliating retreat or a nuclear war. To adopt that kind of course in the nuclear age would be evidence only of the bankruptcy of our policy—or of a collective death wish for the world.

To secure these ends, America's weapons are nonprovocative, carefully controlled, designed to deter, and capable of selective use. Our military forces are committed to peace and disciplined in self-restraint. Our diplomats are instructed to avoid unnecessary irritants and purely rhetorical hostility.

For we can seek a relaxation of tensions without relaxing our guard. And, for our part, we do not need to use threats to prove that we are resolute. We do not need to jam foreign broadcasts out of fear our faith will be eroded. We are unwilling to impose our system on any unwilling people, but we are willing and able to engage in peaceful competition with any people on earth.

Meanwhile we seek to strengthen the United Nations, to help solve its financial problems, to make it a more effective instrument of peace, to develop it into a genuine world security system—a system capable of resolving disputes on the basis of law, of insuring the security of the large and the small, and of creating conditions under which arms can finally be abolished.

At the same time we seek to keep peace inside the non-Communist world, where many nations, all of them our friends, are divided over issues which weaken Western unity, which invite Communist intervention, or which threaten to erupt into war. Our efforts in West New Guinea, in the Congo, in the Middle East, and in the Indian subcontinent have been persistent and patient despite criticism from both sides. We have also tried to set an example for others—by seeking to adjust small but significant differences with our own closest neighbors in Mexico and in Canada.

Speaking of other nations, I wish to make one point clear. We are bound to many nations by alliances. Those alliances exist because our concern and theirs substantially overlap. Our commitment to defend Western Europe and West Berlin, for example, stands undiminished because of the identity of our vital interests. The

United States will make no deal with the Soviet Union at the expense of other nations and other peoples, not merely because they are our partners but also because their interests and ours converge.

Our interests converge, however, not only in defending the frontiers of freedom but in pursuing the paths of peace. It is our hope—and the purpose of Allied policies—to convince the Soviet Union that she, too, should let each nation choose its own future, so long as that choice does not interfere with the choices of others. The Communist drive to impose their political and economic system on others is the primary cause of world tension today. For there can be no doubt that, if all nations could refrain from interfering in the self-determination of others, the peace would be much more assured.

This will require a new effort to achieve world law, a new context for world discussions. It will require increased understanding between the Soviets and ourselves. And increased understanding will require increased contact and communication. One step in this direction is the proposed arrangement for a direct line between Moscow and Washington, to avoid on each side the dangerous delays, misunderstandings, and misreadings of the other's actions which might occur at a time of crisis.

We have also been talking in Geneva about other first-step measures of arms control, designed to limit the intensity of the arms race and to reduce the risks of accidental war. Our primary long-range interest in Geneva, however, is general and complete disarmament, designed to take place by stages, permitting parallel political developments to build the new institutions of peace which would take the place of arms. The pursuit of disarmament has been an effort of this Government since the 1920's. It has been urgently sought by the past three administrations. And however dim the prospects may be today, we intend to continue this effort—to continue it in order that all countries, including our own, can better grasp what the problems and possibilities of disarmament are.

The one major area of these negotiations where the end is in sight, yet where a fresh start is badly needed, is in a treaty to outlaw nuclear tests. The conclusion of such a treaty—so near and yet so far—would check the spiraling arms race in one of its most dangerous areas. It would place the nuclear powers in a position to deal more effectively with one of the greatest hazards which man faces in 1963, the further spread of nuclear arms. It would increase our security; it would decrease the prospects of war. Surely this goal is sufficiently important to require our steady pursuit, yielding neither to the temptation to give up the whole effort nor the temptation to give up our insistence on vital and responsible safeguards.

I am taking this opportunity, therefore, to announce two important decisions in this regard.

First: Chairman Khrushchev, Prime Minister Macmillan, and I have agreed that high-level discussions will shortly begin in Moscow looking toward early agreement on a comprehensive test ban treaty. Our hopes must be tempered with the caution of history, but with our hopes go the hopes of all mankind.

Second: To make clear our good faith and solemn convictions on the matter, I now declare that the United States does not propose to conduct nuclear tests in the atmosphere so long as other states do not do so. We will not be the first to resume. Such a declaration is no substitute for a formal binding treaty, but I hope it will help us achieve one. Nor would such a treaty be a substitute for disarmament, but I hope it will help us achieve it.

Peace and Human Rights

Finally, my fellow Americans, let us examine our attitude toward peace and freedom here at home. The quality and spirit of our own society must justify and support our efforts abroad. We must show it in the dedication of our own lives, as many of you who are graduating today will have a unique opportunity to do, by serving without pay in the Peace Corps abroad or in the proposed National Service Corps here at home.

But wherever we are, we must all, in our daily lives, live up to the age-old faith that peace and freedom walk together. In too many of our cities today the peace is not secure because freedom is incomplete.

It is the responsibility of the executive branch at all levels of government—local, State, and national—to provide and protect that freedom for all of our citizens by all means within their authority. It is the responsibility of the legislative branch at all levels, wherever that authority is not now adequate, to make it adequate. And it is the responsibility of all citizens in all sections of this country to respect the rights of all others and to respect the law of the land.

All this is not unrelated to world peace. "When a man's ways please the Lord," the Scriptures tell us, "he maketh even his enemies to be at peace with him." And is not peace, in the last analysis, basically a matter of human rights—the right to live out our lives without fear of devastation, the right to breathe air as nature provided it, the right of future generations to a healthy existence?

While we proceed to safeguard our national interests, let us also safeguard human interests. And the elimination of war and arms is clearly in the interest of both. No treaty, however much it may be to the advantage of all, however tightly it may be worded, can provide absolute security against the risks of deception and evasion. But it can, if it is sufficiently effective in its enforcement and if it is sufficiently in the interests of its signers, offer far more security and far fewer risks than an unabated, uncontrolled, unpredictable arms race.

The United States, as the world knows, will never start a war. We do not want a war. We do not now expect a war. This generation of Americans has already had enough—more than enough—of war and hate and oppression. We shall be prepared if others wish it. We shall be alert to try to stop it. But we shall also do our part to build a world of peace where the weak are safe and the strong are just. We are not helpless before that task or hopeless of its success. Confident and unafraid, we labor on—not toward a strategy of annihilation but toward a strategy of peace.

56. EMOTIONAL AND MOTIVATIONAL ASPECTS OF THE DISARMAMENT PROBLEM*/ JEROME D. FRANK

Western nations today seem to be caught up in a maladaptive response to threat which seems analogous to that shown by certain mental patients in that the methods used to deal with a problem aggravate instead of solve it. The problem facing all nations today is how to assure human survival and achieve security in the face of massive, unprecedented threat posed by nuclear weapons. It is generally agreed that disarmament must be part of any solution. As

* Jerome D. Frank, "Emotional and Motivational Aspects of the Disarmament Problem," *The Journal of Social Issues*, Vol. 17, No. 3 (1961), pp. 20–27. Reprinted by permission.

the unanimous resolution of the United Nations Assembly of November 2, 1959 puts it: "the question of general and complete disarmament is the most important one facing the world today." So far, attempts to solve this question have consisted not of moves towards disarmament, but of the competitive development and accumulation of nuclear, chemical, and biological weapons of mass destruction. Thus the means by which nations try to diminish the peril posed by modern weapons serve to increase it. Never have the nations of the world spent so much on armaments in an effort to achieve security, and never have they been so insecure.

One can find similar behavior in psychiatric patients, like the alcoholic who increases his anxiety and depression by trying to combat these feelings through drink, which aggravates them. It therefore may be worthwhile to explore possible parallels between the motivations and behavior of nations and individuals, recognizing, of course, that such analogies have only limited applicability (Frank, 1960).

The Nature of the Nuclear Threat

The unprecedented nature of the threat lies in the literally unlimited destructive power of nuclear weapons. This means that there can never be an adequate defense against them. There can be no passive defense because the attacker can always mount an attack sufficiently powerful to overcome it. By setting up certain arbitrary limitations, such as that the size of a nuclear attack shall be limited to 2500 megatons, it is possible to show that if certain drastic conditions are met—in itself highly unlikely—a country might survive a nuclear war. But the enemy is not bound by these limitations. America and Russia might choose to mount a 10,000 megaton attack against each other, in which case 75% to 80% of Americans and Russians would be killed outright and the rest would die within 2 years of radiation poisoning. "You might as well cross off both Russia and the United States from the map." (Glass, 1960, p. 11.)

Nor is it likely that there will ever be a successful active defense against these weapons, for the same thought processes which perfect a defense against a weapon at the same time devise ways of thwarting the defense. For example, we are now trying to develop a system for intercepting missiles through plotting their trajectories, and at the same time developing missiles which do not follow predictable trajectories. We boast of our means of confusing Russian radar, but they, of course, will be able to confuse ours equally well.

In the days of conventional weapons, a defense which worked reasonably well was good enough. Because of the massive destructive power of nuclear weapons, this is no longer true. Now a defense would have to be at least ninety percent effective—a level of effectiveness never achieved in history; and the likelihood of its being achieved when technology is advancing at such a fantastically rapid rate seems extremely remote.

Finally, the knowledge of how to make nuclear, bacteriological, and chemical weapons will never be lost. Therefore even if universal disarmament were achieved, it would always be possible for a nation secretly to build a few and blackmail its unarmed neighbors with them.

These considerations and others force one to a drastic conclusion, which has been succinctly stated in the following unanimous statement of 28 leading scientists from 8 nations: "In the end, only the absolute prevention of war will preserve human life and civilization in the face of chemical and bacteriological as well as nuclear weapons. No ban of a single weapon, no agreement that leaves the general threat of war in existence, can protect mankind sufficiently." (Proceedings of the Pugwash Conference, 1959, pp. 5–6.)

Some Maladaptive Responses to the Nuclear Threat

Before considering the possibilities that mankind might achieve the goal of the abolition of war, it may be well briefly to review some of the current responses to the threat posed by modern weaponry which are steadily propelling humanity towards disaster. These may be grouped into responses which have always beeen maladaptive, unreasonable, and known to make trouble, and those which always worked in the past but now for the first time in human history will not work any longer.

The grossly maladaptive responses have been described elsewhere (Frank, 1960; Osgood, 1959; Singer, 1958) so they will be merely mentioned here. Particularly important ones are:

1. *Ignoring* the danger. This is easy to do because it lies outside the experience of most of humanity. The human imagination has a

remarkable capacity to make remote contingencies real, but it seems unable to grasp the immediacy and extent of the danger posed by weapons which do not impinge on any of the senses and whose full devastating power has never been actually experienced. The tendency to ignore the threat is reinforced by habituation and denial.

2. *Habituation.* Over and over again in the past 15 years we have initially recoiled in horror from a weapons development, only to accept it calmly a few years later. We finally managed to become inured to the deaths of tens of thousands in a firebomb raid by the end of World War II. Now we consider with equanimity the deaths of millions. The point scarcely requires elaboration.

3. *Denial.* One common response to an overwhelming threat is "denial" in the clinical sense—that is, a refusal to admit the threat into awareness. Denial is not always pathological. The inability of most persons to contemplate their own deaths may be psychologically healthy. But denial in the form of failing to face the threat posed by modern weapons seriously impedes efforts to resolve the problem they present. Denial in this sense may take subtle forms. One is what David Riesman has termed "one man chess." (Personal communication, March 1960.) Each country plots its moves without considering what the moves of the enemy might be. For example, Senator Aiken, when told of the Russian threat to our bases abroad, is quoted as saying: "The first rocket to fall on the soil of our allies would be the signal for a rain of rockets on Russia." (Aiken, 1960, p. 1.) One looks in vain for the remainder of the thought "and a rain of Russian rockets on us."

A more subtle form of denial is a fallacious appeal to history: With the advent of each new weapon alarmists prophesied that it would destroy mankind and they were wrong; so those who say that nuclear, biological, and chemical weapons threaten the existence of humanity are probably also wrong. The fallacy lies in the proportionate increase in destructive energy made available by splitting the atom. At the dawn of history, when men killed each other with clubs and stones, a blow could scarcely kill more than one person. By 1944 mankind had so improved the destructiveness of weapons that an average firebomb raid on Japan killed four thousand. Thus the killing power of weapons increased by a factor of four thousand over half a million years or so. Today a moderate nuclear raid could kill fifty million people and nuclear weapons could be made in sufficient quantity to wipe out the entire human

race. This represents an increase in destructive power over the most
deadly non-atomic weapons by a factor of somewhere between
12,500 and infinity in a scant half-generation. Those who prophesy
disaster, and their like-minded forebears, are in the position of the
boy who cries "Wolf" too often, so that when the wolf really comes
no one believes him.

4. *The effects of strong emotion.* To the extent that we do not
succeed in ignoring or denying the threat of modern weapons of
mass destruction, we are made anxious by them. As is well known,
anxiety and other forms of emotional tension tend to diminish
flexibility of thinking and lead to a narrowing of alternatives. They
also shorten the time perspective so that the anxious or emotionally
aroused person clutches at measures which afford immediate relief
despite the certainty that they will lead to increased suffering in the
future. Like the alcoholic who uses alcohol to gain brief but
immediate relief even though he knows it will eventually kill him,
nations respond to each new threat by increasing the arms budget,
which yields momentarily heightened feelings of security at the cost
of increasing the likelihood and magnitude of ultimate disaster.

At the group level emotional tension is most seriously reflected
in the formation of the stereotype of "the enemy." Whoever we are
and whoever the enemy is, we gradually assume all the virtues and
they become the incarnation of everything evil. Once we have cast
another group in the role of the enemy, we know that they are to be
distrusted. We then tend to twist all their communications to fit our
belief.

The mutual distrust of enemies has two dangerous consequences. First, it tends to disrupt communication between them.
Since the enemy is viewed as so diabolically clever, each side fears
that the other will be able to use improved communications to its
advantage. I am not suggesting that some enemies do not deserve to
be mistrusted. But disruption of communication prevents gaining
information which would help to rectify any incorrect perceptions
of one's opponent. The second and greatest danger of the mutual
stereotype of the enemy is that it tends to make itself come true by
virtue of the mechanism of the "self-fulfilling prophecy" (Merton,
1957), which operates at both individual and group levels. Enemies
may not be untrustworthy to begin with, but if the mutual posture
lasts long enough, they eventually become so, as each acts in such a
way as to justify the other's suspicion.

"Adaptive" Responses to the Nuclear Threat

The pathological, maladaptive nature of the responses described above is readily apparent. Therefore they are relatively easy to identify. More difficult to detect, and therefore perhaps ultimately more difficult to deal with, are responses to threat which have been highly adaptive in the past. Therefore they appear eminently reasonable and right today, though they are as maladaptive as the others in the face of weapons of limitless destructive capacity. Three of these warrant special comment because they are evoked by all conflict situations. They represent very deep-seated aspects of human nature, and any scheme for the abolition of war must include ways of taking them into account. They are the belief that superior destructive force is the final arbiter of conflict, the propensity to fight for one's ideals to the point of death, and the fact that any sign of weakness or fear encourages an opponent to attack.

1. *International relations since time immemorial have been based on the fact that in a showdown, conflicts are won by the side possessing superior destructive force.* Although behavior guided by this premise has regularly led to war, outcomes of armed conflicts have confirmed it, at least until the twentieth century. The intellectual conviction that no one can win a nuclear war in the sense of gaining the ends for which he fought can make little headway against agelong human experience to the contrary. So national leaders still speak of winning the nuclear arms race as if this statement made sense.

2. *In a conflict one must be prepared to give one's life for one's ideals and beliefs.* Whether in the long run the willingness of people to die for their ideals has been good or bad for mankind is debatable. The world would certainly be a poorer place today were it not for religious, national, and intellectual martyrs who sacrificed their lives for their convictions, but this propensity has also led to catastrophic conflicts over differences in ideologies which now seem utterly trivial, such as whether God is Unitarian or Trinitarian. None the less, when patriotic orators evoke the image of Patrick Henry, who preferred death to loss of liberty, most Americans feel a responsive thrill. Unfortunately a man can no longer die in battle for his ideals without dragging millions of people after him who have no choice

in the matter. Nor can his death in a nuclear war possibly preserve the ideals for which he gave his life. However, any solution to the problems posed by weapons of mass destruction must permit people to sacrifice their lives, if necessary, for their beliefs, but in such a way that there is some hope of the sacrifice succeeding.

3. *One must not show fear in the face of the enemy.* There is no question as to the soundness of this principle, for fear undoubtedly encourages aggression. The time-hallowed way to maintain one's courage in the face of the enemy is to proclaim one's willingness to die for his cause, and demonstrate by shows of strength and other means that he will not be intimidated. The series of Russian and American reactions precipitated by the shooting down of the U-2 illustrate this response all too clearly. Each truculent gesture on one side evokes a corresponding one from the other, as a demonstration to itself and the other country that it cannot be intimidated. A world from which war has been abolished would have to include means for showing that one is not afraid, other than piling up arms.

Psychological Aspects of a World Without War

The crucial first step, psychologically, towards the ultimate abolition of war is the acceptance of the falsity of the first premise on which the policy of all nations today is based—that superior destructive force is the ultimate means of settling conflict. That is, one must begin one's thinking by ruling out resort to violence. The challenge is to devise non-violent means for resolving problems hitherto solved by war. This does not mean the abolition of conflict, but rather placing one's faith in the development of non-violent means of persuading, or even coercing, an opponent which have a chance of succeeding even if he has and is prepared to use superior destructive force.

The major ground for hope that this goal can be achieved lies in the actual demonstrations in recent years of the effectiveness of non-violent methods against an opponent who possessed and was prepared to use superior force. These include the non-violent campaigns in Norway and Denmark which demoralized the Nazi troops so badly that they had to be frequently rotated, the refusal of some Russian soldiers to fire on unarmed East Germans at the cost of their own lives, and, above all, the success of two large-scale,

carefully planned non-violent campaigns—Gandhi's for Indian independence and Martin Luther King's for bus desegregation in Mont-
gomery, Alabama. It seems probable that these leaders achieved a
genuine break-through in human affairs, which we have barely
begun to exploit. After the fact it is easy to explain away the success
of these campaigns on the basis of certain special circumstances. The
significant point is that in two different cultures both worked, when
no one would have predicted their success in advance. This at least
raises the hope that other successful non-violent ways of waging
conflict can be developed for other situations, including even the
arena of international conflict.

Because of the special conditions surrounding these campaigns,
it is unwise to generalize from them, but in terms of this discussion
they have at least demonstrated the possibility of meeting the needs
mentioned above without threat of or resort to violence. Both these
campaigns showed that non-violent methods of conducting conflict
require as great a degree of dedication as violent ones, including the
sacrifice of one's life. And the martyr would at least know his
sacrifice might help to realize the aim for which he made it, as
sacrifice of one's life in a nuclear war cannot.

Gandhi and King also succeeded in creating a set of group
standards which made refusal to resort to violence a means of
demonstrating one's fearlessness, thereby removing it from the
context of cowardice.

Thus commitment to non-violent ways of resolving international disputes would immediately take disarmament out of the
context of weakness and surrender. Disarming would become part
of an over-all plan of promulgating our ideals, rather than a move
away from them.

Finally, commitment to non-violence would take the teeth out
of the threat of nuclear blackmail. That is, a world organized along
non-violent lines would contain very powerful deterrents against
any nation which was tempted to reinvoke the specter of superior
destructive force. In such a world institutional means of resolving
conflicts peaceably would have been developed, the standard of
living would be rapidly rising as resources formerly squandered on
armaments were expended for human welfare, and all peoples would
be rejoicing in their release from fear of annihilation. Any government that contemplated taking advantage of the general disarmament to blackmail another country through threat of force would

face extremely unpleasant consequences. First of all, such a move would have a profoundly demoralizing effect within the country that made it. Even an absolutely ruthless dictatorship cannot make major changes in policy overnight without consideration of the feelings of the population. An even more serious consequence would be that every country of the world would rearm as rapidly as possible and the aggressor would be the enemy of them all. Since the countries would still know how to make weapons of limitless destructive power and since some of these weapons—notably bacteriological ones—are very cheap and easy to produce, the government which threatened violence would have to be prepared to police the entire world. Finally, she would know that she would meet stubborn non-violent resistance in the countries she occupied.

There are powerful positive and negative incentives for applying ourselves to the development of means of non-violent solution of conflict. The negative incentive is that modern weapons of mass destruction have left no other alternative. As Dr. C. F. von Weizsacker, the eminent German physicist-philosopher, put it at a recent conference: "Renunciation of violence is no longer a pious hope but a necessity. The only question is whether it will come before or after a catastrophe." (Personal communication, July 1959.)

The positive incentive is the dazzling vista that opens up for mankind once our imaginations, freed from preoccupation with mutual annihilation, can turn to developing the constructive potentialities of the vast power now at our disposal.

References

1. AIKEN, GEORGE D. *Baltimore Evening Sun*, May 30, 1960, p. 1.
2. FRANK, JEROME D. Breaking the thought barrier: psychological challenges of the nuclear age. *Psychiatry*, 1960, **23**, pp. 245–266.
3. GLASS, H. BENTLEY. *Baltimore Morning Sun*, May 14, 1960, p. 11.
4. MERTON, ROBERT K. *Social Theory and Social Structure*. Glencoe, Illinois: Free Press, 1957.
5. OSGOOD, CHARLES E. Suggestions for winning the real war with communism. *Journal of Conflict Resolution*, 1959, **3**, pp. 295–325.
6. *Proceedings of Pugwash Conference of International Scientists on Biological and Chemical Warfare*. Pugwash, Nova Scotia, August 24–30, 1959.
7. SINGER, J. DAVID. Threat-perception and the armament-tension dilemma. *Journal of Conflict Resolution*, 1958, **2**, pp. 90–105.

part V

PROSPECTS

17
THE FUTURE OF WORLD POLITICS

What are the prospects for international politics in the coming decades? It is often extremely difficult to understand past and present international events, and it is even harder to forecast the future. Nevertheless, it is important to try to analyze which directions future developments may take.

The first two selections in this chapter are predictions made in the nineteenth century, that have turned out to be highly accurate. Alexis de Tocqueville (1805–59) made his famous prediction of the rise of the two superpowers in the first volume of his *Democracy in America*, published in 1835.

An equally interesting but less well-known prediction is Friedrich Engels' prophetic vision in 1855 of the line that the Iron Curtain would follow across the map of Europe after the Second World War.

The remarks by Engels (1820–95) are particularly interesting, because the aims of the Panslavist movement which he described and
condemned, have been largely realized by the Soviets who claim to
follow Marx's and Engels' teachings.

A contemporary statesman who was fond of making predictions
was Nikita S. Khrushchev, Chairman of the Council of Ministers of
the Soviet Union and First Secretary of the Communist Party until
his involuntary retirement in 1964. One of his boasts that Communism would eventually rule the world is contained in an article that
he wrote for *Foreign Affairs*. The third selection consists of the
relevant passages from this article.

The chapter closes with an intensive and stimulating analysis of
the future of world politics by Karl W. Deutsch, a leading theorist
in the field of international relations. Deutsch is Professor of Government at Harvard University and the author of numerous books
and articles. He served as President of the American Political Science
Association in 1969–70.

57. *TWO GREAT NATIONS MARKED OUT TO SWAY THE DESTINIES OF HALF THE GLOBE* */ ALEXIS DE TOCQUEVILLE*

I am approaching the close of my inquiry; hitherto, in speaking of
the future destiny of the United States, I have endeavored to divide
my subject into distinct portions, in order to study each of them
with more attention. My present object is to embrace the whole
from one point of view; the remarks I shall make will be less detailed,
but they will be more sure. I shall perceive each object less distinctly,
but I shall descry the principal facts with more certainty. A traveller
who has just left a vast city climbs the neighboring hill; as he goes
farther off, he loses sight of the men whom he has just quitted; their
dwellings are confused in a dense mass; he can no longer distinguish
the public squares and can scarcely trace out the great thorough-
fares; but his eye has less difficulty in following the boundaries of

* Alexis de Tocqueville, *Democracy in America*, trans. Henry Reeve, rev.
by Francis Bowen (Cambridge, Mass.: Sever and Francis, 1863), Part I, Chap.
18, Conclusion.

the city, and for the first time he sees the shape of the whole. Such is the future destiny of the British race in North America to my eye; the details of the immense picture are lost in the shade, but I conceive a clear idea of the entire subject.

The territory now occupied or possessed by the United States of America forms about one twentieth part of the habitable earth. But extensive as these bounds are, it must not be supposed that the Anglo-American race will always remain within them; indeed, it has already gone far beyond them. . . .

It must not, then, be imagined that the impulse of the British race in the New World can be arrested. The dismemberment of the Union, and the hostilities which might ensue, the abolition of republican institutions, and the tyrannical government which might succeed, may retard this impulse, but they cannot prevent the people from ultimately fulfillling their destinies. No power upon earth can shut out the emigrants from that fertile wilderness which offers resources to all industry, and a refuge from all want. Future events, whatever they may be, will not deprive the Americans of their climate or their inland seas, their great rivers or their exuberant soil. Nor will bad laws, revolutions, and anarchy be able to obliterate that love of prosperity and spirit of enterprise which seem to be the distinctive characteristics of their race, or extinguish altogether the knowledge which guides them on their way.

Thus, in the midst of the uncertain future, one event at least is sure. At a period which may be said to be near—for we are speaking of the life of a nation—the Anglo-Americans alone will cover the immense space contained between the polar regions and the tropics, extending from the coasts of the Atlantic to those of the Pacific Ocean. The territory which will probably be occupied by the Anglo-Americans may perhaps equal three quarters of Europe in extent.[1] The climate of the Union is, upon the whole, preferable to that of Europe, and its natural advantages are as great; it is therefore evident that its population will at some future time be proportionate to our own. Europe, divided as it is between so many nations, and torn as it has been by incessant wars growing out of the barbarous manners of the Middle Ages, has yet attained a population of 410 inhabitants to the square league.[2] What cause can prevent the United States from having as numerous a population in time? . . .

[1] The United States alone cover an area equal to one half of Europe. The area of Europe is 500,000 square leagues; its population is 205,000,000. (Malte-Brun, Vol. VI, Bk. 114, p. 4.)

[2] See Malte-Brun, Vol. VI, Bk. 116, p. 92.

The time will therefore come, when one hundred and fifty millions of men will be living in North America,[3] equal in condition, all belonging to one family, owing their origin to the same cause, and preserving the same civilization, the same language, the same religion, the same habits, the same manners, and imbued with the same opinions, propagated under the same forms. The rest is uncertain, but this is certain; and it is a fact new to the world—a fact which the imagination strives in vain to grasp.

*   *   *   *   *

There are at the present time two great nations in the world, which started from different points, but seem to tend towards the same end. I allude to the Russians and the Americans. Both of them have grown up unnoticed; and whilst the attention of mankind was directed elsewhere, they have suddenly placed themselves in the front rank among the nations, and the world learned their existence and their greatness at almost the same time.

All other nations seem to have nearly reached their natural limits, and they have only to maintain their power; but these are still in the act of growth.[4] All the others have stopped, or continue to advance with extreme difficulty; these alone are proceeding with ease and celerity along a path to which no limit can be perceived. The American struggles against the obstacles which nature opposes to him; the adversaries of the Russian are men. The former combats the wilderness and savage life; the latter, civilization with all its arms. The conquests of the American are therefore gained by the plough-share; those of the Russian by the sword. The Anglo-American relies upon personal interest to accomplish his ends, and gives free scope to the unguided strength and common sense of the people; the Russian centres all the authority of society in a single arm. The principal instrument of the former is freedom; of the latter, servitude. Their starting-point is different, and their courses are not the same; yet each of them seems marked out by the will of Heaven to sway the destinies of half the globe.

[3] This would be a population proportionate to that of Europe, taken at a mean rate of 410 inhabitants to the square league.

[4] The population of Russia increases proportionately more rapidly than that of any other country in the Old World.

58. *THE DIVISION OF EUROPE* / *FRIEDRICH ENGELS*

The immediate objective of Panslavism is the setting up under Russian domination of a Slavic empire from the Erzgebirge and the Carpathians to the Black, Aegean and Adriatic Seas, an empire that would embrace about a dozen Slavic languages and dialects in addition to the German, Italian, Magyar, Wallachian, Turkish, Greek and Albanian languages. The whole is to be held together not by those elements which formerly held together and developed Austria, but rather by the abstract property of Slavdom and the so-called Slavic language, which, to be sure, is common to the majority of the inhabitants. . . .

We have been assured by the best sources that the present Russian Czar has sent a telegram to certain Courts wherein, among other things, it is stated that: "The moment Austria shall irrevocably ally herself to the West, or commit any overt act of hostility against Russia, Alexander II will place himself at the head of the Panslavist movement, and change his title of Emperor of all the Russians into that of Emperor of all the Slavs." This declaration of Alexander's if authentic is the first plain-spoken word since the war began; it is the first step toward giving the war, frankly and openly, that European character which has hitherto been lurking behind all sorts of pretexts and pretences, protocols and treaties, Vatel phrases and Puffendorf quotations. Turkey's independence and existence is thrown into the background. Who is to rule in Constantinople is no longer the question, but who is to command all Europe. The Slavic race long divided by internal contests, repelled towards the East by Germans, subjugated, in part, by Turks, Germans, Hungarians, quietly reuniting its branches, after 1815, by the gradual rise of Panslavism, for the first time asserts its unity, and, in doing so, declares war to the knife against the Romano-Celtic and Germanic races which have hitherto ruled Europe. Panslavism is not a movement which merely strives after national independence; it is a movement which aims to undo what a thousand years of history have

* Karl Marx and Friedrich Engels, *The Russian Menace to Europe: A Collection of Articles, Speeches, Letters and News Despatches,* selected and edited by Paul W. Blackstock and Bert F. Hoselitz (London: George Allen and Unwin, 1953), pp. 62, 84–85, 87. Reprinted by permission of George Allen and Unwin Ltd. and The Macmillan Company.

created; which cannot realize itself without sweeping from the map of Europe Hungary, Turkey, and a large part of Germany. Moreover, it must subjugate Europe in order to secure the stability of these results, if they are ever obtained. Panslavism is now, from a creed, turned into a political programme, with 800,000 bayonets to support it.

It leaves Europe only one alternative: submission to the Slavic yoke or destruction forever of the center of its offensive strength—Russia. . . .

To restore all originally Slavic soil and territory to the Slavs, to convert Austria, with the exception of the Tirol and Lombardy, into a Slavic Empire—the goal of the Panslavists—is to declare null and void the historical development of the last thousand years, is to cut off a third of Germany and all of Hungary, and to change Vienna and Budapest into Slavic cities—a process with which the Germans and Hungarians who own these districts cannot exactly sympathize.

59. *COMMUNISM WILL ULTIMATELY BE VICTORIOUS* / NIKITA S. KHRUSHCHEV*

The Communist Party of the Soviet Union at its Twentieth Congress made it perfectly clear and obvious that the allegations that the Soviet Union intends to overthrow capitalism in other countries by means of "exporting" revolution are absolutely unfounded. I cannot refrain from reminding you of my words at the Twentieth Congress: "It goes without saying that among us Communists there are no adherents of capitalism. But this does not mean that we have interfered or plan to interfere in the internal affairs of countries where capitalism still exists. Romain Rolland was right when he said that 'freedom is not brought in from abroad in baggage trains like Bourbons.' It is ridiculous to think that revolutions are made to order."

* Nikita S. Khrushchev, "On Peaceful Coexistence," *Foreign Affairs*, Vol. 38, No. 1 (October 1959), pp. 1–18 (excerpts). Copyright by the Council on Foreign Relations, Inc., New York. Reprinted by permission.

We Communists believe that the idea of Communism will ultimately be victorious throughout the world, just as it has been victorious in our country, in China and in many other states. Many readers of *Foreign Affairs* will probably disagree with us. Perhaps they think that the idea of capitalism will ultimately triumph. It is their right to think so. We may argue, we may disagree with one another. *The main thing is to keep to the positions of ideological struggle, without resorting to arms in order to prove that one is right.* The point is that with military techniques what they are today, there are no inaccessible places in the world. Should a world war break out, no country will be able to shut itself off from a crushing blow.

We believe that ultimately that system will be victorious on the globe which will offer the nations greater opportunities for improving their material and spiritual life. It is precisely socialism that creates unprecedentedly great prospects for the inexhaustible creative enthusiasm of the masses, for a genuine flourishing of science and culture, for the realization of man's dream of a happy life, a life without destitute and unemployed people, of a happy childhood and tranquil old age, of the realization of the most audacious and ambitious human projects, of man's right to create in a truly free manner in the interests of the people.

But when we say that in the competition between the two systems, the capitalist and the socialist, our system will win, this does not mean, of course, that we shall achieve victory by interfering in the internal affairs of the capitalist countries. Our confidence in the victory of Communism is of a different kind. It is based on a knowledge of the laws governing the development of society. Just as in its time capitalism, as the more progressive system, took the place of feudalism, so will capitalism be inevitably superseded by Communism—the more progressive and more equitable social system. We are confident of the victory of the socialist system because it is a more progressive system than the capitalist system. Soviet power has been in existence for only a little more than 40 years, and during these years we have gone through two of the worst wars, repulsing the attacks of enemies who attempted to strangle us. Capitalism in the United States has been in existence for more than a century and a half, and the history of the United States has developed in such a way that never once have enemies landed on American territory.

Yet the dynamics of the development of the U.S.S.R. and the

U.S.A. are such that the 42-year-old land of the Soviets is already able to challenge the 150-year-old capitalist state to economic competition; and the most farsighted American leaders are admitting that the Soviet Union is fast catching up with the United States and will ultimately outstrip it. Watching the progress of this competition, anyone can judge which is the better system, and we believe that in the long run all the peoples will embark on the path of struggle for the building of socialist societies.

You disagree with us? Prove by facts that your system is superior and more efficacious, that it is capable of ensuring a higher degree of prosperity for the people than the socialist system, that under capitalism man can be happier than under socialism. It is impossible to prove this. . . .

Prior to the Second World War the U.S.S.R. was the only socialist country, with not more than 17 percent of the territory, 3 percent of the population, and about 10 percent of the output of the world. At present, the socialist countries cover about one-fourth of the territory of the globe, have one-third of its population, and their industrial output accounts for about one-third of the total world output.

This is precisely the explanation of the indisputable fact that throughout the past years, hotbeds of war breaking out now in one and now in another part of the globe—in the Near East and in Europe, in the Far East and in Southeast Asia—have been extinguished at the very outset.

What does the future hold in store for us?

As a result of the fulfillment and overfulfillment of the present Seven Year Plan of economic development of the U.S.S.R., as well as of the plans of the other socialist countries of Europe and Asia, the countries of the socialist system will then account for a little more than half of the world output. Their economic power will grow immeasurably, and this will help to an even greater extent to consolidate world peace: the material might and moral influence of the peace-loving states will be so great that any bellicose militarist will have to think ten times before risking going to war. It is the good fortune of mankind that a community of socialist states which are not interested in new war has been set up, because to build socialism and Communism the socialist countries need peace. Today the community of socialist countries which has sprung up on the basis of complete equality holds such a position in the development of all branches of economy, science and culture as to be able to exert an influence towards preventing the outbreak of new world wars.

Hence we are already in a practical sense near to that stage in the life of humanity when nothing will prevent people from devoting themselves wholly to peaceful labor, when war will be wholly excluded from the life of society. . . .

60. *THE FUTURE OF WORLD POLITICS** / *KARL W. DEUTSCH*

Surveying the theories of international politics, as we find them in textbooks, in scholarly writings, and at a second or third remove in various popularisations by newspaper columnists and other writers, it appears that much of current thought about international politics can be described as utopian.

Four Utopias of International Politics

Broadly speaking, we find in many of these writings two chief kinds of utopias—utopias oriented to the future and utopias oriented to the past. The utopias oriented to the future or past, respectively, can be divided further into optimistic and pessimistic ones, so as to produce altogether four kinds of utopias of international politics.

The future-oriented and optimistic utopias are essentially utopias of harmony. The world, it is said, is becoming one. Conflicts are becoming unimportant. World trade is superseding national economies. A world literature is taking the place of national literature. Jet aircraft will carry people—most of them paying passengers, to be sure—in a few hours across the ocean. National sovereignties are becoming outmoded, international organisations are multiplying and so are federations, and soon all the antiquated nonsense of nation states and national governments will go into some museum of recent archaeology.

* Karl W. Deutsch, "The Future of World Politics," *The Political Quarterly*, Vol. 37, No. 1 (January–March 1966), pp. 9–32. Reprinted by permission.

There are also, however, pessimistic utopias which do not see the future in harmony but, rather, in conflict, somewhat in the manner of the old Manichean sect in the days of St. Augustine. They envisage the world as a huge battleground between light and darkness, day and night. The children of goodness are contending implacably against the children of evil. Monolithic ideological blocs are being formed and these blocs must become ever tighter and ever better organised. Neutrality between these blocs or even independence, according to this new Manichean creed, is clearly a sign of fuzzy-minded thinking, if not indeed of moral weakness.

The late John Foster Dulles in the United States held to something of this view, but by now such a view seems to be held with even greater strength in Peking and other capitals. By those who share this vision on each side of the cold war, it is felt that the tightness of one's own bloc must be increased, that countries not wholeheartedly sticking to the discipline of that bloc must be looked upon with suspicion and that independent or neutral countries will gradually disappear, being shown the error of their ways, or else collapsing by the ineptness of their unrealistic policies. Eventually the whole world thus will be neatly divided into two camps; and then clearly one's own righteous and superior side is destined to win a clear-cut victory, unless timid, cowardly, soft-minded statesmen should fritter it away.

There are also mixed utopias, where this picture of ever-increasing unity is projected for one's own camp whilst one triumphantly forecasts the dissolution of the camp of the adversary. The inner contradictions of capitalism—one is told in Marxist language—will clearly put all the non-Communist countries at sixes and sevens until they all fight each other whilst the Marxists will triumphantly go from unity to unity. On the other hand, more recently, anti-Communist writers, taking often the Marxist phrases verbatim, with only the signs reversed, have been describing how Communist régimes contain the seeds of their own destruction, and how the European federation will triumphantly progress while utter confusion will smite the camp of the totalitarians.

For purposes of exposition, I have simplified these lines of argument close to the point of caricature. Nonetheless, we all remember having read these arguments not once but many times, and it seems safe to predict we shall read them many times in the future. There is an old newspaperman's saying to the effect that if you have a good story you ought to run it once in a while, and the same seems true of a good folk theory of international relations.

But against these globe-girdling utopias of harmony or of conflict, oriented to visions of a future which is confidently expected to arrive, there are other utopias oriented to the past. According to these past-oriented utopias, the international politics of today and tomorrow will still be, in essence, the international politics of Machiavelli and of Bismarck. They will be the politics of irreducible national sovereignty, of conflicts among nation states pursuing nothing higher and nothing more worthy than their national interest; and, indeed, according to this school of thought there ought not to be anything higher than the national interest of each nation.

These national interests, then, have to be backed by power. Diplomacy, according to these utopias, becomes more effective if backed by power. The more guns or ships or bombs a country has the more likely it is, according to this theory, to get its way in international negotiations. More bombs thus ought to equal more diplomatic successes, roughly speaking, and assuming equal diplomatic skill on the part of each prince. To be sure, a prince or minister who is unskilled in diplomatic negotiations (which are seen as similar to some kind of horse trade or poker game of bluff and counter-bluffs, threat and counter-threat), may indeed even with six bombs in his arsenal only get four bombs' worth of concessions in the negotiations, whereas another, more skilful, man may be able to raise the military equivalent of two deuces into the diplomatic equivalent of a successful poker bid.

In this form of utopia it is believed that national armaments can be translated into national prestige and national power in influencing the course of international events. It is, moreover, believed that national interests are clear-cut, historically and geographically given, and readily discernible. At least it is believed that they are discernible by a small élite of statesmen, preferably of noble origin but also including professors and newspapermen who have spent many diligent years in their consideration. It is important, of course, to keep out the mob of ordinary voters and of the general populations of the countries concerned, since these might disturb the diplomats by intruding the ugly processes of popular emotions and of domestic politics, and thus disturb the rational calculations of the balance of power.

The balance of power, according to this belief, dominates politics now and will do so in the future. Under the balance of power one's strongest ally of today is one's most dangerous enemy of tomorrow. Present-day opponents become future allies. Present-day allies become future rivals. Princes, as Machiavelli wrote, ought to keep their word only as long as it is to their own interest, but since the prince on the opposing side also must be presumed to have read Machiavelli, he will know when the interest constellation changes and just when a solemn promise will be broken.

Translated into specific perspectives, this again can become the vision of optimism, a past-oriented utopia of harmony, or else a past-oriented utopia of conflict. In the past-oriented utopia of harmony, a future is seen roughly similar to the Europe after the Congress of Vienna in the early nineteenth century. Wise and enlightened statesmen, such as the late Prince Metternich, will keep their peoples in order; they will negotiate carefully with their counterparts in other countries; and the balance of power will preserve harmony, and will contain any unruly or overly-ambitious power. In this manner a "Europe of the Fatherlands", led by a particularly brilliant and enlightened general, will exercise a beneficent leadership in a world of sovereign nations. This world of sovereign nations will be characterised by balance of power whereby each nation develops national armaments and national nuclear weapons, both against possible nuclear enemies and as a prudent re-insurance against their neighbours and their allies. The politics of the balance of power and the strategy of national deterrents will be supplemented by the domestic politics of authoritarian leadership, of great impressive leaders, keeping the mass of voters at a respectful distance and preventing them from exercising undue influence over important matters of foreign policy, and this in turn will be supplemented by economic policies worded deliberately so as to revive vague memories of the gold standard. Most of these period pieces of economic and political thinking thus seem well matched in their style.

There are, however, past-oriented utopias of conflict in which we are shown much of the same world, but where we are asked to think no longer of the relative peace that characterised European politics between 1820 and 1840, and again between 1890 and 1900, but to think of the results which the same system of national states, national armaments and the balance of power produced in the 1860s and in 1870, and again in 1914. These pessimistic utopias of conflict point out that in the past there were always conflicts among the nation-states. They stress that in the end national states always had to invoke the decision of arms in pursuit of the national interests, and that the patriotic statesmen could only do their duty to their countries by getting the most efficient weapons available at each time, such as breech-loading rifles in 1871, Big Berthas, poison gas and submarines in 1914, and nuclear weapons, obviously, for the wars of the future. Here the European politics of the 1860s, of 1914, and of the 1930s are held to be the inevitable model for the politics of the future. This clearly is pessimism, but to a professional observer this also clearly looks utopian.

Of course, the utopias oriented to the past often are offered under the label of realism. They are no less utopian, I submit, than the visions of complete peace and harmony in the near future. In general, these pseudo-realistic utopias tend to overestimate the effects of particular interests and factors, as well as the effects of will and national morale. They greatly overestimate the rationality of decision of statesmen. They overestimate the ease with which national interests can be clearly discerned and people can foresee the future. At the same time they tend to underestimate the impact of popular initiatives and popular participation.

Basic Errors in Decisions

Such seemingly realistic utopias also tend to underestimate the effects of communication overload on the ability of governments to make decisions, and they tend to underestimate the very large margins of error which are inherent in many substantive decisions involving war and peace. If one looks over the major decisions about initiating war—decisions made by responsible statesmen in the last half-century, on all sides and in all countries, Communist and non-Communist, Western and Axis—the probability of a major decision being realistic may well have been less than one-half, on the average. That is to say, if in the last half-century statesmen made major decisions on matters of war and peace, the chances were better than even that the particular decision would be wrong. This is true of the German decision to go to war in 1914. It is true of the Austrian decision in 1915 to refuse Italy the concession of Trieste; and it is true of the Italian decision expecting great gain and booty out of the first world war. It is true of Hitler's decision in 1939 to go to war against England. It is also true of Hitler's decision in going to war in 1941 against Russia; and it is true of Stalin's expectation in the same year, first that the Nazis would not attack, and then that his own troops would contain them many hundreds of miles away from Moscow.

There is no need to labour the point. The frequency of major, fundamental and bloody errors during the last half-century has been so large that a statesman whose decision on matters of war and peace were right half of the time probably was doing better than many of his colleagues.

Finally, some utopias of *Realpolitik* underestimate the difference between the effect of the risks taken once and the cumulative effect of risks taken repeatedly. If a driver speeds up at a street corner so as to deter a rival who is coming out of the intersection, he may indeed have a 90 per cent chance of succeeding and getting his right of way. If he repeats this behaviour at two intersections, however, his chances of survival are $.9 \times .9$ which is roughly equal to .81 or eight-tenths. If he goes on doing this sort of thing at seven intersections, his chances of survival are less than one-half. If he does it for a hunderd intersections, his chances of survival are small indeed.

That is to say, the same policy and the same risk which it may be rational to take once, are less rational to take twice, far less rational to take five times, and suicidal to take a hundred times. Mathematicians know one version of this law as the law of gambler's ruin. It is not yet sufficiently appreciated among professional students of international politics.

But the most important point, the point that does make the past-oriented utopias, utopias, and that also leads us to doubt the future-oriented utopias of solid conflict among blocs, or else of universal harmony, consists in the actual facts of the transformation of the international systems that are observable before our eyes. What are these observable transformations, or at least some of them?

Some Transformations of the International Political System

The first transformation consists in a simple fact. For the first time since the invention of writing, roughly 3000 B.C., the majority of mankind is literate. According to the best estimates, mankind passed the 50 per cent mark in literacy about 1955. There has never been anything like it since writing was introduced.

The second transformation is now under way. By the end of the century it is very likely that the majority of mankind will no longer be employed in agriculture, for the first time since agriculture was invented. In the world at large, one-half of 1 per cent of the work force in most countries is shifting out of agriculture into non-agricultural employment. Every ten years 5 per cent more of a country's work force are leaving agriculture and going into non-agricultural employment. In thirty years this would amount to 15 per cent of the work force. France in 1957 had 26 per cent of her work force in agriculture. If this trend goes on it would therefore take little more than forty years to reduce France's agricultural work force to 5 per cent the present level of England. For Japan, which in 1959 had 40 per cent of her work force in agriculture, and where the rate of shift into non-agricultural employment was a little more than 4 per cent per decade, the same result would be reached in less than ninety years, or within three generations.[1]

Even the population remaining on the land is becoming different. Many years ago Clemenceau once said that war was too serious a business to be left to generals. We might now add that perhaps food production is becoming too serious a business to be left to peasants. For millenia, peasant agriculture has been the handicraft stage of food production, but now we are witnessing the technical transformation of agriculture in very many ways, and those who used to be peasants are becoming increasingly alert political voters, fathers of sons going to agricultural colleges, readers of newspapers and periodicals, and members of efficiently organised political pressure groups.

About one-third of mankind now is urban, again more than ever in all human history. Probably by the end of the century the majority of mankind will consist of city dwellers, again for the first time since there have been towns, at the end of the Stone Age.

It will be a mankind that is literate, a mankind that works in non-agricultural employment (which is largely industry and services), a mankind that lives in towns, a mankind with unprecedented amounts of capital goods and mechanical energy at its disposal for production or destruction. Within the nations everywhere in the world, class distinctions are declining. Karl Marx, as you may remember, predicted for the industrial workers in the advanced industrial countries a law of increasing misery. For Marxist theorists this has become a source of increasing embarrassment. The differences in real wages between the working classes and the middle classes in most countries are declining. They are serious enough in

[1] Most of these and the following figures are from Bruce M. Russett, H. R. Alker, Jr., K. W. Deutsch and H. D. Lasswell, *World Handbook of Political and Social Indicators*, New Haven, Yale University Press, 1964, or from the files of the Yale Political Data Programme.

many parts of the world, and the differences between town and country, and between the well-to-do landowner and the poor peasant or the farm hand are still heart-breaking and dangerously high in many countries. Yet a survey of many countries shows that these differences are declining. The data for Europe shows this. This trend has come about partly by taxation, partly by welfare services, partly by the effort of labour unions and labour parties, and partly by the effects of full employment.

Whatever the reason—and I am now speaking of the non-Communist countries of the world—there is a decline in the inequality of income. The great majority of the work force of America works within an income span of the order of about one to ten, that is to say, including highly skilled managers, the great majority of middle management and executive personnel in the United States do not earn more than ten times, at most, of the income of the average industrial worker. Much the same is the case for many other countries, and much the same seems to be the case, interestingly enough, in capitalist and Communist countries, insofar as comparable data are available.

It seems that modern industry has built into itself a certain bias that works against complete equality of incomes, because this destroys incentives, and against extreme inequality because that destroys harmony and co-operation; and somewhere in the range of one to ten most of the incentive requirements and teamwork requirements of modern industry can somehow be accommodated. The countries where inequality is strikingly outside this range are the countries with the highest loss of life from domestic political violence, and the highest record of political instability in the last fifteen years. On the whole, the distinction of income within countries is not disappearing but is becoming more moderate.

In the international field, from 1900 to 1950, the opposite could be observed. Between 1900 and 1950, the most advanced countries advanced much faster than the poor countries and the developing countries. In the world of international trade and international economics, from 1900 to 1950, the rich were getting richer and the poor, not absolutely but relatively speaking, were getting poorer.

Since 1950 this trend may have been reversed. From 1950 to 1960, using income data for sixty-eight countries, we find in this latest decade that the difference between the poor and richer countries has been slightly declining. By 1975 the gap may be somewhat less. By 2000 it is likely to be still less, although even then, if the trend towards greater equality does not accelerate, the amount of international inequality among countries at the end of this century probably would still be higher than the present levels of domestic income inequality within such countries as Mexico, Guatemala or Ceylon. The post-1950 data, however, are inconclusive, and more research is needed.

This projection is based on *per capita* incomes, and it already takes into account the birth rates of the different countries, including the relatively high birth rates of some of the developing countries. On the whole, however, perhaps luckily, the high population growth rates of 3 per cent and more are found most often in small developing countries, whereas the large ones—such as India and China—rather seem to have been growing somewhere in the neighbourhood of 2 per cent.

Nevertheless, we will have about six billion people in the world by the end of the century, double the three billion people we have now. Still, the six billion people will be less unequal in income than they are now, and their average income will be at least double of what it is today. All these changes we may reasonably expect, and we can even make a forecast of some psychological and political changes that are likely to come with them.

The Growth of Politics

As incomes increase—and I am speaking now of the future of non-Communist countries—and as technology and industry increase, there increases the need for public services. When a peasant lives in a hut by a little brook, to get drinking water is not a political problem. On a city block in Bombay, Calcutta, Rome or Tokyo, drinking water is a political problem, and so is sewage disposal, and public health, and a hundred other matters of the mechanics of daily living. This applies to the simplest needs for living, health and human dignity. If you live in a large family in a village and get sick, you have numerous relatives to care for you. If you are a worker in a city and should fall ill, you need a hospital and health insurance. This, again, is a political problem.

The human needs of industrialisation, therefore, are giving direct rise to human needs for public service. Human needs for public service give rise directly, with only small time-lags, to political demands for public service, explicit or tacit, and therefore they give rise to potential political support for governments and leaders supplying some or many of these services. This applies both to the tangible services that supply the growing material needs of people, and to the flow of symbols and experiences that supply strengthened feelings of affiliation, identity and dignity to uprooted people who need them.

The result has been that the government sector in economic life has been increasing, and so has the government sector in the daily behaviour of individuals and families. If we think of those of our actions which we perform or modify in response to tradition as one part of our life, then a second part consists of the actions we carry out in response to the market mechanism of buying and selling, and a third section comprises the actions we perform or modify in response to some regulation of the government. If we apply this primitive threefold division to the history of modern or developing countries, then it can be said that the tradition-directed sector of human behaviour has been steadily shrinking. The market sector has been somewhat growing; and the public sector has been growing steadily.

A measure for the growth of the public sector is the proportion of all government budgets—national, provincial, and local, and of public service corporations such as posts, railroads, or social security agencies—to the gross national product.

In the most advanced non-Communist countries, the share of this government sector is now 25 per cent or more. It is 28 per cent for the United States, over 40 per cent for France, West Germany, the United Kingdom and Japan, and over 50 per cent for Sweden. As capitalism has been creeping forward, socialism has been creeping along with it.

The theoretical prediction that these two systems invariably would be opposed does not quite stand up in the light of the empirical facts for a large number of non-Communist countries. More success in industrialisation under private enterprise auspices brings with it more demands for public services and, therefore, eventually a higher amount of public taxation and public spending.

Politicisation of the Masses

This in turn means that the stakes of politics increase; and this in its turn means that the interest of people in politics increases; and as needs for political services grow, the stakes of politics increase, the interest in politics increases, and political participation increases all around the world. We see for the first time in world history the politicisation of the masses of mankind. In the 1890s an American farm leader, Mary Lease of Kansas, advised the farmers of Kansas to raise "less corn and more hell." Ever since, the farmers of the world have followed that instruction. They have discovered that the prices of their products depend less on the weather than on their votes, and on the state and efficiency of their political organisation. Farm prices are political. Wages are political. Welfare conditions are political. The world is getting more political than it has ever been.

This political change has been going hand-in-hand with a psychological transformation. As countries move from traditional apathy into the early stages of political and social mobilisation, people are interested in getting oriented, in knowing what to do, in getting an image of their condition in their world. Experiments by psychologists have shown that people of scant education are more thoroughly convinced and more satisfied if they are offered only one side to a question. Psychologists speak of the authoritarianism of the poor.

Tests carried on by the United States Army showed that soldiers who had only elementary school education—that is, no more than six years of schooling—preferred to hear only one side to an argument, but soldiers with twelve years or more of education preferred hearing both sides. That is to say, just as there is an authoritarian predisposition among the illiterate or less educated, so there is a liberal tradition—with a small "l"—among the highly educated. There is a feeling of impatience and frustration among highly educated people if they are given only one side of an argument, if they are subjected to endless repetition, or confronted with dogmatic authority.

This effect of the level of education works to some extent independently of any particular ideology. It is simply that, as education increases, the desire to hear more than one opinion, to see more than one side of a question, spontaneously increases in the minds of the new and more highly educated generation.

For the world as a whole this means that for the next thirty or fifty years, we will find at the same time that some of the developing countries, such as India or China, may well be becoming more authoritarian, whilst at the same time many of the more highly developed countries of Europe—as well as Japan and many of the Latin American countries—may well be becoming more liberal. We see some of this process at work in the public opinion data in the United States. Mr. Goldwater did not believe in this trend. Mr. Johnson did, and won the 1964 election by a landslide.

Its Effect on International Politics

This trend has practical effects on international politics. As more and more people take part in politics and make demands on government, they make claims upon the time and attention of their rulers. Since a modern ruler's day, whether he is a democratic prime minister or a dictator, still has only twenty-four hours, it means that the increasing burden on his time from domestic politics must reduce the time and attention available to him for foreign policy; and we find all over the world that governments are in increasing danger either of being so attentive to foreign policy and world-wide alliances that they lose their popularity at home, or of being so solicitous of preserving their popularity at home that they begin to give less and less attention to international affairs. This is not an accident but a necessary dilemma, produced by the fact that the millions of subjects can no longer be governed with quite as little attention and care as they could be governed twenty or fifty years ago; and this dilemma is certain to get worse in the future.

Communication overload presses upon all central governments, Communist and non-Communist alike. A Communist Party secretary in Peking fifteen years ago could make a choice. He could spend several hours a day reading *Pravda* and maintaining his expert knowledge of the international versions of Marxism as interpreted in Moscow, or he could spend the same amount of time forgetting about *Pravda* and learning to know every Communist Party secretary in Peking by his first name. Which of the two party secretaries would be likely to make a better career in the Chinese Communist Party?

I asked, in effect, this question in a paper I wrote in February 1953 before Stalin's death, and I came to the conclusion that the Communist bloc was going to loosen or break up, not because of accidents but because of the necessary operation of the process of communication overload. In each major Communist country there was so much to pay attention to, so much to think about, so much

to decide about, that something had to be given up. Either the
Chinese leaders in Peking were going to pay less attention to Russia
and more attention to China, or they would become unpopular in
China; and the same held for leaders in Russia. Mr. Khrushchev
had to spend more attention on Russia, and as it now seems, he did
not pay quite enough attention to internal Russian politics at that.
It follows that the Communist parties of the different countries are
going to become diversified, if they are to maintain that minimum
degree of responsiveness to their populations which they must maintain if they are to keep in power.

But the same process—the increasing burden of domestic matters
which demand attention and, therefore, the increasing dilemma
between domestic popularity, and the partial neglect of international
commitments—is at work in the non-Communist countries.

If you compare a list of French politicians who in 1950 identified themselves prominently with Europe, with another list of those
who quietly stuck to the politics of France, you may well find that
those French officials who invested their future in France have more
power today than those French who invested their future in Europe.
Some of the latter may be now prominent in Brussels. They are
not prominent in Paris.

The same process is likely to be at work in other countries. Let
me illustrate it with a figure. The ratio of foreign trade to gross
national product was at its maximum in the world around 1913.
Since 1913, that is, for the last half century, in most countries of
the world sooner or later the ratio of foreign trade to gross national
product has begun to fall. This includes Japan. Japan had a peak
of its foreign trade ratio around 1928, but England had its peak, or
rather its plateau, between 1871 and around 1914. America had its
peak about the time of George Washington. Today in most countries the ratio of foreign trade to gross national product is declining.
Foreign trade clearly should not be abandoned, but it does not weigh
as much in the economic picture of many nations as it did in 1913
or 1928; and the interest groups linked to foreign trade, therefore,
have less of a power base to use in domestic politics than was the
case twenty or fifty years ago.

The world is therefore becoming somewhat more insulated,
somewhat more nationally self-preoccupied. At the same time, since
people take much more of an active part in politics, it follows that
most countries are becoming harder to govern. They are harder to
govern for their own traditional rulers. They are harder to govern

by new national governments, and they are still harder nowadays to govern by foreigners. The difficulty of government from abroad is getting ever larger.

The Rising Cost of Intervention

In 1830, 30,000 Frenchmen conquered Algeria. In 1958, twenty times as many Frenchmen—600,000—failed to hold Algeria. In the Congo, which in the late fifties was in some respects not far from where Algeria had been in 1830, one armed man, usually a Congolese soldier under Belgian command, was sufficient to maintain order among 500 natives. The police ratio in the Congo then was 1 to 500. In Algeria in the same year, 1958, one armed Frenchman was unable to maintain order among fifteen natives. The police ratio had shifted from 500 to fifteen. This is a measure of possible change. The world is becoming perhaps thirty times as hard to govern as it used to be. My countrymen are making this unhappy statistical discovery at this moment in South Vietnam. It is not a process particular to one country or one ideology alone. In any country, it can be aggravated by foreign intervention. Ideologists in neighbouring or distant countries can take advantage of this process, but the process itself is world-wide, and it is deeply inherent in the social transformations which industry and technology are bringing to the whole world.

The cost of intervention in the internal affairs of other countries is steadily rising, therefore, both in manpower and in money, as well as in risk.

In 1776 the founding fathers of America wrote in the Declaration of Independence that governments are getting their just powers from the consent of the governed. In 1976 it should be safe to say that governments are getting most of their effective powers from that source.

The Reduced Effect of Threats

This, in turn, leads to an increasing counter-productivity of the tactics of threat and the tactics of retaliation. It is increasingly difficult to intimidate a country, for two reasons. Large countries today are very complicated communication systems. Threats from the outside can only be transmitted to a small part of their population. Even if they were broadcast or scattered in leaflets, the population usually is accustomed to believe, at most, what their own countrymen tell them. They certainly are not in the habit of believing what foreign governments tell them. It is, therefore, almost useless to try to tell a population directly or at large that they are threatened; this produces next to no response. One must, therefore, try to speak to the élite. The élite in turn, however, have their own preoccupations, and as we saw, these preoccupations are increasingly domestic. Élites make peace or go to war more often because they calculate what the domestic political effect of such a step will be than because they have made a careful and painstaking assessment of international strategy. Professor Masao Maruyama of the University of Tokyo has shown how to some degree the Japanese decision to go to war at Pearl Harbour was made by civilian statesmen who were greatly worried about what the army would do to them, rather than being worried about how many ships and airplanes the United States could build after a Japanese attack. This is an extreme case, but the same tragedy is potentially present in every major country in the world today, Communist and non-Communist as well.

Every country in the world today is similar to a giant with a hearing aid—a hearing aid which frequently is out of order. What is more, if you try to shout threats into the hearing aid it is likely to be turned off. Shouting dire threats is, therefore, not practical. The nationalist or realist who says force or threats are the only things to make those foreign people understand—and if threats will not do, a few bombs will—is unconsciously developing a theory of two kinds of human beings—foreigners who can be intimidated, and his own countrymen who could only be provoked. If you ask someone "How would your countrymen react if such and such a thing were done to them?" he may reply with indignation, "They would rise like one man and would say 'we would rather die than submit to such scandalous threats and behaviour' ". If you then ask him, "How do you expect those foreigners over there to react?" he may say, innocently, "Oh, that is quite different". Experience in conflict after conflict shows, however, that human beings, fortunately or unfortunately, are not all that much different.

It is becoming increasingly impractical to use under modern conditions the same methods used fifty and eighty years ago, the methods of the punitive expedition, the method of shelling or bombing or burning foreign countries or cities as a technique of deterrence or persuasion. British troops successfully burned the Summer Palace in Peking in 1860, as they did earlier the city of Washington in 1813—it was an old tradition of dealing with recalcitrant colonial or ex-colonial populations—and similar methods were used by many powers in the Boxer affair in China in 1900. In those days energy and toughness often paid off. Today they may not do so. I do not think that their worst critic could charge either the German or Japanese army of the Second World War with having lacked firmness and resolution in trying to suppress guerrillas or civilian resistance in the various countries which they occupied. But we find that these methods did not bring the results expected. Why did they fail? Because people are no longer the same kind of people. If most people do not care about politics, and most people stay at home in their villages, the few strange deviant characters who take part in politics can indeed be shot. If most people take an interest in politics, then a bomb, a reprisal, the burning of a village are more likely to increase their bitterness.

This need not be taken just as a prediction of one scholar. I hope that experts in many countries, both academic scholars and conscientious military men, will sit down and try to calculate as precisely as possible the rate of attrition inflicted upon guerrillas by more or less precise or imprecise area bombing, and the rate of enemy recruitment which results from the popular resentment afterwards. If their hearts will not give an answer to these conscientious investigators, perhaps their slide rules will.

It is essential in forecasting the future of a guerrilla war to calculate the rates of recruitment and attrition on both sides, and it is then possible to project to some degree by mathematical methods what the situation will be one or two or five years in the future, taking also into account the size of the initial populations on both sides. Exhortations might increase the fervour and effectiveness of one side by 5 or 10 or 15 per cent, and a hard core of trained cadres may help more, but neither of these things are all-powerful, and some reasonable estimates and calculations could still be made.

The important point is that a basic constant has changed, namely human apathy, or the human belief that one cannot and should not participate, in politics; and so long as technology and science will go on in this century, these human constants will continue to change. They will continue to change in the direction of greater popular participation and, therefore, of greater national intractability in politics.

A World of Irreducible Nation-States?

This, in turn, may mean a prediction that the blocs and alliances on both sides of the world's ideological divisions are likely to loosen. This is true of both sides of the traditional East-West bloc, which is now loosening in front of our eyes. General De Gaulle is giving an impressive performance of loosening the Western alliance system at this time, and Mr. Mao Tse-tung has been busy giving a similar performance on the Communist side, taking the spotlight away from the earlier prologue of the same play as performed by Mr. Tito. It is possible that temporary crises will bring some of the Great Powers together again for a time, but the basic processes driving countries toward more divergent national politics are likely to stay at work. We of the Western countries would have to work very hard indeed to restore and cement a Sino-Soviet alliance.

But the same is true of the famous North-South division between the more- and the less-developed countries. The Afro-Asian bloc is not showing increasing solidarity, nor will any other bloc, since again and again statesmen respond more to domestic pressures than to international ones.

What is more, the different ideological blocs, in order to increase their military power and to reduce the burden on the principal member of each bloc, have been trying to promote a militarisation of lesser members of the bloc. They have tried to persuade the lesser members of the bloc to make bigger military contributions. This effort in many countries has been successful. National military establishments have increased in many countries on both sides of the world. What has been the result? In many cases, the greater the national military establishment became, the more it became a force for the pursuit of supposed national interests, contrary to bloc solidarity. It was the Hungarian army which became a major factor in the anti-Soviet uprising in Hungary in 1956. It has been the growing military power of China that has made China more independent from Russia, and it was the growing military strength of Yugoslavia between 1945 and 1948 which similarly made Yugoslavia less responsive to Moscow's direction.

The NATO-supplied aeroplanes of Turkey were firing in 1964 at Greeks in Nicosia. And Greeks and Turks in early 1965 still are using their NATO equipment to threaten one another. So are India and Pakistan. And I have heard in conversation a very able young Japanese scholar explaining to me how important it would be for Japan to have much stronger military forces because then national diplomacy and national interest could be backed up with power. I was asking him then whether he could give me some examples of such national interests involved, and he mentioned Japan's disputes with South Korea.

One may thus expect that, as the different bloc members become somewhat more strongly militarised, this will accelerate the disintegration of blocs, and it will increase the shift toward national policies rather than international ones.

These considerations lead us to an image of the future as a world of irreducible nation-states. But what kind of nation-states will these be, and what kind of politics will there be among them? The first and perhaps most critical question is: Will all these nation-states have atomic bombs or not? Will we, in other words, be entering an age of nuclear proliferation?

Nuclear Weapons: Must They Spread?

The first nuclear power emerged in the world in 1945. After twenty years, there are now five such powers. On the average one power has been added to the number of nuclear powers every four years. In thirty years we may, therefore, have another seven or eight nuclear powers. We may have to live then in a twelve-power world, and if the rate does not speed up—as it well may—we would have by the end of the century about fourteen or fifteen nuclear powers. By the year 2030, we might then very easily have two dozen, but if this process of diffusion speeds up, as automobiles, telephones and other technical innovations have speeded up in their diffusion in their later stages, we may very well have a forty- or fifty-power nuclear world before this century is out. Will we have that many decades to contemplate international politics and to comment on them?

As the number of nuclear powers increases the amount of attention each country can pay to any one rival declines. What is more, the more nuclear powers there are, the easier it is for any one country to counter a threat from another not only by speeding up its own armament but by adjusting its alliances.

From these two viewpoints, then, the danger of conflict goes down as the number of powers increases. From this viewpoint, therefore, nuclear proliferation would somewhat increase the chances for peace.

However, there is a second process at work. In every country there is a possibility of miscalculation. One hopes it is small. It may well be much smaller than it was in the last fifty years, but even if it were only one-fifth, if modern statesmen were five times as clever as the statesmen of the last fifty years, there would still be one chance in ten of some important decision going wrong.

Moreover, there is the possibility in many countries of insubordination. There are some countries, such as the United States and Britain, where in a conflict between a general and the civilian head of state, it is the general who retires, as General Douglas MacArthur did in the Korean war. There are other countries where in such cases the civilian head of state retires; and there are still others where in such cases the civilian head of state is likely to get killed.

But we find that, as you project to the future the acquisition of an atom bomb by the Government of Indonesia, the Government of Egypt, the Government of Syria, the Government of Iraq, the Government of Israel, the Government of Albania, and many others, the likelihood of something blowing up somewhere becomes ever larger. In other words, with the increased number of nuclear powers there is an increased possibility of war by miscalculation, malfunction, misjudgment or domestic instability. The two danger curves, the declining curve from the broadening balance of power system and the rising curve from the instability of ever more nuclear powers, intersect. The aggregate curve of the total danger from both processes is then perhaps roughly shaped like a U, with a minimum somewhere in the middle, perhaps at the point where there are not more than five powers.

It would be my best judgment that a world of five or six nuclear powers, five preferably, can be managed. A world of many more than ten nuclear powers cannot. We have, therefore, a zone somewhat between the present five powers, and preferably no addition, or very few additions, in which we can maintain world peace.

We might be able for a short time to keep peace by deterrence, but we cannot keep it by coercion. We cannot get a world government for the next ten or twenty or thirty years, and we cannot get an international authority with power to compel anybody. The Russians cannot compel China. The Chinese cannot compel the Russians. The United States cannot even compel effectively Vietnam. Nobody can compel anybody very effectively in the international world of today, and in a nuclear world even less so. Certainly no one can compel France at this moment in regard to anything that concerns her vital interests.

It follows that we have a few years, ten or twenty at the most, during which we can stabilise a world on the basis of a very few nuclear powers. After that, and failing such stabilisation, might well come the deluge.

A Possible Five-Power World?

What can we do during this period? One possibility would be an agreement based on the United Nations Charter which would, on the initiative of the non-nuclear powers of today, limit nuclear weapons to the five permanent member countries of the United Nations Security Council. International law gives these five countries a position different from other countries. No new precedent would have to be set to state these responsibilities. What is more, such an agreement would be in accord with existing facts because these are, in fact, the five countries which have nuclear weapons at this time.

Let me add, with all sympathy for the republic that is now established on the island of Taiwan, I cannot pretend that it is in charge of the mainland of China. Sooner or later, as a practical pragmatic matter of calling spades at least instruments for digging, we shall have to find a way of dealing with Communist China as one of the Great Powers whose status in the weapons balance of the world must be provided for.

If five countries have nuclear weapons, this does not necessarily mean that all have to like each other or help each other. They might not even at times talk to each other. The important thing is that at least some of them on each side are agreed to make sure that no one else gets nuclear weapons, and that they are backed up in this by the moral sentiment of mankind as represented in the United Nations.

The outstanding countries, the candidate countries, the countries whose technology would most easily qualify them to acquire nuclear weapons but whose historic experience and popular political preference today make them opposed to nuclear weapons, are Germany and Japan. These two countries might now be in a natural position to take the moral and political leadership of world opinion, in the campaign against nuclear proliferation. If this can be accomplished, it is possible that later on, for civilian and non-military purposes, some of the old plans of an international atomic energy authority, the old Baruch Plan, might be modified and revised for voluntary co-operation and acceptance among non-Communist countries. We might eventually get a Free World Atomic Energy Authority, run perhaps by a board representing the ten leading industrial countries of the free world; and it might be possible to adjust voting rights in various ways proportionate to industrial output or national income of each country, and to readjust the quotas from time to time, or to find some weighted compromise between population and income, acceptable to all participants.

In the meantime, if we manage at all to slow down or to stop the race to a nuclear proliferation, we may live to observe what Stanley Hoffman has called the gradual atrophy of war. By "the atrophy of war" I mean that it is not practical now, and will be less practical in the future, to use nuclear threats to obtain political or economic objectives. Two years ago when China had no atom bomb, she almost got a Japan Export-Import Bank credit. In February 1965 China had an atomic device and no Japanese credit. Possession of a bomb had not spectacularly increased the bargaining power of China's diplomats.

The United States has found itself in much the same position. Secretary MacNamara has reported that in early 1965 the American armed forces have four times the nuclear fire power of a few years ago. I do not think anybody would claim that we have four times as much control of world affairs as we had a few years ago. A few years ago France had no atomic bomb and could control Algeria. Today France has an atom bomb and cannot control Algeria. The indications of the increasing political impotence and inapplicability of nuclear weapons are becoming fairly clear.

As a result, political objectives can at most be sought by conventional weapons; and even conventional weapons are becoming increasingly impractical for such purposes, because of the increasing political participation ratio and the rising resistance of local populations, and thus of the increasing cost of intervention. It turns out that the Mediterranean countries, the Arab world and Southeast Asia are not inhabited by "power vacua" but by people, and what has been called a power vacuum has existed more in the heads of some observers than in the countries and areas concerned.

Toward More Safety for a Changing World

Thus, it is quite likely that some parts of the world may turn out not to be susceptible to very effective control in the name of ideology. Other parts of the world may very well at the same time move on a voluntary and popular basis towards gradual integration.

Western Europe shows slow, halting, and by now distinctly lagging steps, but still steps, toward a partial integration. Ten years from now Western Europe is almost certain still to be a Europe of six nation-states, but a generation will have grown up who will have become accustomed to the idea that Europe is somehow one, and also accustomed to the idea that at least some things can be carried on quite well by supranational organisations.

When these people will be parents of families, they may well be shocked by their youngsters who in 1985 may suggest that European integration might very well be moving a little faster. But it is safe to say that the road to a supranational integration in Western Europe, in Central America, among the Arab countries, in the Caribbean and elsewhere, will be long and slow.

In the meantime, we may very well have two other techniques to rely upon. One will be the improvement of national intelligence systems. The day may yet come when intelligence services will become worthy of their names, when the decision-making systems of countries will be improved, so as to cope somewhat better with the ever-growing problems of communications and decision-making overloads, and when the communication and control system of countries will be made far more precise, perceptive and reliable.

The United States Government has, I think it is well known, worked very hard in the last five years to increase the reliability of its command and control system with regard to nuclear weapons and other devices, and similar efforts will have to be made both in the field of weapons systems and of political and social engineering in every modern country.

In general, international politics may very well become a science or art developed in the image of safety engineering or collision engineering. The expert traffic engineer is the man who can advise an aeroplane or a stream of aeroplanes how to go where they want to go without crashing head-on into somebody else going somewhere else.

The Revival of the Problem of Peaceful Change

Since it will become impractical to use force in order to produce major change, and since the need for some changes will continue, we will begin to face some very serious problems. Some countries and some populations will experience increased needs for land. A country like Japan is one of the most densely populated in the world. At the moment, Japan's birth rate is low, but we must remember that France and America had similarly low birth rates in the depression years of the 1930s. There is no forecasting with any great precision what Japan's population growth will be a few years in the future. Even the present-day Japanese population is growing at 1 per cent and if this should go on, the population will double in seventy years. If the growth stops earlier, the peak might come, as one demographer says, at 138 million at some time in the future. But what happens in Japan will happen to an increased extent in Pakistan, in India, and in many other countries.

We shall, therefore, have the problem of what to do with such land as there is in the world, and perhaps our diplomats may rediscover a standard procedure of diplomacy from the Middle Ages until the 1860s. The purchase of Alaska by the United States from Russia in the 1860s was the last great peaceful real estate transaction in history. But if there are countries in the world which are rich in land but poor in capital, and other countries which are rich in capital and poor in land, it would be strange if people sooner or later, ten, twenty or fifty years from now, will not begin again to wonder whether a trade could perhaps be made.

I could imagine, if I may for a moment daydream of a time twenty or thirty years in the future, that some day the United Nations might receive a bid from the Government of Japan to take over and develop the island of New Guinea. A suitable price might come out of the proceeds of Japanese industry. This price might be divided partly among other overseas countries with major population pressure, such as Indonesia, Pakistan and India, all of which have large underdeveloped land reserves in their national boundaries, but all of which badly need capital goods. The remainder of the price would be set aside for the welfare and development of the Papuans—

the 700,000 stone-age aborigines—so as to develop a part of the huge island for their reservation, and for the welfare and education of themselves and their descendants.

Eventually this could very well be done with the blessings of the United Nations. The jungles of New Guinea could come to look like the terraced hills and the garden-like agriculture of Japan. I do not know whether this will come to pass, but it would not surprise me if it happened sooner or later.

We cannot ever expect again to redistribute the lands of the world by violence. They would be too radioactive to be very useful. On the other hand, we cannot expect that the coming of nuclear energy should freeze forever the historic accidents of the settlement patterns and the land distribution of 1945. Eventually, as within every national state so in the world, more land will be given to those who can make the most creative and productive use of it, provided that they can provide fair and adequate compensation to the interests of all concerned.

With the enormous productivity of modern industry, with the actual and still greater potential growth of national incomes, in industrial countries, this should not be impossible. This is not a problem for today or tomorrow, but if the study of international politics and its future does include an effort to look twenty or thirty years ahead and to see what future options may be open to mankind, then this would not be a wholly idle speculation.

The Self-Transforming Societies

At the end of this development, we may well enter the stage of what I should like to call self-transforming societies. The most advanced countries of the world are now beginning to move there. If you extrapolate the rates of economic growth of Germany, France, Britain, the United States, Canada, and others—and the speed of growth of Japan will soon put her there within thirty years or so —we find that by the end of the century some countries will have approximately $3,000 to $5,000 *per capita* income. We will have about a third or possibly one-half of the young people going to the universities. The secondary school will then be the elementary school of the future, and the university will be what we today call the secondary school, and the intellectual equivalent of today's graduates of the Sorbonne, or of Oxford, or of Tokyo University will then go on to specialised study.

We may find that by that time we have a large preponderance of urban and industrial employment, and we may find more people employed in scientific research than in farming. In the United States this is almost certain. We have after all less than 10 per cent of our work force in agriculture and perhaps 2 or 3 per cent by now in scientific research. If you extrapolate growth trends to the end of the century, we are likely to have more people in the research laboratories than on farms. In England and Japan this seems likely to happen, too, if recent rates of change should continue.

Such societies will have nuclear energy for peaceful purposes in plenty. They will have significant capabilities for interplanetary transportation; and they may very well have photosynthesis and other methods for getting at least some food from the sea and from chemical processes.

These societies will be unlike anything we have seen so far. Yet we are moving toward their attainment at a calculable speed. We are shifting something like 0.5 per cent of our social reality each year in this direction. We are thus very likely to get there somewhere between the years 2000 and 2020 if we do not blow up the world on the way.

We are going now through a period of extreme danger and high hope. We are shooting the rapids on the river of history. Or, if I may change the image, we are now engaged in helping mankind in the dangerous and painful but infinitely promising process of growing up.